ANGLICAN HUMANITARIANISM
IN
COLONIAL NEW YORK

ANGLICAN HUMANITARIANISM

IN

COLONIAL NEW YORK

By

FRANK J. KLINGBERG

BOOKS FOR LIBRARIES PRESS

FREEPORT, NEW YORK

First Published 1940
Reprinted 1971

INTERNATIONAL STANDARD BOOK NUMBER:
0-8369-5896-9

LIBRARY OF CONGRESS CATALOG CARD NUMBER:
71-164612

PRINTED IN THE UNITED STATES OF AMERICA

To

PROFESSOR CHARLES MCLEAN ANDREWS

WHOSE WRITINGS ON COLONIAL HISTORY HAVE
RESTORED THE AMERICAN COLONIES TO THEIR
RIGHTFUL PLACE IN ENGLAND'S FIRST EMPIRE

ANGLICAN HUMANITARIANISM
IN
COLONIAL NEW YORK

PREFACE

THE AUTHOR, while collecting materials in Great Britain for *The Anti-Slavery Movement in England, A Study in English Humanitarianism*, covering the years from 1770 to 1833, became convinced that a further analysis of earlier sources of humanitarian opinion was clearly indicated. The development of the eighteenth century humanitarian mood was not in itself sufficient to explain great reservoirs of sentiment favorable to the protection of native peoples. Organized ameliorative activities, even if originally at least partially a product of the new mood, obviously in turn intensified humanitarian sentiments and made effective action possible. Outstanding among such humanitarian bodies were the older Anglican missionary societies, founded at the opening of the eighteenth century.

The richness of the Society for the Propagation of the Gospel records for historical purposes, British as well as American, was first stressed by Professor Charles M. Andrews in the *American Historical Review*, in an article entitled, "Materials in British Archives for American Colonial History," which appeared in January, 1905. And three years later, the value of religious records for the study of "the broad story of American culture," and "a full understanding of American character and spirit," was ably stated by the late Dr. J. Franklin Jameson in a presidential address, "The American Acta Sanctorum," which was published in the *American Historical Review* in January, 1908.

A scrutiny of the voluminous documents of the Society has revealed an intensity and continuity of effort in Great Britain and in the colonies, for the Christianization and education of the Negro and the Indian from the very beginning of the eighteenth century, comparable to that of the great Roman Catholic orders.

As already stated, the collection and analysis of this material has been made with the purpose of following not only the migration of ideas and Anglo-colonial social and intellectual contacts, but also the progress of the humanitarian attack developed by the Society for the Propagation of the Gospel. Quite intentionally, the Society and its allied Societies, the Society for the Promotion of Christian Knowledge, and the Bray Associates, worked for the enrichment of colonial life by founding libraries, schools, and colleges, and by establishing new and active centers of the Church in the colonial world, all of which were in effect outposts of British civilization.

The treatment in this volume is limited to the province of New York before the American Revolution, and is confined to the Indian and the Negro, with but incidental mention of the white colonists. Promoting the work in every colony were the ecclesiastical trustees of the Society in London, with their Executive Secretary, who usually served for years and was comparable to the Secretary to the Board of Trade in the governmental field. Each year an eminent ecclesiastic, usually a bishop— Berkeley, Butler, Fleetwood, Secker, Shipley, Warburton—was chosen to deliver a sermon, an occasion for an evaluation of past achievements and for stating a challenging prospectus for future efforts. While the volume covers but a part of the whole body of the S. P. G. materials, it may be regarded as a representative presentation of the methods used and the objectives attained by the Society in all of its work. The laboratories of education for whites, blacks, and Indians, set up in any area, the methods of questionnaires and answers, the development of literary aids and the distribution of literature, and the careful adaptation of the Society's program to each center, all are characteristic of the experiment on its wide front throughout the ‚British western world. Momentum was gained and skill developed so that a setback at one point became a valuable experience for another area. The American Revolution, of course, was such a crisis in the affairs of the Society.

The accumulation of small facts necessary to establish larger outlines, in this case the study of the minutiae of the painstaking field work records of the missionaries, and of the annual sermons preached in London, imposes a severe discipline upon the investigator, and at times perhaps equally upon the reader. But these "samplings" and probings from the materials furnish convincing evidence of the Society's humanitarian activity in that difficult, bewildering period, the eighteenth century, when provincialism flourished side by side with expansion, and profiteering with humanitarianism.

Three monographs, which have appeared in the *Historical*

Magazine of the Protestant Episcopal Church, are incorporated in this volume. Because written and printed separately, they overlap in some measure. For this reason, the footnotes necessarily contain bibliographical information and show some variety of form. Moreover, due to the great quantity of the Sir William Johnson material, a more compact arrangement of footnotes was used in Chapter III than in the other portions. The immense and long-time labor of winnowing documents, a task which is never ended, and the necessity of surveying all related literature, have been made possible only by annual research grants from the University of California, which, over a period of years, have led to the production not only of this work but of earlier volumes, a group of related monographs dealing with the West Indies, and additional studies shortly to appear or approaching completion. To the President of the University, Dr. Robert Gordon Sproul, to Professor Herbert E. Bolton, and to Dean Charles Lipman for their understanding of a new field of discovery, I am grateful. I thank the Librarian, Mr. John E. Goodwin, and his staff for constant help in making available the resources of the University of California at Los Angeles library, and for assistance in interlibrary loans. To Dr. St. George L. Sioussat of the Library of Congress and his aides, particularly to Dr. Thomas P. Martin and Miss Grace Gardner Griffin, and to Director Max Farrand for ready access to rich materials at the Huntington Library, my thanks are especially due. I am indebted to my research assistant, Florence Cook Fast, who helped in an early survey of the Huntington Library sources, as did Dr. Dallas D. Irvine, Richard I. Shelling, and my colleague, Dr. Louis K. Koontz, in the Library of Congress.

The Social Science Research Council supported the investigation by a grant which was invaluable not only in the initial exploration of material but in laying the foundation for the present volume and for other monographs as well.

To the Church Historical Society for access to its archives, to its President, Dr. Walter Herbert Stowe, for critical editorial advice and unstinted assistance of all kinds, to Dr. Edgar Legare Pennington of Miami, Florida, for generous access to all his materials, the fruit of many years' work, to Dr. G. MacLaren Brydon, of Richmond, Virginia, for his care and skill in reading the proof, my indebtedness is gratefully acknowledged. I am under obligations also to many other scholars, more particularly, Professors Merle Curti, Albert T. Volwiler, Charles Kingsley Webster, R. B. Mowat, Reginald Coupland, and Dr. George

Peabody Gooch, all contributors in the field of the transit of ideas and the formation of opinion, who have been a stimulus to me in my work. To Dr. Carter G. Woodson, whose help and advice are always at the service of his fellow scholars, I have been in debt for many years.

I owe especial obligations to Dr. William Thomas Manning, Bishop of New York, and to Dr. Frederic Sydney Fleming, Rector of the Parish of Trinity Church in the City of New York; to Dr. Cameron J. Davis, Bishop of Western New York; to Dr. G. Ashton Oldham, Bishop of Albany; and to Dr. Ernest Milmore Stires, Bishop of Long Island, for their generous support and their recognition that ecclesiastical records are a part of the social, political, and cultural history of the Anglo-American world.

Dorothy Klump Jones, who has served for four years in the capacity of archivist of the author's thirty-year collection of books and manuscripts, has rendered invaluable assistance in keeping in order the accumulating masses of material, with all the care, eager interest, and zeal of a gifted curator.

And finally, for constructive help and encouragement over a period of many years, I wish to express my gratitude to Professor Charles M. Andrews by dedicating this volume to him.

FRANK J. KLINGBERG.

University of California, Los Angeles.
August 1, 1940.

TABLE OF CONTENTS

BOOK ONE

ANGLICAN HUMANITARIANISM
IN
COLONIAL NEW YORK

ANGLICAN HUMANITARIANISM IN COLONIAL NEW YORK

INTRODUCTION

A DDITIONAL light on the social order of the Anglo-American world in the eighteenth century, particularly the difficult first half, is much needed. The activities of the instruments of government were so severely limited that it has been well said that the eighteenth century was one of meager institutions and of great men. It is, nevertheless, true, that, while governmental institutions in numbers and in functions were restricted in comparison with modern times, private initiative, expressing itself either individually, or in partnerships, or in corporations, was a characteristic feature of the age. It is necessary, therefore, to study the records of private or semi-private bodies, whose strength animated or permeated the outward governmental activities or which even served as complete substitutes. And in certain instances, such as those of the East India Company and the Hudson's Bay Company, empires were founded and governed by business corporations. Although speaking of a later period, Lord Haldane equally well described the elements of the eighteenth century order when he said,

> Indeed, the civic community is more than a political fabric. It includes all the social institutions in and by which the individual life is influenced—such as are the family, the school, the church, the legislature, and the executive. None of these can subsist in isolation from the rest; together they and other institutions of the kind form a single organic whole; the whole of which is known as the Nation.[1]

The weight of the Society for the Propagation of the Gospel in Foreign Parts,[2] as it operated in the Anglo-American world, is not to be assessed solely by the numbers of its converts, nor by the stamina of its missionaries, nor by the size of the collection and the disbursement of funds, but also by the fact that it functioned in a civilization, which, in the last two centuries, has in all aspects of human endeavor played a

[1]*Lord Richard Burdon Haldane, Higher Nationality; a Study in Law and Ethics, an Address delivered before the American Bar Association at Montreal on September 1, 1913, found in the series International Conciliation, Vol. IV, No. 72, p. 15. (Published in New York City by the American Bar Association for International Conciliation, 1914.) This address can also be found in "The London Times," Tuesday, September 2, 1913, pp. 7-8.*
[2]*Hereafter referred to as the S. P. G., or the Society.*

major part. The powers of the S. P. G., and those of the Society for the Promotion of Christian Knowledge[3] as well, are, therefore, to be measured not in isolation but must be assessed as vital parts of an expanding world culture. If these Societies contributed to making this Anglo-American world more humane, to mitigating the effects of expansion on backward peoples, or stimulated and extended intellectual development, or if they aided or retarded imperialism, they were doubly significant because they were operating in one of the most virile of modern civilizations. For quite obviously, an individual cannot be evaluated standing alone, but must be viewed as a part of the nation to which he belongs. Thus the S. P. G., an incorporated missionary and humanitarian enterprise, could exert an influence beyond that possible to a similar organization working in a small state or backward nation, remote from the stream of modern events.

The Society's effort, in the northern and middle colonies, is of additional interest because there at least it was an Anglican minority movement in a non-conformist region, where dissent was all but overwhelming and strong enough to prevent the establishment of an Anglican bishop until after the Revolution. In a majority position and legally established in England, the Anglican found himself in most of the continental colonies in a reversed position, functioning in a middle class environment which put him on his mettle, developed his hardihood, and in many instances threw him into the Revolution as a Loyalist. He survived this ordeal and established his own independent Episcopal Church.[4]

During the decade of the 1780's, an American episcopate was secured; a constitution satisfactory to the Church in all the thirteen states and the nation was adopted; and a Book of Common Prayer was adapted to meet the needs of a politically independent people. A distinctive feature of this creation of a free church in a free state was the admission of laymen into diocesan and general conventions. As part of the legal disestablishment of the Church of England, state subsidies, for example in Virginia and Maryland, were cut off and support from the S. P. G. naturally was discontinued.

Although most S. P. G. men suffered expulsion during the Ameri-

[3]*Hereafter referred to as the S. P. C. K.*
[4]*See the Historical Magazine of the Protestant Episcopal Church, VIII, No. 3, September 1939. This number includes: Edgar Legare Pennington, "Colonial Clergy Conventions," pp. 178-218; Walter Herbert Stowe, "The State or Diocesan Conventions of the War and Post-War Periods," pp. 220-256; William Wilson Manross, "The Interstate Meetings and General Conventions of 1784, 1785, 1786 and 1789," pp. 257-280; Percy Varney Norwood, "Constitutional Developments since 1789," pp. 282-303.*

can Revolution,[5] their several achievements lived on as a part of the new independent society. For example, King's College (now Columbia University) and other educational enterprises were continued under American leadership. The policy of conservation of native people as an imperial, rather than as an individual colony's responsibility, was left as a legacy on which the Federal government of the United States built its Indian policies.[6] As the Indian dwindled and vanished westward, the S. P. G. gave increasing attention to the multiplying Negroes. The economic and political implications of the Negro's gain of religious rights before he secured freedom and civil rights, inherent in the S. P. G. program discussed in Chapter IV, had to do with the basic assumption, underlying all the educational programs and all the steps of Christianization, that the Negro would, when civilized, work for his own economic survival and security for exactly the same reasons that actuated the white man. This predication, opposed by the owners and planters wherever the Negro was in contact with the white man, was the key to the later slavery controversy. Efforts made by Lincoln to remove experimental groups of free Negroes to the West Indies, were based on the perhaps unconscious feeling that the whites and Negroes could not, or would not, live together in the South in a free, wage-economy social order.

An early correct appraisal of the Negro's eventual contributions to American life, involving his ability to learn and to work as a free man, animated the program of the Society in New York. That freedom and the freeman's motives were not to be secured in a moment, however, was revealed in many penetrating comments from the Society's workers and stressed in annual sermons. Just as the argument that education would make the poor white man presumptuous and unruly, the objection to education maintained in Great Britain in the eighteenth and nineteenth centuries,[7] it is to be noted that identical arguments were used against the education of the black man as soon as that was undertaken. This idea that education would make the Negro dissatisfied with his status in slavery and unwilling to work, arose wherever instruction began in the West Indies and in the American continental colonies.[8] These arguments as to the dangers of education

[5]*Although there was a Revolutionary purge of 100,000 Loyalists, the minority tradition was maintained, and under American auspices, Anglicanism revived, and adapted itself to the changed conditions.*

[6]*Frank J. Klingberg, "The Anglican Minority Movement in Colonial Pennsylvania with Particular Reference to the Indian and the Negro." (Not yet in print).*

[7]*M. G. Jones, The Charity School. A Study of Eighteenth Century Puritanism in Action (Macmillan, 1938).*

[8]*The obstacles to Negro conversion in the colony of Virginia are typical. See for example, Mary F. Goodwin, "Christianizing and Educating the Negro in Colonial Virginia," in Historical Magazine of the Protestant Episcopal Church, I,*

continued until, as often occurred in social changes, public opinion and the public administrator made universal in New York what private effort had begun.[9]

Financial appeals were made to all elements of the community, particularly to those men who had made money in trade and shipping, to support educational work for "heathen" on the ground that profits of empire trade must make some return to its victims, "Savage Natives," and "Savages in Bonds." Every parish was solicited for funds, and, in the New World, established parishes were expected to take up the Mission program as soon as finances allowed the parish to become independent of the Society. Thus the Society encouraged the colonists in home rule.

The comparisons of literary and organization techniques with those later used by the Methodists, the Unitarians,[10] and earlier by the Jesuits and other Roman Catholics[11], are interesting but cannot be surveyed here.[12] However, it may be stated that the S. P. G. missionary eventually found, as did the Jesuits, Franciscans, Dominicans, and other Roman Catholics, that the processes of Christianity depended as a final solution upon the use of the white man's languages, rather than upon the attempts of the white man to recreate in native tongues the concepts and ideas of Christianity.

The two chapters of this volume dealing with the Indians convey the author's impression that "the cult of the noble savage" was based on the Indian rather than on the Negro. The samplings of the annual sermons in Chapter I confirm this conclusion. Paradoxically, the difficulties of civilizing the Indian on the frontiers contributed to the idealization of savage man, and to the extensive body of controversial literature on primitive peoples and their cults. The problem of a practical Indian program was left to the Federal government as another permanent legacy by the Society, especially through its joint work with

No. 3, Sept. 1932, pp. 143-152. For hindrances to Indian conversion, see Frank J. Klingberg, "The Indian Frontier in South Carolina as Seen by the S. P. G. Missionary," in Journal of Southern History, V. No. 4, November, 1939, pp. 479-500.

[9]The S. P. G. records, some 200,000 documents up to 1783, will, when fully studied, throw further light upon the humanitarian backlog in Great Britain. Also, further studies, such as the analysis of financial support, are indicated.

[10]Robert F. Wearmouth, Methodism and the Working-Class Movements of England, 1800-1850, (London, Epworth Press, 1937); Raymond V. Holt, The Unitarian Contribution to Social Progress in England, (Allen and Unwin, 1938).

[11]Michael Trappes Loman, Bishop Challoner: A Biographical Study, derived from Dr. Edwin Burton's "The Life and Times of Bishop Challoner." (Longmans 1936). The Roman Catholic Bishop in London faced many of the Anglican problems in his relation with the British colonies.

[12]Comparisons of the colour bar in Anglo-Saxon countries including South Africa with Latin-America have been made by Marais, and by Wyndham. J. S. Marais, The Cape Coloured People 1652-1937, (Longmans, 1939); H. A. Wyndham, The Atlantic and Slavery, (H. Milford, 1935).

Sir William Johnson. In Chapter IV the first but fundamental step, the Negro's gain of religious rights, in the long story of his progress toward civil rights, a process not yet ended, is discussed. The destiny of the Negro was to become an individual member of the community; that of the Indian to remain for decades in his tribe as a ward of the government.

In Chapter I the author presents materials indicating a re-evaluation of the Anglican Church and its intellectual and social achievements in the eighteenth century. Can it be that the dramatic achievements of the Wesleys and Whitefield (themselves priests of the Anglican church) in preaching, in the use of mass hymn singing, and in organization, have obscured a precise and well balanced appraisal of the intellectual and social contributions of those who remained faithful to the Anglican communion? The mere mention of the names—Berkeley, Butler, Warburton, William Law[13]—hints at the intellectual range of the Church, its social consciousness, and its profound readjustment to the needs of the people of England as they drifted into a new industrial age, with the problems incident to the rapid rise of population and the migration of the overflow to the cities and to America.

Perhaps the complete reorganization of the English State and Anglican Church, which occurred in the third and fourth decades of the nineteenth century, makes the structure of both in the eighteenth century seem to our age so archaic that it is surprising to realize that men in the eighteenth century lived happily under the many inequalities as between one bishopric and another and between bishop and parish rector. In this age of stability, Parson Woodforde fitted into his rural surroundings and met the needs of village life so completely that any other personality would have been disruptive.[14] Can it be that the tremendous propaganda necessary to reform both Church and State have left us

---

[13]*William Law (1686-1761), declined to take the oaths of allegiance and abjuration to George I, and throughout his life, Law retained his non-juring principles. Although Law early influenced the Wesleys, he later came into opposition with them because of his mystical tendencies. His mystic conceptions also led Law to oppose the rationalism of John Locke, and to attack the Divine Legation of Bishop Warburton. Law's most famous book is, no doubt, his Serious Call to a Devout and Holy Life, Adapted to the State and Condition of all Orders of Christians (1728). For works on Law see Canon Overton, William Law, Nonjuror and Mystic (1881); Richard Tighe, Life and Writings of William Law (1813).*

[14]*James Woodforde, The Diary of a Country Parson: The Reverend James Woodforde . . . 5 vols. Edited by John Beresford. (London: H. Milford, 1924-1931). The Diary covers the years 1758-1802. "In the company of Parson Woodforde, the reader will enter into that country peace" of rural England. The Parson found dinner with a Bishop and a Baronet rather a strain but on the other hand rejoiced in the "Society of his farmers at the tithe-frolic, or in the more cultured society of the poet Cowper's cousins, the Bodhams and the Donnes." Introduction, Vol. II, ix and xi.*

with only half the picture, the indictment rather than the harmonious features of this earlier society?

Reverting for a moment to the eighteenth century British constitution, the overwhelmingly enthusiastic statements made by Sir William Blackstone and Burke seem to the modern reader almost satirical. Blackstone's statement, "so wisely contrived, so strongly raised, and so highly finished [that] it is hard to speak with that praise which is justly and severely its due,"[15] and Burke's very similar views are well known, as is the tribute of the Duke of Wellington, uttered in the debates on the Reform Bill of 1832.

It is of interest that the Wesley-Whitefield and other eighteenth century criticisms of the constitution of the Church preceded by at least a generation the criticism of the State, but that the reform of the State occurred somewhat earlier than that of the Church. Both reorganizations, necessary for a more complex society, may in part at least account, as already indicated, for retroactive indictment of the Church at a time when it fitted the conditions of eighteenth century life. A study of the activities of the S. P. G. in Great Britain in the eighteenth century suggests, not that the Church was an arm of the State, in the usual view, but rather that the State and Church were more nearly co-equals, and that in the 1830's, to glance ahead, both were reorganized at approximately the same time, to meet the needs of the new industrial society.[16]

As stated above, the annual sermons before the S. P. G. contain a mine of information about the intellectual and philosophical conceptions of the time. The attempts to thresh out a proper philosophy for the Society to cover the conflicting interests, in the colonies and at home, of the British trader, the white settler, the imported Negro, and the endangered Indian, can be distilled from the sermons, a battle forum for the reconciliation of Christian idealism, imperial interests, and business profits. Religion and trade, it might be said, were both props of empire, but in opposition on the ethics of dealing with primitive people. The Society was critic, reporter, and ameliorative agent. It was the trader and his goods, rather than the soldier, who prepared the way for the settler and who represented Britain in the wilderness; and the missionary followed wherever the trader penetrated. The march of empire in the new world, where the Indian was pushed aside to make room for the white man and the Negro was introduced to aid the white

[15]*Quoted in Basil Williams, The Whig Supremacy, 1714-1760, (Oxford: Clarendon Press, 1939), p. 55.*
[16]*Whether the French Revolution was responsible for delaying these reorganizations for a generation cannot be discussed here, nor can the body of controversial literature on that topic be surveyed.*

man in the mastery of the continent, is sensed throughout the records. The wide range of the Society's efforts, the close direction of each missionary from London, the constant exchange of personnel and ideas, reflect the steady transit of ideas from frontier to London, from London to the outposts. Almost any page from the Abstract of Proceedings, in the mere routine of business, bounds the Atlantic in quick succession from Africa, to the West Indies, Mosquito Shore, South Carolina, Pennsylvania, New York, New England, and Nova Scotia.

To sum up, the whole story cannot be seen in any one frontier laboratory, but each experiment must be evaluated as a part of the whole century-long achievement, and, with this view accepted by the reader, the pattern of these reports falls into a common unity. The work in colonial New York, however, is of sufficient variety and was carried on with enough energy for three quarters of a century to justify its presentation as a significant unit in the empire scope of the Society.

CHAPTER I

LEADING IDEAS IN THE ANNUAL S. P. G. SERMONS

THE sermon had great political significance during the bitter constitutional conflicts and civil wars of the seventeenth century; and, as one of the chief, if not indeed most important, means of communication, it was inevitably a weapon which political and religious antagonists attempted to seize and control. In fact, during the religious and political revolutions of Tudor and Stuart times, "tuning the pulpits" became the rule. Attendance at church services was compulsory until 1688, and the sermon served not only for the announcement of extraparochial events, but it often gave the only authoritative information as to the policy of the national government. "The golden age of the pulpit" in Elizabeth's time and the changes of the seventeenth and eighteenth centuries, including its relative decline in modern times, are well described by Bishop Hensley Henson of Durham in a recent work.[1]

By the opening of the eighteenth century the dominant constitutional questions had been settled in favor of the supremacy of Parliament as against the King, and Anglicanism had been re-established in a secure position with toleration granted to dissenters, at first de facto, and gradually legally. With these burning home controversies largely ended by a series of compromises, the sermon was restored to its religious and social functions. It is by no means an accident that Thomas Bray's work in the creation of the S. P. G. and the S. P. C. K. was essentially contemporaneous with the softening of the bitter internal political and religious controversies.[2] Not only was Anglicanism the Established faith of Englishmen, it was also the religion of an overwhelming majority. Missionary and educational activities were natural

[1] For the general significance of the sermon, as a form of literature, as an historical document, as a picture of life and manners, and as an element in "the long discipline of the English character" see the excellent "Introduction" by the Rt. Rev. Hensley Henson, the Lord Bishop of Durham, in Selected English Sermons, Sixteenth to Nineteenth Centuries, (London, 1939); see also a summary of political sermons by Godfrey Davies, "English Political Sermons, 1603-1640," in Huntington Library Quarterly, III, No. 1, October 1939, pp. 1-22.

[2] The dynastic and constitutional crises of 1688 and 1714, when James II was replaced by William and Mary, and Anne was succeeded by George I, produced a number of nonjurors in the former case and a few additional supporters of the exiled Stuarts in the latter, such as Atterbury. Whenever possible, Churchmen aided their colleagues by securing positions or recognition for them in the world of scholarship in order to enable them to function without violence to their conscientious scruples. For example, Bishop Fleetwood assisted a number of scholarly nonjurors.

developments under these conditions.[3]   In short, the Anglicans, and the dissenters as well, were now free to devote themselves more fully to the original purposes of the Church at home, to its young branches in the New World, and to the Indian and the Negro.

The English Church at its best, which had become "representative of the finest spirit of England" in the age of Elizabeth, is described by T. S. Eliot as meeting the highest ideals, which he defines in striking terms,

> " . . . a church is to be judged by its intellectual fruits, by its influence on the sensibility of the most sensitive and on the intellect of the most intelligent, and it must be made real to the eye by monuments of artistic merit."[4]

It may be well to note that, while it is true that the sermon was being joined by new means of communication, such as the newspapers in the city of London, the fundamental reasons for the earlier vogue of the sermon continued in force in the first three-quarters of the eighteenth century.   The parish remained a chief center of local government even as late as the time of Parson Woodforde's *Diary*.[5]   The English parson was the leader in his parish, due in good part to the fact that a great mass of people could not yet read and write and were therefore dependent upon oral communication as a means of keeping abreast of the times in local and national matters.   Under Anglican organization and practice, the parson was closely interwoven with the life of his village community, and was bound on the other hand by canon law and tradition to the wider life of his diocese and province.   Although largely dependent for intellectual stimulus upon the Charges and the directions emanating from his superiors, often men of vision and of weight in the spheres of philosophy and of world affairs, the parson also had his occasional journey to London and his visitors from a distance.   Even when not an Oxford or Cambridge man, he was nevertheless, because of his position, one of the clerical order, and presumably eager to remain in the scholastic circle of his fellow-clergy.

Under these circumstances of eager receptivity, a good or brilliant sermon was a local or even a national event.   It was carefully prepared for

[3]*Indispensable for the student of the eighteenth century is the volume by the Rev. Norman Sykes, Church and State in England in the Eighteenth Century (Cambridge, England, at the University Press, 1934).   For a recent summary of the churches in Great Britain in the eighteenth century, see Basil Williams, The Whig Supremacy, 1714-1760 (1939), pp. 66-97.*

[4]*For an appreciative appraisal of the culture of the English Church see an essay by Thomas Stearns Eliot on Lancelot Andrewes in Selected Essays, 1917-1932, p. 290, (New York: Harcourt Brace, c 1932).*

[5]*James Woodforde, The Diary of a Country Parson: the Reverend James Woodforde . . . 5 vols.   Edited by John Beresford.   (London: H. Milford, 1924)-.   The Diary covers the years 1758-1802.*

delivery, usually of great length, and was revised for publication. In its first part the S. P. G. sermon at least often embodied a rich selection of direct quotations from the Bible for those parishioners unable to read for themselves or not able to make the pertinent Biblical selections; and it then customarily developed the theme of the occasion.

The decision, then, to have an annual sermon preached[6] in February, in London, by distinguished clergymen, and to have it bound, usually with the Abstracts of Proceedings, and widely distributed in Great Britain and in the colonies, was in recognition of all the factors set forth above.

While the seventeenth century conflicts had mellowed into religious toleration and the spiritual forces of the Church could accordingly be directed into humanitarian and social reforms at home and abroad, the S. P. G. sermons, although directed to the frontiers of missionary enterprises, were more than narrow missionary appeals, and admitted new themes from year to year. The new scientific conceptions, dating from Newton and others, had brought a new enemy on the home front, philosophical deism,[7] which immediately migrated to the New World, as did also the indictments made in reply by Bishops Berkeley and Butler, in their annual sermons. Thus the many-sided intellectual mood of the century shows itself. Empire building is reflected in Bishop Warburton's sermon of 1766, and political controversy, with a Whig point of view, is shown in Shipley's sermon of 1773.[8]

Naturally, the later sermons repeat the key themes developed by Dean Willis and Bishop Williams, but differ from each other in the

[6]*At the second meeting of the Society July 8, 1701, the Bye-Laws and Standing Orders, were adopted. Among them was an order stating "That there be a Sermon preacht before the Society on the third Friday in every February, and that the Preacher and Place be appointed by the President". In 1830 the fixing of the time was also left to the President. All dates in the text are Gregorian.*

"From 1702 to 1853 (excepting 1703, 1843, and 1849, not printed) the Sermons formed part of the Annual Reports. Since then they have been only occasionally printed. The Places selected have been:—From 1702 to 1839, St. Mary-Le-Bow, excepting in 1706 and 1806, when St. Lawrence Jewry was substituted. From 1840 to 1901, St. Paul's Cathedral.

"The Months—From 1702 to 1831, February; 1832-49, May; 1850-92, June; 1893-95, 1897-9, May; 1896, June; 1900-01, April.

"For the first twenty-five years or more the hour chosen was generally 8 A. M.—on a few occasions 9 A. M. Of recent years the hour has been 11 A. M. and the occasion has been marked by a celebration of the Holy Communion."

See C. F. Pascoe, Two Hundred Years of the S. P. G. Vol. II, p. 833. Also see David Humphreys, An Historical Account of the Incorporated Society for the Propagation of the Gospel in Foreign Parts, p. 347, London 1730.

[7]*Dr. Robert R. Palmer has thrown new light on the intellectual life of France during the eighteenth century in his, "The French Jesuits in the Age of Enlightenment," The American Historical Review, October, 1939, Vol. XLV, No. 1, pp. 44-58.*

[8]*For Locke's many-sided influence in the United States see Dr. Merle Curti, "The Great Mr. Locke, America's Philosopher, 1783-1861" in Huntington Library Bulletin, April 1937.*

emphasis derived from the movement of events, from the changing interests of the country, and from the exigencies of the Society's own history, such as the Codrington gift for Negro education in Barbados, or the weight of a great personality upon the scene as in the case of Sir William Johnson.   Inevitably also, the sermons reflect the philosophical or practical bias of the notable men invited to address the Society.

Out of the approximately 75 sermons, of the pre-Revolutionary period, three have been selected for reproduction, others for extensive quotation, but they must be read in their entirety to get the full measure of the contemporary effect.   The sermons as a whole are closely reasoned, based on a particular text, and are thoroughly documented with Scriptural quotations pertinent to the main theme.   The material is usually divided into an introductory part, doctrinal or theoretical, followed by the applications of the speaker's ideas to the S. P. G. dominion in all parts of the world.[9]

The earliest sermons, for example, the very first one by Dr. Richard Willis,[10] Dean of Lincoln, in 1702 and that by Dr. Williams, Bishop of Chichester, in 1706, present the problems and the plans[11] of the Society.   Dean Willis outlined explicit aims:

> The design is, in the first place, to settle the state of religion, as well as may be, among our own people there, which, by all accounts we have, very much wants their pious care, and then to proceed in the best methods they can toward the conversion of the natives: both these are works that will require a great expence—the sending ministers thither, and maintaining them in many places where they have no settled maintainance; the procuring libraries to encourage ministers to go thither, and to enable them to do their duty the better when they are there; the breeding up of persons to understand the great variety of languages of those countries, in order to be able to converse with the natives, and preach the Gospel to them.
> . . .

[9]*An analysis of the list of Sermons from 1702-1901 shows 142 Sermons preached by English bishops, 29 by Welsh, 6 by Irish, 5 by Americans, 1 by an Indian bishop (1901) and the remaining 17 by clergymen in priests' orders.   See C. F. Pascoe, Two Hundred Years of the S. P. G., II, p. 835.*

[10]*For a representative collection of Sermons made by the Society, but without any interpretations, see Twelve Anniversary Sermons Preached Before the Society for the Propagation of the Gospel in Foreign Parts, pp. i-xi, 1-205, London: T. B. Sharpe and J. A. Hatchard, 1845.   Included in this edition are the sermons for 1702, 1706, 1707, 1732, 1739, 1741, 1745, 1771, 1776, 1783, 1795, 1822.   At the end of the volume is a folded chart of work in process in 1703.   These dates are Gregorian.   See pp. 1-13, for Sermon of Dr. Richard Willis, Dean of Lincoln.*

[11]*Twelve Anniversary Sermons preached before the Society . . . , pp. 15-37. Dr. Williams took Acts xvi 9 as his text: "A vision appeared to Paul in the night: there stood a man of Macedonia, and prayed him, saying, come over into Macedonia, and help us."*

Both Willis and Williams pointed out that the home front must support the whole new enterprise by religious solidarity, or philosophical deism would be successful in destroying religion in Great Britain. Deism, Williams defined as 'natural religion' which implied that each people had its own religion, and that the faith of natives was best suited to them. Of this religious equalitarianism, which had produced indifferentism, he declares "If this be the case, the labours of the missionaries will be an end, and all the expense of sending them abroad may be saved, for what is left is not Christianity but Deism."[12] An appeal to the wealth of England, particularly that of the great city of London, so largely the result of American trade, was made in realistic terms. The moral improvement of the white colonists and Negro slaves was presented as an economic advantage, not only to these two groups themselves, but also to the people of England who would benefit economically from a more harmonious new world order. And, he concluded, the Indian, dangerous in the hands of the French and Spaniards, might well become an ally for the English.

Bishop Williams clearly perceived the problems of the depth and fixity of native cultures and therefore the difficulties of the Christianization of Indians and slaves. He presented a Negro program which survived the whole century, namely, that Christianization, the goal of all the Society's effort, did not mean emancipation, documenting his thesis from the Bible. Although hinting that he did not approve of slavery,[13] he took the ground that the master had it in his power to Christianize his slaves, greatly to the advantage of both parties,

> Here we may reasonably expect a greater success in the conversion of such than of natives [Indians], because they are wholly in the power of their masters, and are not in a condition to refuse whatever they demand of them; . . .

[12]*Dr. Williams (1706) put the argument into the mouth of a noble savage, who stated the case thus " . . . I [a native] grant what you say, that the christian religion doth propose many excellent advantages to those that believe and embrace it; but I have been otherwise educated, and cannot easily part with what all my progenitors have lived and died in, and must have very convincing reasons to oblige me to forsake it: . . . give me a plain and positive answer, whether a heathen, continuing so to be, may not be saved, if he take nature and reason to be his guide, and live soberly and virtuously? And why must all the world submit to you? And are all to be damned that believe not as you do believe? . . .*
Then saith the native, let the fault lie upon me, and if I may be saved in the religion of my own country, I shall need no further instructor, nor shall I desire any change."

[13]*Dr. Williams stated, "I know nothing as to Christianity that alters men's rights for the sake of it; but such as they were, so they remained till altered by a human law: and the practice of this hath been continued throughout all ages in the most parts of the world where liberty has been restrained by laws, or parted with by voluntary surrender, or seized by conquest and forfeiture, or lastly, been transferred by sale and purchase." See Twelve Anniversary Sermons . . . , p. 25.*

What a security will this be to their masters, when those
that they now fear more than an enemy are in one and the same
interest, when there will be a mutual trust and confidence, and
they that are now watched and guarded for fear of doing mischief will be a safeguard to their masters for preventing it.[13a]

Although pointing out that in many places the Church was wanted,
he used words that became familiar in later sermons and in the letters
of the missionaries, in speaking of the white colonists,

. . . the degeneracy of which from Christianity is much
to be lamented, as it is easy to be observed, in too many of
them: and it is the more to be lamented because it is a degeneracy . . . But those whom we are now treating of
are born and bred up in the Christian religion, admitted into
the Church by baptism, and cannot but have heard in some
measure what they are obliged to by virtue of it; and yet by
a shameful apostogy are little better than infidels.[14]

The Bishop brilliantly presented the entire thesis of the noble
savage, following in the footsteps of Las Casas whom he quoted point-
edly. In his own burning indictment of Spanish cruelty, he observed,

The Indians in those parts were capable of receiving the
impression of Christian religion, and easily inclined to embrace
it, for they were of a tractable, sweet, and gentle disposition,
and endued with all those good qualities which fitted them for
it; and when the missionaries came first amongst them, they
received them as messengers from heaven, and some were disposed to be baptized. But upon the barbarous usage of those
natives, who were destroyed without any provocation, when
whole countries were made desolate like a wilderness, and the
cities and town depopulated, when by tortures they were com-
pelled to turn Christians without any previous instruction, they
had an abhorence of the Christians, and bestowed no better
a name upon them than 'Yares' that is devils, as the Bishop
of St. Martha relates in his letter to the King of Spain in
anno. 1541; . . .[15]

13a*Twelve Anniversary Sermons . . . pp. 26-27.*
14*Ibid., p. 29.*
15*Twelve Anniversary Sermons, pp. 29-30. In the letters of the venerable Dr.
Francis Le Jau, a missionary for the Society at Goose Creek, South Carolina, 1706-
1717, can be found a similar opinion regarding the English trader. On December
2, 1706, Dr. Le Jau wrote to John Chamberlayne from Goose Creek (S. P. G.
MSS. (L. C. Trans.), A3, No. LXVIII) that the Indians were "very quiet, sweet
humored, and patient, content with little, which are dispositions to be true christians." But three years later he was complaining of the wicked lives of the traders
and other whites which was hindering conversion. He wrote, " . . . if anything
opposes the publishing of the Gospel among the Indians it shall be the manner how
our Indian trade is carried on, chiefly the fomenting of war among them for our
people to get slaves. . . . interest has a great power here and does occasion injustice*

A comparison of Anglican with Roman Catholic methods led the Bishop to state in a short sentence his conclusion that "The men shall teach over again in their lives what they have before taught in their principles;" and that such men, enthusiastically supported by England, will be able to overcome the reputed advantage of the Roman Catholic priests in performing miracles,[16] and the generosity of many donors will overcome by their support the use of the great funds of the Roman Catholic orders as well as the mobility and devotion of their personnel.

The sermons of the first decade of the Society's history staked out the primary activities.   Faced with the problems of securing funds and decisions as to the emphasis upon and division of work among the Indians, white colonists, and Negroes, Bishop Gilbert Burnet in 1704, wisely anticipated much that practical experience revealed on every front.   Pointing out that new methods of carrying on the work must be developed and that wild natives would not be convinced by the same arguments as could be used in England, he urged that " 'our design upon infidels' must begin in the instruction and reform of our own people, in opening schools, sending over books, and preparing labourers to go into that field.   For the grown natives who do not speak English and are past their youth, it is not easy to say what to do with them but just dealing might in time dispose them to think well of us and our religion and make them friends and allies."

In a Word, while our Colonies are as so many Mines of Wealth to us, and while such vast Numbers of Seamen are imployed in so many hundreds of Ships . . . While we have so many Blessings coming home daily, shall we take no Care to secure those Blessings to us and to our Brethren in those Plantations? . . . Shall we export nothing for the good of their Souls, while we import so much for the raising our own Wealth from their Industry.[17]

too visibly . . . " See Francis Le Jau to John Chamberlayne, St. James Goose Creek, South Carolina, October 20, 1709, in S. P. G. MSS. (L. C. Trans.), A5, No. 49. For a detailed study of the work of the Society with the Indians in South Carolina, see Frank J. Klingberg, "The Indian Frontier in South Carolina as Seen by the S. P. G. Missionary" in Journal of Southern History, V, No. 4, November 1939, pp. 479-500.

[16]*Twelve Anniversary Sermons, p. 36, Williams states, "But on the other side, as our missionaries have not the 'advantage' of comprising their doctrine by miracles and extraordinary powers, so they are not under the advantage of extraordinary provisions and means of subsistence."*

[17]*Gilbert Burnet, Bishop of Sarum, Sermon Preached before the S. P. G. in St. Mary le Bow, London, 1704, p. 20. (Huntington Library) Burnet's most famous work was published after his death in 1715. It was the History of his Own Times, 2 vols. Volume one was printed in 1723, volume two in 1734. There is also a Clarendon Press edition (1823 and 1833) which gives a full list of Burnet's writings.*

Bishop Beveridge, in his sermon three years later, spoke of the
initial liberal contributions of the officers and members of the Society,
and urged his listeners to be "so fully assured of the truth of . . .
religion, . . . [to] think nothing too great to be done or suffered for
it." Bishop Beveridge continued:

> For there is such beauty and lustre in all true Christian
> zeal and virtue, that it allures the eyes of those who behold it,
> and affects their hearts with a holy emulation and ambition to
> embrace and follow it, as appeared not only in the first propaga-
> tion of our holy religion, but likewise in the reformation of it
> after it had been corrupted in these parts of the world. How
> did the zeal of some few princes, and other learned and good
> men, provoke and stir up people of all ranks and qualities,
> yea, whole nations, to venture their lives and fortunes in re-
> storing it to its primitive purity in doctrine and worship!
> But we need not go so far back for instances of this nature:
> we have a great one now before us—the Society for propagating
> the Gospel in Foreign Parts, which was no sooner incorporated
> by his late Majesty, but the President and Members of it con-
> tributed and subscribed so liberally to the carrying on this most
> Christian design, that many were thereby stirred up to tread
> in their steps, and some without letting their left hand know
> what their right hand doth; insomuch, that the first year they
> were able to lay out upon it above four hundred pounds; in the
> second, above five hundred; in the third, above eight hundred;
> and in the next, above thirteen hundred pounds. So mightily
> did this apostolical fund increase and multiply, from the zeal of
> the first promoters of it, and that among themselves,—besides
> the influence it hath had upon foreign churches,—so that I may
> truly say to you, as St. Paul here saith to the Corinthians,
> "Your zeal hath provoked very many;" and I hope it will still do
> so, every day more and more.[18]

William Stanley, Dean of St. Asaph, in 1708, re-emphasized the
seriousness of the undertaking.[19] William Dawes, Bishop of Chester,
1709, discussed the technicalities of securing information from traders,
who could not only transport the missionaries but aid them in their
settlement, for the missionary would be a protection to all parties, amidst
the unsettled conditions.[20] Dr. Charles Trimnell, Bishop of Norwich,
in 1710, reiterated that doctrinal disputes must not be introduced to
the Indians, the whites must show a "better" religion than that already

[18]*Twelve Anniversary Sermons Preached Before the Society for the Propagation of the Gospel in Foreign Parts, p. 48.*
[19]*William Stanley, Dean of St. Asaph, Sermon preached before the S. P. G.
in St. Mary le Bow, London, 1708, pp. 1-8. (Huntington Library).*
[20]*William Dawes, Bishop of Chester, Sermon preached before the S. P. G. in
St. Mary le Bow, London, 1709, pp. 1-16 (Huntington Library).*

possessed by the Indians, and that the merchants trading with America should furnish the money.[21]

While these necessary preliminary moves were being made, Colonel Codrington appeared with his famous gift of the Codrington estates, making the Society itself a slaveholder of 300 Negroes, committed to their amelioration and Christianization.[22] Bishop William Fleetwood (1656-1723), in 1711, preached a sermon which became a blueprint for the process of Christianization and education of the Negro. A master of the sermon, with a genius for the presentation of just such a case as this, he reached all levels of society in Great Britain, and also in New York and other colonies. Although a Whig, Queen Anne, as well as William and Mary, had appointed him Royal Chaplain. Descendant of an ancient family, and educated at King's College, Cambridge, he received his Bachelor of Arts degree in 1679, Master of Arts in 1683, and Doctor of Divinity, 1705. He first won deserved recognition as a preacher in 1689, when he delivered a sermon in King's College Chapel, commemorating the memory of its founder, Henry the Sixth.

Queen Anne installed William Fleetwood in a canonry at Windsor in 1702, and six years later appointed him to the see of St. Asaph. An ardent Whig, Fleetwood attacked the peace of Utrecht, made by the Tories, and denounced them as Jacobites. The Tories caused all of Fleetwood's published sermons against the government to be publicly burned.[23] He was an authority on pagan inscriptions, the value of money and commodities, war, and peace, his work often appearing anonymously.[24] Throughout his lifetime he liberally assisted the Angli-

---

[21]*Charles Trimnell, Bishop of Norwich, Sermon preached before the S. P. G. in St. Mary le Bow, London, 1710 (Huntington Library).*

[22]*For a detailed account of the Codrington Estates and College, see Frank J. Klingberg, "British Humanitarianism at Codrington" in Journal of Negro History, XXIII, No. 4, October 1938, pp. 451-486.*

[23]*These Sermons were those preached by Fleetwood on the deaths of Queen Mary, of the Duke of Gloucester, of William III, and at the accession of Queen Anne. They were immediately issued as No. 384 (May 21, 1711-12) of the "Spectator" and Fleetwood said that thousands of copies were put into people's hands that would never otherwise have seen them.*

[24]*Some of his best known works are: (1) A collection of pagan and Christian inscriptions, with many original notes, entitled, Inscriptionum Antiquarum Sylloge (1691) 8 vols.; (2) Research on value of money and commodities for previous six centuries, published anonymously, entitled Chronicon Pretiosum, London 1707; (3) An Essay on Miracles in two Discourses: those of Moses and Jesus Christ, dedicated to Dr. Godalphin, provost of Eton, 1701; (4) Anonymous Sermon on Ps. lxxviii, 30, on the Fast Day, Jan. 16, 1711-12, against such as delight in war. By a Divine of the Church of England. London 1712; (5) Sixteen Practical Discourses on Relative Duties with Three Sermons upon the Case of Self-murther, addressed to the parishioners of St. Austins and St. Faith. London, 1705. 2 vols., 8vo.
A collection of Fleetwood's works was published in a folio volume, in 1737, with a prefatory memoir by his nephew, Dr. W. Powell, dean of St. Asaph and prebendary of Ely.
The biographical material is, of course, taken primarily from the Dictionary of National Biography.*

can Church with money and books. He was also an interested patron of letters, encouraging such men as George Hickes, Thomas Hearne, and Browne Willis.

For decades following 1711, Fleetwood's sermon before the Society[25] was widely used by the missionaries in trying to win over the whites to a program of Negro conversion. Thousands of copies were printed and distributed throughout the colonies, the S. P. G. workers in the West Indies alone receiving two thousand at one time for distribution.[26] Fleetwood's position, that of a small minority convinced that the Negroes possessed potentially the same intellectual powers as the whites, was in opposition to that of the populace in England, as well as to the opinion of whites in the colonies, who believed in the racial inferiority of the Negro mind. The missionaries of the S. P. G., confronted with the gulf between native and European cultures, often raised questions as to the feasibility of their work with the Negroes.[27]

The rapid Europeanization of the Negro race, in a long-range perspective, is a phenomenon that would perhaps have surprised the bishop himself. This sermon is in contrast to the customary reprimand of the whites for their crimes in capturing and enslaving the "down-trodden," "wretched," and "ignorant" Negroes. On religious grounds

[25]*Dr. William Fleetwood, Lord Bishop of St. Asaph, Sermon Preached before the Society for the Propagation of the Gospel in Foreign Parts, at St. Mary le Bow, Friday, February 16, 1710-11. (London: Joseph Downing, 1711) (Huntington Library).*

[26]*Letters written by missionaries to the Society asking for Fleetwood's Sermon can be found in the S. P. G. MSS. and Journals. See, for example, Thomas Temple to [Philip Bearcroft]. Hempsted, New York, May 17, 1742, in S. P. G. MSS. (L. C. Trans.), B. 10, No. 91, in which this school teacher wrote in part " . . . one thing more I crave . . . that I may have the Benefit of the late Bishop Fleetwood Sarmon [sic] preached in the year 1711 concerning ye instruction of Negroes . . . "; William Becket to David Humphreys, Philadelphia, September 25, 1729, in S. P. G. MSS. (L. C. Trans.), B 6, No. 248, also id to id., Lewes, Pennsylvania, July 1, 1731 in ibid., B 6, No. 238, in which Becket wrote that he was convinced that this and other Sermons were effective in his work; Fleetwood's Sermon was also gratefully received by the catechist to the Negroes in Philadelphia, Mr. William Sturgeon, see letters from him to the Society, February 3, 1741/48 in Journal of S. P. G. (L. C. Trans.) XI, May 20, 1748; July 26, 1750, in ibid., November 16, 1750; April 26, 1751 in ibid., July 19, 1751.*

[27]*See a letter of Thomas Standard to David Humphreys, West Chester, New York, November 5, 1729 in S. P. G. MSS. (L. C. Trans.), B1, No. 50, in which he states that one thing the Society should realize was "That few of them [Negroes] are capable of being instructed"; Joseph Ottolenghe, catechist to the Negroes in Georgia, wrote to the Society on September 9, 1751 that "in general they [Negroes] are slow of apprehension, of a dull understanding, and soon forgetting what they have learned," in S. P. G. MSS. (L. C. Trans.), B19, No. 149; see also Abel Alleyne to Philip Bearcroft, Consets, Barbados, December 9, 1741, in S. P. G. MSS. (L. C. Trans.), B8, No. 51, in which Alleyne, although commenting on the good demeanor of the Negroes, states his belief that it was difficult for many black men to understand the principles of education.*

he asked the colonists to save their own souls[28] by good works, asking what the reluctant masters could answer upon arriving at the gates of Heaven. This part of the sermon provoked in America a retort belonging obviously to an earlier era than that of the "black mammy" tradition which arose only after years of familiar servant-master relationship. A white owner exclaimed that she would not care about going through the gates of Heaven if she saw black faces peering out.[29]

The bequest of the Codrington Estates in Barbados to the Society was made just one year before the Fleetwood sermon. New York was a chief center not only for Indian but also for Negro work and, with Codrington, furnished voluminous records for the Society's vaults. Codrington was a yard-stick experiment for all the colonies, inasmuch as the Society there owned slaves on a plan of model management. It was a frequent subject of the bishops throughout the century; discussed, for example, by J .Wynne, (1725), William Warburton, (1766), Shute Barrington, (1775), and Beilby Porteus, (1783),[30] whose remarkable sermon will be discussed by way of a final summary; and John Warren, (1787).

To acquire a taste for eighteenth century sermons a Lewis Carroll direction might be, "Read one." The first ten pages of Bishop Fleetwood's sermon arrays the Scriptural texts and phrases he has carefully assembled. The sermon then gets up steam and theme and grips attention throughout with its facing up to the "Interests" of that day.[31]

In the sermon here, in 1711, are to be found all the later arguments used for the emancipation of the Negro, clearly and emphatically

[28]*The missionaries in the American colonies and the West Indies from 1702 to 1783 complained constantly of the reluctance of masters to have their Negroes baptized. A typical example can be found in Thomas Hasell to David Humphreys, St. Thomas Parish, South Carolina, May 12, 1726 in S. P. G. MSS. (L. C. Trans.), B4, No. 200, in which he wrote to the Secretary "few masters and mistresses will be convinced that it is their duty to instruct them [the Negroes] or have them instructed, nor will they be persuaded to take the necessary care and pain in order to do it"; see also John Usher to David Humphreys, Bristol, New England, December 27, 1726 in S. P. G. MSS. (L. C. Trans.), A 19, pp. 459, 460, Usher said his hopes for Negro Christianization had vanished "by reason of the total aversion of the inhabitants . . . to it"; for an earlier instance, see trans. of Elias Neau to John Chamberlayne, New York, August 24, 1708 in S. P. G. MSS. (L. C. Trans.), A4, No. 68.*

[29]*This incident is described by Dr. Francis le Jau in a letter to the Society, dated St. James, Goosecreek, South Carolina, September 18, 1711 in S. P. G. MSS. (L. C. Trans.), A6, No. cxlii.*

[30]*Beilby Porteus, Bishop of Chichester and later Bishop of London, urged the Society to try new expedients to better the existence of slaves, and declared that almost the only attempts, up to 1783, to deliver Negroes from their state of ignorance had been those of the S. P. G. Porteus suggested that on the Estates, the S. P. G. give its slaves some benefits of society, attach them to the soil, give them some rights and privileges, and after this, much progress in religion would be sure to follow. Porteus' Sermon preached before the S. P. G. in St. Mary-le-Bow, February 21, 1783, pp. 1-34 (Huntington Library).*

[31]*Bishop Fleetwood's sermon is given in full in this volume, Book II, p. 195.*

put: that the Negro was not inferior to the white man, that he would work for wages, that low prices for tropical products did not justify slavery. He made the concession to the slave owner that baptism did not free the Negro, but again because of that fact slavery was not justified. The strong words, the Negroes "were equally the Workmanship of God with themselves [the planters] ; endued with the same faculties and intellectual powers; Bodies of the same Flesh and Blood, and Souls certainly immortal," made this forceful sermon the choice for wide distribution, for reprinting throughout the eighteenth century and of fresh interest to the twentieth century.

On the matter of the Codrington Estates, his point was that if all other slaves were infidels, *"yet ours alone must be Christians."*[32]   His sagacity did not dodge the problems of the necessity for the work of time, or that mature counsels, comprehensive views and able heads would be needed for solutions. His argument is a model of firmness and persuasiveness. From his distance in London as from an elevation above other men's prejudices, he penetrated with a flash of intuition to what would eventually be the solution of slavery. He knew in his own time of Neau's pupils gathering in their night schools in New York, and of the other catechists at work throughout the colony, and possibly of the slaves in Virginia learning the alphabet from the labels on merchandise and from other such accidental primers teaching other slaves to read.[33] But in this early sermon he encompassed all that would follow and was, in that sense, the discoverer of the race and its future in the Americas.

The sermons following Fleetwood for thirty years include several notable discussions of the deistic controversy, of which Sherlock's in 1716, Berkeley's in 1732, Butler's in 1739. are among the better known. The Society, in brief, confronted the successive problems inherent in the native missionary program in the new world, and also waged the ideological battles of the age, particularly those of deism, whose proponents took the position that natural religion was sufficient, and Christianity unnecessary. Sherlock published a tract, "Tryal of the Witnesses of the Resurrection of Jesus,"[34] which was a defense of the his-

[32]*Dr. William Fleetwood, Lord Bishop of St. Asaph, Sermon Preached before the Society for the Propagation of the Gospel in Foreign Parts at St. Mary-le-Bow, Friday, February 16, 1710/1711, (London: Joseph Downing, 1711), p. 32 (Huntington Library).*

[33]*The Negro History Bulletin III, No. 2, November 1939, has two excellent articles written by Carter G. Woodson on Negro Education. "Educating the Negro before the General Emancipation" pp. 17-19, and "Snatching Learning in Forbidden Fields" p. 21.*

[34]*This book was published anonymously in 1729, and in 1749 a sequel to* it came out, attributed to Sherlock. *Other works of Sherlock include Remarks on the Bishop of Bangor's Treatment of the Clergy and Convocation, London 1717; The Use and Intent of Prophecy 1725 (also other editions). The latter book contained six Sermons preached by Sherlock in the controversy with the Deists.*

torical occurrences of miracles given in the strange form of a trial and acquittal of the Apostles in the Inns of Court, on the charges of giving false evidence.

More famous, however, was the work of Bishop Berkeley who stated in his sermon that the immortality of the soul "is a fundamental doctrine as well of natural religion as of the Christian"[35] and he argued that "life and immortality were brought to light by the Gospel."[36]   In this sermon he developed, as was to be expected, the general obligation of Christians to carry on missionary work, and surveyed the program of the S. P. G. He argued that, ". . . if we have not Miracles, we have other advantages which make them less necessary now,"[37] which advantages were to be used to the full, in a modern world where Christianity so largely prevailed. He based his specific observations on a residence of three years in Rhode Island where Indians and Negroes were few, and were disappearing under, he said, the influence of strong liquor and smallpox, so that 1000 Indians were left, and about 1500 Negroes who, he was glad to note, were not freed by baptism.

He commented on the superiority of the Roman Catholic policy among the French and Spaniards whose settlers intermixed with the Indians and instructed the Negroes in religion, and who had bishops and seminaries for the clergy in their colonies. Under the circumstances his main attention was given to the settlers who had welcomed S. P. G. missionaries and would profit by additional labourers. His concern about the home front is graphically expressed in these words: " . . . in order to propagate the gospel abroad, it is necessary we do it at home, and extend our charity to domestic infidels, if we would convert or prevent foreign ones."[38]

Bishop Butler, in 1739, took up the same problem from a more abstract and philosophical angle. Leading quickly to the obligations of all Christians to protect Christianity at home and spread it abroad, particularly among slaves and natives, he made surprisingly downright, blunt suggestions, as unequivocal in tone as an anti-slavery speaker's a century later:

> Of these our colonies, the slaves ought to be considered as inferior members, and therefore to be treated as members of them, and not merely as cattle or goods, the property of their masters. Nor can the highest property possible to be acquired in these servants cancel the obligation to take care of

[35]*Twelve Anniversary Sermons Preached before the Society . . . Sermon IV* by *Dr. George Berkeley, Dean of Londonderry (afterwards Bishop of Cloyne) in 1731* [1732], *p. 52.*
[36]*Ibid., p. 53.*
[37]*Ibid., p. 58.*
[38]*Ibid., p. 67.*

their religious instruction. Despicable as they may appear in our eyes, they are the creatures of God, and of the race of mankind for whom Christ died; and it is inexcusable to keep them in ignorance of the end for which they were made, and the means whereby they may become partakers of the general redemption. On the contrary, if the necessity of the case requires that they be treated with the very utmost rigour that humanity will at all permit, as they certainly are, and, for our advantage, made as miserable as they can be in the present world; this surely heightens our obligation to put them into as advantageous situation as we are able with regard to another.

The like charity we owe to the natives,—we owe to them in a much stricter sense than we are apt to consider, were it only from neighbourhood and our having gotten possessions in their country. For incidental circumstances of this kind appropriate all the general obligations of charity to particular persons, and make such and such instances of it the duty of one man rather than another. We are most strictly bound to consider these poor uninformed creatures as being in all respects of one family with ourselves, the family of mankind, and instruct them in our common salvation, that they may not pass through this stage of their being like brute beasts, but be put into a capacity of moral improvements, how low soever they must remain as to others, and so into a capacity of qualifying themselves for an higher state of life hereafter.

And as to ways and means, he remarked:

. . . And thus navigation and commerce should be consecrated to the service of religion, by being made the means of propagating it in every country with which we have any intercourse. And the more widely we endeavour to spread its light and influence, as the forementioned circumstances and others of a like kind open and direct our way, the more faithful shall we be judged in the discharge of that trust which is committed to us as Christians, when our Lord shall require an account of it.

. . . And it is an obligation but little more remote, to assist in doing it in our factories abroad, and in the colonies to which we are related by their being peopled from our own mother country, and subjects (indeed very necessary ones) to the same government with ourselves. And nearer yet is the obligation upon such persons, in particular, as have the intercourse of an advantageous commerce with them.[39]

[39]*Joseph Butler, Bishop of Bristol, Sermon preached before S. P. G. in St. Mary-le-Bow, London 1739 (Huntington Library) pp. 14-16. Twelve Anniversary Sermons Preached before the Society . . . , Sermon V, Dr. Joseph Butler, Bishop of Bristol, 1739, pp. 76-77. Dr. Butler's text was taken from Matt. xxiv. 14. "And this gospel of the kingdom shall be preached in all the world for a witness unto all nations." For an excellent recent discussion of Butler see "The Analogy of Religion, 1736-1936, Joseph Butler's Achievement" in "The London Times Literary Supplement," No. 1784, Saturday, April 11, 1936, pp. 305-306.*

With Berkeley, Butler admonished Christians to proceed without miracles, to be satisfied with small beginnings, and expressed the hope that serious men of all denominations would join in the work, and would remember that the nature of the Society required some cooperation with others.[40] Of education of the children he hoped " . . . good men separately, can do nothing proportionable to what is wanting in any of these ways; but their common united endeavors may do a great deal in all of them."[41] Throughout he expressed toleration, appealed to the will of all good men, and breathed confidence that good will would prevail and Christianity triumph.

The overwhelming majority of the sermons from Fleetwood's to Secker's (1711 to 1741) dealt with the profits of American commerce, including of course the sugar islands, and the justice, equity and Christian duty of making a fair return to the colonists, the natives, and the Negroes. Sir Humphrey Gilbert in 1583 perhaps first suggested this restitution in his famous essay "On the Advantages of Colonies."[42] Among the annual speakers, the sermons of Bishops Leng, 1727, Egerton, 1729, Maddox, 1734, Herring, 1738, make characteristic references to planters and traders as debtors to the slaves and natives, and to England's heavy obligations to the colonies for the great economic advantages derived from them. Whatever the prevailing theories of contemporary economists on the financial advantages or disadvantages of colonial possessions, the sermons are unanimous in stressing the thesis that much of the wealth of England was derived from colonial sources. Egerton's words were firm:

> As we are therefore engag'd in Commerce with these People, and have our Settlements amongst them, and by these Advantages have many opportunities of instructing them in the Principles of our Holy Religion, and recommending it to them by our Good Examples, we ought not to neglect any of the means that are put into our Hands, of bringing them over to the practice of it. And I cannot but think it a just debt, with which we are oblig'd to charge ourselves to do this for the many Benefits which in the Business of our Trade we reap from them. . . . [43]

Bishop Maddox after a long discussion of the necessity of keeping missionaries for the English population in the colonies, referred particularly to the obligation to the Negroes:

[40] *Twelve Anniversary Sermons Preached before the Society . . . , Sermon V,* Dr. Joseph Butler, Bishop of Bristol, in 1739, p. 80.
[41] *Ibid., p. 82.*
[42] *Found in A. E. Bland, P. A. Brown, R. H. Tawney (comps. and eds.) English Economic History; Select Documents (London: G. Bell and Sons), 1924.*
[43] *Henry Egerton, Bishop of Hereford, Sermon Preached before the S. P. G. in St. Mary le Bow, London, February, 1728, pp. 13-14 (Huntington Library).*

The harder State of Bondage these poor Creatures, engaged in Labour for our Pleasure and Advantage, must now endure, the more reasonable it is to alleviate the Distress, by furnishing their Minds, with good Principles.[44]

Bishop Herring, referring to strength of empire, pointed out, "For every convert to Christianity, or member secured to our Establishment upon Gospel and Protestant Principles, is a Friend to our Country and Government, as well as to our Religion."[45] The "wild and barbarous" Indians appear in almost every sermon, described in words similar to Bishop Green's " . . . and many of the barbarous ignorant *Indians,* both the Neighbours to these & those that have been made use of for the Service of the Plantations have been instructed . . . and brought into the Christian Fold by Baptism."[46] Bishop Claggett dealt with the presence of Indians on the borders of the colonies at some length and discussed the aversion shown by them to Christianization. He continued by reminding his hearers that the S. P. G. was not prevented by this from pursuing its efforts. Missionaries had been sent them, scriptures put into their own languages, schools opened, "But after all the pains we have taken with them, and the use of the kindest methods of treating them, that were possible, we cannot say of the Indians we have been concerned with . . . that we have found them . . . easy to be taught."[47] His statement that the Indians were so backward that the missionaries had to put into them the first rudiments of reason, and of the religion of nature, indicates an early differentiation between the Indian and the Negro races.[48]

Just as in the anti-slavery movement the phrases "Christian humanity" and "sound policy" recur, the linked ideas of Christian idealism and good business appear tellingly in the sermons. This union is nowhere more clearly expressed than by the able Bishop Benson, in February, 1740, who in his sermon, instead of generalizing widely, made pointed concrete observations to appeal to the practical instincts of the country,

For were we but wise enough to consider only the Advantages of our Trade in *America* yet for the Sake of That we should take care to propagate the Christian Revelation: which

[44]*Isaac Maddox, Dean of Wells, Sermon preached before the S. P. G. in St. Mary le Bow, London, February, 1733, p. 28 (Huntington Library).*

[45]*Thomas Herring, Bishop of Bangor, Sermon preached before S. P. G. in St. Mary le Bow, London, February 1738, p. 27 (Huntington Library).*

[46]*Thomas Green, Lord Bishop of Ely, Sermon preached before S. P. G. in St. Mary le Bow, London 1723, pp. 32-33 (Huntington Library).*

[47]*Nicholas Claggett, Bishop of St. David's, Sermon preached before the S. P. G. in St. Mary le Bow, February 1736, London, p. 30 (Huntington Library).*

[48]*Ibid., p. 30ff.*

teaches Industry, Honesty, Sobriety, Temperance, Frugality; which enjoins all those Virtues that make Commerce gainful, and prohibits all those Vices that bring poverty in their Rear.[49]

Benson declared that besides the general obligation the English were under to propagate the Gospel, they were in duty bound to the colonies in America, both on account of the great benefit received from them, and by reason of the many opportunities of making this recompense:

> Do we imagine that if these People have no Faith towards God, they will have any Fidelity to their King? If they lost all Regard to right behaviour in the common relations of life at home, do we fancy they will retain still a filial Reverence to their remote Mother Country?[50]

The trader, Benson believed, should be especially concerned in promoting religion, for the trader would then be encouraging those virtues without which "Trade must sink to nothing and with which it must flourish and increase."[51]

Although Bishop Benson believed that the first obligation was to the English colonists, he urged that the Society should help the Indians. Civil life and the arts should be introduced; the manner in which the Georgia Indians had been handled was praised. The Indians in this colony, he observed, were treated with justice and humanity, and no liquor was proffered them.[52]

In regard to the Negroes, Bishop Benson deplored the opposition to their instruction shown by the masters. The whites were afraid, he said, that, if the slaves were instructed in eternal things, they would damage the material affairs of their masters, an opinion making it difficult for him to decide whether the wickedness or folly of the masters was the greater.[53] He also lamented, as did many others, the lack of a bishop in America, and believed this was an important hindrance in colonial conversion.[54] He bluntly stated that England was now engaged in a war the success of which chiefly depended on strength gained from America. He asked how England could prosper with her colonies unless religion and virtue were flourishing.[55]

Fortunately for the student of these sermons Bishop Secker, at

[49]*Martin Benson, Bishop of Gloucester, Sermon preached before the S. P. G. in St. Mary le Bow, London. February 1740, p. 10 (Huntington Library).*
[50]*Ibid., p. 13.*
[51]*Ibid., p. 13.*
[52]*Ibid., p. 17.*
[53]*Ibid., p. 19.*
[54]*Ibid., p. 22.*
[55]*Ibid., p. 22.*

the half way point between the organization of the Society and the Revolution, summed up in a heartening way the achievements of the first four decades. As was usual he called for intensified effort along the lines of the issues of that day, and voiced in confident words his further hopes in regard to the now well-developed objects and problems of the Society.

Thomas Secker (1693-1768), Archbishop of Canterbury (1758-1768), born in Nottinghamshire of pious nonconforming parents, educated at a dissenting academy in Attercliffe, studied under Samuel Jones with the object of entering the ministry. Among his classmates were Joseph Butler, later Bishop of Bristol, Isaac Maddox, Dean of Wells, and Samuel Chandler, the nonconformist writer. Being unable after six years of study to make up his mind as to the ministry, Secker decided to study medicine, and attended lectures in London and Paris. In Paris he became acquainted with his lifelong friend and future brother-in-law, Martin Benson, Bishop of Gloucester, referred to above. Before entering the ministry Secker received his M. D. degree at Leyden on March 7, 1721.

Under the influence of Butler and Benson, Secker became an Anglican. He was ordained deacon in December, 1722; and in March, 1723, was advanced to the priesthood by Dr. Edward Talbot, Bishop of Durham, and a friend of Butler. From 1724 to 1727 he was parish priest of Houghton-le-Spring, and in 1727 became rector of Ryton and prebendary of Durham. In 1732 he received appointment as chaplain to the king, and, after various advancements, he was consecrated bishop of Bristol in 1735; in 1737 he was translated to the see of Oxford; and, in 1758, became Archbishop of Canterbury.

In politics Secker supported the Hanoverian government, and was a staunch friend of George II and George III. A man of tolerance and enlightened education, he had among his friends many dissenters, including Philip Doddridge, Nathaniel Lardner, and Samuel Chandler. For his independence in making representations in favor of granting an episcopate to the American colonies he was attacked by critics, including Horace Walpole and Bishop Richard Hurd.

Archbishop Secker was generous with his money and his time, often taking over the task of revising the manuscripts of his friends. His writings include 140 sermons, four volumes of which were published during his lifetime, and the others after his death.[56] In his

[56]*Following is the list of some of Secker's works:*
(1) Five Charges delivered by him as Bishop of Oxford to his clergy in 1738, 1741, 1750, 1753. (2) Three Charges as Archbishop of Canterbury, 1758, 1762, 1766; (3) Lectures on the Church Catechism, 1769, 2 vols; (4) An Answer to Dr. Mayhew's Observations on the Charter and Conduct of the Society for the Propagation of the Gospel in Foreign Parts, 1764; (5) Letter to the Right Hon. Horatio

S. P. G. sermon of 1740-41,[57] Secker's emphasis upon the mission of
the Church for the white colonists was so impressive that his view
appeared frequently in the following years.[58] His penetration and grasp
of the questions before the Society are shown in his picture of the
success of the S. P. G. in its work from 1701 to 1741 : 100 churches
had been built in the colonies; 10,000 Bibles and Common Prayer Books
were sent out; 100,000 small tracts, sermons, and addresses had been
given the missionaries for distribution; seventy missionaries were in the
field; hundreds of Negroes and Indians had been made Christians; out of
230 Negroes on the Codrington Estates, 70 had become Christians.[59]
This bird's-eye view was refreshing as a change from the routine laments
as to the things not accomplished. Emphasis upon specific results produced, too, a generous mood, for the financial appeal which followed.[60]

*Walpole, Esq., dated Jan. 9, 1750/51, but not published until after Secker's death.
The answer to Mayhew and the Letter to Walpole both favor sending bishops
to the American colonies. All of Secker's works were collected and published
in four octavo volumes in 1792. There is a life of Secker by Bishop Beilby Porteus,
A Review of the Life and Character of Dr. Thomas Secker, Archbishop of Canterbury, 1770.*

[57]*For this Sermon in full, see below, Book II, p. 213.*

[58]*Earlier exhortations had been made by Charles Trimnell, Bishop of Norwich
in 1710, who said that the Negroes and the Indians could never be converted unless
the English exhibited "better" religion. This same idea was also presented by St.
George Ashe, Bishop of Clogher in 1714; by Joseph Wilcocks, Bishop of Gloucester
in 1726, who believed that by sending missionaries among the English, the necessary
groundwork could be laid for instruction of the heathen; by Frances Hare, Bishop of
Chichester, in 1734 who said that the first business of the S. P. G. was "to maintain religion and virtue" among the colonists; by John Lynch, Dean of Canterbury
in 1735 who stated that the chief aim of the S. P. G. was "to keep up religion and
piety among the English" in the plantations, and then to care for the heathen.*

[59]*In the nineteenth century, the fruits of the Codrington enterprises were evi-
denced. For example, in 1855, John H. A. Duporte, a Negro from Codrington
Mission, was selected to go to the Pongas country in Africa by the Missionary
Association for the Furtherance of the Gospel in West Africa; in 1860, Antigua
filled the vacancy left by the death of Bishop Rigaud, by the appointment of Rev.
W. W. Jackson, a former student of Codrington College; from 1830 to 1840, of the
whole number of persons ordained by the bishop, 49 deacons and 22 priests had
been educated at Codrington. See Frank J. Klingberg, "British Humanitarianism
at Codrington," in Journal of Negro History, XXIII, No. 4, October, 1938; pp.
451-486.*

[60]*For other examples of appeals for money, see the sermons delivered by William Stanley, Dean of St. Asaph in 1708, using as his text, "The harvest truly is
plenteous, but the laborers are few"; Thomas Hayley, Canon Residentiary of Chichester, in 1716, had urged that the work of the S. P. G. could surmount any difficulties by "a greater number of subscriptions, larger benefactions"; George Stanhope, Dean of Canterbury in 1714, commented on the wealth of London and its
ready support of charitable projects and hoped that the Society would not be
neglected. William Dawes, Bishop of Chester, in the Annual Sermon for 1709,
stated that the merchants and traders were reaping huge material profits from
the colonies; the same idea was stated by Charles Trimnell, Bishop of Norwich,
1710, and Edward Chandler, Bishop of Coventry and Lichfield, 1718; John Leng,
Bishop of Norwich in 1726 expressed his belief that the traders and merchants of
London who had become wealthy through the colonies should contribute to the
work of the S. P. G. as a thank-offering for their own success. Henry Egerton,
Bishop of Hereford, 1728, said, "And I cannot but think it is a just debt, with*

The forthright common sense of the man is shown again in his contention that if the colonists were not won over to the Anglican faith they could easily be made dissatisfied by rivals, "And we shall well deserve their revolting from Us, if we take no care of their obeying God;" and again, the colonists, by "agreeing in the same Faith and Worship with us will be an everlasting Motive to civil Unity also."

Secker, in speaking of the Indians, said that since the brown men had yielded their land to the English, the English in return should give them a way of living in the remaining territory; the colonists had introduced diseases and vices, therefore they should give the Indian Christian living in return.[61] Furthermore, Secker realized "that every single Indian, whom we make a Christian, we make a friend and ally at the same time."[62]

As to the Negroes, Secker's words described with convincing reasonableness the very effort made in New York, declaring that it was the duty of every Christian to make their lives happier, to help them with religious studies, teach them the Gospel, and lay for them a foundation in secular studies. Secker did not argue against the slave trade, as Warburton did 25 years later, but stated, "The Scripture, far from making any Alteration in Civil Rights, expressly directs, that *every Man abide in the Condition wherein he is called, with great Indifference of Mind concerning outward circumstances.*"[63] Less abstract than Berkeley or Butler, Secker was nevertheless a man of vision, as well as a genius in the especial gift of visual perception of a scheme or subject, and he possessed intelligent understanding of all the elements of a problem. This grasp upon the whole of his subject illuminates his sermons, and the reader gains the impression that he, who had never been

---

which we are obliged to charge ourselves to do this [propagate religion] for them, were it only in return for the many Benefits which in the business of our trade we reap from them."

[61]*John Waugh, Dean of Gloucester, 1722, expressed the same idea when he said that the English should promote Christianization in the colonies in order to repay the "poor infidels" for temporal riches gained by the Indian's cession of lands and trading privileges.*

[62]*Three years earlier, Thomas Herring, Bishop of Bangor, had stated almost the same idea, "For every Convert to Christianity, or member secured to our Establishment upon Gospel and Protestant principles, is a Friend to our Country and Government, as well as to our Religion." Samuel Lisle, Bishop of St. Asaph in 1748 also stated that the Negroes and Indians would be won away if efforts were not increased, and the result would be an assault upon English settlements. "Our own Safety therefore should spur us on to list these people in the Service of Christ . . ."*

[63]*Similar impressions were given by other Bishops: for example, John Green, Bishop of Lincoln, in 1768, commented: "As partakers with us of the same nature, they [Negroes] are already entitled to all acts of humanity; and if they were more nearly connected by a profession of the same faith, they might reasonably expect milder usage, they would not . . . be released from any engagements of servitude . . . Christ did not make or propose to make any change in the personal condition and privileges of men."*

in America at all, was more keenly conscious through his imaginative insight of actual conditions there, than was Bishop Berkeley who, after considerable colonial residence, conveys no such sense of the atmosphere of the life of the frontier in his academic discussion.

Dr. Philip Bearcroft, Secretary of the Society,[64] in his sermon in 1745 made a most valuable factual summary of the Society's work, indicative of the years of arduous committee meetings, the constant sessions of the trustees, and the close supervision of the field. Surveying carefully the colonies in turn, he reports of New York and New Jersey:

In the province of *New York* appear no footsteps of any attempt towards a settlement in religion earlier than in the year 1693, when, because [Vide "Trot's" Laws of the *British* Plantations in America. p. 263] "profaneness and licentiousness had overspread the province, for want of a settled ministry throughout the same," it was ordained by Act of Assembly "that six Protestant ministers should be appointed therein;" but this Act began not to operate till four years later, in 1697, when they set about building the church at *New York,* which they speedily and happily effected, and chose that worthy person [The Reverend Mr. Vesey, Commissary of New York] their rector, who continues to this day the careful pastor thereof. But as for the other five churches to be built in the other parts of the province—the salaries, from the public, for the incumbents to be appointed to them, were so small, as not to be a sufficient maintenance without the charitable aid of this Corporation, which gives salaries to nine missionaries in this province, in which there are about twenty churches and chapels with crowded congregations. And it hath been remarked, *[Vide Historical Account of the Society, p. 35] to the honour of the inhabitants of this province, that they have thrown off all their former rudeness, and become a religious, sober, and polite people, and, as traders to *New York* assure us, resemble the English very much in their open behaviour and frank sincerity of spirit.

In *East* and *West Jersey,* now united into one, there was a very wretched appearance of religion; and the principles of the poor people were so corrupted, and their practices so debauched, as to suffer them "to commit all manner of iniquity with greediness. They generally spent the Lord's day throughout the province at public houses, where they got their fill of rum, and then went to fighting and to running races;" [Colonel Morris's Memorial concerning them] but now, through the blessing of God upon the charitable endeavours of the Society, there is a great reformation of manners among them; and the "grace

64 *The Charter of the S. P. G. provides for one Secretary. The office was filled up to 1778, by the following: John Chamberlain (or Chamberlayne) 1701; William Taylor, 1712; David Humphreys, 1716; Philip Bearcroft, 1739; Daniel Burton, 1761; Richard Hind, 1773; William Morice, 1778.*

of God which teaches us that, denying ungodliness and worldly lusts, we should live soberly, righteously, and godly in this present world," hath so far wrought upon them, that they have built ten churches, besides chapels, in which the word of God, which giveth wisdom and understanding, is well attended on every Lord's day by populous congregations, and the blessed Sacraments duly administered by five missionaries from this Society.[65]

In terms not unlike the phrases used in 1737 by Bishop Claggett, Bearcroft says of the Indians:

As to the wild Indians bordering on our colonies, they are rather to be styled tribes than nations, for they are not numerous, seldom above one hundred or two in a company speaking the same dialect, and those frequently at enmity, if not open war, with their next neighbours: and by the best proof, that of experience, it is found to be to no purpose to talk to these Indians about our religion in their wild native state; they must be reduced from their barbarity, I had almost said brutality, and be made men, that is, rational, considerate creatures, before they will become Good Christians.[66]

The vital relationship of the S. P. G. to the white colonists is treated at length in 1754 by Bishop Robert Drummond, who, with many others, raised the question of the English attitude toward them. How did

[65] *Twelve Anniversary Sermons Preached before the Society . . . , Sermon VII, by Dr. Philip Bearcroft in 1744 [1745], pp. 113-114. (Words in brackets are the footnotes cited by Bearcroft). Other colonies are also passed in rapid review by Bearcroft. He first gives the number of inhabitants and their churches as found in 1701: In Newfoundland were 500 families without any public worship; New England had 70,000 in Massachusetts Bay, 30,000 in Connecticut, 3,000 in New Hampshire, 1,000 in Maine, with only one church in Boston; in Rhode Island and Providence were 5,000 people with only a beginning of a church in Newport; Narraganset had no form of religion for its 3,000 inhabitants; New York had 25,000 with one church; East Jersey, 8,000 and West Jersey, 5,000 with a few places of public worship, but not one Church of England; Pennsylvania, 15,000 with one church; North Carolina, 5,000 plus Negroes and Indians, no Church; South Carolina with 7,000, one church. Dr. Bearcroft then gives the work of the Society in these colonies. "In Newfoundland two missionaries . . . are and have been maintained for many years, at the expense of the Society . . ." "In New England . . . nineteen missionaries are supported . . . and . . . they must . . . double the number, 'so mightily grows the word of God . . .' there are at least thirty churches and chapels in this province, under the care of our missionaries . . ." ."In Pennsylvania are people of almost all persuasions . . . There is one flourishing church at Philadelphia, and not less than twenty churches and chapels more, served by eight missionaries in this province . . ." ."In North Carolina . . . the Society hath lately added a third missionary . . ." ."South Carolina is much better settled . . . ten parishes are furnished with missionaries from the Society . . ." " . . . the Society have done all in their power to encourage the setting up of schools . . . they give salaries to three catechists and twelve schoolmasters . . . they have furnished the churches with Bibles and Common Prayer Books, fixed parochial libraries, and given away books . . . tracts." See pp. 110-118, passim.*

[66] *Twelve Anniversary Sermons Preached before the Society . . . , p. 119.*

Churchmen picture their transplanted fellows? Were they semi-savages, or Englishmen in danger of losing their allegiance? Urging that the care of the white people in the colonies was necessary, not only from a religious standpoint but from prudence as well, Drummond designated as the objects of the Society's care, the inhabitants of all the American colonies, except Virginia, Maryland, and the islands. In these latter the Church of England was better established and ministers labored under more settled conditions. Outside of these, in the remaining continental colonies there were more than 100 S. P. G. churches and chapels, and nearly 70 missionaries and catechists employed, of whom some were paid wholly, some partly, by the S. P. G.[67]

Drummond stated firmly, to summarize somewhat in his own words, that the primary concern was for the S. P. G. "to prevent our own people" (implying a close sense of nationalism) from sinking into barbarism. Then [good] manners would have an effect upon the Negroes and Indians. If left without such care from England, the whites would lose the feeling of kinship with the home country, become extravagant and abandoned in living. In discussing the problems of Christianizing Indians and Negroes, he made an analysis of the difference in their respective problems as the Society perceived them to be, remarking, " . . . and the conversion of any body of *Indians* seems to be much more out of our power, than that of the Negroes."[68] He described the initial success with one tribe, the Mohawks, and mentioned widespread Roman Catholic activities among the Indians. After depicting the barbarism of the North American Indians, he recommended more free intercourse with them, the introduction of civil life, and the learning of the Indian language. Contrary to Sir William Johnson's convictions, he believed that the savages must be reduced to "gentle and just manners in a settled society, before we can hope to win any number of them to Christianity."[69]

These obstructions to Indian work, however, did not hold equally in the case of the Negroes, because they were under the eyes of the planters, " . . . and it seems to lye at the doors of Masters, that the slaves are not allowed to partake of the Common Salvation."[70] Drum-

[67]*Dr. Bearcroft in 1745, also stated similarly, "For, as to Maryland and Virginia, and the islands of the West Indies, they were found to be so well settled and provided with churches and incumbents under the care of the right reverend ordinary, as not to stand in need of assistance from the Society." But in the following colonies there was no form of worship in 1701: Newfoundland, Narraganset, North Carolina; in the Jerseys there were a few places of worship but not one according to the Liturgy of the Church of England. See Twelve Anniversary Sermons . . . pp. 110-111.*

[68]*Robert Drummond, Bishop of St. Asaph, Sermon Preached before S. P. G. in St. Mary le Bow, London, 1754, p. 16 (Huntington Library).*

[69]*Ibid., p. 17.*

[70]*Ibid., p. 18.*

mond declared, "These poor creatures are brought by a strange traffick from *Africa* to cultivate America, which the Europeans have dispeopled by their cruelty, and the vices introduced by them among the natives." The Negroes in the English plantations, he continued, were very little, if anything, worse in their outward condition by the change from their own country, and, if the English did their duty toward them, they might be much better in their minds. The common error that Christianity made the Negroes free had been so often refuted by the colonial laws and by juster reasoning upon the laws both of the realm and of the Gospel, that this objection, he believed, was probably either worn out or insincerely made use of. Or, expressed in his words, "If there are those who studiously hinder their slaves from becoming Christians, or who refuse them the means of opportunity, or encouragement to be instructed; we cannot attribute this hard usage to any other principle than avarice, inhumanity, or irreligion." Drummond pointed out that Christianization would calm the Negroes' spirits and induce sobriety, which would be all to the master's advantage.[71] He concluded his appeal for sincerity and zeal with a comment on tolerance, "No one can justly complain now that the Church of *England* does not maintain the Toleration upon the most extensive principles."[72]

In 1756, during the Seven Years War, Bishop Frederick Cornwallis expressed fears that unless Anglicans increased their efforts among the colonists, Papists would win them away, "And if our colonies change their Communion, we shall be in Great Danger of losing the Fruits of the Industry."[73] Characteristic of the references to the Indians, which occur again and again around the half century mark, was his view that the Indian's untutored mind could scarcely be expected to understand the precepts of the Gospel, and the barbarian must be civilized by friendly intercourse and gentle treatment. They must see and partake of the good effects of Christianity in honesty and justice. Such examples of fair dealing would calm their savage dispositions, reduce them from wildness and then find them prepared for the reception of Christianity.

Bishop James Johnson, in 1758, however, in a hopeful vein, used the phrase, "these *Indians* with whom this Society has had the longest correspondence and the most Influence, have been found the most faithful of all the Tribes, and the most steady Friends in this Country."[74] He is emphatic as to the value of the work in

[71]*Robert Drummond, Bishop of St. Asaph, Sermon Preached before S. P. G. in St. Mary le Bow, London 1754, pp. 18-19 (Huntington Library).*
[72]*Ibid., p. 27.*
[73]*Frederick Cornwallis, Bishop of Lichfield and Coventry, Sermon Preached before the S. P. G. in St. Mary le Bow, London 1756, p. 17 (Huntington Library).*
[74]*James Johnson, Bishop of Gloucester, Sermon Preached before the S. P. G. in St. Mary le Bow, London, 1758, pp. 12-13 (Huntington Library).*

" . . . our several Colonies in *America,* with whom we have constant Intercourse and to whom it is more immediately in our Power to impart it [religion]; who are the Source of our Wealth, from whom our Commerce receives its very life, and Existence, and our Naval Strength its continual Supply and Increase; and who are intitled to our first Care and Consideration, by every motive of Interest and Duty.[75]

Five years after Drummond's sermon, Bishop Anthony Ellis, although urging that white colonists needed attention, placed as of prime importance the instruction of heathen natives, Negro and Indian, that border on the colonies.[76] In demanding contributions to support the work he said, " . . . If cruelty has been used by masters towards their unhappy slaves, the former can hardly make fitter amends or give better proofs of their repentance for these sins . . . than by proportionate contributions to be employed to the glory of God and the spiritual benefit of those injured by them." Ellis cited discussions in former Abstracts about Papist dangers to Carolina and Mohawk Indians. Probably still sensing the dangers of the Seven Years War, he drew a picture of all the colonies falling under Roman Catholic control, "As the great importance of these colonies to this kingdom is now understood, it is easy to conceive what their loss would be to us, especially should they come into the possession of any enemy solicitous to impair and, as far as possible, ruin, our commerce . . . ". He continued, "They [the colonists] will be more loyal subjects to the King, more able and . . . willing to defend themselves from their bordering enemies, or any others, and more attached to this, which may properly be accounted their principal Country, by the strong bond of the same religion." He stressed the wisdom of making good Christians of the Negro slaves. He believed that as their obstinacy and eagerness for revenge were abated, they would become better servants and fewer revolts would be started.[77]

Bishop Philip Yonge's sermon, in 1765, is a conventional statement on the slave trade and a denial of the Indians' title to their lands. Bishop William Warburton, the next year, in his fiery rebuttal of the usual slave trade arguments may have had this Yonge sermon in mind. Yonge states the manifest destiny argument for the white man and even suggests a justification for bringing the Negro from Africa to help in this

[75] *James Johnson, Bishop of Gloucester, Sermon Preached before the S. P. G. in St. Mary le Bow, London, 1758, p. 10 (Huntington Library).*
[76] *Anthony Ellis, Bishop of St. David's, Sermon Preached before S. P. G. in St. Mary le Bow, London, 1759 (Huntington Library).*
[77] *Ibid.*

evolution of the new world.[78] Not only did he justify the slave trade, but he defended the white man's seizure of the Indian lands:

> It has been objected to the first *American* Settlements, that they were in themselves acts of rapine and lawless power. But this is without reason; for the law of nature gave no right to the Indians, of prior occupancy except to what lands could be, and actually [were] used by them. And if they, who bring men from Africa, in a state of slavery, can be as well vindicated as they who fertilize tracts, otherwise useless, in America; yet as neither of them will be able to find moral reason for withholding from those rude people the light of the Gospel, so will it be impossible . . . to cultivate in their understandings the reasonable faith and hope of a Christian, unless he [the missionary] can enforce his doctrines by the example of those who already have received them.[79].

More liberal was Yonge's instruction to the missionaries that when they wished to convert heathen, they must begin with the principles of natural religion.

[78]*Thomas Thompson, a missionary for the Society in New Jersey (1745-1750) and on the coast of Africa (1752-1756), curiously also accepted and defended the slave trade. Due to the historical and bibliographical interest of Dr. Walter H. Stowe, rector of Christ Church, New Brunswick, New Jersey, An Account of Two Missionary Voyages (1758) by Thomas Thompson, A. M., was reprinted in facsimile with introduction and notes (1937) from the copy owned by Rutgers College. The Account was published by the Society for the Promotion of Christian Knowledge for the Society for the Propagation of the Gospel in Foreign Parts. Although the S. P. G. had originally purchased 500 copies, 150 years later it owned no copy. In the United States, Rutgers and Huntington Library had copies. The obstacles in religious and commercial enterprises on the Guinea Coast are emphasized in this account. The oppressive climate, native rites, Mohammedanism, and the mixed population are vividly described by Thompson. For Thompson's approval of the slave trade, see the Dictionary of National Biography. His pamphlet in favor of the trade (1772) was answered by Granville Sharp.*

[79]*Philip Yonge, Bishop of Norwich, Sermon preached before the S. P. G. in St. Mary le Bow, London, February 15, 1765, pp. 22-23 (Huntington Library). This idea was taught as late as 1834 at the University of Virginia in the law class of Professor Davis. See Frank J. Klingberg, Old Sherry: A Portrait of a Virginia Family (Richmond, Garrett and Massie), appendix B, "On Benjamin Franklin Wysor's Lecture Notes," pp. 212-218. On p. 216, Wysor's Notes for September 30, 1834, say "The discovery of America has given rise to the celebrated question— Have nations a right to take possession of part of a great uncultivated country inhabited only by erratick tribes who cannot find use for the whole. The question then as it regards America comes up on which issue is joined—Had its first discoverers under the circumstances a legal right to take possession of it by force or otherwise. There are two points . . . 1st under the abstract principles, . . . 2nd under the right established by the custom of nations with regard to discovered territories . . . Under the first of these propositions may be regarded the general command unto mankind to multiply and replenish the earth . . . It follows from this, . . . the first discoveries of America . . . had a right . . . to take possession of it and fulfill . . . the obligation imposed by the above command. . . . Tribes or nations of men, who endeavour to support by hunting and fishing have no right to, & may be driven from all lands except what is necessary to support them by cultivation. The tribes of North American Indians could not be said to possess or occupy the country; Because their settlements were not permanent . . . "*

Bishop Warburton's early life and academic training were determining factors in producing the independence of mind which prompted him to oppose the slave trade. William Warburton (1698-1779), Bishop of Gloucester, attended grammar school for a few years at Oakham, Rutland; in 1714, for five years, he was put under the supervision of John Kirke, an attorney, under whose tutelage he developed an eagerness for miscellaneous reading, especially theological literature. In 1723, he was ordained deacon by the Archbishop of York, began his active writing career, and was given a Master of Arts degree from Cambridge.

Warburton's advancement was rapid. In 1738, he became chaplain to the Prince of Wales; in 1754, one of the King's chaplains in ordinary, he obtained the Doctor of Divinity degree from the Archbishop of Canterbury; and in 1755, he was a prebend at Durham, at £500 a year. Supported by William Pitt, two years later he became dean of Bristol; and, in 1759, probably again through Pitt's influence, he rose to be bishop of Gloucester.

Throughout his career, Warburton wrote voluminously on varied subjects, including the alliance between Church and State, with commentaries on the *Essay on Man,* Bolingbroke's philosophy, and religious topics.[80] In 1747, he brought out an edition of Shakespeare, which was much criticized, and, in 1751, as Pope's literary executor, he published an edition of the poet's works. His books were often severely criticized by his contemporaries, because, in writing, his legal training made him highly controversial and coloured his religious and philosophical ideas. His legal point of view is especially noticeable in his *Divine Legation. of Moses.* His work shows wide knowledge and is stamped by a strong personal character, and, in style, it is provocative and bold. Three of his sermons were published during the Re-

[80]*Some of Warburton's best known works are: (1) The Alliance between Church and State; or the Necessity and Equity of an established Religion and a Test Law demonstrated from the Essence and End of Civil Society . . . 1736, other editions include 1741, 1748, 1765, 1746. This book represents many contemporary opinions and largely accepts the principles of John Locke. (2) The Divine Legation of Moses Demonstrated on the principles of a Religious Deist, from the Omission of the Doctrine of a Future State of Rewards and Punishments in the Jewish Dispensation. In six books, published first in January 1737/38, also other editions; (3) A View of Lord Bolingbroke's Philosophy in four Letters to a Friend, 1754 (first two letters), 1755 (other two). (4) A . . . Commentary on Mr. Pope's "Essay on Man" in which is contained a Vindication . . . , 1739. This was rewritten, in part, in 1742, and issued as A Critical and Philosophical Commentary on Mr. Pope's "Essay on Man," in which is contained a Vindication. (5) Two volumes of sermons called, Principles of Natural and Revealed Religion, 1753, 1754. Warburton's widow, in 1788, under the supervision of Hurd, published a collective edition of Warburton's Works, 7 vols. 4to. In 1794, Hurd published a Discourse by way of a general Preface to the Quarto Edition, chiefly a life of Warburton. Only 250 copies were printed. In 1811, the Works and the Discourse were published together in 12 vols.*

bellion of 1745; two volumes of sermons that he had preached at Lincoln's Inn, called *Principles of Natural and Revealed Religion,* were printed in 1753 and 1754; and another sermon was issued in 1767, following his famous sermon of 1766 before the S. P. G.[81]

Discussing the problems of the Indian and the Negro in the British colonies, the sermon of 1766 is first an appeal for more thorough preliminary training for the missionaries to the Indians and, second, a fiery blast of denunciation against the slave trade. Fleetwood and Secker both preached during war times, and in the light of the anxiety of war conditions; Warburton at the close of a successful war.

Beginning with the duty, not the charity, of preaching the Gospel to the new world,[82] he found the Jesuits the most successful, and the reader will note how brilliantly he surveys the Latin-American world: Paraguay, the island of California, and all the works of man, mostly evil, in the known regions of both hemispheres are covered. His practical suggestion that the Society found a college for young men entering the mission field goes beyond the more general suggestions for the training of missionaries often brought forward by bishops in other sermons,[83] and by the Society's workers in the field.[84] The fruit of Sir William Johnson's teaching is seen in Warburton's demand that men must be found who are willing to live among the savages.[85] The missionaries in the colonies had also for years, in their letters, dealt with the dream of living and moving with the Indians as the French missionary did.[86] Warburton's observations that the Indians' property and

---

[81]For *Warburton's S. P. G. Sermon of 1766 in full, see below, Book II, p. 235.*

[82]*Samuel Lisle, Bishop of St. Asaph, Sermon preached before the S. P. G. in St. Mary le Bow, pp. 1-33, London, 1748 (Huntington Library). Bishop Lisle said that it was not only a religious duty bequeathed the English, but a political one, because if the English failed, the heathen nations would fall into the hands of other missionaries and then turn around and assault the English settlements.*

[83]*Edmund Law, Bishop of Carlisle, in his Sermon preached before the S. P. G. at St. Mary le Bow, February 18, 1774 (Huntington Library), p. 16, urged the Society carefully to instruct its workers as to their duties and obligations, such as trying to learn an Indian language if necessary, avoiding controversial subjects, interfering with other societies, and so forth.*

[84]*For example, Dr. Francis le Jau, a missionary for the Society at Goose Creek, South Carolina, 1706-1717, continually asked for missionaries who would learn the Indian language, who could be taught the tribal customs, and who would sacrifice themselves to live among the tribes. For an account of the work done in South Carolina by the S. P. G. for the Indians, see Frank J. Klingberg, "The Indian Frontier in South Carolina as Seen by the S. P. G. Missionary," in Journal of Southern History, V, No. 4 November, 1939, pp. 479-500.*

[85]*The prevalent idea of civilizing the native before converting him was not upheld by John Waugh, the Dean of Gloucester, who, in his Sermon before the S. P. G., February, 1722, asked the Society to send forth missionaries who would instill nothing into the minds of the natives but pure doctrine and Gospel.*

[86]*The common belief of the missionary in regard to the Indian was stated ably by John Checkley in a letter to Philip Bearcroft, Providence, New England, October 26, 1743, in S. P. G. MSS. (L. C. Trans.), B11, No. 48, "The Indians are a*

temporal interests had been abused were, of course, supported by the missionary reports on the trader, and on the settler who engaged in unfair practices.[87]

In regard to the Negroes, Warburton, unlike other bishops in their sermons, spent no time on the methods of Christianizing them, but delivered his fiery argument condemning the slave traffic. The rush and force of the argument is overwhelming: he declares that stealing Negroes, to be sacrificed "to their great Idol, the God of Gain, is a crime;" that there is no property right in rational creatures; that one man cannot judge another's happiness; that therefore a white man cannot say that the Negro was happier in the colonies than in Africa; and that the traffic infringes "both divine and human law." The closely linked blows of this argument mark his legal turn of mind, his literary skill, and his wrath. One could perhaps date this sermon from its contents and assess both the character and temperament of the speaker. Other bishops, in the sermons, often denounced the traffic, yet did not find it contrary to all law. John Green, Bishop of Lincoln, in 1768, for example, said, " . . . this dealing in men seems a very unnatural kind of Traffick, and any treatment of them [Negroes] . . . cannot plainly be justified, yet I know not that we are warranted by any precept delivered in the Gospel, or by any example recorded in the Apostolick writings, to say that this practice is expressly forbidden there."[88]

People who must be taken . . . their own way, and Managed by One who understands their Language and Customs, and can lodge a Night or two upon the Ground with them in the Woods, when he visits them."

[87]*For example see, Thomas Barton to Secretary Huntingdon, Pennsylvania, November 8, 1756 in W. S. Perry, Historical Collections, II, pp. 278-279 in which Barton related that although the English had given Indians presents, they saw to it that they never carried the gifts far before the traders came after them, to cheat them and give them a little rum. "Whereas the French always paid them well for their skins, etc.; built houses for them; instructed their children and took care of their wives when they went to war." See also the Sermon by Shute Barrington, Bishop of Llandaff before the S. P. G., 1775, in which he said " . . . if our people . . . are careful to display in their various intercourse with the neighboring Indians those engaging virtues, which pure Christianity naturally inspires; what favorable impressions may be made upon them!" Frederick Cornwallis, Bishop of Lichfield and Coventry, in the Sermon for 1756, stated that the Indians should be allowed to see and partake of the good effects of Christian honesty and justice. Samuel Frink, a missionary for the S. P. G. in Augusta, Georgia, wrote to the Society in this year of Warburton's Sermon [Journal of S. P. G. (L. C. Trans.), XVII, July 18, 1766] that he had lost hope of instilling the principles of Christianity into the Chickasaw Indians because many of the white people were "as destitute of a sense of religion as the Indians themselves."*

[88]*John Green, Bishop of Lincoln, Sermon preached before the S. P. G. in St. Mary le Bow, London, 1768, p. 19 (Huntington Library). The safe and prevalent middle course of opinion was expressed in most of the Sermons, and was ably stated by the Bishop of St. David's, Richard Trevor, in 1750, when he said, " . . . opportunity is presented for the Exercise of our Charity . . . among the unhappy Negroes, who, by a sort of Traffick not easy to be vindicated, being reduced to a state of bodily Slavery for the purposes of our Colonies have certainly the justest claim upon us for every Instance of Compensation that is in our Power, especially . . . the communication of the Gospel Light."*

Bishop Warburton, the friend of Pope, described by Macaulay as an intellectual bully, was familiar with the legal and literary world of the day and by temperament suited to make such a ringing attack upon the slave system. His words were indeed weapons. Eighty years later when both the slave trade and slavery in the British colonies were abolished, it is of interest that the Society reprinted his sermon, in 1845, when anti-slavery forces were gathering strength in the United States.

At the immediate time, the American Revolution was but a decade away and in 1773, seven years after Warburton spoke, Bishop Jonathan Shipley's Whig sermon reflected, as Warburton's did not, Burke's and Franklin's point of view. Shipley's sermon[89] is a most interesting example of Whig liberalism, in which he sketches American destiny in Benjamin Franklin's most expansive mood and much as it now has come to be. The American continent, in his view, was destined for the white man, and with friendly cooperation across the Atlantic, it would be mastered. His phrases could be borrowed by present day groups working for Anglo-American solidarity.

The friend of Franklin, Chatham, and Burke, he was a bitter opponent of the British policy which led to the Revolution, and of the separation of the colonies. He saw no reason for a conflict; he opposed, whenever he spoke in the House of Lords, the regulations closing the port of Boston, and other war producing measures. This Whig sermon, praised by Chatham, and the most famous of Shipley's, reflects his broad views, and the atmosphere of the Johnson circle to which he belonged. He had an intimate knowledge of the early struggles of the colonials, and devoted himself on this occasion to the white settlers, dismissing the Indians as having "an untameable, savage spirit." Unable to understand their disregard for the "discipline" of the white man's law and religion, he says of them:

> The first object of our zeal was the conversion of the Indians; and it should seem no difficult task to influence the minds of men, who have few religious notions of their own growth, and appear to have no strong prejudices in favour of them. Such minds one would think might easily be led to receive a religion of the most simple form, consisting of a few great luminous principles, and inculcating plain rules of life and conduct, which must approve their usefulness in deserts, as well as in cities. Such doctrines, founded on Divine authority, would, in all appearance, be particularly welcome, where the restraints of law and government have but little force.

[89]*Jonathan Shipley, A Sermon Preached before the Incorporated Society for the Propagation of the Gospel in Foreign Parts at their Anniversary Meeting in St. Mary le Bow, Friday, February 19, 1773. (London: T. Harrison and S. Brooke, MDCLXXIII) (Huntington Library).*

Yet it has happened contrary to our hopes, that the preaching of the gospel has been of small efficacy amongst the Indians. The sagacity for which they are remarkable seems to be of a partial kind, and to partake more of instinct than of reason. They can employ great art to obtain their ends; to procure what they desire; or to gain a superiority over an enemy; but their passions and habits proceeding always in one narrow track, they have neither relish nor discernment for the clearest truths to which they have not been accustomed. After shewing the greatest address and courage in subduing or surprising an enemy, they cannot comprehend that it would be generous not to torture him; and that it would be wise to give such treatment as they would wish to receive. They have besides an untameable savage spirit, which has refused to hear the voice of instruction; which has obstinately rejected the arts and improvements of the Europeans, and has hitherto only adopted the most beastly of their vices.

For these reasons, though we ought not to remit our endeavours, yet I fear we have little reason to hope for their conversion, till some great change in their manners has made them abandon their savage vagrant life, and prepared them for the discipline of law and religion.[90]

This sermon is delightful to read, with its praise of all the accomplishments of the colonies and the mother country. It was bought and eagerly read in Boston, New York, and Philadelphia. It outlines the British Commonwealth of Nations, expressing ideas not unlike Burke's, but in words of simplicity and charm. He gives an unforgettable picture of the ties between the two countries, of the British heritage, and

[90]*Jonathan Shipley, Sermon preached before the Society . . . , 1773, pp. iv-vi (Huntington Library). Shute Barrington, Bishop of Llandaff, in his Sermon preached before the S. P. G. in St. Mary le Bow, London, February 17, 1775, p. 21, (Huntington Library) eulogized Sir William Johnson's work in New York, and speaking of his benevolence, intercourse, and interest with the Indians, he declared "By these means long and steadily exerted by a late distinguished native of the American continent to whom this Society is not less indebted for his active labours in the cause of Religion, than the community at large is to his eminent services in the field, and the introduction of the arts of civil life among a rude and barbarous people, some Indian tribes were at first gained over to our interest, and then became converts to our faith."*

For examples of other opinions expressed by the later bishops, see the Sermon by Thomas Thurlow, Bishop of Lincoln, 1786, in which he cited the reception given Stuart by Mohawks after an absence of seven years, with eagerness to have their children baptized. This interest of the children gave a well-grounded hope of a more general establishment of Christianity among Indians under British control, he declared. James Cornwallis, Bishop of Lichfield and Coventry, 1788, was not so optimistic. He said that nothing effectual could be accomplished in converting the savages unless a degree of civilization be brought about, which some had recommended by trying to introduce them to agriculture, others by different means. Samuel Halifax, Bishop of Gloucester, 1789, stated that the Indians were too uncivilized to be susceptible to religion, impatient of any settled habitation, engaged in frequent wars, were ignorant of morality, and even of decencies of be-

of an Anglo-American future, expressing the hope that the wise and good on both sides shall prevail:

> Our mutual relation was formed, and has hitherto sub-sisted, by a perpetual communication of benefits. We want the produce of soils and climates, that differ so much from our own; and they will long have occasion for the fruits of our arts, our industry and our experience. And should they ever cease to want our protection, which as long as we render it beneficial to them they never will; yet we may still continue united in in-terest, in commerce and the grateful remembrance of old services . . . To countries so closely united it is needless, and even dangerous, to have recourse to the interpretation of charters and written laws. Such discussions excite jealousy, and intimate an unfriendly disposition. It is common utility, mutual wants and mutual services, that should point out the true line of submission and authority. Let them respect the power that saved them; and let us always love the companions of our dangers and our glories.[91]

Drawing positively on the past for his expansive picture of the possibilities of the future, he says further:

> Perhaps the annals of history have never afforded a more grateful spectacle to a benevolent and philosophick mind, than the growth and progress of the British colonies in North America, We see a number of scattered settlements, formed at first for the purposes of trade, or from a spirit of enterprize; to procure a maintainance, or to enjoy the exercise of their re-ligion, which in those unhappy days was refused them at home,

haviour. In spite of this, the S. P. G. had several times tried to introduce them to the white man's way of life. But in spite of all S. P. G. care, little had been done and in a short time they would relapse into barbarism. "Before then we attempt to submit the manners of a barbarous people to the restraints of Religion, we . . . should first instruct them in the arts of life . . . " He cited Bishop Warburton's view that "Civilizing and saving" should be one effort. Sir George Tomline, Bishop of Lincoln, 1792, summed up the results of work among Indians. In some cases the work proved entirely fruitless and in other instances, the effect was of short duration. He cited the Mohawks as examples of the success of Christian teaching, and the affection with which they received the missionary as proof that Indians were not incapable of comprehending principles of religion. William Cleaver, Bishop of Chester, in 1794, said that experience had taught that a degree of civilization was requisite to make religion acceptable. Late reports related that the Indians in western settlements were beginning from necessity to apply them-selves to the arts of civilization. In this case, one might hope that missionaries could find an opportunity to bring religion to them. Charles Manners-Sutton, Bishop of Norwich, 1797, repealed former opinions that as long as the Indian was nomadic, it was almost impossible to make an impression on him. One remedy was early education. He mentioned the establishment of a seminary in the Mohawk village. Latest returns from there, though far from satisfactory, did not justify giving up of the attempt.

[91]Jonathan Shipley, Sermon preached before the Society . . . , 1773, pp. xiv-xv (Huntington Library).

growing by degrees under the protection of their mother-country, who treated them with the indulgence due to their weakness and infancy, into little separate common-wealths. . . . Had they been left to shift for themselves, they would have perished . . . Had they been planted by any kingdom but our own, the inhabitants would have carried with them the chains and oppression, to which they had been inured at home; they would have been subject to the schemes of ministers and favourites, and have suffered more from their ignorance than from their rapine. At best they could only have hoped to be considered as the live stock upon a lucrative farm, which might sometimes be suffered to thrive for the sake of its produce. But Britain . . . has not sold them her protection at the price of their liberty . . . and has sought no other advantage from so generous a conduct, but the mutual benefit arising to distant countries from the supply of each other's wants. Adhering to these maxims, she has continued to reap the fruits of her own wisdom and moderation in a surprising encrease of national greatness; while her prosperous colonies are spreading without interruption over a vast continent, that may in a few centuries rival the commerce, the arts and the power of Europe.[92]

Thus appealing to the ambitions and imaginations of his countrymen in advancing his theme of benevolent control, he proceeds to enlarge upon the future of the colonies:

The colonies in North America have not only taken root and acquired strength; but seem hastening with an accelerated progress to such a powerful state, as may introduce a new and important change in human affairs. Descended from ancestors of the most improved and enlightened part of the old world, they receive as it were by inheritance all the improvements and discoveries of their mother-country . . . They may avail themselves not only of the experience and industry, but even of the errors and mistakes of former days. . . . May we not reasonably expect that a number of provinces, possessed of these advantages, and quickened by mutual emulation, with only the common progress of the human mind, should very considerably enlarge the boundaries of science. The vast continent itself, over which they are gradually spreading, may be considered as a treasure, yet untouched, of natural productions, that shall hereafter afford ample matter for commerce and contemplation. And if we reflect what a stock of knowledge may be accumulated by the constant progress of industry and obser-

[92]*Jonathan Shipley, Sermon preached before the Society* . . . , *1773, p. vii (Huntington Library). For a recent appraisal of Shipley, see "A Georgian Prelate, Jonathan Shipley and his Friends," "London Times Literary Supplement" July 24, 1937, p. 533-534. Franklin was the most favored guest there and wrote most of his autobiography in Shipley's garden at Twyford. The war did not break their friendship, and Franklin spent much of his last visit there.*

vation, fed with fresh supplies from the stores of nature, assisted sometimes by those happy strokes of chance, which mock all the powers of invention, and sometimes by those superior characters which arise occasionally to instruct and enlighten the world; it is difficult even to imagine to what height of improvement their discoveries may extend.[93]

But not only from the standpoint of natural and human resources does he see the destiny of the colonies. An enlargement of the "equitable principles" which in the homeland were gained at "the price of civil wars, and the reward of the virtues and sufferings of our ancestors, descend to them as a natural inheritance," and seem to him the natural birthright of the new land:

> May not a method be invented of procuring some tolerable share of the comforts of life to those inferior useful ranks of men, to whose industry we are indebted for the whole? Time and discipline may discover some means to correct the extreme inequalities of condition between the rich and the poor, so dangerous to the innocence and the happiness of both. They may fortunately be led by habit and choice to despise that luxury, which is considered with us as the true enjoyment of wealth. They may have little relish for that ceaseless hurry of amusements, which is pursued in this country without pleasure, exercise, or employment. And perhaps after trying some of our follies and caprices, and rejecting the rest, they may be led by reason and experiment to that old simplicity, which was first pointed out by nature, and has produced those models which we still admire in arts, eloquence and manners.[94]

That the S. P. G. could play an important part in the development of this Utopia he did not doubt:

> That sober and reasonable sense of duty, which has been taught under our direction to a few scattered villages, may give its character hereafter to the religion and morals of a powerful state. The weak and imperfect fruits we reap at present may bear no higher proportion to the future benefits that may arise, than that of a few scattered seeds to the fulness of the harvest.[95]

And again:

> We presume not to instruct our rulers in the measures of government; but it is the proper office of a preacher of the

[93] *Jonathan Shipley, Sermon preached before the Society* . . . , 1773, *pp. ix-x* (Huntington Library).
[94] *Ibid., p. xii.*
[95] *Ibid., p. xiii.*

gospel of peace, to point out the laws of justice and equity which must ultimately regulate the happiness of states as well as of individuals; and which are no other in effect than those benevolent christian morals which it is the province of this Society to teach, transferred from the duties of private life to the administration of publick affairs.[96]

It had been the policy of the Society from the beginning to transfer its activities to the colonials as soon as possible. In New York, as well as in the other colonies, the colonists were to take over the work of the local churches, releasing S. P. G. funds for other areas. This encouragement of home rule, and the policy of promoting independence in colonial enterprises, is rather remarkable, and was a course steadily pursued in all the colonies.[97]

Bishop Porteus,[98] an Evangelical, a friend of Hannah More, gave his sermon ten years after Shipley's, when the loss of the colonies was certain, and the Empire destined to be brown and black in the vast majority[99] of its people, with the government in the immediate future centered more fully in London. Naturally he turned his attention to the remaining vast areas of S. P. G. interest, particularly to the West Indies and Canada. Although the chief European settlements of the Empire had been lost, the empire of commerce with Negroes, Indians, and the people of India remained.

Bishop Porteus in his sermon, therefore, not only exhibited the rallying powers of the Society promptly put to work in new fields, but, in a sense, returned to the original aims as he summed up the achievements of the past and turned to the future. He believed that a Negro peasantry could be created in the West Indian Islands, and that the

[96]*Jonathan Shipley, Sermon preached before the Society . . . 1773, p. xix (Huntington Library).*

[97]*For instance, for an account of American support of humanitarian enterprises, and of Franklin's early interest in the Bray Associates, see Richard I. Shelling, "Benjamin Franklin and the Dr. Bray Associates" in The Pennsylvania Magazine of History and Biography, July, 1939, pp. 282-293. As President of the Pennsylvania Society for Promoting the Abolition of Slavery, he signed a memorial of the Society presented to Congress, February 12, 1789, followed by an "Address to the Public, from the Pennsylvania Society for Promoting the Abolition of Slavery, and the Relief of free Negroes unlawfully held in Bondage," November 9, 1789; and "Plan for Improving the Condition of the Free Slaves," October 26, 1789, in [Albert H.] Smith, [ed.] op. cit. [The Writings of Benjamin Franklin] X, 66-68; 127-129," (see Shelling, p. 292, footnote 50). In 1763, after visiting with Sturgeon the Negro School in Philadelphia, Franklin observed, in almost the words Bishop Fleetwood used in 1711, "I then have conceived a higher opinion of the Natural Capacities of the black Race, than I have ever before entertained. Their apprehension [is] as quick, their Memory as Strong, and their Docility in every Respect equal to that of the White Children . . . " Quoted by Shelling, p. 288.*

[98]*Beilby Porteus, a Sermon preached before the S. P. G. in St. Mary le Bow, London, February, 1783 (Huntington Library).*

[99]*About two-thirds of the English speaking people of the world are in the United States today.*

loss of the thirteen colonies would release the funds for this purpose; which indeed proved to be the case, as the funds afterwards increased beyond the income of the pre-Revolutionary years. The release of trained men for an intensified program of Negro civilization and Christianization in the West Indian Islands, was still to be a major objective of the Society.[100] New York and Codrington had previously been the important centers of attention. The former was no longer under the Society. The placement of the missionaries left without posts in the thirteen revolting colonies was not unlike the familiar transfers which occurred in the normal course, when Thomas Thompson went from New Jersey to Africa, Christian Post from Delaware to the Mosquito Shore, other men to and fro between the islands and the continental colonies.

Bishop Porteus made a telling point as to the practical efforts of the S. P. G.,

> . . . Almost the only considerable attempts that have been made to deliver them [Negroes] from this deplorable state of ignorance have been made by this venerable Society; who have had this object, among many others, constantly in view, and, in the prosecution of it, have not been sparing either of labour or expense. But it must be owned that our endeavours have not hitherto been attended with the desired success. This, however, has been owing not to what some are willing to suppose, an impossibility in the nature of the thing itself; not to any absolute incapacity in the Africans to receive or retain religious knowledge; but to *accidental,* and I trust, surmountable causes,—to the prejudices formerly entertained by many of the planters against the instruction and conversion of their slaves; to the want, which the latter have experienced, of sufficient time and opportunity for this purpose; to the abject, depressed, degraded, uncivilized, unbefriended, immoral state, in which the negroes have been so long suffered to remain; to the very little attention paid to them on the part of the Government; to the almost total want of laws to protect and encourage them, and to soften, in some degree, the rigours of their condition; [The regulations that have been occasionally made in the British Islands respecting the slaves breathe a spirit of extreme severity

[100]*Frank Wesley Pitman, The Development of the British West Indies, 1700-1763 (New Haven: Yale University Press, 1917); Lowell Joseph Ragatz, A Guide for the Study of British Caribbean History 1703-1834, including the Abolition and Emancipation Movements, (Washington, D. C.: United States Government Printing office, 1932). Strangely enough, this program has come true in the United States more fully, perhaps because of the higher white-Negro percentage. In America the Negro is not more numerous than is the White, except in one or two areas. In the West Indies with ten to one preponderance of the Negro, the collapse of the planter class, due to economic conditions in the sugar trade and other factors, produced conditions which in spite of the fact that emancipation was a generation earlier, slowed economic solutions to a point behind the United States.*

and rigour. There are laws in abundance to punish and restrain, but scarce any to secure them from oppression. Some,
undoubtedly, meet with kind and indulgent masters, whose natural humanity stands in the place of laws; but the greater part
of them, it is to be feared, feel most sensibly the want of legal
protection.] to the necessity, in short, which the Society themselves have hitherto been under, of listening to other claims of a
very pressing and important nature, and of employing a large
share of their fund in disseminating religious knowledge, and
providing for the maintenance of public worship in other parts
of His Majesty's dominions, where their assistance was much
wanted, and most earnestly and repeatedly solicited.[101]

By 1783 the Anti-Slavery forces were on the march, under the
leadership of Granville Sharp,[102] having won the Somerset case in 1772
which emancipated the slaves in England and Ireland, and the Joseph
Knight case in 1778 which emancipated the slaves in Scotland. The
new mood of the country reflected in those judicial decisions was doubtless in part the product of the S. P. G. in its 75 years of presenting
the case of native peoples. Bishop Porteus, in this pointed sermon, reviewed the success of the Society and its adjustment to the loss of the
thirteen colonies, and outlined the new program which was to make
the slave free, not legally but *de facto*: for peasant proprietorship of
land, legal marriage, and the possession of personal property left him
protected in important matters and attached to the land in feudal fashion:

. . . If ever, then, we hope to make any considerable
progress in our benevolent purpose of communicating to our
negroes the benefits and the blessings of religion, we must
first give them some of the benefits and the blessings of society
and of civil government. We must, as far as is possible, attach
them and their families inseparably to the soil; must give them
a little interest in it, and indulge them with a few rights and
privileges to be anxious for; must secure them, by fixed laws,
from injury and insult; must inform their minds, correct their
morals, accustom them to the restraints of legal marriage, to
the care of a family, and the comforts of domestic life; must
improve and advance their condition gradually, as they are
able to bear it; and even allow a certain number of the most
deserving to work out their freedom by degrees (according
to the plan said to be established in some of the Spanish settlements), as a reward of superior merit and industry, and of
an uncommon progress in the knowledge and practice of Christianity.[103]

[101]*Twelve Anniversary Sermons Preached before the Society . . . , pp. 160,
161.*
[102]*E. C. P. Lascelles, Granville Sharp and the Freedom of Slaves in England.
(London, 1928), passim.*
[103]*Twelve Anniversary Sermons . . . p. 165.*

48 ANGLICAN HUMANITARIANISM IN COLONIAL NEW YORK

In brief, Porteus made a blueprint of a more advanced regime on the Codrington estates, which, in the program of the Society, was to serve as a model for all the British slave-holding colonies, and was similar to Burke's famous code.[104]

From the very foundation of the S. P. G., the annual sermon was an outstanding ecclesiastical event and no greater honor could be conferred upon an eighteenth century Churchman than to be invited to address the Society. Like the Government's speech from the throne on the state of the nation, the sermon was a survey of the state of the Church at home and abroad; it drew the attention of all men to the missionary engaged in distant fields, in contact on the frontiers with native peoples and with the puzzling problems of empire expansion. In fact, the sermons all but uniformly tied up the home front and the foreign field as one and inseparable. The activities of the missionary, the catechist, and the rector in New York are therefore envisioned as part of the whole undertaking, and the deist, equally an enemy whether at home or abroad in the colony, was merely one of the many common preoccupations.

New York has been chosen as a center where all the factors involved in these colonial cooperations were set in interesting juxtaposition. To appreciate the scope and field problems of the Society, which began its work in this colony in 1702, and expanded its contacts with the Indian still there in full force, and with the Negro brought in by ship-loads, the period before the Revolution is sufficiently long to estimate the degrees of failure or of success. The following chapters will deal first with the Indian and then with the Negro.

[104]*Letter to the Right Honourable Henry Dundas, one of His Majesty's principal Secretaries of State, dated Easter Monday Night, 1792; with the "Sketch of a Negro Code,"* in *The Works of the Right Honourable Edmund Burke (A New Edition, London, 1826), IX, 278-318.*

See also Frank J. Klingberg, *The Anti-Slavery Movement in England: A Study in English Humanitarianism (New Haven and London, 1926) pp. 321-335,* for a somewhat abridged copy of the Code. Burke wrote Dundas that he had drafted the Code in 1780, and it therefore antedates the Porteus Sermon. The ideas of Sermon and Code have much in common, but by this time the influences of Granville Sharp, John Woolman, Anthony Benezet and the leaders and workers of the S. P. G. probably cannot be sharply separated.

CHAPTER II

THE NOBLE SAVAGE AS SEEN BY THE MISSIONARY OF THE SOCIETY FOR THE PROPAGATION OF THE GOSPEL IN COLONIAL NEW YORK 1702-1750

THE four bidders for the Indian's loyalty were the British Government, which desired him as a fighter and an outpost of empire; the trader who wanted him as a consumer of alcohol and other goods, and as a supplier of furs and various products; the colonist who craved his lands; and the missionary who wished his conversion to Christianity and who in fact softened the impact of the new order. Without him as a religious and social teacher, "a secularized native", bewildered by commercial and military pressures, would have suffered even more severely from the barbaric effect of a strange civilization upon a native culture.

While it is true that these imperial forces were centered in London, where the great fight against France in the second hundred years war (1689-1815) was being planned and waged, colonials were inevitably active participants, and the European continent contributed its contingents of 3000 Palatinates and many scattered Huguenots to this pioneer and frontier society of mixed nationalities and many religious faiths. The S. P. G.[1] was not only the latest arrival of these four forces, but, as a pioneer Protestant missionary Society, it could not be expected to adapt itself quickly to a large scale program in every part of the British Empire in the western world. Under the circumstances, the effort to Christianize the Iroquois took the form of individual survey, individual contact, and first hand reporting of conditions in the American forest of New York in the early decades of the eighteenth century. These documents are therefore to be regarded as first hand, contemporary contributions to an evaluation of Protestant cultural contacts with natives, which are suggestive illustrative of problems occurring wherever the white man's world meets native cultures whether in the early eighteenth century or in more recent times.

In these early letters, the missionary reporter showed himself as an excellent observer and as a competent analyst of problems met in the wilderness for which he had no advance preparation or handbook, and which his superiors in London could perhaps not fully comprehend. These early annalists are therefore to be read for their contribution to "the cult of the noble savage," and are to be regarded as laboratory or field men, collecting factual data for the testing of theory by

[1]In this monograph, the S. P. G. and The Society are the two abbreviations used for the Society for the Propagation of the Gospel in Foreign Parts.

actual experiment.   Their amazing insight will be referred to from time to time in this study.

The hotly debated question of the superiority or inferiority of the noble savage was one of endless interest to eighteenth century men and not merely to Dean Swift and Defoe.[2]   Occasionally, as these letters show, the missionary could in his letters vie with the interest aroused by the stories of pirates and explorers.   It is only necessary to remember that the first edition of Robinson Crusoe, with its instant success and many imitations, appeared in 1719 for the reader to recapture some of the contemporary impressions of interest in the world wide discovery, imagined or real.   Dampier (1652-1715), buccaneer, logwood cutter, privateer, and explorer held the world spell-bound with his publications of entertaining cruises and voyages around the world; and he and Woodes Rogers (d. 1732) were at the height of their fame.   Such historic rescues as that of Alexander Selkirk rivalled the popularity of Gulliver's Travels (1726).

The ideas regarding noble savages brought home by travellers and missionaries were occasionally checked by visits of natives to London such as that of Joseph Brant from the Iroquois, Philip Quaque from Africa, Omai from the South Sea Islands, and many others.   These natives, at times presented at court and painted by the noted artists of the day, aroused great curiosity.   It was in this eighteenth century atmosphere and mood that these letters from the wilderness were received and read in London.

However, in this paper, it is intended to omit imperial and certain other aspects of Indian affairs in colonial New York in the first half of the century and to concentrate on the daily activity of the S. P. G. missionaries in Christianization and education, and, as indicated above, to regard them primarily as pioneer observers and reporters to whom the individual Indian was a human being, neither hero nor devil.[3]   This

---

[2]*H. Neale Fairchild, The Noble Savage, A Study in Romantic Naturalism, 1928, passim; and Chauncey B. Tinker, Nature's Simple Plan, 1922, passim. A suggestive bibliography is to be found in R. S. Crane's review of Professor Tinker's book in Modern Language Notes, XXXIX, No. 5, pp. 291-297. A helpful account of the origin of the ideas regarding primitive people is given by Miss Lois Whitney, "English Primitive Theories of Epic Origins," in Modern Philology, XXI, May, 1924. For a fine analysis of the work of the leading poet of Evangelicalism and humanitarianism, see Lodwick C. Hartley, "William Cowper, Humanitarian", 1938. The notes are a very valuable bibliography. Professor Charles M. Andrews, winner of the Pulitzer Award for 1935, author of "The Colonial Period of American History", 4 vols., called attention to and gave an evaluation of the S. P. G. and allied records for the historian in his "Materials in British Archives for American Colonial History" in The American Historical Review, Jan., 1905.*

[3]*No attempt has been made in this study to incorporate the observations of other contemporary or later students of the Indian but rather to make the reports of the S. P. G. Missionary available. For the part played by the Iroquois in the Anglo-French and Anglo-American conflicts, see John Wolfe Lydekker, The Faithful Mohawks, reviewed by Frank J. Klingberg in The Mississippi Val-*

contemporary zeal of the day appears at the very beginning in the request of the Rev. John Talbot, chaplain on the ship, "Centurion," that he go to Boston with the Rev. George Keith, the first itinerant S. P. G. missionary sent to the New England colonies in 1702. In an early report to a friend in England, Mr. Talbot, who at once started work among the Indians, explained their impressions of a squaw sachem,

> I have baptized several persons . . . indeed in all places where we come, we find a great ripeness and inclination amongst all sorts of people to embrace the Gospel, even the Indians themselves have promised obedience to the faith, as appears by a conference that my Lord Cornbury the Governor here, has had with them at Albany, 5 of their sachems or kings told him they were glad to hear that the sun shined in England again since King William's death, they did not admire at first what was come to us, that we should have a squaw sachem vizt a woman king, but they hoped she would be a good mother, and send them some to teach them religion, and establish traffic amongst them that they might be able to purchase a coat and not go to church in bear skins, so they send our queen a present, 10 beaver skins to make her fine, and one for muff to keep her warm.[4]

Rev. Mr. Talbot continued by commenting that the Papists had been very zealous and diligent in converting these Indians, through the sending of priests and Jesuits. The Jesuits had suffered much for Indian conversion, and should inspire the Church of England to further efforts.

However, a letter sent from Nova Scotia the following year to the Secretary of the Society, John Chamberlayne, suggests the controversy among the missionaries of diverse faiths and the strain imposed upon the Red Man by conflicting counsels:

> It is the common opinion that the Jesuits debauch the Iroquois (which is the common name of the 5 nations) from their fidelity to the Crown . . . for among the Five Nations there is a great number of French that are incorporated by adoption into their tribes, and as such, they ostentatiously as-

ley Historical Review, December, 1938, pp. 398-399; and by Robert H. Nichols in Church History, December, 1938. For S. P. G. work among the Iroquois from 1749 to 1774, see Chapter III, p. 87.

    [4]*Rev. John Talbot to Mr. Richard Gillingham, New York, Nov. 24, 1702, in S. P. G. MSS. (L. C. Trans.), A 1, No. LVI. For an excellent recent study of John Talbot which includes his biography and his letters, see Edgar Legare Pennington, Apostle of New Jersey, John Talbot, 1645-1727, (Church Historical Society, Philadelphia, 1938).*

sume . . . Indian names, and the poor silly Indians considering themselves as persons of their own blood, do entirely con-
fide in them and admit them into their councils from whence
you may judge what fine work the Jesuits make with their affairs.[5]

To offset the intrigues, as French efforts were regarded, in New
York and surrounding territory, the S. P. G. was urged, through a
memorial by Robert Livingston, Secretary of Indian Affairs, to send
Protestant ministers to the Five Nations.[6] Livingston attended a meet-
ing of the Society and gave an account of the needs of the natives. By
October 1703, the members had agreed upon two missionaries, the Rev.
Thoroughgood Moore, and the Rev. Mr. Smith.[7] The Society wrote
to the Lords of Trade and Plantation regarding finances as follows:

> . . . the said Gentlemen [are allowed] 100£ per annum each,
> over and above which they will have 20£ a piece to buy them
> utensils for the little Caban they are supposed to have among
> the Indians, and 10 or 15£ for books etc. Now, My Lords, I
> am to tell you that the Society having done so much . . .
> they would gladly know what assistance they may expect in an
> affaire, that does at least as much concerne the State as the
> Church . . .[8]

The Lords of Trade were asked to present the situation to the
Queen and to the Government of New York. The Society explained
that four additional missionaries were immediately needed in New York,
three more for the Five Nations and one for the River Indians.[9] Moreover, it was imperative that each missionary have a well built home, se-
curely barricaded, for fear of the insults of drunken Indians. Other
items of expense would be necessary presents for the Indians and pay
for personal servants.[10]

In reply to this application, the Secretary to the Lords of Trade
wrote,

[5]*Translation accompanying a letter in French from Godfrey Dellius to John
Chamberlayne, Halsteren, N. S., May 17, 1703, in S. P. G. MSS. (L. C. Trans.)
A 1, No. LXXII.*
[6]*Journal of S. P. G. (L. C. Trans.) I, April 16, 1703; Ibid., September 17,
1703.*
[7]*Journal of S. P. G. (L. C. Trans.), I, October 15, 1703.*
[8]*John Chamberlayne to Lords of Trade, Westminster, February [1] 1703/4,
in E. B. O'Callaghan (Ed.), Documents Relative to the Colonial History of the
State of New York, IV, 1077. (Documents originally selected by J. R. Brod-
head.)*
[9]*The River Indians, however, Secretary Chamberlayne believed, were no
longer formidable, most of them having been killed in former wars.*
[10]*John Chamberlayne, to Lords of Trade, Westminster, February [1] 1703/4,
E. B. O'Callaghan (Ed.), in Documents Relative to the Colonial History of the
State of New York, IV, pp. 1077-1078.*

. . . the Lords Commss[rs] for Trade and Plantat[ns] . . . have ordered me to acquaint you that her Majesty does allow £20 a piece to all Ministers going to the Plantations for their passage; that they are of opinion it will be a great incouragement to such Ministers if they can be assured of a Benefice in England after so many years service (as may be thought reasonable) among the Indians . . . their Lord[pps] will take care to recommend the said Ministers to the Lord Cornbury, Governour of New Yorke.[11]

Mr. Moore asked for and obtained £40 in addition to the usual £60 for his support.[12]   He arrived in Albany in the fall of 1704, and began his preliminary work at once.   To win the confidence of the Indians proved difficult, so that by November, 1705, he had not been accepted because, in his opinion, he was an Englishman, to whom the Indians ". . . bear no good will but rather an aversion, having a common saying among them that an Englishman is not good."[13]   He analyzed this Indian hostility as due to,

1. The behavior of the English of New England towards them which has been very unchristian, particularly in taking away their land from them without a purchase.

2. The example of the garrison at Albany (the only English in this province that many Indians ever saw) which may justly have given them a prejudice against us not easily to be removed.

3. The continual misrepresentations of us by the Dutch which are the only inhabitants of that part of the province that borders upon the Indians, and the only persons that trade with them, who as they never had any affection towards us, so they have always shown it to the Indians, though I must say I have . . . received many civilities from some of them particularly Col. Schuyler and Mr. Lydius the Dutch Minister.[14]

Anticipating the eventual Americanization of the colonies by means of common language, Mr. Moore and Governor Cornbury quaintly asked the Society to use its interest towards making the Dutch better subjects by prevailing with the Lords of Trade in London that there

[11]*Secretary Popple to John Chamberlayne, Whitehall, February 3, 1703-4, in E. B. O'Callaghan (Ed.), Documents Relative to the Colonial History of the State of New York, IV, p. 1078.*
[12]*Journal of S. P. G. (L. C. Trans.), I, Sept. 17, 1703.*
[13]*Thoroughgood Moore to John Chamberlayne, New York, November 13, 1705, in S. P. G. MSS. (L. C. Trans.), A 2, No. CXII.*
[14]*Ibid.*

be no more Dutch schools in New York, and by persuading the Queen that there be no more Dutch ministers sent from Holland. If the Society did not take an interest in these suggestions, fatal consequences would ensue, and the Governor stated that ". . . without a command, if the Queen would only give him leave he would never suffer another Dutch minister to come over."[15]   However, the Society, though remote from the scene, realized that such extreme measures would be detrimental and it encouraged two Dutch ministers, the Rev. Mr. Dellius and the Rev. Mr. Lydius, in their work with the Indians. Mr. Lydius, of Albany, was presented with books worth £10 by the S. P. G. in consideration for his ". . . promoting the Christian Religion among the Indians of the 5 Nations bordering on New York,"[16] and Mr, Dellius translated several prayers into the Mohawk language and transmitted them to the S. P. G.

Rev. Mr. Moore after patient efforts with the Indians at Albany and Schenectady, in November, 1705, decided to leave for the twofold reason that the Indians were difficult to Christianize, and the barbarous white colonials needed missionary care first.[17]   He thus reflected the division of opinion regarding the chief aims of the Society in a pioneer world. Should major attention be centered on natives or on the colonists? He was convinced that to begin Christianizing the Indians before the whites was preposterous, ". . . for 'tis from the behavior of the Christians here that they have had and still have their notions of Christianity, which God knows has been and generally is such that I can't but think has made the Indian hate Christianity."[18]   The English, he declared, were a very thriving and growing people, whereas it was the opposite with the Indians.

> They waste away and have done ever since our first arrival amongst them (as they themselves say) like snow against the sun, so that very probably forty years hence there will scarce be an Indian seen in our America. God's providence in this matter seems very wonderful and no cause of their decrese visible unless their drinking Rum, with some new dis-

[15]*Thoroughgood Moore to John Chamberlayne, New York, November 13, 1705, in S. P. G. MSS. (L. C. Trans.), A 2, No. CXII.*
[16]*Journal of S. P. G. (L. C. Trans.), I, March 17, 1703/4.*
[17]*Robert Livingston, Secretary of Indian Affairs, said there was some mismanagement on Moore's part also, see a letter from Livingston to John Chamberlayne, January, 1706, in S. P. G. MSS. (L. C. Trans.), A 2, No. CXXXVI.*
[18]*Thoroughgood Moore to John Chamberlayne, New York, November 13, 1705, in S. P. G. MSS. (L. C. Trans.), A 2, No. CXII.*

tempers we have brought amongst them. Indeed the Christians selling the Indians so much rum as they do is a sufficient bar, if there were no other, against their embracing Christianity.[19]

This penetrating observation at this early date of the fate of the Indian north of Mexico stamps Moore as a man of keen prophetic insight, and as a pioneer of the cult of the white man's manifest destiny.

Concurrently with Mr. Moore's selection as a missionary, Mr. Elias Neau was appointed as a catechist for the province of New York with a salary of £50 a year.[20] Mr. Neau was as conspicuous for his work in New York as Dr. Le Jau was in South Carolina. French Huguenots, they had gifts for analyzing problems clearly and quickly, and imaginative and practical qualities as well. On July 10, 1703, Mr. Neau accepted the position and wrote the Society " . . . desiring that he may be allowed to teach the Negroes as well as the Indians."[21] Although Mr. Neau's work with the Negroes was successful,[22] he soon perceived the discouraging features of the Indian work. In November, 1705, he wrote the Society that the slaves were more numerous than the Indians, and if he were capable of giving advice to the Society, he would not waver in saying that one could make more proselytes of the Negroes than of the Indians. In striking phrases, he declared:

> . . . and since charity well ordered begins at home, I believe God would sooner bless the works of pious persons who employ themselves at this work than to run up in the woods after miserable creatures who breath nothing but blood and slaughter, that are but a few and are moreover prejudiced by covetous persons who traffic with them for their skins and furs. In a word, they are people who have nothing but the figure of men and I am not surprized if the good and pious Mr. Moore has been obliged to say as St. Paul, "Since you refuse the light which I would have given you I shake off the dust of my feet, and I leave you in your dismal unbelief."[23]

This realistic evaluation of Indian life and manners, with its clearly expressed impression of the Negroes, states the missionary problem as it so often revealed itself to men actively at work on the ground, in divers parts of the colonies. Nevertheless, Mr. Neau did teach a few

[19]*Thoroughgood Moore to John Chamberlayne, New York, November 13, 1705, in S P. G MSS. (L. C. Trans.), A. 2, No. CXII.*
[20]*Report of Committee for Establishing Catechists in the Plantation in Journal of S. P. G. (L. C. Trans.), I, January 15, 1702/3.*
[21]*Elias Neau to [Secretary], New York, July 10, 1703, in Journal of S. P. G. (L. C. Trans.), I, Oct. 15, 1703.*
[22]*For a good account of Neau's labors see William Webb Kemp, The Support of Schools in Colonial New York by the Society for the Propagation of the Gospel in Foreign Parts, pp. 234-261.*
[23]*Translation of Elias Neau to John Chamberlayne, New York, November 15, 1705, in S. P. G. MSS. (L. C. Trans.), A 2, No. CXXV.*

Indians, and in March 1706, he wrote to the Society that he was continuing ". . . to instruct the Negroes and Indians"[24] who came to his house, and asked the members for an Indian catechism for a Mr. Osterwald, of Neufchatel, who took a great interest in the Indians.[25]

Governor Cornbury, however, was not discouraged by Mr. Moore's lack of success; he still was confident of Indian conversion. In 1707, he asked the S. P. G. to send a minister to Albany, one who could teach school as well as ". . . make the Mission to the Indians effectual, . . . I would appoint one of the Interpreters to attend him by which means he might learn something of the Indian Language, then there might be some hopes of his doing some good among these Heathen, but for a Minister of the Church of England to convert the Indians to Christianity by a Dutch Interpreter, will never do."[26] The Indians declared that they had been the neighbors of the English for many years, yet had never been taught religion, ". . . but as soon as the French came we [Indians] learnt it of them, and in that we will live and dye, let them look to this that have as much favor in their hands, but not that zeale to stretch them forth to do good."[27]

In addition to this critical letter, the Society received one from Rev. William Urquhart of Long Island in which he related the murder of the William Halliot family, including husband and wife, and five children by two slaves, one Indian and one Negro, stressing the fact that the Indian had been brought up by Mr. Halliot from the age of four.[28]

Another disillusioning report from Long Island came from the Rev. John Thomas of Hempstead (Hamstead). He explained that the Society had a very imperfect notion of the native Indians; it was impossible to impart any Christian impression, education, moral or otherwise, because the ". . . Indians are wholly given up to drink and sottishness, rum and strong liquor being the only deities they now care [for] or are solicitous to worship."[29]

The following year, 1710, four Iroquois Sachems[30] went to England to appear before Queen Anne, asking that someone be sent to their country to instruct them. The proposal was laid before the Archbishop of Canterbury by the Earl of Sunderland, who, in turn, presented it to the Society so that its members ". . . may consider what

[24]*Translation of Elias Neau to John Chamberlayne, New York, March 1, 1706, in S. P. G. MSS. (L. C. Trans.), A 2, No. CLIX.*
[25]*Ibid.*
[26]*Lord Cornbury to John Chamberlayne, New York, November 29, 1707, in S. P. G. MSS. (L. C. Trans.), A 3, No. 155.*
[27]*Rev. John Talbot to John Chamberlayne, Rhode Island, December 13, 1707, in S. P. G. MSS. (L. C. Trans.), A 3, No. 158.*
[28]*Rev. William Urquhart to John Chamberlayne, Jamaica, Long Island, February 4, 1707/08, in S. P. G. MSS. (L. C. Trans.), A 3, No. 176.*
[29]*John Thomas to John Chamberlayne, Hamstead [Long Island], June 12, 1709, in S. P. G. MSS. (L. C. Trans.), A 5, No. IX. Also spelled Hempsted.*
[30]*Their names were Henrique, John, Brant, and Etchwa Caume.*

may be the more proper ways of cultivating that good disposition these Indians seem to be in for receiving the Christian faith, and for sending thither fit persons for that purpose . . ."[31] Mr. Chamberlayne at once wrote the Society regarding the affair, and enclosed an address by the Sachems to the Society which read in part:

> 'Tis with great satisfaction that the Indian sachems reflect upon the usage and answers they received from the chief ministers of Christ's religion in our great Queen's dominions, when they asked their assistance for the thorough conversion of their nations. 'Tis thence expected that such of them will ere long come over and help to turn those of Our subjects from Satan unto God as may by their great knowledge and pious practices convince the enemies to saving faith that the only true God is not amongst them.[32]

A Select Committee of the S. P. G. then met at Lambeth, and agreed upon several resolutions. First, that the design of propagating the gospel in foreign parts related primarily to the conversion of the heathen, and therefore that branch of work should be prosecuted preferably to all others; next, that immediate steps were to be taken to send itinerant missionaries to preach among the Six Nations; and last, that no more missionaries be sent among the white Christians except to those places where the ministers were dead or removed, unless the Society had enough funds for both projects.[33] After consulting Col. Francis Nicholson, Col. Peter Schuyler,[34] and the Indian Sachems themselves, the following resolutions were passed for the more practical administration of the new policy of concentrating on the natives, by providing for two ministers (single men) and an interpreter, who were

[31]*Earl of Sunderland to the Archbishop of Canterbury, Whitehall, April 20, 1710, in S. P. G. MSS. (L. C. Trans.), A 5, No. LXXXVI.*

[32]*Indian Sachems to the Venerable Society for Propagation of the Gospel in Foreign Parts (n. d.) in S. P. G. MSS. (L. C. Trans.), A 55, No. LXXXVIII (enclosed in Archbishop of Canterbury to John Chamberlayne, April 20, 1710, q. v.).*

[33]*Report of Select Committee on the Six Nations of Indians, Journal of S. P. G. (L. C. Trans.), I, April 28, 1710.*

[34]*Col. Schuyler (1657-1724) had accompanied the Indians to England. In 1686, he had been made mayor of Albany, and, as such, became head of the Board of Indian Commissioners. His constant object was to cement friendly relations between the Five Nations and the English. Both Col. Schuyler and Col. Nicholson are best known for their parts in the British expeditions for the conquest of Canada, especially Port Royal, 1710. Nicholson (1655-1728) began his career in the colonies as captain of the troops sent to New England under Sir Edmund Andros, became a Member of the Council for the Dominion of New England, and in 1688, Lieutenant Governor. Nicholson's varied career included the governorships of Maryland, Virginia, South Carolina, and Nova Scotia. Col. Nicholson was an enthusiastic member of the S. P. G., and on his death left most of his estate to the Society. Col. Nicholson, after Governor Cornbury, was instrumental in convening a conference of the Anglican clergy in New York to discuss Indian conversion and education shortly after Rev. Mr. Moore's arrival as missionary.*

to live at Dynderoogby, the chief Mohawk village, at a salary of £50 a year for each minister and £60 for the interpreter. Moreover, a chapel, house, and a fort for their defense were to be built; specific instructions were to be given to the ministers, and the Indian children were to be taught in English; a brief history of the Bible or New Testament, a Catechism, some prayers and psalms were to be translated into the Indian language, printed and distributed among the Indians, in which errors in the French Quebec Catechism were to be noted; laws against intoxicating liquors were to be strictly enforced, in accordance with the wishes of the Indian chiefs themselves; and lastly, a plea to the Queen for an Anglican Bishop was to be made, based in part on the success of the French under a Roman Catholic Bishop at Quebec.[35]

The Indian Sachems were again brought before the Society, and, through an interpreter, these resolutions were explained to them. The Indians expressed satisfaction, promised to care for the Ministers sent to them, and agreed not to admit any Jesuits or French priests among them. It was then decided to give each Indian a Bible and Common Prayer, handsomely bound in red turkey leather.[36] In a letter of May 2, 1710, the Indians thanked the Society and hoped for the early arrival of the ministers.

Political as well as religious arguments for missionaries were repeatedly used. On May 22, Col. Francis Nicholson wrote to the Archbishop of Canterbury,

> I was in hopes before I left Great Britain to have received her Majesty's . . . commands concerning the chapel and house for the missionaries which were to be in an Indian fort, as likewise about an interpreter. . . . These things being promised, the Indians, . . . fully rely thereupon and nothing will convince them but occular demonstration . . . if there be not a speedy beginning made I fear they will at least suspect that what was promised them will not be performed and that will not only be a point of ill consequence of religion but of state also. . . .[37]

Steps were soon taken to fulfill these promises. In 1709, the Rev. Thomas Barclay who had been appointed minister at Albany and incidentally to instruct the neighboring Indians, was at once given an Indian boy by the Commissioners of Indian affairs, to be trained as a na-

[35]*Select Committees Resolutions for effective converting of the Indians, Journal of S. P. G. (L. C. Trans.), I, April 28, 1710. This is one of the first pleas for a Bishop for the colonies, the appeal continued in vain for the duration of the Society's connection with the American colonies.*

[36]*Journal of S. P. G. (L. C. Trans.), I, April 28, 1710, and May 19, 1710.*

[37]*Col. Francis Nicholson to the Archbishop of Canterbury, on board her Majesty's ship Draggon, 100 leagues from Lands End, May 22, 1710, in S. P. G. MSS. (L. C. Trans.), A 5, No. XCIV, see also a letter regarding same from Col. Schuyler, ibid., A 5, No. XCV.*

tive teacher.[38] The boy was the son of a French Christian Indian, and consequently a promising pupil. A little later, the expressions of English missionary nationalism naturally occurred as the English came into contact with French and Dutch religious activity. Rev. Mr. Barclay reported the death of Mr. Lydius, the Dutch minister, who had been working among the Indians, and believed that a minister especially for the Indians was sorely needed because the Indians that had come under Mr. Lydius' care were "so ignorant and scandalous that they can scarce be reputed Christians."[39] Moreover, Barclay observed that in his opinion Prince Hendrick, who was so honored in England did not have ten Indian followers, and that the other three Indians were not Sachems. In short, the Society and Her Majesty had been imposed upon,[40] a view which the Society was unwilling to accept.

In Great Britain much interest was aroused in favor of the Indian mission. An anonymous contributor gave £20,[41] and several missionaries were suggested. A Mr. Henderson was the first candidate recommended but he was rejected because he was not a native Englishman.[42] Mr. Barclay and Col. Robert Hunter recommended the Rev. Mr. Freeman of the Dutch Congregation who had translated part of the Liturgy into the Indian language. The Bishop of Salisbury suggested Mr. Edward Bishop of Somersetshire;[43] William Cordiner wished a Mr. Hunt to go to New York;[44] but none of these applicants was approved, and it was not until 1712 that a missionary to the Indians was appointed, a discouraging delay often met with in eighteenth century negotiations.

During the interval, various encouraging reports concerning the New York Indians found their way to England. In May, 1711, Governor Robert Hunter wrote that "the Indians are solicitous for their missionaries and forts promised them. The Lord Bishop of London

[38]*Thomas Barclay to the Bishop of London, New York, July 5, 1709, in S. P. G. MSS. (L. C. Trans.), A 5, No. 1.* Mr. Barclay said that it cost him £15 for the boy's diet and schooling, so he asked for an increase in salary. In 1710, an allowance was asked for the boy. See a letter from Barclay to John Chamberlayne, Albany, September 26, 1710, in S. P. G. MSS. (L. C. Trans.), A 5, No. CLXXVI.

[39]*Thomas Barclay to [Secretary], Albany, September 26, 1710, in Journal of S. P. G. I, January 19, 1710/11.*

[40]*Ibid.*

[41]*Richard King to John Chamberlayne, Exon, October 4, 1710, in S. P. G. MSS. (L. C. Trans.), A 5, No. CLVI.*

[42]*Bishop of London to John Chamberlayne, [London], June 18, 1710, in S. P. G. MSS. (L. C. Trans.), A 5, No. CXIV, and ibid., September 15, 1710, A 5, No. CXXVII.*

[43]*Journal of S. P. G. (L. C. Trans.), I, January 5, 1710/11.*

[44]*William Cordiner to John Chamberlayne, London, February 23, 1711, in S. P. G. MSS. (L. C. Trans.), A 6, No. XII,* Mr. Bishop said that he understood the mission to the Iroquois was the best preferment in America. See a letter from him to John Chamberlayne, Somerset, April, 1711, in S. P. G. MSS. (L. C. Trans.), A 6, No. LIX.

writes me about the Queen's bounty for that purpose, but I have as yet heard nothing of it. . . ."[45] The Society had, however, received £136 of the sum of £400 promised by the Queen for building a house, chapel and fort, and Colonel Nicholson had been empowered to draw upon other funds for the rest of the sum in case it was not paid out of the Treasury.[46]

Aided by the colonial Governor, Rev. Thomas Barclay zealously endeavored to bring the Indians into the Anglican Church, and was encouraged in several conferences with the Chiefs at Albany and Schenectady.[47] Mr. Barclay told of his own successes with the Indians,

> The proselytes have accepted of My Ministry, and on the 23 of My [May] last in our English Chapel at Albany, I christened a child of one of their chief Sachems, and on the 9 of this Month I had a Meeting . . . in the Church of Schenectady, to the number of 50 and upwards. They have been converted to the Christian Faith by the Popish Missionaries and by Monsieur Dellius, Freeman, and Lydius. After I had Catechized several of them, I found three fit for receiving the Sacrament, and the day following being Sunday, they very devoutly received it at My hands. The same day I christened two of their children. . . .
> The Indian interpreter hath been assisting to me in bringing the proselytes and I have promised him 15 or 10£, at least for the first year.[48]

To the Society Colonel Schuyler reported the gratitude of the Indians for the notice taken of them and their eager expectancy in the arrival of the missionaries. He had laid a plan for the fort and chapel with an estimated expense of about £900 sterling.[49] A little later, Governor Robert Hunter announced that he had her Majesty's orders ". . . in conjunction with Col. Nicholson, to build forts and chapels, not exceeding the value of £1000 New York money."[50]

[45]*Governor Robert Hunter to John Chamberlayne, New York, May 7, 1711, in S. P. G. MSS. (L. C. Trans.), A 6, No. LXX.*
[46]*Journal of S. P. G. (L. C. Trans.), II, March 22, 1710/11.*
[47]*Hendrick, the Indian Sachem, was not at the meeting of the Proselytes at Schenectady. See Thomas Barclay to Secretary, Albany, July 3, 1711, in S. P. G. MSS. (L. C. Trans.), A 6, No. CXXIXa.*
[48]*Thomas Barclay to Secretary, Albany, June 12, 1711, in S. P. G. MSS. (L. C. Trans.), A 6, No. CXXIX. In this letter can also be found an account of the opposition given Barclay by Mr. Debois, minister of the Dutch congregation.*
[49]*Col. Schuyler to [Secretary], Albany, May 4, 1711, in Journal of S. P. G., II, June 22, 1711, also S. P. G. MSS. (L. C. Trans.), A 6, LXXI.*
[50]*Gov. Robert Hunter to Secretary, New York, September 12, 1711 (Postscript) in S. P. G. MSS. (L. C. Trans.), A 6, No. CXXXII; also in Journal of S. P. G. (L. C. Trans.), II, November 29, 1711.*

Mr. Barclay wrote hopefully, "I need not tell you that a fort is a building in the Mohogs [sic] country and will be finished in July next. The Chapel is to be 24 foot square. There is a house . . ordered for the Missionaries. . . ."[51] He contemplated a visit to the fort, which was only twenty eight miles above Schenectady and could be reached in one day from Albany. Mr. Barclay urged that the Society send men with zeal and courage, because the French Indians were bold and committed bloody murders.[52]

The Rev. John Sharpe, a former missionary in New Jersey, also joined in words of warning:

> I am sorry there is so little hopes of doing good among the Indians. We received the news of their being of late very insolent, and that they have chased away the carpenters who were (at their own request) sent to build a fort and chapel in their country. . . . They speak . . . as they are moved by liquor and presents. . . . Those who pass in England for emperors were not representatives of the Five Nations, but Mohawks of the nearest Nation to Albany. The French have their priests now among the Senecas and Onondagoes. . . . [53]

Under these circumstances, Mr. Barclay naturally pressed the need for liquor laws, ". . . and if a law be not promoted at home against selling strong liquors to the Natives in any of her Majesty's Colonies in America, there is no possibility of doing any good to them."[54]

To facilitate Indian conversion, Mr. Barclay asked Mr. B. Freeman, of the Dutch congregation at Flatbush, to send to the Society part of his Indian translation of the liturgy of the Church of England. Mr. Freeman supplied the Morning and Evening Prayer, Creed of Athanasius, and the Litany in the dialect of the Mohawks, the first of the Five Nations although it was understood by all Five Nations.[55]   In

[51] *Thomas Barclay to [John Chamberlayne], Albany, Nov. 21, 1711, in S. P. G. MSS. (L. C. Trans.), A 7, pp. 130-131.*

[52] *Mr. Barclay relates how the French Indians, not far from Albany, barbarously murdered a whole family of twelve. This frightened the farmers and forced them to leave their homes and flocks. See Barclay to [Secretary], Albany, Nov. 21, 1711, in S. P. G. MSS. (L. C. Trans.), A 7, pp. 130-131.*

[53] *John Sharpe to [William Taylor], New York, June 23, 1712, in S. P. G. MSS. (L. C. Trans.), A 7, pp. 214-215. Regarding the French, Mr. Sharpe said that they had imposed upon ". . . them to believe there were instructions found in a chest drove ashore from some of the fleet that were cast away in Canada River which directed, that after the reduction of Canada the Continent being in the hands of the English, all the Indians should be destroyed. They have upon this met together which they never presumed to do without the consent of the Government till now."*

[54] *Thomas Barclay to William Taylor, New York, May 31, 1712, in S. P. G. MSS. (L. C. Trans.), A 7, p. 206.*

[55] *Mr. Barclay transmitted these to the Society, in May, 1712, see a letter from him to William Taylor, New York, May 31, 1712, in S. P. G. MSS. (L. C. Trans.), A 7, pp. 204-206.*

August, 1700, Lord Bellomont ordered Mr. Freeman to instruct the
Mohawks. He explained his plan for converting the Indians, and his
success and methods in making the translations.

> I had one Indian constantly by me of whom I gathered
> several words, but afterward out of their language I found 16
> alphabetical letters. . . . By this alphabet I taught that Indian
> to read and write perfectly . . . besides what I have trans-
> lated of your liturgy, I have done in the Indian tongue the
> Gospel of St. Matthew . . . and the 1. 2. 3. Chapters of Gene-
> sis, as also 6. 7. 8. 9. 11. 17. 18. 19. of the same book . . . the 1.
> 5. 6. 7. 8. 9. 10. 11. 12. 13. 14. and 20 of Exodus. I have like-
> wise translated the 1. 5. 6. 15. 22. 32. 38. Psalms, besides the
> whole . . . of St. Mathew. . . . A short explanation of the
> Ten Commandments, the Apostles Creed . . . a short system
> of Theology. . . .[56]

The Indians, he continued, had a great veneration for the English liturgy, especially the Litany, "at the reading of which they frequently did tremble." Mr. Freeman was happy that Anglican missionaries were coming to the Indians, and he placed his translations
and papers at their disposal.[57]

In February, 1712, Mr. Barclay's load was reduced by the appointment of Mr. William Andrews as missionary to the Indians of
New York.[58] He had been in the plantations, had some understanding
of the Indian languages, and possessed a character well suited to this
work. He was to receive £80 per year and his interpreter £60, and,
upon his entering speedily on his duties in the Mohawk country, he
was to be paid £50.[59]

The Queen, the Archbishop of Canterbury, and the S. P. G. gave
generously to help out the mission. Queen Anne donated a communion cloth, altar cloth, cushions, a Bible, and several other items.
The Archbishop of Canterbury furnished copies of the Commandments,

[56]B. Freeman to [William Taylor], Flatbush, May 28, 1712. (Read to the Society October 10, 1712) in S. P. G. MSS. (L. C. Trans.), A 7, pp. 204-205. Mr.
Freeman also translated other texts of scripture in relation to Birth, Passion, Resurrection and Ascension, and some of his writings discussed the errors of the Church
of Rome.

[57]Mr. Freeman said he had no consideration for his work among the Indians,
the Government had promised him £75 per annum but failed to pay him.

[58]Journal of S. P. G. (L. C. Trans.), II, February 22, 1711/12.

[59]Testimonial of William Andrews, Missionary to the Six Nations, London,
April, 1712, in S. P. G. MSS. (L. C. Trans.), A 7, pp. 102-104; William Taylor
to Gov. Robert Hunter, London, May 23, 1712, in S. P. G. MSS. (L. C. Trans.),
A 7, pp. 289-290.

Lord's Prayer, and some prints; and the Society sent a painting of its arms, and sixty sermons.[60]

By August, the fort and chapel had been finished and garrisoned by the Governor. Pending the arrival of Andrews, Barclay went among the Mohawks and was kindly received by them. Sixty Indians came to hear him preach [61] and two children were baptized.

In October, the Rev. Mr. Andrews landed in New York, and, on November 13, he arrived at Albany. Barclay gave an account of his reception by the Indians:

> . . . at his arrival he was welcomed by the five principal Sachems, viz. Sachan, or (Amos), Henrick, Taqueinant, Tarjoris, and a fifth whose name I have forgot. There were also present several of their chief squas [sic] and young men. . . . The 15 Nov. the Commissioners for Indian affairs being met and the five sachems with them . . . the sachems . . . promised him all civil and kind usage. . . . Hendrick . . . expressed . . . their highest gratitude to Almighty God who had inclined the . . . Queen . . . to send them one to lead them on the way to Heaven, they being in the dark full of dismal fears and perplexities, not knowing what shall become of them after this life. Next he returned their humble thanks to the most religious Queen Anne, to their ghostly Father, his Grace the Archbishop, and the rest of the Spiritual Sachems of that Godly body (as they were pleased to call the Society)

[60]*William Taylor to Gov. Robert Hunter, London, Saturday, July 26, 1712, in S. P. G. MSS. (L. C. Trans.), A 7, p. 267. The exact gifts were as follows:*
  Gifts for the Mohawk Chapels given by Queen Anne,
    1 communion Table Cloth
    2 Damask Napkins
    1 Carpet for the Communion Table
    1 Altar Cloth
    1 Pulpit Cloth
    1 Large cushion with tassels
    1 Small cushion for the desk
    1 Holland surplice
    2 Common Prayer Books, one for each Chapel
    1 Book of homilies
    4 of Her Majesty's Arms . . .
    1 large silver salver
    2 large silver flaggons
    1 silver dish which is a drawer under the other plate
    1 silver cup
  Gifts given by the Archbishop of Canterbury,
    2 tables of the Commandments and Lord's Prayer
    97 prints of the Queen's effigies, arms, etc., to be distributed among the Indians
  Gifts given by the Society,
    1 Society's arms painted to be put up in the Chapel
    50 Octavo
    10 Quarto
Sermons to be distributed in the Province
[61]*The sermon was taken from Matthew 21:18, "It is written my house shall be called the house of prayer."*

who had been pleased to send them a father . . . and last of all to the minister who had travelled so far for their good.[62]

Hendrick, however, voiced some suspicion and requested that none of the Mohawks' land be clandestinely bought from them, for to do so would only cause their enmity. He also hoped that the rumor that one-tenth of the Indian goods was to be taken from them for the support of the minister was false. Andrews assured him that he and the English had no such design.[63] On November 20, Mr. Andrews set out for the Mohawk country, accompanied by Robert Livingston Jr., Mayor of Albany, Captain Mathews, a Churchwarden, Justice Strooman of Schenectady and Mr. Barclay. Mr. Andrews entered upon his duties at once preaching and baptizing two Indian children. However, the interpreter was a Dutchman, unacquainted with the English tongue, therefore a Mr. John Oliver was hired to translate Mr. Andrews' sermon into Dutch for the interpreter to render into Indian. Mr. Oliver was hired to teach in the Indian School.[64]

One of the first letters written by Mr. Andrews to the Society read, in part,

> . . . I find, I thank God, most of the Indians that are at home (for the greatest part of them as they tell me are abroad which I have not yet seen) very well disposed to embrace those Christian doctrines which are delivered to them, as appears from their diligence in coming to Church and their seeming good attention and devotion when there, and where we have commonly 50 or 60 every Lord's Day, but I hope when the others come home we shall have a great many more. I had 18 at the Sacrament on Christmas Day. I have baptized 8 of their children and a young Man about 24 years of age.[65]

Two months later he again wrote that the Dutch as well as the English traders were not keen on having a minister settle among them, and the "extortion, deceitful dealing, lying and cheating" of the Traders had a bad influence on the Indians.[66] He deprecated the utter lack of real concern for the Indians baptized by priests, for they never instructed the Indians previous to baptism. A school was greatly needed, and Mr. Andrews asked the Society's advice as to whether to teach the

[62]*Thomas Barclay to William Taylor, Albany, December 17, 1712, in S. P. G. MSS. (L. C. Trans.), A 8, pp. 125-128.*

[63]*Record of meeting of Commissioners of Indian affairs in Albany, November 15, 1712, in S. P. G. MSS. (L. C. Trans.), A 8, pp. 254-256.*

[64]*Mr. Oliver was formerly a clerk to Mr. Barclay, and had always been a communicant of the Church. He was to be paid out of the interpreter's salary.*

[65]*William Andrews to William Taylor, Fort Hunter, January 13, 1712/13, in S. P. G. MSS. (L. C. Trans.), A 8, pp. 227-228.*

[66]*William Andrews to William Taylor, Queen's Fort near Mohawk Castle, March 9, 1712/13, in S. P. G. MSS. (L. C. Trans.), A 8, p. 144.*

children in their own language or in English. Andrews himself did not favor English because it gave the Indians "opportunity of conversing the more with the English as also with Dutch who speak English, and so to learn their vices."[67] To encourage education, Mr. Andrews requested the Society ". . . to order the value of 5 £ in some triffling things such as coarse beads, small knives, small scissors, small brass rings and the like. . . ."[68] At first he described the Mohawk Nation as numbering about 260,[69] but by September, 1713, he thought there must be 580[70] adults and many children. Their life was a roving one, and their language was the most difficult to learn because the words were so long, the language was imperfect in adverbs, conjunctions, and interjections, and so much had to be supplied by the understanding of the hearer.

In other words, Andrews almost at once faced all of the major problems of Indian conversion and civilization. Some of these were: the evil influence of the trader, Dutch and English; French rivalry and hostility from Canada; matters of religious education as to what stage when baptism should occur; what should be taught in the school and in what language, a pressing problem in Africa today, always related to whether learning a white man's language opens a road to culture or to vice; and the task of learning a native language by grown up men. Just as classical Latin in the first centuries had to be seriously modified to express the ideas of Christianity, so now to teach the new religion in the Indian language might well discourage the most stout hearted. The life and habits of the Indians were interestingly described by Mr. Andrews.

> Their chief town or Castle . . . stands by the fort, consisting of 40 or 50 wigwams or houses, palisaded around. Another of their chief towns, between 20 and 30 houses is three or four and twenty miles distant from this. They have several other little towns, 7 or 8 houses in a town, and single houses up and down pretty near their Castle, next to the fort. Their houses are made of mats and bark of trees together with poles about 3 or 4 yards high. Their clothing is a match coat, like a mantle, either a blanket or a bear's skin. They paint and grease themselves . . . cut the hair off from one side of their heads and some of that on the other, they tie up in knots upon the crown with feathers, tufts of fur upon their ears, and some of them wear a bead fasten to their nose, with a thread hang-

---

[67]*William Andrews to William Taylor, Queen's Fort near Mohawk Castle, March 9, 1712/13, in S. P. G. MSS. (L. C. Trans.), A 8, p. 146.*
[68]*William Andrews to William Taylor, Queen's Fort near Mohawk Castle, March 9, 1712/13, in S. P. G. MSS. (L. C. Trans.), A 8, p. 146 ff.*
[69]*William Andrews to William Taylor, Queen's Fort near Mohawk Castle, March 9, 1712/13, in S. P. G. MSS. (L. C. Trans.), A 8, p. 147.*
[70]*Ibid., September 7, 1713, S. P. G. MSS. (L. C. Trans.), A 8, p. 185.*

ing down to their lips, bead and wampum about their necks and waists. The men are slothful and lazy enough. The women laborious, true servants of their husbands—carry all the burdens fetch the venison . . . the wood . . . carry the children . . . on their backs, hoe the ground, plant the corn, wait upon their husbands when they eat and take what they leave them. Yet for all this . . . the women court the men when they design marriage. . . . The vices they are most guilty of is drinking . . . especially rum, and changing their wives when they are weary of them. . . . I have been at great expense in treating them, especially at my first coming among them, and am still frequently giving them victuals and drink for they are constant visitors when they are well used."[71]

Despite these difficulties, thirteen baptisms were reported for the period from November 22, 1712 to March 9, 1713.[72] A schoolmaster was much needed, for the assistant to the Interpreter was of slight use, and the Indians had built a school and were anxious to send their children, who numbered in this vicinity about forty.[73] Some of the pupils, however, were sixteen to eighteen years of age. So urgent was this problem that he had hired a teacher, in addition to the interpreter, pending the Society's approval. The Mohawks were apt pupils but needed printed books because the parents wished to have them educated in their own language. As early as February, 1714, Andrews transmitted to the Society, for the printer, manuscripts of the Church Catechism, Morning and Evening Prayer, Litany, Psalms, and English

[71]*William Andrews to William Taylor, Queen's Fort near Mohawk Castle, March 9, 1712/13, in S. P. G. MSS. (L. C. Trans.), A 8, pp. 146-147. Mr. Andrews said that changing of wives was not a common practice and as a rule, husband and wife were kind to one another, and shared possessions peaceably.*

[72]*Complete list of baptisms was inclosed in William Andrews to William Taylor, Queen's Fort near Mohawk Castle, March 9, 1712/13, in S. P. G. MSS. (L. C. Trans.), A 8, p. 257.*

Name	Age	Date Baptized	Parents
Aaron	Infant	Nov. 23, 1712	Peter and Cornelia
Cornelius	Infant	Nov. 23, 1712	Sachtachrogi & Anne
Catherine	Infant	Jan. 11, 1713	Simon and Josiena
Elizabeth	2 years	Jan. 11, 1713	Onagsakeartet & Maria
Luke	4 years	Jan. 11, 1713	Phillin and Anne
Ezra	22 years	Jan. 11, 1713	. . . .
Solomon	2 years	Jan. 25, 1713	Tinliheraroungswo & Sara
Anne	4 years	Jan. 25, 1713	Uttagrarondagrough & Anne
Sarah	Infant	Jan. 25, 1713	Uttagrarondagrough & Anne
Zachariah	4 years	Feb. 22, 1713	Joseph Sagcot & Hannah
Hannah	Infant	Feb. 22, 1713	Joseph Sagcot & Hannah
Aron	Infant	Feb. 22, 1713	Ezra and wife
Mary	Infant (?)	March 8, 1713	Ezra and Maria

[73]*Andrews said he would willingly undertake it but his other work took up all of his time. He strongly recommended Mr. Oliver because he spoke both English and Dutch and knew the Indian language as well as his own, as he had been taken a prisoner by the Indians when a mere child.*

Hornbooks.[74] He also requested three reams of writing paper for the Indians, six dozen inkhorns, and as many pens. He recommended a minimum of £30 for the schoolteacher because of necessities of living,

> There is no manner of pleasure to be proposed by living here, but only the hopes of doing some good among those poor dark ignorant creatures, for in the winter season for 4 or 5 months we can scarce stir abroad by reason of . . . coldness . . . and in summer tormented with flies and mosquitoes . . . and snakes. . . . In the next place the transporting of provisions to this place is very chargeable. The nearest towns to us of the Christian inhabitants, where we by what we want, is Schenectady and Albany. The one about 24 and the other about 44 miles [distant].[75]

His record of baptisms, from March 8 to September 3, 1713, totalled 32; sixteen received the Sacrament at Easter and twenty-four the fifth Sunday after Trinity.[76]. Moreover, the next year he visited the Onondaga Indians and baptized several. The father or mother of these had been baptized by the French Missionaries in Canada. The sachems of this tribe refused to have a fort among them, whereas the rank and file were willing to have both a fort and a minister.[77]

Although Mr. Andrews' first reports on the school were favorable, it soon appeared that, after three or four months, many of the Indians wearied of book learning and their parents would not compel them to conform and adapt themselves to the white man's aims and plans. He hoped, however, that when the parents saw the progress of the persistent pupils, who were beginning to read and write their own language, they would keep their children at school. He was teaching three or four of them English, and had taken two into his own house. The trinkets, such as beads, cord, knives, buttons, etc., were of great help.[78]

[74]*He said that if the Society could not have them printed in England without mistakes, it should be done in New York where some one could be with the printer. It was decided that the Prayers should be printed in England, but the Hornbook should be printed in the colonies to show respect to the Indians. See the Journal of S. P. G. (L. C. Trans.), II, March 4, 1713/14.*

[75]*William Andrews to William Taylor, Queen's Fort by the Mohawk's Castle, September 7, 1713, in S. P. G. MSS. (L. C. Trans.), A 8, p. 184.*

[76]*List of those baptized can be found enclosed in William Andrews to William Taylor, September 7, 1713, in S. P. G. MSS. (L. C. Trans.), A 8, pp. 304-305. Ages range from infants to 75 years.*

[77]*Mr. Andrews to [Secretary] Queen's Fort by the Mohawk Castle, May 25, 1714, in Journal of S. P. G. (L. C. Trans.), III, Oct. 15, 1714.*

[78]*Invoice of Sundries shipped on Board the "Drake", John Tucker, Master, for New York, on the proper account and risk of the Honorable and Reverend Society . . . and goes consigned to Rev. Mr. William Andrews . . . in S. P. G. MSS. (L. C. Trans.), A 8, pp. 306-307. Among Articles sent were: 2 bundles of black and green beads; 2 bundles of crystal and amber colors [sic]; 4 bundles small red; 8 bundles larger red; 6 dozen sizers; 1 doz. knives; 1 doz. forks; 2 dozen boys knives; 3 dozen feather quilts; 2 dozen pictures in guilt frames; 2 dozen small stone rings and three cards colored sleeve buttons. The total price, including transportation, was 5£, 13s, 10d.*

Opposition to Mr. Andrew's education was instigated by Dutch traders. He wrote to the Society,

> . . . the Dutch traders, a sordid, base sort of people . . . are continally suggesting notions to the Indians to make divisions and factions among them to make them dislike my being among them. One while telling them that the design of the English in building forts among them is only to get their land from them another while caluminating me, telling them that I am an ill man, that I preach a Popish religion to them and that there are none so fit to instruct them as the Dutch. . . ."[79]

Many of the Dutch informed the Indians that religious instruction was worthless, and they told Mr. Andrews that Indian Christianization was hopeless. But he affirmed that as far as he understood the Indian tribal customs and, "considering they have no laws among them, they are, many of them, better Christians than they [Dutch] themselves are."[80]   Mr. Andrews particularly opposed Dutch liquor selling and Sunday trading, and the Dutch, in turn, attempted to drive him away. But the Society steadfastly encouraged him, and in June, 1714, sent him three dozen gilt hornbooks, three dozen gilt primers, one ream Dutch paper, one ream fine writing paper, one ream ordinary paper, six dozen leather inkhorns, and six dozen pen knives.[81]   In order to solve the language difficulty, the missionary urged the Society to send him two English boys, between the ages of 9 and 12 to be trained as interpreters. Although his work with children and women went on with success, the men were too often carried away by drink. When asked why they got drunk, the Indians often replied, why do you Christians sell us so much rum.[82]   He implored the Society to use its influence to procure a Queen's Proclamation or an Act of Parliament to restrain all the provinces from selling strong liquors to the Indians.[83]   For example, when he visited the Onondagas all of them were drunk on liquor just received from Albany, and consequently would not let him preach. But he believed that if the So-

---

[79]William Andrews to William Taylor, Queen's Fort near the Mohawks, May 25, 1714, in S. P. G. MSS. (L. C. Trans.), A 9, pp. 123-125.

[80]William Andrews to William Taylor, Queen's Fort near the Mohawks, May 25, 1714, in S. P. G. MSS. (L. C. Trans.), A 9, pp. 123-125.

[81]Invoice of a box shipped on board the "Antelope", John King, Master, for New York, on Account and Risk of the . . . Society . . . goes consigned to Rev. Mr. William Andrews, June 20, 1714, in S. P. G. MSS. (L. C. Trans.), A 9, p. 72.

[82]The Dutch traders were selling rum by the wholesale, since the act of assembly against it had expired, and it was not thought likely to be renewed, because the argument was that if it were, the Indians would go into another province to buy it. However, such an act was passed in 1717, see Journal of S. P. G. (L. C. Trans.), III, September 20, 1717.

[83]Mr. Andrews to [Secretary], Mohawk Castle, October 15, 1714, in Journal of S. P. G. (L. C. Trans.), III, June 17. 1715.

ciety would send him a large box of pipes to give the kings of the nations, these could be used as inducements for the Indian Sachems to allow him to preach. Strangely enough it was even difficult for him to count the Indians, because if they believed anyone were trying to count them, they would move away, imagining some ill design.

In 1715, Mr. Andrews had about 100 of the baptized Indians coming to his church constantly, when they were at home;[84] many more had been baptized, but were no better nor lived otherwise than the heathen Indians. The first flush of success was being followed by a period of apathy, and his school was also diminishing, and only six or seven came to learn their language. To encourage the Indians, he asked the Society to adopt a system of prizes of blankets, shirts, and stockings for regular school attendance. In his opinion, if they did not come for this promise, it would be useless for the Society to be at any more expense either in printing books, or in continuing the schoolmaster.[85] The scheme failed and on October 18, 1717, the schoolmaster was discharged. Henceforth the missionary himself was to teach the few remaining pupils.[86] Governor Hunter was disappointed with this action, for he believed that the best way to convert the Indians was to erect schools among them, and teach the young the English language and the Christian religion at the same time. The Governor correctly diagnosed a main difficulty when he pointed out to the Society that religion in the Indian language sounded oddly, the idioms of the two being widely different. He continued, "What we say in one short word costs them a long sentence which causes the mistake of writing down words of yards length in all translations."[87] Roman Catholics in their Indian work usually followed the procedure of carrying on their religious work in an European language, rather than attempting to make an Indian language over into an adequate medium for the expression of Christian culture.

For the next few years, Mr. Andrews made little progress, and complaints against him were sent to the Society. One Rev. Thomas Haliday, who objected to Mr. Andrews' methods, declared that the prayers which had been printed in New York were not true Indian. He asked to be appointed Indian missionary.[88] The Society at once, upon

[84]*Mr. Andrews to [Secretary], Kings Fort, Mohawk Castle, October 17, 1715, in Journal of S. P. G. (L. C. Trans.), III, January 11, 1716/17.*
[85]*Mr. Andrews thought it proper to defer printing the Catechism and Vocabulary until the school increased.*
[86]*The discharge for the schoolmaster was sent to the Governor of New York, not to Mr. Andrews.*
[87]*Governor Hunter to [Secretary], New York, October 2, 1716, in Journal of S. P. G. (L. C. Trans.), III, September 20, 1717, see also Journal of S. P. G. (L. C. Trans.), IV, February 13, 1718/19.*
[88]*Thomas Haliday to [Secretary], Elizabeth Town, New Jersey, July 13, 1715, in Journal of S. P. G. (L. C. Trans.), III, February 3, 1715/16. Mr. Haliday was formerly of New York.*

the receipt of this letter, wrote to Governor Hunter to ascertain the facts. He replied that, although little progress had been made by Andrews, his relative failure was not due to his want of care or attendance upon his duties, but nevertheless, he believed that a new man should be put in his place.[89] The Society decided to discontinue his salary. At the end of two centuries and for the same reasons which baffled Mr. Andrews in these early days, the solution of Indian education has not been found.

Without an outlet for use of the white man's culture, the average Indian could not interest himself in alien studies. Neither force, nor the unlovely example of the white man's life and his unintelligible customs, supplied the inner motive power which alone could make him struggle to exchange his racial independence for the white man's economy.

On July 11, 1719, Mr. Andrews wrote that he had received his order to leave in case he had no better success among the Indians. He explained that he had given up hope, as they still continued in drunkenness, and filthy living,[90] and he would leave shortly for Virginia. He left all the plates, books, and other furniture at the chapel, and a large Common Prayer Book he loaned to Mr. Barclay. The interpreter was given the manuscripts in the Indian language, and he gave an Indian lad and four girls several of the books that were printed in their language.[91] All of the other books were left with Mr. Jenney, chaplain at the garrison in New York.

At Mr. Andrews' departure, the Rev. Thomas Barclay asked to combine the Mohawk Mission with his Albany work, but the Society decided to withdraw his allowance also.[92] Barclay's financial distress apparently affected his mind, for on July 5, 1722, the clergy of New York wrote to David Humphreys, asking help for Barclay's family. This letter clearly related the missionary's devotion to his duties and revealed the pathetic condition to which he and his family had been reduced:

> He hath been all along diligent in his cure and hath taken
> great pains in catechizing Indian infidels in a place where they
> are very numerous, but of late many misfortunes successively

[89]*Governor Hunter to [Secretary], New York, November 4, 1718, in Journal of S. P. G. (L. C. Trans.), February 13, 1718/19.*
[90]*William Andrews to [Secretary], New York; July 11, 1719, in Journal of S. P. G. (L. C. Trans.), IV, December 18, 1719. However, he said the Indians were talking of moving ten or fifteen miles further from the Christian inhabitants, in order to be nearer to another Mohawk Castle; if this were done, Mr. Andrews believed a great deal of the lewdness and swearing would be eliminated.*
[91]*Mr. Andrews believed they would soon forget what they had learned because they took no interest in their books.*
[92]*Thomas Barclay to David Humphreys, Albany, New York, June 13, 1721, in S. P. G. MSS. (L. C. Trans.), A 15, pp. 93-94.*

attending him have at length brought him to an outrageous dis-
traction such has obliged his friends to confine him to a dark
room and in the mean time the small salary which allowed him
not being paid, his family (a wife and 4 children) are reduced
to extreme poverty.[93]

Several years passed before another missionary was appointed at
Albany.   However, work with the Indians in other sections of the
colony was progressing.   From Richmond the Rev. Eneas MacKenzie
wrote to the Society, that he had baptized an Indian man, twenty-two
years of age, and a native of the province.   He wrote about the Indian
thus,

> Coming accidentally upon this island he was induced to
> learn to read English and then was desirous to understand
> something of the Christian religion.   I hope he will bring no
> scandal upon his holy profession, for he is a sober and seem-
> ingly serious young man, and there is not any reason of sus-
> pecting that he desired baptism upon any view of temporal in-
> terest or respect (it being one of the crying crimes of the gen-
> erality of this country not only to discourage but to ridicule the
> baptizing of negroes and Indians)[94]

Mr. Elias Neau reported the baptism of an Indian woman in May
1722;[95] Rev. James Wetmore, of Brookhaven[96] reported 554 native Indians in his county of Suffolk, most of them being brought up in English families, but inasmuch as no care was taken to bring them over to
Christianity, he hoped a missionary could be sent them.[97]

In New York city, Mr. William Huddleston, a schoolmaster, was
catechizing the Indian slaves on Sundays, Wednesdays, and Fridays.[98]
After Mr. Huddleston's death, in 1724, another catechist was requested
to take care of the 1400 Indian and negro slaves.[99]

[93]Clergy of New York to David Humphreys in behalf of Mr. Barclay, New
York, July 5, 1722, in S. P. G. MSS. (L. C. Trans.), A 16, pp. 206-207.   Mr. Barclay was supposed to receive £50 pension from the Crown, but for four years it
had been unpaid.
[94]Eneas MacKenzie to David Humphreys, Richmond [New York], August
22, 1720, in S. P. G. MSS. (L. C. Trans.), A 14, p. 135.
[95]Elias Neau to David Humphreys [New York, summer 1722], in S. P. G.
MSS. (L. C. Trans.), A 16, p. 204; ibid., New York, May 22, 1722, in Journal of
S. P. G. (L. C. Trans.), IV, February 15, 1722-23.
[96]Rev. Mr. Wetmore's mission was at Staten Island, but he said he could do
no service there so he removed to Brookhaven, see S. P. G. MSS. (L. C. Trans.),
A 18, pp. 173-174.
[97]James Wetmore to David Humphreys, Brookhaven, Long Island, May 11,
1724, in S. P. G. MSS. (L. C. Trans.), A 18, pp. 173-174; Journal of S. P. G.
(L. C. Trans.), V, September 19, 1724.
[98]William Vesey to David Humphreys, New York, November 8, 1725, in
S. P. G. MSS. (L. C. Trans.), B I, No. 85.   Mr. Huddleston passed away two
years after Mr. Elias Neau, in 1724.
[99]The Rector, Churchwardens, and Vestry of Trinity Church, New York, July
5, 1726, in S. P. G. MSS. (L. C. Trans.), B I, No. 73; Journal of S. P. G. (L. C.
Trans.), V, September 16, 1726.

In 1728, six years after Mr. Barclay's misfortune, the Rev. John Miln was sent to the Albany mission. In the summer of 1729, he baptized three Mohawk children, and administered the communion to ten.[100] He wrote to the Society,

> The Indians seem very well disposed to receive the blessed Gospel among them. Everytime I go there they meet me with acclamations of joy, at some distance from their Castle where they discharge a volley of shot. I meet with much respect, kindness and civility from them. Some of them have been pretty well instructed in the grounds of Christianity by Mr. Andrews, the late Missionary to the Society am[ong] them, and indeed, they very much regret the loss of th[at] good man. At divine service where the interpreter reads the prayers and a sermon in their own language they behave themselves decently and devoutedly.[101]

Mr. Miln states that he would continue to visit the Mohawks until a missionary was sent them, but, as the labor was great and hiring an interpreter expensive, he wished the Society would grant him a consideration. The Society accordingly gave him £10 for his services among the Indians.[102] He visited them at least four times yearly, each time remaining four or five days, offering the Indians the Sacrament, baptizing the children, and preaching to them in their own language through an interpreter. His special care was for those that were already Christians. The number of constant communicants among the Mohawks was fourteen, and his hearers about fifty.[103] The Society's charitable assistance, Mr. Miln declared, could be no better answered than among the Indians. At Easter, in 1731, fifteen Mohawks were present as communicants and twelve children and two Indian women were baptized.[104]

Although Mr. Miln was enthusiastic concerning his work among the Indians, he felt that he could not in addition do justice to his parish at Albany. He wrote as follows to Commissary William Vesey of New York,

> I have often informed the Society of the propensity and inclination of the Mohawk Indians, to receive the Gospel; and I have taken pains and employed all the time I could spare from the exercise of my function in Albany to instruct them,

[100]*John Miln to David Humphreys, Albany, November 3, 1729, in S. P. G. MSS. (L. C. Trans.), B I, No. 53.*
[101]*Ibid.*
[102]*Journal of S. P. G. (L. C. Trans.), V, January 16, 1729.*
[103]*John Miln to Secretary, Albany, November 4, 1730, in S. P. G. MSS., A 23, pp. 85-86.*
[104]*John Miln to David Humphreys, New York, November 2, 1731, in S. P. G. MSS. (L. C. Trans.), A 23, p. 345.*

since it pleases God to still [store] up in their hearts a desire
to receive Christianity. . . . That good work can be furthered
by nothing so much as to have a proper person instructed in
their tongue.   Since ideas can but be perfectly conveyed to
them, by the means of an interpreter whose immoral life con-
tributes to lessen the impression of his dictates.

Now, sir, as the son of the Revd. Mr. Barclay . . . is
desirous of acquiring their language, designs to live amongst
them for sometime and instruct them, I hope you'll recommend him to the Society's bounty.[105]

In 1735, the state of Mr. Miln's health obliged him to go to England.[106]   The following year an account of the state of the Church at
Albany and the Mohawk Indians was laid before the Society by Lieutenant Walter Butler, commander of the British garrison at Fort Hunter.   He testified that the Mohawk Indians were becoming civilized,
the result of the industry of the Rev. Mr. Miln in teaching them the
Christian Religion.   The communicants exceeded twenty.   The Mohawk Indians, as well as the Canajoharies, had often asked Lieut. Butler to try to persuade Mr. Miln to come oftener.[107]   The Society had
allowed him £10 per annum for his services among the Indians in 1730
and 1731, and he now requested £10 a year for his last four years
work, which compensation was agreed to by the Society.[108]

From the time of Mr. Miln's retirement to the appointment of
his successor, Henry Barclay, in 1737, the work with the Mohawks
temporarily broke off, but the work with Indians in other parts of New
York continued.   For example, Mr. Edward Davies, schoolmaster of
Southampton on the Island of Nassau in New York, taught several
Indian children;[109] Rev. Mr. Charlton of New York city had a number of Indian catachumens; Rev. William Harrison baptized ". . . in
a religious French family . . . one Indian woman . . .";[110] and
similar letters were received by the Society from James Wetmore of

[105]*John Miln to William Vesey, New York, November 14, 1732, in S. P. G.
MSS. (L. C. Trans.), A 25, p. 42.   Mr. Barclay had spent four years at the college at New Haven, and made excellent progress in education, and Mr. Miln
believed he would become "an ornament to the Church."*
[106]*Mr. Miln's mission was temporarily supplied by Mr. Orem, chaplain to
the Four Independent Companies, see Journal of S. P. G. (L. C. Trans.), VI,
January 16, 1735/36.*
[107]*The Indians often had to come to Albany to have their children baptized,
or to be married.   Certificate of Mr. Miln's services among the Mohawk Indians,
delivered to the Society, January 16, 1735/36, in S. P. G. MSS. (L. C. Trans.),
A 26, p. 4.   The certificate is signed by Walter Butler and sworn before James
De Lancey, October 26, 1735.*
[108]*S. P. G. MSS. (L. C. Trans.), A 26, p. 1; Journal of S. P. G. (L. C.
Trans.), VII, February 20, 1735/36.*
[109]*Edward Davies to David Humphreys, Southampton, New York, November
6, 1733, in S. P. G. MSS. (L. C. Trans.), B I, No. 9.*
[110]*William Harrison to David Humphreys, Staten Island, November 20,
[1735], Journal of S. P. G. (L. C. Trans.), VII, April 16, 1736.*

Rye and Mr. Jacob Eblig of Canajoharie. The latter stated that the Indians were very numerous in his parish.[111]

Although Mr. Henry Barclay, son of Rev. Thomas Barclay, was not appointed missionary to Albany and the Mohawks until October 21, 1737,[112] he had been appointed as catechist to the Fort Hunter Indians on May 29, 1735.[113] In his first letter to the Society,[114] he stated that the Indians desired instruction in Christianity, and the following year in a letter to the Secretary gave details of his regime,

> I have made myself master of the pronunciation of their [Indian] tongue, and do perform Divine Service therein every Sunday, which they constantly and very devoutedly attend; and understand me perfectly well. I daily teach above forty young men and children to read and write their own tongue, most of whom make vast progress. I also keep a Catechetical school, every evening, which all—both young and old attend. I read an exposition of the Catechism (translated for . . . Mr. Andrews) every Sunday. There are but three or four adults remaining unbaptized at Fort Hunter, and 25 infants have been baptized since my residing among them, by the Rev. M. Oël, a German Episcopal Minister. The number of communicants [is] above 40. . . .[115]

Mr. Barclay, as was to be expected, found the language extremely difficult,[116] and had to have an interpreter, and recommended the one formerly employed by Mr. Andrews.

In the spring of 1737, Mr. Barclay went, as was necessary, to England to receive Holy Orders, and, on October 21st of the same year, was appointed missionary to the Mohawk Indians and to Albany, with a salary of £50 a year. For the translation of parts of the Scripture and of the Common Prayer Book, he was granted £5.[117] With one-half his time devoted to the Indians, his early reports told of a steady reformation of manners and an increase in virtue. In No-

[111]Jacob Eblig to [Secretary] Canojarhare, September 30, 1734, in Journal of S. P. G. (L. C. Trans.), VII, May 21, 1736. Mr. Eblig asked for some recompense for his instruction of the Indians.
[112]Journal of S. P. G. (L. C. Trans.), VII, January 20, 1737/38.
[113]Henry Barclay to David Humphreys, Fort Hunter, November 11, 1735, in S. P. G. MSS. (L. C. Trans.), A 26, pp. 71-72.
[114]Dated November 11, 1735, in S. P. G. MSS. (L. C. Trans.), A 26, pp. 71-72; Journal of S. P. G. (L. C. Trans.), VII, July 16, 1736.
[115]Henry Barclay to David Humphreys, Fort Hunter, August 31, 1736, in S. P. G. MSS. (L. C. Trans.), A 26, pp. 283-284; Journal of S. P. G. (L. C. Trans.), VII, December 17, 1736. In this letter, as well as his first, i. e., November 11, 1735, he asks for more money, as his board alone cost him £15 a year, and it was necessary for him to buy a house and hire an interpreter. He had been allowed £20 a year by the Society.
[116]The verbs were varied, and the conjugations numerous.
[117]Journal of S. P. G. (L. C. Trans.), VII, January 20, 1737/38. This £5 allowance was made instead of the usual one for the buying of small tracts, etc.

vember, 1738, he said he had 500 Indians under his care, 50 of whom were communicants,[118] but his two following "Notitia Parochialis", dated June 3, 1739[119] and November 18, 1739,[120], showed slight increases, including the baptism of two adult Indians.[121]

About the middle of August, 1740, the Governor of New York had a conference with representatives of the Six Nations at Albany, to renew their League of Friendship, and Mr. Barclay was asked to preach to them.[122]

> The Mohawks, (of whom there were above Seventy present) did then for the first Time make the Responses in the Prayers, and perform'd in So decent and Devout a Manner as Agreeably Surprised all that were present. The Governor also observed to them the great happiness they enjoy'd in having the means of Instruction afforded them and earnestly exhorted them to persevere in their profession.[123]

In his analysis of this conference, Mr. Barclay emphasized the necessity of stationing a schoolmaster among the Indians because the Society could not be readily effective unless the youth were taught to read in their own language.[124]

At the very time that Mr. Barclay asked for an interpreter, an unknown benefactor gave the Society £50 for work with the Mohawks;[125] the Society added £10 to this amount for a translation into Mohawk of one of the Gospels, and the Bishop of Man's Essay on the Instruc-

[118]*Rev. Mr. Barclay to [Secretary], Albany, November 10, 1738, in Journal of S. P. G. (L. C. Trans.), VIII, April 13, 1739. His "Notitia Parochialis" contained:*

Number of inhabitants in the City and County	*10610 whites*
Slaves or blacks	*1110*
Indians under his care	*500*
Communicants at Albany	*35*
Communicants among Indians	*50*
Professors of Church of England	
(besides Indians and garrisons)	*110*
Baptized within half year	*20 infants*
Admitted to Holy Communion	*8*

[119]*S. P. G. MSS. (L. C. Trans.), B 7, Pt. I, pp. 127-128.*
[120]*S. P. G. MSS. (L. C. Trans.), B 7, Pt. II, p. 139.*
[121]*Ibid.*
[122]*The sermon had to be composed with the assistance of the interpreter; however, Mr. Barclay received much satisfaction in knowing that he was well understood.*
[123]*Henry Barclay to Philip Bearcroft, Fort Hunter, October 15, 1740, in S. P. G. MSS. (L. C. Trans.), B 7, Pt. II, p. 141; Journal of S. P. G. (L. C. Trans.), Vol. VIII, March 20, 1740/41.*
[124]*Barclay's greatest hopes were built on the Indian youths, and he had tried several ways to obtain an allowance for a teacher, but to no avail.*
[125]*Additional light has been thrown on the great generosity of British people during the middle years of the eighteenth century in a recent study, W. S. Lewis and Ralph M. Williams, Private Charity in England, 1747-1757, p. 28, 1938, Yale University Press.*

tion of the Indians.[126]   The Society also gave Barclay instructions to appoint an Indian schoolmaster. Barclay was delighted with the new aggressive policies. He found the drunkenness of the Indians much decreased. He had not seen above ten drunken people all summer, whereas on his first coming, he saw at least that many every day. Besides, his Communicants had increased from 50 to 58.[127]   Strangely however, just at the moment of success in America, the debate within the Society in England was renewed on the matter of spiritual care for Indians versus the claims of the white colonists. This question was reopened by Dr. Henry Stebbing, who, in 1742, preached the annual Sermon, asserting that the first object of the S. P. G. was not to convert heathen in the colonies but to care for its own people. He declared, "The Converting of Heathens is a *secondary, incidental* Point," and he saw no great likelihood of the conversion of the Indians, mentioning the Mohawks especially.[128]

In America, Mr. Barclay proceeded with his plans, and, with the advice and consent of the Governor and Commissioners, appointed two schoolmasters at ten pounds New York currency to each.

> One *Cornelius* a Sacheme at the Lower and One Daniel att the Upper Town. The Former is very faithful and Diligent and vastly Successful; and so is the Latter. . . . The Society will be pleased to Observe, that there are two hunting Seasons, when the Indians take all their Families with them; at these times the Schoolmasters have leave to go a hunting and are Commonly Two Months Out at a time.
>
> The Building of the Church and my own house, and a great Scarcity of Provisions among the Indians, which has Obliged them to be much abroad; have prevented my catechising as usual. . . .[129]

The schoolmasters were obliged to write their own manuscripts for instruction, for there were of course no Indian books for that purpose, and besides, the interpreter and translator that Mr. Barclay had engaged had died. Encouraging was the fact that another present of five guineas was given to this work; and to Mr. Barclay, the Society

[126]*Henry Barclay to Rev. Dr. Berriman (Fellow of Eaton College, London), Albany, December 7, 1741, in S. P. G. MSS. (L. C. Trans.), B 9, No. 83.*

[127]*Henry Barclay to [Philip Bearcroft], Albany, November 9, 1741, in S. P. G. MSS. (L. C. Trans.), B 9, No. 81-82; Journal of S. P. G. (L. C. Trans.), IX, February 19, 1741/42.*

[128]*Sermons preached before S. P. G. in St. Mary Le Bow, February 19, 1742, by Henry Stebbing, Chancellor of Sarum. (Huntington Library).*

[129]*Henry Barclay to Philip Bearcroft, Albany, November 17, 1742, in S. P. G. MSS. (L. C. Trans.), B 10, No. 112.*

gave a gratuity of £50 because of "the expensiveness and laboriousness of the mission."[130]

But in the midst of King George's War, smooth sailing was not to be expected. In fact, about the middle of January, 1745, a severe disturbance occurred among the Indians. Six Indians coming home from Schenectady, alarmed the whole Indian town by telling them that the white people were coming "to cut them all in Pieces." This caused most of the Indians to flee into the woods. Mr. Barclay gave the following account to the Society,

> As Soon as I heard It, I call'd . . . many of them together . . . which had a good Effect. . . . But the Authors of the Sedition, opposed us with Violence, . . . and warn'd them [the Indians] . . . that I was the chief Contriver of the Destruction intended against them. . . . I was a very bad man and in League with the Devil who was an Author of All the Books I have given them. Very few of the Lower Mohawks could be brought to believe in this. . . . But the Upper Town was all in a Flame. . . . I gave notice to Commissioners of Indian Affairs . . . who . . . prevailed with . . . them. . . . They promised to lay aside all thoughts of It for the Future. . . .[131]

This affair produced much uneasiness, and was reputed to be work of French who had some emissaries endeavoring to corrupt the Indians away from the British allegiance.

Amidst all this confusion, Barclay exerted himself vigorously, and in October, 1745, was able to report baptisms of three Tuscarora Indians, one of the Oneida tribe, and the attendance of seven Mohawks at Communion in the past six months.[132] In his absence, he engaged "some of the better sort of Indians" to read prayers on Sundays. Their salary was paid out of a benefaction of £35 given to him for use in the Indian work.[133] About this same time, he was asked to accept the

[130]*Philip Bearcroft to Henry Barclay, [Charterhouse, London], June 14, 1743, in S. P. G. MSS. (L. C. Trans.), B. 10, No. 196. In addition, the Society recommended that Mr. Barclay receive his father's pension of £50 per annum for officiating to the Garrison at New York. The petition was granted. See S. P. G. MSS. (L. C. Trans.), B 13, p. 38.*

[131]*Henry Barclay to [Philip Bearcroft], Albany, March 12, 1744/45, in S. P. G. MSS. (L. C. Trans.), B 13, pp. 314-315. For a survey covering the whole period of the Iroquois alliance with the English, see John Wolfe Lydekker, The Faithful Mohawks, 1938, Macmillan; reviewed by Frank J. Klingberg, Mississippi Valley Historical Review, 25, No. 3, 398-399, December, 1938.*

[132]*Henry Barclay to Philip Bearcroft, Albany, October 21, 1745, in S. P. G. MSS. (L. C. Trans.), B 13, p. 317; Journal of S. P. G. (L. C. Trans.), X, November 15, 1745.*

[133]*Henry Barclay to Philip Bearcroft, New York, December 9, 1746, in S. P. G. MSS. (L. C. Trans.), B 14, p. 99. This £35 had been given several years previous and Mr. Barclay said he had forgotten "to mention the Benefaction."*

call of Trinity Church, New York, as Commissary Vesey had died.[134] At first he hesitated because of his interest in the Indians, but his efforts were thwarted and his safety endangered on account of the war (1740-1748). In fact, the flourishing county of Albany had become a near wilderness, deserted by its inhabitants and almost laid waste by the French Indians.[135] Governor Clinton felt that the removal of Mr. Barclay from Albany would be bad policy and so informed Secretary Philip Bearcroft,

> . . . considering Mr. Barclay's situation amongst the Indians, whose assistance might have been of use in the intended Expedition against Canada; Their uneasiness at Mr. Barclay's removal must evidently appear from a petition I have since had from the Indians, and which I have transmitted to the Ministry with proper remarks: that petition will show how ill grounded the excuse is, which some of his friends have trumped up for calling him from them, that he is in danger of his life amongst them, which is contrary to truth.[136]

Nevertheless, Barclay remained in New York, but promised faithfully to make the Mohawks his special concern and care, and offered to try to find a proper person as his successor.[137] He asked the Society to give a small sum to a German clergyman of his Church, a Mr. Oël, who lived in the Indian country between the Upper and Lower Mohawk Towns. Mr. Barclay explained, "This Gentleman administers the Sacraments to the Indians Some of whom, I also learn, continue to meet together every Lord's Day."[138]

During this decade, from 1740 to 1750, work with the Indians was also under way in other parts of New York, but these cells of activity were on a small scale. The Rev. Thomas Temple, school teacher at Hempstead, was teaching one Indian to read his Testament;[139] the fol-

---

[134]*Letter from Churchwardens and Vestry of Trinity Church, New York, December 5, 1746, in Journal of S. P. G. (L. C. Trans.), X, February 20, 1746/47; S. P. G. MSS. (L. C. Trans.), B 14, p. 93.*

[135]*Henry Barclay to [Secretary], [New York], November 2, 1746, in Journal of S. P. G. (L. C. Trans.), X, February 20, 1746/47. The Mohawks could not be prevailed upon to join the English but kept up a secret correspondence with the French Indians.*

[136]*George Clinton to Philip Bearcroft, New York, December 20, 1746, in S. P. G. MSS. (L. C. Trans.), B 14, p. 91.*

[137]*Henry Barclay to Philip Bearcroft, New York, July 18, 1747, in S. P. G. MSS. (L. C. Trans.), B 15, fol. 93.*

[138]*Henry Barclay to Philip Bearcroft, New York, April 16, 1748, in S. P. G. MSS. (L. C. Trans.), B 16, No. 46. Mr. Oël started from Germany as minister to the Palatines, was ordained in London by Bishop Robinson, thus alienating many of his people. After the Palatine settlement in New York dispersed, he bought a small plantation at Canajoharie, where he lived and administered Sacraments to the Indians.*

[139]*Thomas Temple to Philip Bearcroft, Hempstead, December 14, 1741, in S. P. G. MSS. (L. C. Trans.), B 10, No. 90.*

lowing year one Indian boy learned to count up to ten, almost painful evidence of the difficulties encountered;[140] the Rev. Isaac Browne of Brookhaven said that some Indians came often to his Church,[141] and, in September, 1743, he wrote, "I have Christened . . . an Indian Woman, after proper Instruction. She is a remarkable Instance of one reclaimed from a prophane. . . . Course, to a Life of Religion and Piety."[142] Thomas Colgan, of Jamaica, had a few Indians in his parish, as did the Rev. Thomas Standard of Westchester.

In 1748, Barclay designated Mr. John Ogilvie[143] as a proper person to go among the Mohawks.[144] After spending some weeks in New York with Mr. Barclay, learning the Indian language, he took up his duties in March, 1750.[145] Mr. Ogilvie was received warmly by the principal inhabitants at the time of his arrival. Many Indians were away from home, so he did not visit the Mohawks until Easter week, where he ". . . was kindly received by Col. Johnson, a gentleman of the greatest influence and interest in these parts.[146] Sir William Johnson's interest in Mr. Ogilvie is an early example of his coöperation with the Anglican missionaries. From 1749, until his death in July, 1774, Sir William, Government Superintendent of Indian Affairs in America, pressed steadily for the Christianization and civilization of the Indians. Consequently, the history of the Mohawk and Albany missions from the time of Mr. Ogilvie's appointment up to the very eve of American Independence is necessarily intertwined with the career of Sir William. A detailed account of his coöperation with the missionaries, John Ogilvie (1749-62), J. J. Oël, assistant from 1750-1777, Thomas Brown (1760-1766), Harry Munro (1768-1775), and John Stuart (1770-1778) has been given recently;[147] therefore, only a brief summary is given here.

[140]*Thomas Temple to Philip Bearcroft, Hempstead, May 17, 1742, in S. P. G. MSS. (L. C. Trans.), B 10, No. 91.*

[141]*Mr. Browne characterized the heathens as a "Miraculous compound of Paganism and Methodism." Isaac Browne to Philip Bearcroft, Brookhaven, March 25, 1743, in S. P. G. MSS. (L. C. Trans.), B 11, No. 138.*

[142]*Isaac Browne to Philip Bearcroft, Brookhaven, September 25, 1743, in S. P. G. MSS. (L. C. Trans.), B 11, No. 140.*

[143]*Mr. Ogilvie was a native of New York, educated at Yale, and in 1747 became lay-leader to Dr. Samuel Johnson, Rector of Stratford, Connecticut. In 1748, Mr. Ogilvie was ordained in London, in order to become a missionary for the S. P. G.*

[144]*Henry Barclay to [Secretary], New York, November 7, 1748, in Journal of S. P. G. (L. C. Trans.), XI, February 17, 1748/49; S. P. G. MSS. (L. C. Trans.), B 16, No. 71.*

[145]*John Ogilvie to [Secretary], Albany, July 27, 1750, in Journal of S. P. G. (L. C. Trans.), XI, January 18, 1750/51; S. P. G. MSS. (L. C. Trans.), B 18, Nos. 102-103.*

[146]*John Ogilvie to [Secretary], Albany, July 27, 1750, in S. P. G. MSS. (L. C. Trans.), B 18, Nos. 102-103.*

[147]*For a detailed account of the co-operation between Sir William Johnson and The Society, see Chapter III, p. 87.*

In June, 1750, Mr. Ogilvie again visited the Indians, and was met with congratulatory addresses from the principal Sachems; yet he found the Indians universally degenerated, and, since the war, entirely given up to drunkenness. The only hope was in the rising generation, and he asked the Society to send a schoolmaster,[148] preferably someone from Yale. In the meantime, he was instructing nearly twenty Indian children daily in reading and writing.

At the Upper Castle, the Indians were not so addicted to drink, which vice was decried by a pious Indian named Abraham. Abraham neglected his hunting in order to instruct his brothers in religion, and, while others were away he conducted Divine Service among the aged people and children. Many more such Indian teachers were needed, Mr. Ogilvie explained, to offset the wiles of the French priests to gain the Indian's affection.[149] To give a brief word of what was to follow after the mid century it may be said that the Society, in England, at this time intensified its interest in Indian education, as is shown by the Bishop of Carlisle's Sermon before the S. P. G. in 1752. He argued that the Indians were capable of instruction, and added, "Can we doubt then, but by proper Instruction, they are capable of making Improvements in every Branch of Knowledge; and that the Truth of the Christian Religion, when communicated to them, would be received by them?"[150] The Bishop agreed with all the foregoing missionaries to the Indians, that a worker among the natives should attain a competent knowledge of their language.

Many of the white men of New York, who could converse with the Indians, had a bad effect upon Indian morale. Mr. Ogilvie wrote to the Society,

> The generality of the professors of Christianity who have any considerable dealings with the Indians by their conduct give the most convincing proof that they regard them only as mere *Machines* to promote their secular interest; and not their fellow creatures, rational and immortal agents, equally dear to the Father of Spirits, capable of the same improvement in virtue, and the purchase of the same precious blood; in short, *the salt of the Earth hath* (in these parts) *lost its savour;* and not one thing that I can mention as a circumstance of encouragement in this momentous undertaking I have made use of

[148]*Mr. Ogilvie mentioned an Independent schoolmaster of New England, who for some time had been soliciting the Indians under his mission without his knowledge, and therefore would not consent to send to the teacher the Indians in his territory.*

[149]*Mr. Ogilvie mentioned the fact that while he was visiting the Upper Castle, the Indians received a belt of money from a Popish priest of Codroghque (Fort Frontenac), inviting them to embrace the true religion and expressed concern at their being heretics. The Mohawks refused compliance.*

[150]*Richard Osbaldeston (Bishop of Carlisle), Sermon preached before S. P. G. in St. Mary Le Bow, February 21, 1752, pp. 1-20. (Huntington Library.)*

everything that had the least probability of being serviceable to the main end. I've only been as it were, rowing against stream, and have not been able to stem the Torrent by reason of the extravagant quantities of rum that is daily sold to these poor creatures.

It is impossible for me to express . . . the shocking effects of strong drink upon these people. They commit the most barbarous actions. . . .[151]

In other words, the consensus of opinion was that the best chance for success lay in the education of the young. Mr. Ogilvie, on Sir William's advice,[152] recommended one Petrus Paulus as schoolmaster for the Indian children. Paulus was accordingly appointed by the Society with a salary of £7. 10 sterling per year.[153] This appointment was in line with the more aggressive instructions sent to America in 1756 while the fate of the continent hung in the balance. The part relating to the Indians admonished the missionaries,

That, as far as Circumstance render it practicable, you embrace every Opportunity of exerting your best Endeavours for the Conversion of the Indians to the Christian Faith, which good work is not only pious and Charitable in the more important Views of Religion, but highly beneficial likewise in a Civil View, as promoting the security and Interest of the American Colonies. An Advantage of which our Enemy's are by no means insensible or negligent; That for the more effectual Accomplishment of this good Work, You earnestly recommend an honest, human, and Friendly Treatment of these poor people. . . .[154]

In short, then, as in later generations, the native was to be not merely a Christian but a "Warlike Christian Man," ready to fight for the white man's security. Indeed, Paulus was so diligent and successful as a schoolmaster, teaching above 40 children daily, that the Rev. Mr. Ogilvie thought a similar project should be started with the Indians of the Lower Castle, a plan agreed to by the Society.

Mr. Ogilvie's reports of baptisms and sacraments administered to Indians kept a steady pace. In addition to his work as missionary, he was an army chaplain as well. In the latter capacity, in February, 1760, he wrote an exceptionally interesting and important letter con-

[151]*John Ogilvie to Philip Bearcroft, Albany, June 29, 1752, in S. P. G. MSS. (L. C. Trans.), B 20, No. 55.*
[152]*Sir William Johnson to [Secretary], New York, October 3, 1749, in S. P. G. MSS. (L. C. Trans.), B 17, No. 117.*
[153]*John Ogilvie to [Secretary], New York, July 19, 1753, in Journal of S. P. G. (L. C. Trans.), Dec. 21, 1753.*
[154]*Instructions for the missionaries in America formulated by the Special Committee, in Journal of S. P. G. (L. C. Trans.), XIII, March [11?], 1756.*

cerning the French and Indian War to the Society. He accompanied the Royal American Regiment on the expedition to Niagara. The Mohawks were all in this service and almost all of the Six Nations, numbering 940 fighters at the time of the siege.[155] He officiated constantly for the Mohawks and Oneidas, choosing exhortations suitable to the emergency. The Oneidas met him near their Castle, and brought ten children to be baptized. During the campaign, he had an opportunity of conversing with some representative member of every one of the Six Nation Confederacy, and in every nation he found a few who had been instructed by the priests of Canada and appeared zealous Roman Catholics. From good authority, Mr. Ogilvie was informed,

> . . . that there is not a Nation bordering upon the five great lakes, or the banks of the Ohio, the Mississippi, all the way to Louisiana, but are supplied with priests and schoolmasters, and have very decent places of worship. . . . How ought we to blush at our coldness, and shameful indifferences in the propagation of our most excellent religion? The Harvest truly is great but the labourers few. The Indians themselves are not wanting in making very pertinent reflections upon our inattention to these points!
> The possession of . . . Niagara . . . gives us a . . . opportunity of . . . cultivating a friendship with those numerous tribes . . . who inhabit the borders of *Lakes Erie, Huron, Michigan, and even Lake Superiour.*[156]

In May of the same year, 1760, Mr. Ogilvie lamented the fact that the leading men of the country did not countenance the conversion and education of the Indians with adequate zeal or application. He wrote they did nothing to oppose it, but he never ". . . met with any actual countenance in this service from any of them, excepting *Sir William Johnson,* who, I must do him justice to say, has been very much my patron and friend, which has been of no small consequence to me among the Indians."[157]

As a crusader against the French, Mr. Ogilvie reported in this same letter that he was preparing again· to march with the troops to Canada, and, as all the Mohawks were going, he would still be acting as their missionary. Proceeding to Oswego under General Amherst, Mr. Ogilvie tarried at Fort Hunter for three days, preached twice and baptized several white and Indian children, and at Oneida Town, on

[155]*John Ogilvie to [Philip Bearcroft], Albany, February 1, 1760,* in *S. P. G. MSS. (L. C. Trans.), B 2, No. 105.*
[156]*John Ogilvie to [Philip Bearcroft], Albany, February 1, 1760,* in *S. P. G. MSS. (L. C. Trans.), B 2, No. 105.*
[157]*John Ogilvie to [Secretary], Albany, May 20, 1760,* in *S. P. G. MSS. (L. C. Trans.), B 2, No. 106.*

July 18th, he also officiated and baptized six adult Indians,[158] fourteen children, and married nine couples.

In the absence of Mr. Ogilvie, the Rev. Thomas Brown was sent to Albany and the Mohawk Castle.[159] The Rev. Mr. Oël, assistant to Mr. Ogilvie, continued his labors, although he had reached the age of 72. He wrote to the Society, in November, 1761, that a school had been erected in the Upper Fort for the instruction of all who desired it; this gave the Indians an opportunity of being taught in their own language by one of their kinsman, who took great pleasure in teaching thirty youths reading and writing. However, as the teacher was receiving no compensation, Mr. Oël felt that this good work would have to be discontinued.[160] Mr. Brown, although he began to officiate in 1760, was not appointed missionary until Mr. Ogilvie had been given the position of chaplain to one battalion and made deputy to several others,[161] and consequently was unable to attend to his congregation at Albany, or to serve the Mohawk Indians. The Rev. Mr. Brown's first reception was favorable, but soon his congregation was in dissension, ". . . arising from the deep laid schemes of the Presbyterian minister and others to destroy the good harmony. . . ."[162] Therefore Mr. Brown felt it best to resign, because, he said, "I must acknowledge that I think my residence in this place will by no means answer the Society's good intentions."[163] The year of Mr. Brown's resignation, 1767, Sir William Johnson was made a member of the Society, and he was asked by its members to suggest schemes of Indian conversion. Sir William replied suggesting a mission to the Lower Mohawk Castle, urging that the missionary reside constantly among the Indians, and not have the care of the Albany congregation, as formerly. In December, 1767, the S. P. G. granted £150 for the establishment of a school for Indian

[158]*These were three men and three women, whom he afterwards married. They had lived together many years as man and wife according to the Indian custom.*

[159]*Thomas Brown to Philip Bearcroft, New York, November 15, 1761, in S. P. G. MSS. (L. C. Trans.), B 3, No. 103. Rev. Mr. Brown asked for a small gratuity for his services. The S. P. G. allowed Mr. Barclay to draw for him.*

[160]*The Indian, in addition to teaching, had to engage in another occupation to support his family. See two letters written in Latin from Mr. Oël to the Society, one dated November 1, 1761, in Journal of S. P. G. (L. C. Trans.), XV, March 19, 1762, and the other July 1, 1762, in ibid., December 17, 1762.*

[161]*Petition from congregation of St. Peter's Church, Albany, New York, May 5, 1764, in S. P. G. MSS. (L. C. Trans.), B 3, No. 110.*

[162]*Thomas Brown to Daniel Burton, Albany, July 2, 1766, in S. P. G. MSS. (L. C. Trans.), B 3, No. 114, see also S. P. G. MSS. (L. C. Trans.), B 3, No. 113. The Controversy started when Mr. Ogilvie, returning to Albany, refused to give Mr. Brown the books belonging to the mission, because the latter did not have his papers under the seal of the S. P. G. Therefore many people believed that the Society disapproved of him.*

[163]*Thomas Brown to Daniel Burton, Albany, New York, March 24, 1767, in S. P. G. MSS. (L. C. Trans.), B 3, No. 115.*

boys on the Mohawk river. This was to be under the supervision of Sir William Johnson.

In 1767, the vacancy in the Albany mission was filled by the Rev. Harry Munro of Philipsburg.[164] Mr. Munro wrote the following favorable account of his work in January 1770,

> Baptized during the last half year, sixty eight . . . one Indian adult. . . . In September last I preached at Sir William Johnson's; baptized six, and married one couple. I am now again just returned from visiting Sir William and the Indians at Fort Hunter, where I preached last Sunday, and administered the Sacrament; and am now preparing for another journey to Conojoharee, the Upper Castle, being seventy miles from Albany, there to preach and administer the Sacrament . . . at the request of some old Indians who are communicants, and could not attend at Lower Castle.
>
> Besides these journeys in October last, I made an excursion into the woods, to the eastward of Albany, and visited the new settlements of Langsingburg, St. Choack, Shaftsbury, Arlington, Cambden, White Creek, Saratoga, and Stillwater, being a journey of one hundred miles and upwards.[165]

In 1770, Rev. John Stuart, after endorsement by Sir William, was appointed to the Mohawk mission at Fort Hunter. Sir William helped him in every way, had the chapel floor renewed, and provided Mr. Stuart with a new pulpit, reading desk, communion table, windows and a bell.[166]

Sir William did not confine his interest to the work of the Albany mission, but he collaborated with the Rev. Charles Inglis, then assistant in Trinity Church, in working out a scheme for Indian conversion, which did not gain the support of the home government because of more pressing problems.[167] He encouraged the growth of Johnstown close by his own residence of Johnson Hall. A school and church were built

[164]*Churchwardens and Vestry of St. Peter's Parish to John Ogilvie, Albany, February 22, 1768, in S. P. G. MSS (L. C. Trans.). B 3, No. 119; another to Harry Munro, February 22, 1768, in S. P. G. MSS. (L. C. Trans.), B 3, No. 118; and one to Daniel Burton, July 11, 1768, in S. P. G. MSS. (L. C. Trans.), B 3, No. 120.*

[165]*Harry Munro to Daniel Burton, Albany, January 5, 1770, in S. P. G. MSS. (L. C. Trans.), B 3, No. 270. For interesting glimpses of the religious life on the frontier, and for the obstacles common to all colonial churches, see a recent study by Thomas Jefferson Wertenbaker, The Founding of American Civilization, pp. 89-92. (Scribner's, 1938.)*

[166]*S. P. G. MSS. (L. C. Trans.), B 2, No. 98. Stuart said that Johnson did everything to render his life agreeable, and his ministry useful.*

[167]*Charles Inglis was at this time, 1770, assistant to Dr. Samuel Auchmuty, rector of Trinity Church, New York, and later was consecrated the first colonial bishop. For the career of Rev. Mr. Inglis see John Wolfe Lydekker, Life and Letters of Charles Inglis, His Ministry in America and Consecration as First Colonial Bishop, from 1759-1789; New York; Macmillan, 1936. Reviewed by Frank J. Klingberg in American Historical Review, 42; 558-59, April, 1937.*

in the village and Johnson asked the Society for a clergyman to officiate;[168] at Canajoharie he erected the historic chapel for the Mohawks
and hired a teacher out of his own funds for the Indians. He engaged
in similar noteworthy projects, up to the time of his death on July 11,
1774, which event together with the reverberations of the Revolution
close the foregoing brief word of epilogue to the story of the first half
century of varied experiment.

Two centuries ago, the missionary sent these first hand, contemporary reports from Upper Castle, Lower Castle, Albany, and elsewhere to London. From these outposts in America during the first
half of the eighteenth century, the S. P. G. agents reached the Indian
on his own ground, when he was still possessed of his lands and of his
tribal organization. Such field reports as these illuminating letters yield
facts of social history before tribal life and customs had melted away
and before the Iroquois had been ground to pieces by the Anglo-French
and Anglo-American conflicts. The startling phrases, "the Mohawks
are all going along" (to Canada), and, "the Indians are abroad," or
are firing a shot to welcome the missionary after long absence, seize
the imagination and sweep the reader along on campaigns of military
conquest and on far flung journeys in quest of food. In one capacity,
the Indians accompany the troops as invisible advance scouts, independent of compass, or "communications," or a base of supplies, masters of the forests and of distances; while in the other view of their activities, these realistic reports show them as hungry and victims of
great hardships when the hunting was poor, and the weather severe.
Curious about the white man's God, courteous in their welcome to the
itinerant clergymen, they were, nevertheless, if drunken after contact
with traders, sullen, dangerous, and unwilling to listen to missionaries
and teachers.

Missionary opinion in comparing the Indian with the Negro, early
perceived, perhaps without realizing the full import of the matter, that
the latter in his industry, his willingness to work, and in his energy,
shared in the white man's enterprise and yet appreciably remained himself. His special racial philosophy and his imaginative gifts were to remain his own, while he adapted himself to the white man's world,
shared his objectives, aims, and valuations. Lord Hailey, in the recent
monumental survey of Africa, finds that the present African folk are
in mind and character not unlike other peoples, and clears away much
of unfounded legend myth and mistaken reports about the Negro race.[169]

[168]*Samuel Seabury, the Society's missionary at East and West Chester and
later the first American Episcopal bishop, was considered, but Seabury finally declined because of the insecurity of the mission after Johnson's death, and because
of an insufficient salary offered to him.*
[169]*Lord Hailey, An African Survey, Oxford University Press, 1938.*

The firm conviction of Mr. Neau and others that the white man's effort in running "up in the woods after miserable creatures [Indians]" was a lost cause, and that the black and white settlers should be the chief objective, and similar opinions from early Society missionaries elsewhere, show that it was clear to these pioneers from the beginning that the destiny of the Indian was as alien from that of the white man as that of the Negro was identified with it. The Indian herein pictured, as dwindling in numbers from no visible cause, suspicious, alien, fleeing into the woods, frightened by rumors of wars, was to the fact-hunting missionary, both noble and savage. The observations of these educated men contributed to the cult of natural happiness but also checked the growth of the wholly idealized primitive man of Rousseau and other eighteenth century critics of the ills of civilization. The question, then as now, was, did the American Indian, north of Mexico, while in touch with white races, have sufficient inner motive power and strength to maintain and develop an independent civilization? Early in the eighteenth century the negative answer was being formulated for the Anglo-Saxon world. The North American Indians, even the sturdy Iroquois, as is well known, were too few in number, too different in culture, to resist the on-rushing multiple attack of imperial agents, sharp traders, and land hungry settlers. The devoted missionaries reported but could not prevent the catastrophe. Strategically located for purposes of tribal destruction, the Iroquois benefited from the humanitarian mitigation of the missionaries, but with weight of the other forces against them, even though a viceroy of the strength of Sir William Johnson was on their side, the Indians' fate was sealed. Strong as "the cult of the noble savage" might be in Great Britain, it did not dominate the mood of frontier society. Nevertheless, what has been called the final and Attic tragedy of the North American Indian is here revealed in miniature by the S. P. G. missionary in the first half of the eighteenth century when the Red Man came into a many sided contact with the swarming visitors upon his continent.

In conclusion, attention may be called to what is obvious throughout this study, that the S. P. G. missionaries and teachers were keeping the home front in touch with the far flung frontiers and were inevitably strengthening British humanitarian sentiments in their early stages, a subject reserved for later detailed analysis.

CHAPTER III

SIR WILLIAM JOHNSON AND THE SOCIETY FOR THE PROPAGATION OF THE GOSPEL (1749-1774)

THE co-operation of Sir William Johnson, imperial viceroy to the Indians, as he might be called, and the Society for the Propagation of the Gospel,[1] during the quarter of a century from 1749 to 1774, forms a striking and significant chapter in the use of the mission as an agent of empire. The crusading strength of the Protestant missionary societies during the last two and one-half centuries has not been as fully assessed as that of the great Roman Catholic orders. The Protestant powers were about a century late in European expansion, and for still another century lacked the very effective assistance of the great present-day missionary organizations in meeting their problems with the natives, and in effect proceeded in colonization without the help or hindrance of large scale mission activity. The very fact that English expansion was so largely a joint stock company undertaking, rather than a royal enterprise, doubtless helped, with other factors, to delay missionary effort as a parallel development of penetration into new lands. It is, perhaps, pertinent to recall, in passing, that the English East India Company kept all British missionaries out of its part of India for 200 years, until the end of the eighteenth century, in striking contrast to the permission given the Jesuit, Saint Francis Xavier, to survey the whole Portuguese Asiatic Empire, as early as 1541.

Under the circumstances of the time, it was to be expected that in England missionary work would follow the precedent of business enterprise and would take the form of individual initiative or company organization. This fact is strikingly illustrated by the amazing achievements of Thomas Bray, who was largely responsible for the organization of three missionary bodies: The Society for the Promotion of Christian Knowledge, in 1699; the S. P. G., in 1701; and the Bray Associates in 1723, which together, in scope and longevity, are comparable to the Roman Catholic orders. The purpose of this particular study is to analyze the S. P. G. as a pioneer of empire in its relationship to Sir William Johnson, Superintendent of Indian Affairs in America. It was clear to Johnson that Protestant, and particularly Anglican, Christiani-

[1]*Hereafter referred to either as The S. P. G., or The Society.*

zation was necessary with the Six Nations, not merely as an end in itself, but also as a weapon against French Jesuit penetration from Canada on the one hand, and later against revolutionary religious dissent on the other, as represented, for example, by Wheelock from New England. It will be brought out later that Johnson at first favored Wheelock and New England Congregational and other non-Anglican work among the Indians, but eventually made up his mind that New England dissent represented revolution against British authority, and then he would have none of it. He therefore came to stand for King and Church, as the king's representative and administrator, and lay champion of the Anglican Church as an aggressive member of the S. P. G. The prodigious effort Johnson made to have the Indians Christianized and educated stamps him, even if partly self-interested, as an outstanding proponent of Anglicanism in the British imperial world. The story must be followed with patience because eighteenth century individualism in economics, government, and religious persuasion worked through trial and error, used argument and discussion rather than autocratic orders and imperial instructions. It is always necessary to remember that the new world in which Johnson worked had its large majority of Protestant dissenters, its self-governing assemblies, its pioneering frontier traditions, as well as long range pressure from the loosely knit imperial organizations. Besides, the England of Johnson's time, in point of view and tradition, was a country far removed from the Latin countries, France, Spain and Portugal. The British national government was to a great degree an oligarchy of big business and of great landlords who cloaked their management in the guise of self-government. Big companies in Lombard Street carried commerce to the seven seas. These business companies early learned to deal with Indians as tribes rather than as incorporated individuals of the state, in contrast with Spanish policy.[2]

Inevitably, the bitter wars with France intensified Johnson's interest in religion as an imperial force, and, as early as 1749, he was ready to use Protestant missionary assistance in holding his Indian allies loyally to the British cause. After the French were defeated, as has been intimated, his Anglican preference showed itself in the conflict with Wheelock and the New England contingent.

The minutiae of missionary work among the Six Nations for a quarter century will now be presented, and can be regarded as a "sampling" of the larger effort of the S. P. G. as missionary worker and empire builder. During a short initial experiment from 1704-1719,

    [2]For a penetrating analysis of Spanish missionary work, see Herbert E. Bolton, "The Mission as a Frontier Institution in the Spanish-American Colonies," The American Historical Review, Oct. 1917, pp. 42-61.

the Mohawks had been interested in the Anglican faith: (a) through the visits of the Iroquois chiefs to London, and their appearance before the Society where they received red leather bound Bibles; and (b) upon their return, through the erection of a chapel and the settlement of a missionary.[3]

Although the Society discontinued the Mohawk mission in 1719, sufficient progress had been made among the Mohawks to interest them in the Church of England and to tie them to the English rather than to the French interest.[4] Determined efforts to convert the aborigines were continued but success was necessarily slow.[5] At mid-century, stimulated by previous and threatened conflicts with France, and given the active aid of Johnson, the Society became more aggressive, and, in 1756, issued revised imperialistic instructions to all of its missionaries. Even in times of emergency, however, the Society was hampered by lack of funds and by the conviction of many of its members that its first duty was to supply ministers to the white men in the colonies.[6] Besides, many of the Anglican clergymen, hampered by family and other cares, lacked the adaptability and mobility of the French Jesuits in Canada.[7] In spite of all this, however, the Society met with not a little success.

Sir William urged and defended his interest in the spread of religion primarily on the practical grounds of good policy. In almost every letter he wrote to the Board of Trade, or to the Secretary of State, he argued that one decisive way to hold the Indians to the English side was to emulate the French method of stationing missionaries among them. Moreover, the Indians having had some contact with the Church of England missionaries in the early part of the century, felt their withdrawal keenly. Sir William, fully aware of this fact, worked to secure missionaries before the Indians might magnify their absence into a serious grievance. Finding that the S. P. G. could not act rapidly, he encouraged members of various Protestant dissenting sects in their work. This was his policy until 1766-1768, after which time he came,

[3]*Pascoe, C. F., Two Hundred Years of the S. P. G..* I, 65-71.
[4]*McIlwain, C. H. (ed.), Wraxall's Abridgement of the New York Indian Records, 1678-1751, 1915, pp. xliii-xliv. In this work it is pointed out that the Six Nations found it to their commercial advantage to be on the English side.*
[5]*From 1727 on, the Society charged the missionary at Albany to care for the Mohawks when possible, and occasionally appointed catechists to live among the Indians. Pascoe, Two Hundred Years of the S. P. G., I, 71-73. In this study, the earlier S. P. G. work has been severely summarized and the materials reserved for a later monograph.*
[6]*Osgood, H. L., American Colonies in the Eighteenth Century, II, 32.*
[7]*Greene, E. B., "The Anglican Outlook on the American Colonies in the Early Eighteenth Century" in American Historical Review, XX (1914-15), p. 72 says, "Perhaps the practical temper of the English missionary was repelled by the slightness of the results in proportion to the energy expended." In October, 1766, Sir William Johnson in writing to the Society, commented on the superior zeal of the Jesuits. S. P. G. Journal (L. C. Trans.), XVII, Jan 16, 1767.*

for political and other reasons, to regard dissenters with suspicion and to depend upon Anglicans.[8]

Johnson's religious zeal in promoting the spiritual welfare of the Indians is not easily analyzed and evaluated. He can hardly be dismissed as an eighteenth century gentleman who took his religion easily and casually, and consequently had no genuine interest in the spiritual welfare of his wards. The extensive correspondence he carried on with the Society and with its missionaries in America, not only on the subject of Indian conversion but also on other religious topics, involved much thought and labor for a man very busy with Indian affairs, land settlement, and political factions in New York. He was so active in religious matters that his word became law with the Society, and the Anglican missionaries outdid themselves in extolling him as a patron of religion.[9] Doubtless, as his letters show, he was both sincere in his plans for religious progress, and also, at the same time, shrewd enough to realize that evangelical work among the Six Nations would be of distinct political advantage. Stone, an earlier biographer, summed up the situation thus: "It is not contended that his zeal sprang from those higher and purer principles which actuate the true disciple of Christ, for a Christian in its strict evangelical sense, he was not; but that he earnestly desired a higher toned civilization for the red man, from motives of pure benevolence, cannot be doubted."[10] It is not surprising, then, to find him, from 1749 until his death, July 11, 1774, appearing in the records of the Society as a trusted religious adviser.

Turning now to a detailed account, it may be noted that, in September, 1749, Johnson wrote to Governor Clinton of New York for assistance in procuring a gratuity for Abraham, a sachem of Canajoharie,[11] who had read prayers to the Mohawk Indians for several years, and also a salary for his son, Petrus Paulus, as a schoolmaster for the Mohawk children. Johnson observed that these marks of attention would please Hendricks, Petrus Paulus' uncle, ". . . who we are all sensible, has been of the most material service during the late war,

---

[8]*Dictionary of American Biography*, X, 126. *The term dissenter is used throughout the paper for non-Anglican, despite the fact that the Anglican Church was not the official church in many of the colonies.*

[9]*See articles by Young, A. H., "Sir William Johnson, Bart." and "Rev. John Ogilvie" in Ontario Historical Society Papers and Records, XXVII, 575-582; XXII, 309 note.*

[10]*Stone, W. L. (Jr.), Johnson, II, 387. See also Dix, History of the Parish of Trinity Church in New York City, I, 234. A. H. Young, in his article on Johnson, objects to Stone's characterization. Ontario Historical Society Papers and Records, XXVII, 581.*

[11]*The Upper Mohawk Castle, near Fort Hunter. It is also spelled Canjoharie, Canajoharee, Canajohary, Conojahare.*

. . ."[12] Clinton[13] transmitted this letter to the Society with the explanation that Colonel Johnson had the management of all Indian affairs in New York, and added that the employment of Petrus Paulus would do much for the British interest.[14] In London, the Society after considering the request, wrote to the Rev. Henry Barclay, formerly the missionary at Albany, to inquire about Abraham's services to the Mohawks.[15] Barclay replied favorably, so that, on September 21, 1750, one year after the Johnson request, the Society agreed to give the Indian £5 for his past work and to appoint Petrus Paulus as schoolmaster.[16]

This affair is interesting, not only because it marks Johnson's introduction to the Society, but also because it shows how slowly, with division of authority and consultative procedure by sailing vessel as carrier, action could be taken. Johnson, on the scene, occupied every day with Indian matters, felt the necessity of more prompt action. Therefore, while for fifteen years, he worked with the Society formulating plans for the Indian instruction, he countenanced the dissenting missionaries, who were already on hand and eager to attempt to teach and convert the natives. New England dissent did not need to wait upon British ecclesiastical approval.

In 1751, Barclay and John Ogilvie[17] wrote to the Society of an attempt on the part of people in Boston to persuade the Mohawks to leave their homes and settle in the jurisdiction of that government, promising to educate the Indian children. The people of New York disliked the idea but Barclay observed that they did nothing to contribute to Indian education within their own borders.[18] In order to stimulate the Society's interest, he mentioned a legacy left by Sir Peter

[12]S. P. G. MSS. (L. C. Trans.), Series B, Vol. 17, No. 118, Sept. 29, 1749/50.
[13]Governor Clinton was a member of the Society. Ibid., B15, Fo. 94, July 25, 1747.
[14]Journal (L. C. Trans.), XI, Sept. 21, 1750; S. P. G. MSS. (L. C. Trans.), B17, No. 117, Oct. 3, 1749. It should be noted that Journal entries are dates on which letters were considered; received possibly several months previously.
[15]Henry Barclay was then rector of Trinity Church in New York. He was very active in Indian work during his incumbency at Albany and maintained that interest in the Mohawks all his life. Pascoe, Two Hundred Years of the S. P. G., I, 72-73; Ontario Hist. Soc. Papers and Records, XXII, 307 note.
[16]S. P. G. Journal (L. C. Trans.), XI Dec. 15, 1749, Sept. 21, 1750; S. P. G. MSS. (L. C. Trans.), B18, pp. 215-16; B19, p. 8., June 13, 1751—date of letter to Mr. Barclay. It later appeared that, at the time of this appointment, Petrus Paulus had been dead for some time. Ibid., B19, No. 65, No. 72; B20, pp. 34-35; S. P. G. Journal (L. C. Trans.), XII, July 19, 1751, March 20, 1752.
[17]Ogilvie was the missionary at Albany, 1749-1762.
[18]S. P. G. MSS. (L. C. Trans.), B19, No. 72; S. P. G. Journal (L. C. Trans.), XII, March 20, 1752.

Warren[19] for the education of the Mohawk children and hoped that fund would be under the Society's direction, and that the Mohawks would always be under its care.

As a result of this information, the Society, in April, 1752, discussed establishing a school for the Mohawk children. It agreed to write to Johnson and Ogilvie for suggestions and especially for information as to how much aid might be expected from the government of New York in the project.[20]   This matter, characteristically, proceeded with extreme slowness. The following year the Society wrote to Barclay asking him to advise with Johnson and Ogilvie and to prepare a plan jointly with them.[21]   In 1754, Ogilvie reported that he had not yet interviewed Johnson on the matter because of the latter's absence from home at this time.[22]   Johnson at this juncture was so engrossed with military matters that he appears to have had no time to consider the matter of Indian education.[23]   At least there is no evidence of a meeting with the missionaries or of a letter to the Society relative to the scheme.

In January, 1756, the members of the S. P. G. again considered whether any more effectual means could be found for the conversion of the pagans in America.[24]   As a result of these deliberations, the Society proposed a plan for educating a few Indian children in the college in New York and also promised £100 a year to the academy in Philadel-

[19]*Sir Peter Warren was Johnson's uncle and patron. His first contact with the Mohawks came about as a result of his uncle's interest in them. Stone (Jr.), Johnson, I, 57-65; Pound, Johnson of the Mohawks, 21-32. The Stockbridge, Mass., Indian School utilized £700 of the legacy. Johnson Papers, edited by J. Sullivan, I, 353-354.   The secretary of the S. P. G. wrote Barclay in 1753 that Sir Peter Warren's death was a great public loss and a particular one to the poor Mohawk children, for he was very zealous in their instruction. S. P. G. MSS. (L. C. Trans.), B20, pp. 34-35.*

[20]*S. P. G. Journal (L. C. Trans.), XII, April 17, 1752. See also Kemp, W. W., Support of Schools in Colonial New York by the S. P. G., 218.*

[21]*S. P. G. MSS. (L. C. Trans.), B20, pp. 34-35. See also Kemp, Supp. of Schools in Col. N. Y. by the S. P. G., 218.*

[22]*Journal (L. C. Trans.), XIII, Jan. 17, 1755. The hope of obtaining the aid of the New York Assembly in the project was equally disappointing. In 1754, Barclay wrote home that he had presented the Society's request concerning the Indians to the Lieutenant-Governor, who had promised to lay it before the Assembly, but nothing had yet been done because of the dispute over a permanent revenue which obstructed all other business. Barclay, however, said he would remind the Governor of his promise next spring. Ibid., XIII, Jan. 17, 1755; Ontario Hist. Soc. Papers and Records, XXII, 315.*

[23]*Ogilvie wrote to the Society on December 25, 1755, that Johnson was to hold a "treaty" with the Indians preparatory to the intended expeditions (to Lake George and Lake Champlain) and was likely to engage a large number of warriors in the British interest. S. P. G. Journal (L. C. Trans.), XIII, Nov. 19, 1756.*

[24]*S. P. G. Journal (L. C. Trans.), XIII, Jan. 16, 1756.*

phia, and asked the advice of Dr. Samuel Johnson and Dr. William Smith, the respective heads of these institutions.[25]

With the French and Indian War raging over the world, the Society, in 1756, as stated above, approved new imperialistic instructions for its missionaries in America. Article V urged the clergymen in the colonies to do all in their power to convert the Indians " . . . which good Work is not only pious and Charitable in the more important Views of Religion, but highly beneficial likewise in a Civil View, as promoting the security & Interest of the American Colonies: An Advantage of which our Enemy's are by no means insensible or negligent: . . ."[26] They were also charged with recommending ". . . an honest, humane, & Friendly Treatment of these poor people, our ignorant & pitiable fellow Creatures: . . ."[27]

Finally, in 1758, the Archbishop of Canterbury wrote a revealing letter to Dr. Samuel Johnson in New York in which he said, "I suspect that we ought to have more [missionaries] upon the frontiers; at least when it shall please God to bless us with a peace. For Missionaries there might counteract the artifices of the French Papists; and do considerable services, religious and political at once, amongst the neighboring Indians; both which points the Society hath been heavily charged, on occasion of the present war, with having neglected."[28]

So far, then, the Society's success had not been notable. The dissenters, however, showed great energy in Indian missionary work and frequently called upon Sir William[29] to assist them in making contacts with the natives. This he was ready to do, considering the work important ". . . as well in a Religious, as a Political Sense."[30]   With

[25]For a sketch of Dr. Johnson, see Ontario Hist. Soc. Papers and Records, XXII, 307 note, and for a brief notice of Dr. Smith, Pascoe, Two Hundred Years of the S. P. G., II, 852. Smith replied the same year and Johnson at the end of 1757. Dr. Smith wrote to Sir William Johnson for his advice in the matter. S. P. G. Journal (L. C. Trans.), XIII, Feb. 20, 1756, Jan. 21, 1757; XIV, April 21, 1758, May 19, 1758; Perry, W. S., Historical Collections Relative to American Colonial Church, II, 279-280, 562-64, 566. See also a sermon preached by Dr. Smith in May, 1760, on the Conversion of the Heathen Americans, before the trustees and scholars of the academy and convention of the Pennsylvania clergy. Printed in 1760 by W. Dunlop, Philadelphia.

[26]S. P. G. Journal (L. C. Trans.), XIII, March 11, 1756.

[27]Ibid., XIII, March 11, 1756.

[28]Documents Relative to the Colonial History of the State of N. Y., hereafter cited as N. Y. Col. Doc., VII, 347.

[29]Johnson was created a baronet in 1755.

[30]Johnson Papers, III, 586. In 1761 he introduced Samson Occum, an ordained Presbyterian Indian minister to the Oneida Indians. Ibid., III, 585-86; Proceedings of American Antiq. Soc., N. S. XVIII (1907), 37. Acts of Privy Council Colonial (Unbound papers), 342. In 1749 and 1751, Johnson had correspondence with the trustees of the Stockbridge, Mass., Indian School about obtaining Mohawk children for the place. Johnson Papers, I, 233-34, 353-54. In 1753 he entertained Gideon Hawley, a member of this dissenting school, during his journey among the Indians. Documentary History of New York, III, 630 (All references are to the Quarto edition).

Eleazar Wheelock, a leader in Indian work, who was in charge of the Moor Indian-Charity School at Lebanon, Connecticut,[31] Johnson had an extensive correspondence. The distinguishing feature of Wheelock's plan of educating the Indian boys lay in removing them from their homes to Lebanon for the period of instruction. To this end he asked Johnson's aid in securing Mohawk boys. Johnson was responsible for several attending, including the famous Joseph Brant.[32] Wheelock's first success, beginning in 1743, was with Samson Occom, a Mohegan, and this encouraged him to found the Lebanon, Connecticut, school. In 1765, Wheelock sent 10 "graduates" of this school as missionaries and schoolmasters to the Six Nations, who soon reported 127 Indians in attendance at their various schools. In the same year, Wheelock sent Nathaniel Whitaker and Occom to Great Britain where, aided by George Whitefield and others, they raised £12,000, money used later in the establishment of Dartmouth College.[33] Correspondence between the Indian Superintendent and the dissenting school lasted until about 1766-1768,[34] when Johnson began to distrust Wheelock's activities as having a political basis.

In fact, this distrust of dissenters may even have begun earlier on Johnson's part, or Wheelock may have feared the political disturbances of the day would cause Johnson to withdraw his support, for in 1765 he wrote, "And as your Excellency's Influence is great at Home, and, in these affairs, greater than any other Man's, May not I use the Freedom to ask for the Benefit of it toward the Support and Progress of this School? I think it will be a great Pity if Party Names, and circumstantial Differences, in Matters of Religion, should by any Means obstruct the Progress of this so great and important Design of Gospelizing the Heathen."[35] The success of the Wheelock school, initially aided by Johnson, now stimulated the Society to more ambitious plans.[36]

The Society, however, as is well known, was regarded by many of the colonists as merely another imperial institution.[37]. And besides, it

[31]For the origins and aims of the school see Wheelock's Narrative 1762 in Old South Leaflets, No. 22; J. D. McCallum, The Letters of Eleazar Wheelock's Indians, "introduction."
[32]Doc. Hist. of N. Y., IV, 197-98, 222-23; Johnson Papers, III, 832; Stone (Jr.), Johnson, I, 410; II, 173-74; Stone, W. L. (Sr.), Joseph Brant, I, 21.
[33]Article on Nathaniel Whitaker (1730-1795), Dictionary of American Biography, XX, pp. 81-82.
[34]For extent of this correspondence, see, for example, Doc. Hist. of N. Y., IV, 201-232 passim.
[35]Doc. Hist. of N. Y., IV, 223. A little later in the same year, further correspondence elicited from Johnson the remark that Wheelock could scarcely expect royal aid for his project as long as the S. P. G. had so small a fund that they could not maintain as many missionaries in the Indian field as they wished. Johnson Papers, IV, 812. See Ibid., VIII, 229-31, also Ibid., V, 342-43 concerning the establishment of southern schools.
[36]McCallum, Letters of Wheelock's Indians, 20ff.
[37]A. L. Cross, The Anglican Episcopate, passim.

was charged with the double task of civilizing and protecting the Red Man and ameliorating the lot of the Black Man. A large white population, doubling every twenty years, through "manifest destiny" was determined to possess the lands of the Indian and the unrestricted labor of the Negro.

To return to the contemporary details of the S. P. G. experiment, by 1766, therefore, the Society decided to copy the Wheelock plan. On July 31, 1766, Thomas Secker, the Archbishop of Canterbury, wrote to Dr. Samuel Johnson in New York that requests had been made to him and other bishops for approval of and for contributions to Wheelock's Indian School. He had replied that it was intended to set up a similar school, and he hoped that dissenters would support Wheelock's project and churchmen theirs. He had thought, at first, that the Society might support some Indian boys at Wheelock's School, who should later take Episcopal orders and work among their people, but, on reflection, it seemed necessary to set up their own school or be charged with the neglect of duty. He requested an early answer and speedy action.[38]

This letter from the Archbishop, indicating the Society's plans, was really the result of a visit paid by Thomas Barton, missionary in Lancaster, Pennsylvania,[39] to Sir William Johnson, in September, 1765. There he talked to Sir William about the Indians and their need of religious instruction. He wrote an account of this visit to the Secretary of the Society, detailing and endorsing Wheelock's methods of civilization and Christianization.[40] He praised Johnson as a worthy member of the Church of England, and as a man "universally esteemed for his goodness of heart, . . ." Dr. Smith of Philadelphia and Dr. Auchmuty of New York[41] now proposed Johnson for membership in the Society, and on May 26, 1766, the Secretary informed him of his admission to the Society. The Secretary reviewed briefly the Society's efforts for Indian conversion and asked Johnson to suggest ". . . some Scheme of a more extensive Nature."[42] He mentioned Wheelock's

[38]Beardsley, E. E., Life and Correspondence of Samuel Johnson, D. D., 303-04, 308-310; Schneider, H. & C., Samuel Johnson, III, 287-88. See S. P. G. MSS. (L. C. Trans.), B2, No. 19, for a letter from Samuel Auchmuty telling of the Society's intention of setting up an Indian school.

[39]For a sketch of Thomas Barton, see Doc. Hist. of N. Y., IV, 229.

[40]Dr. Samuel Johnson wrote to Archbishop Secker that Wheelock had fallen upon the right method of converting the heathen, by civilizing their children and teaching them sedentary pursuits, while at the same time he taught them Christianity. Beardsley, Life and Corres. of Sam'l Johnson, 308-09; Schneider, Samuel Johnson, I, 380-81. See also Johnson Papers, V, 406-07.

[41]Perry, Hist. Coll. Rel. to Amer. Col. Ch., II, 403-04. Auchmuty urged the Society to ask Johnson to propose a plan for the establishment of missionaries among the Indians in his vicinity. S. P. G. Journal (L. C. Trans.), XVII, Sept. 19, 1766.

[42]Johnson Papers, V, 221.

project thus, "M^r. Wheelock's design is a noble One, which we rejoyce
much in; but this is in a way particular to his own persuasion which
tho' we commend highly yet we cannot support in our Contributions,
our Benefactions being appropriated to the service of the Church of
England."[43]

In October, 1766, Johnson replied to the Society expressing his
pleasure at his admission into the "Venerable Body." He acknowledged that his long residence among the Indians and his special knowledge of them would make his suggestions of value.[44] He now condemned Wheelock's Indian educational enterprise in the following
terms: "M^r. Wheelock's plan seems a laudable one but give me leave
to remark that many of these Schemes which had their birth in New
England have soon appeared calculated with a View to forming Settlements so obnoxious to the Ind^s who have repeatedly declared their
aversion to those who acted on such interested principles; . . ."[45] Johnson also stated that those Indians ". . . brought up under the Care of
Dissenting Ministers became a Gloomy race & lose their Abilities for
hunting . . ."[46]

Sir William carefully outlined his own plan, suggesting a mission
at the lower Mohawk Castle, which would draw the Oneidas and others.
He added that, if the late Dr. Barclay's house and farm[47] were bought,
the missionary's salary might be somewhat lessened. He urged especially
that the missionary should reside constantly among the Indians,[48] and

[43]*Ibid., On the same date the Secretary wrote Wheelock to consult with Sir
William about a plan for the Society to adopt. Ibid., V, 222-23, On Oct. 31,
1766, Barton wrote to Johnson for his advice on the plan. Ibid., V, 401-04. From
time to time the S. P. G. Journal listed benefactions received. Often these were
specifically for work among the Indians. For examples see, S. P. G. Journal
(L. C. Trans.), VIII, Jan. 16, 1740/41; IX, Oct. 21, 1743; X, Nov. 8, 1745; XIV,
March 21, 1760; XVI, March 15, 1765.*

[44]*Dr. Samuel Johnson wrote to Johnson in 1767 that Sir William's perfect
knowledge of the Indians, solicitude for their conversation, etc. made him the
best judge of a method for erecting Indian schools. Johnson Papers, V, 471.*

[45]*Johnson Papers, V, 389; S. P. G. MSS. (L. C. Trans.), B2, No. 86; S. P.
G. Journal (L. C. Trans.), XVII, Jan. 16, 1767.*

[46]*Johnson Papers, V, 389; S. P. G. MSS. (L. C. Trans.), B2, No. 86; S. P.
G. Journal (L. C. Trans.), XVII, Jan. 16, 1767.*

[47]*Dr. Henry Barclay, had, when a missionary at Albany, been granted a
tract of land by the Indians in recognition of his services to them.. He had improved the property somewhat, and, although the land title remained obscure,
Johnson favored the purchase of this property by the Society for the support of
a resident missionary. Barclay, before his death in 1764, agreed to sell his interest for £500 currency. In May, 1768, the S. P. G. agreed to purchase the estate, one corner of which was to be allotted to the use of a schoolmaster among
the Indians. For the extensive correspondence on this matter see, S. P. G.
Journal (L. C. Trans.), XVII, March 18, 1768, May 20, 1768, July 15, 1768;
XVIII, Jan. 20, 1769; S. P. G. MSS. (L. C. Trans.), B2, No. 31, No. 88; Johnson Papers, III, 366, 589ff., 610; IV, 16-18, 47-48; V, 847; VI, 414-16, 746-47.*

[48]*As long as the Indian mission was connected with Albany, the natives could
not often receive attention from the missionary. See Doc. Hist. of N. Y., IV,
196, 257-58, for excuses sent to Johnson by the missionaries at Albany for not
attending to the Indians.*

that he would need to lead an exemplary life. He stressed the importance of converting the Senecas[49] and suggested a mission at Oneida or Onondaga for them where there should be a missionary assisted by a catechist and some qualified Mohawk boys who could act as ushers. He offered, if the King would permit, to ". . . use my Interest with the Indians to obtain a Grant of Lands at a reasonable price for the use of such an Establishment which will in time produce a Revenue sufficient to defray the Expences of so pious an undertaking."[50]

The Society's missionaries and the clergy of New York and Pennsylvania were enthusiastic about Sir William's interest in the problem.[51] In correspondence with his friend, Dr. Auchmuty, of Trinity Church in New York, Johnson further expounded certain parts of his plan. Auchmuty believed that Indian boys destined for the ministry would be more successfully educated away from their home environment, which was the plan adopted by Wheelock.[52] Johnson maintained that the only way to prosecute an extensive plan among the Indians lay in educating them in their own country because of their reluctance to go far from home. His aim was to erect a school where the greatest number might be conveniently reached.[53] By this time, then, Johnson had ceased to have sympathy either with Wheelock's theory or practice.[54]

While waiting for a reply from the Society concerning his plan,[55] Johnson scouted around for proper missionaries for the Indians. Auchmuty wrote that "Great care then must be taken that those [mission-

[49]*The Senecas had 1000 warriors and were usually a source of trouble.*

[50]*Johnson Papers, V. 390; S. P. G. MSS. (L. C. Trans.), B2, No. 86. This plan was sent Oct. 8, 1766 before Barton had consulted with Johnson about the scheme. See Barton's letter of Oct. 31, 1766, Johnson Papers, V, 401-04. In November, Barton informed the S. P. G. that he had written Johnson and expected an early reply. In the meantime he offered his own ideas on Indian education. S. P. G. MSS. (L. C. Trans.), B 21, No. 17.*

[51]*Johnson sent a brief sketch of his plan to Dr. Auchmuty. Johnson Papers, V, 392-93. Auchmuty hoped that as a result of Johnson's activity, the Indians would soon be supplied with ". . . Spiritual Fathers, which both Christianity, and sound policy absolutely require." Ibid., 410. For the address of the convention of the clergy to Sir William, see Ibid., 433, and for Sir William and Dr. Samuel Johnson on the plan see Ibid., V. 438-41; Schneider, Samuel Johnson, 1, 392-93.*

[52]*Johnson Papers, V, 410. Auchmuty feared that Johnson's plan would be too expensive for the Society. He suggested that the S. P. G. petition the government for aid, "Good policy, . . . ought to induce the Government to send a number of clergymen among them [the Indians] . . . ." S. P. G. MSS. (L. C. Trans.), B2, No. 21.*

[53]*Johnson Papers, V, 426-29, 438-41.*

[54]*As early as 1762, Rev. Jacob Oel, a German minister, who acted as one of the Society's catechists to the Mohawks, 1750-1777, was uneasy about the New England plan of taking Indian boys out of their vicinity for instruction. He wrote to Sir William that he feared their designs on the English Church. Doc. Hist. of N. Y., IV, 198-99.*

[55]*Barton wrote in April, 1767, that it was expected that the Society would fix upon the plan suggested by Johnson. Johnson Papers, V, 533. Auchmuty expressed the same idea. Ibid., V, 464.*

aries] the Society send should be Men of exemplary behavior and un-blemished Characters: but how to obtain such men is, & will be a great difficulty."[56] He added a list of reasons why such clergymen would not wish to ". . . set down in American wiles [wilds]. . . ."[57] Dr. Samuel Johnson expressed the same fear and had no suggestion other than, ". . . but I hope providence will provide. . . ."[58]

During this same time, Dr. William Smith, in Philadelphia, was engaged in drawing up a plan, providing for the Christianization of the southern Indians as well, which he sent to Sir William for ap-proval.[59] This particular interchange of letters is important for the light it sheds upon Johnson's views of the Indian response to civilization and Christianity, although the plan itself never matured. On March 16, 1767, Smith sent Sir William the details of his plan. He empha-sized the belief that the work should not be allowed to fall into the hands of dissenters but the whole project of conversion should be car-ried on under the supervision of the British government. Moreover, he maintained that the civilizing process should precede religious in-struction and he presented a scheme for joint white and Indian settle-ment by which this aim would be furthered.[60] Within a month, Sir William sent a cordial reply. In the main, he agreed with Smith's ob-servations. As to dissenters in Indian work, he stated his position un-mistakably: "I am no Enemy to the Membrs of any Religious per-suasion who may from Laudable disinterested motives exert themselves in such a Cause, but I am well aware of the use, or rather Abuse, that some may make of such indulgences, and therefore and for other rea-sons founded on the principles of sound policy I could wish the Church of England exerted itself therein with a Vigour sufficient to render the attention of other Christians unnecessary."[61] As to Indian settlements for the purpose of teaching them agriculture and other civilized pur-suits, Johnson was skeptical. He observed that the Indians of North America had an unconquerable aversion to such occupations ". . . which are indeed inconsistent with their Ideas of Government and policy, . . ."[62] He thought that the Indians, in remaining hunters, would be useful in the Society for another century. Finally, he feared the proposed grants of land to further the settlements would arouse

[56]*Johnson Papers, V, 466.*
[57]*Ibid., V, 466. See also S. P. G. Journal (L. C. Trans.), XVII, Jan. 16, 1767.*
[58]*Johnson Papers, V, 471.*
[59]*Ibid., V, 467, 508.*
[60]*Johnson Papers, V, 510-14. Many of his ideas he seems to have derived from the system used by the Jesuits among the Indians of Paraguay.*
[61]*Ibid., V, 529. See also Ibid., V, 436; VI, 291-94, for similar views expressed at different times.*
[62]*Op. cit. V. 530.*

suspicions of the natives.[63]   He concluded by wishing that time and
health would permit him to visit New York and meet with Smith and
others to exchange views ". . . on a Subject of such Great & Gen¹.
Importance as well Civil as Religious."[64]

By the summer of 1767, the Society took official notice of Johnson's recommendations for the northern Indians and, through Dr.
Auchmuty, informed him of their approval.   They agreed to appoint
missionaries and catechists for the Indians as soon as proper persons
could be secured, and they offered a larger salary than was customary
to men undertaking this work.   Johnson advised £70 sterling per year
and a glebe.   The usual S. P. G. salary for missionaries was £40 sterling.[65]   In December, 1767, the Society also decided to give an allowance, £150 per year, for the establishment of one school for ten Indian
boys on the Mohawk river.   This school was to be under Sir William's
supervision and he was asked to procure a schoolmaster for it.[66]

Early the next year, the Secretary of the Society wrote to Sir William that the members hoped to see some part of the plan put into
effect immediately.   He reported, however, that Dr. Auchmuty, who
had interested himself in obtaining a missionary, had so far been un-
successful.[67]   He ended by assuring Johnson that "The Society are
ready to concur to the utmost extent of their abilities to carry on so
beneficial a design; tho' indeed their income is far too scanty . . . to
forward it in the manner they wish."[68]

[63]*Smith later expressed the hope that hunting could gradually be combined
with more settled pursuits. Johnson Papers, V, 568-70.   See also S. P. G. Journal
(L. C. Trans.), XVII, Aug. 21, 1767; Perry, Hist. Coll. Rel. to Amer. Col. Ch.,
II, 415.*

[64]*Johnson Papers, V, 532.   Smith, Barton, and Auchmuty were not blind to
the material aspect of their correspondence with the Indian Superintendent for each
requested him to assist in obtaining grants of land.   Ibid., V, 530-31; VII, 4-5;
Doc. Hist. of N. Y., IV, 252.*

[65]*Johnson Papers, V, 553-54, 622-23; S. P. G. Journal (L. C. Trans.), XVII,
Jan. 15, 1768; S. P. G. MSS. (L. C. Trans.), B2, No. 23; Johnson Papers VI, 292.*

[66]*The Society allowed the schoolmaster Colin McLeland, £25.   Johnson
Papers, V, 846-47; VII, 290-91; S. P. G. Journal (L. C. Trans.), XVIII, March
17, 1769; S. P. G. MSS. (L. C. Trans.) B2, No. 90.   Professor Kemp in his study
of the Support of Schools in Colonial New York by the S. P. G., 204-06, 225-28,
discusses the Society's schools for Indians in the Mohawk country.*

[67]*See S. P. G. Journal (L. C. Trans.), XVII, Jan. 15, 1768, for Auchmuty's
letter to the S. P. G. on the problem of missionaries.   This letter of the Society
to Johnson was probably an answer to one of Johnson's, of December, 1767, in
which he cited Indian complaints at the lack of a missionary, the importance of the
field, and the necessity for good missionaries.   S. P. G. MSS. (L. C. Trans.), B2,
No. 88.   For other letters of Johnson's on the question of procuring missionaries,
see Johnson Papers, V, 695-96, 755; VI, 11-13.*

[68]*Doc. Hist. of N. Y., 237.   Barton, in a letter to the S. P. G. October, 1768,
said he continued to correspond with Sir William on the subject of Indian schools.
S. P. G. Journal (L. C. Trans.), XVIII, Dec. 16, 1768; S. P. G. MSS. (L. C.
Trans.), B21, No. 18.   Almost a year later he wrote again saying that Johnson
was impatient to have his plan put into execution. S. P. G. MSS. (L. C. Trans.),
B21, No. 21.*

Meantime Wheelock had heard of the Society's intention to set up a mission and school among the Indians and wrote to Johnson about the matter. The former feared with reason that the Society's plans would mean the extinction of his own projects. Johnson replied, confirming the Society's aim to establish a clergyman in the Mohawk country. He would continue to support Wheelock when necessary from the conviction that Wheelock's work would be dictated by a disinterested zeal and prudence. He, moreover, assured the New Englander that the Society approved all efforts which were inspired by principles of charity and not made in an attempt to prejudice the Church of England.[69]

Wheelock's fears, seemingly, were not eased by Johnson's letters, and he, therefore, gave up the hope of Johnson's continued support. His activities became apparent when Sir William negotiated the treaty of Fort Stanwix with the Indians in November, 1768. At that time Johnson found, besides his usual difficulties in handling the Indians, that the New England missionaries, directed by Wheelock, were working in opposition to him, trying to persuade the Indians not to cede their lands.[70] Johnson wrote at length on this unfortunate experience both to the Society and to the government, because the situation gave him a favorable opportunity to point out the necessity of the Society and the home government working together for the conversion of the Indians to Anglicanism.

To Governor Thomas Penn on November 18, 1768, he explained that two missionaries, sent by Dr. Wheelock, delivered a memorial to him to reserve the Indian lands for religious purposes, and also busied themselves among the Oneidas to prevent them from granting the land asked for by Johnson.[71] To the Society he wrote, "The Arguments they made use of in private amongst the Ind[s]. their misrepresentations of our Religion, & the Extraordinary private Instructions of M[r]. Wheelock, of wch I am accidentally possessed would shew them in a

[69]Johnson Papers, V. 683-85. A short time later he wrote to Wheelock that the Society still intended to work among the Six Nations but the difficulty lay in finding proper missionaries for the work. Ibid., V, 779-80. Meantime in a letter to Auchmuty, Johnson mentioned the applications and solicitations to himself in favor of missionaries from New England and wished the English Church could then take advantage of the favorable opportunity to start work among the Indians. Ibid., V, 695-96.

[70]N. Y. Col. Docs., VIII, 122.

[71]Johnson Papers, VI, 472. An abstract of this letter is in the Proceed. of the Amer. Antiq. Soc., New Ser., XVIII, 391-92. For his accounts to Auchmuty, see Johnson Papers, VI, 464-65, 542-44. See Doc. Hist. of N. Y., IV, 249-50, for his letter to General Gage on the matter. Gage replied, "I always apprehended those Missionaries whom you mention, had Lucre more at Heart than Religion, ..." Johnson Papers, VI, 513. See also Ibid., VI, 590. For the activities of the missionaries and their memorial to Johnson, see Doc. Hist. of N. Y. IV, 244-48.

very odd Light, . . ."[72] He requested that this information be held in confidence, for, if the matter were made public, it would draw upon him much abuse from the dissenters, of which they were very free when their schemes were attacked.[73] In the same month, Auchmuty expressed his views in reply to Johnson's account of the Fort Stanwix affair. He was confident the Society would do everything recommended by Johnson for the benefit of the Indians, and that some worthy clergyman would be sent among them before their ". . . Religious principles are debauched by the stupid Bigots that Wheelock is continually turning too [sic] among them."[74] In the course of the same letter he referred to one of "Wheelocks Cubs" and said ". . . Surely such Wretches ought not to be suffered to go among the Indians."[75] He asked Sir William's permission to send an account of their work to the Society. ". . . They will then see the absolute Necessity of sending Missionaries &c, if they have not already, among the Indians . . ."[76]

So far Johnson's contacts with the Society and its clergy in America were chiefly in the field of general plans and methods for Indian conversion. He now gave his attention as well to many details of the project to convert the Six Nations to the Church of England, recommending the appointment of missionaries, catechists, and schoolmasters. He planned a church building at his new village of Johnstown, whose clergyman was to be supplied by the Society.

Johnson, for example, was interested in the work of Cornelius Bennet [or Bennett], who acted as one of the Society's catechists among the Mohawks from 1761-1766. Fifty years old when he decided to work among the Indians, and highly recommended to the Society,[77] Johnson encouraged him, received him in his home, and arranged a

---

[72]*Johnson Papers, VI, 530. See also S. P. G. Journal (L. C. Trans.), XVIII, April 20, 1770.*

[73]*Johnson Papers, VI, 530. Evidently Johnson had no wish to become embroiled in the political confusion of the time. A letter from Johnson to William Franklin, June 1769, indicates he was still disturbed by the activities of these dissenting missionaries, see Illinois Historical Collections, XVI, 546. In January, Joseph Chew, a friend of long standing, wrote to Johnson that he heard in the Connecticut General Assembly that Johnson had ordered all dissenters out of the Indian country and would allow none but the Church of England men to preach to them. Doc. Hist. of N. Y., IV, 253. This was probably a reverberation of the Fort Stanwix dispute.*

Although Wheelock wrote an elaborate eulogy of Johnson in May, 1768, Johnson Papers, VI, 237, the correspondence seems to have ceased after the Fort Stanwix treaty. For one obscure exception, see McCallum, Letters of Wheelock's Indians, "introduction" and pp. 20ff., on this rift.

[74]*Johnson Papers, VI, 455.*

[75]*Ibid., VI, 457.*

[76]*Ibid., VI, 457.*

[77]*S. P. G. Journal (L. C. Trans.), XV, Feb. 19, 1762; S. P. G. MSS. (L. C Trans.), B2, No. 79. He received a salary both from the S. P. G. and from the London Society for Propagating the Gospel in New England. Johnson Papers, IV, 442.*

meeting with the Indians there.[78] Bennet progressed slowly in his work and his sponsors hoped his efforts would soothe the "wild . . . tempers" of the natives and dispose them favorably to the British.[79] He left the Mohawks in 1765 because of a smallpox epidemic, intending to return, but died the next year.[80] Sir William, although ready to support him, did not believe that Bennet's work would solve the problem of instructing the Indians. He wrote to Barton in 1766 that ". . . M[r]. Bennett, . . . seems to be an honest, well meaning Man, but quite unequal to the Task, not knowing how to keep them in order, & so Timerous that he fled from the Smallpox. . . ."[81] He repeated that an ordained resident minister alone would impress the Indians and meet with any success.

Johnson also kept in close touch with Dr. John Ogilvie, who was the Society's missionary at Albany from 1749 to 1762, charged with the duty of ministering, when possible, to the Mohawks.[82] An exceptionally able man, with a clear understanding of the difficulties of Indian conversion, and a keen sense of the value of the English-Indian alliance, his services at Albany were interrupted unfortunately by the French and Indian War in which he served as chaplain, both to the Royal American Regiment and to the Mohawks.[83] He advocated the education of the Indian children as the best means of civilization.[84] On May 20, 1760, Dr. Ogilvie wrote home an analysis of his work. "I could wish that I could say, consistent with the truth, that the propagation of the gospel among the natives of this Continent, was attended to by the leading men of this country, with that zeal and application, the

[78]*Doc. Hist. of N. Y. IV, 199; S. P. G. MSS. (L. C. Trans.), B22, No. 72.*
[79]*S. P. G. Journal (L. C. Trans.), XVI, July 20, 1764, Jan. 25, 1765; S. P. G. MSS. (L. C. Trans.), B22, No. 12. See Kemp, Supp. of Schools in Col. N. Y. by S. P. G., 222-23, for the subjects taught by Bennet.*
[80]*S. P. G. MSS. (L. C. Trans.), B22, No. 71, No. 73; S. P. G. Journal (L. C. Trans.), XVI, Nov. 15, 1765; XVII, Sept. 19, 1766.*
[81]*Johnson Papers, V, 437.*
[82]*For a detailed sketch of Ogilvie's life and correspondence see Ontario Hist. Soc. Papers and Records, XXII, 296-337. See also Johnson Papers, II, 85 note. He was recommended to the Albany mission by Henry Barclay and others. See S. P. G. Journal (L. C. Trans.), XI, Feb. 17, 1748/49; S. P. G. MSS. (L. C. Trans.), B16, No. 71; B17, No. 115, No. 199.*
[83]*Writing to the S. P. G., on Feb. 1, 1760, about the expedition to Niagara, he mentioned the Mohawks and other Indians in the army and stated that he officiated to the Mohawks and Oneidas who regularly attended divine service, "I gave them exhortations suitable to the emergency, ..." S. P. G. MSS. (L. C. Trans.), B2, No. 105.*
[84]*For his views on Indian education and Christianization, see Ibid., B20, No. 55-56; S. P. G. Journal (L. C. Trans.), XII, Dec. 21, 1753; XIII, Nov. 19, 1756; XV, Nov. 21, 1760. For the work of Rev. Jacob Oel see Ibid., VII, Dec. 17, 1736; IX, Oct. 19, 1744; XI., May 20, 1748, July 20, 1750; XII. Nov. 15, 1751; XV, March 19, 1762, Dec. 17, 1762; S. P. G. MSS. (L. C. Trans.), B16, No. 46; B16, No. 243; B17, No. 114. See also Ont. Hist. Soc. Papers and records, XXII, 311 note. Ogilvie sent home some interesting reports as to the activities of dissenters and French priests among the Indians, S. P. G. Journal (L. C. Trans.), XI, Jan. 18, 1750/51; S. P. G. MSS. (L. C. Trans.), B18, Nos. 102-103; B19, No. 71.*

importance of the subject demands.   They do nothing to oppose it, but
I really can't say that I ever met with any actual Countenance in this
service from any of them, excepting *Sir William Johnson*, who, . . .
has been very much my patron and friend, which has been of no small
consequence to me among the Indians."[85]

The appointment of Rev. John Stuart to the Mohawk mission at
Fort Hunter in August, 1770,[86] was the culmination of the Society's
project of setting up a mission among the Indians.   He had been recommended by the leading clergymen of Pennsylvania to Johnson and endorsed by him.[87]   He arrived at his mission early in December, and,
in 1771, began work at once, with marked success.[88]   Both the Indians
and Sir William were pleased with him and the latter wrote to Barton
that " 'Mr. Stuart has been sometime at his Mission where he is much
esteemed not only by the Indians, but by the English and Dutch inhabitants. . . .' "[89]   He had, therefore, great hopes from his appointment.

Stuart, writing to the Society in June, 1771, reported the dis-
repair of the Mohawk chapel.[90]   Early in the next year he requested a
new Prayer Book and a new Bible, which the Society agreed to send
him.   He said that Sir William had had the chapel repaired with a new
floor and provided a new pulpit, reading desk, communion table, windows and a belfry as well as a bell for the latter, and said further that

[85]*S. P. G. MSS. (L. C. Trans.), B2, No. 106; S. P. G. Journal (L. C. Trans.),
XIV, Aug. 15, 1760.   In 1756 Johnson asked the Board of Trade to augment
Ogilvie's salary, in view of his efforts to promote religion among the Mohawks,
N. Y. Col. Docs., VII, 43,   See Ibid., IV, 195, for a letter from Ogilvie to John-
son on military affairs around Albany and S. P. G. Journal (L. C. Trans.), XIII,
Nov. 19, 1756, for marks of favor shown Ogilvie by Johnson.*

[86]*Re the Johnson contacts with Rev. Harry Munro, missionary at Albany,
1768-1775, and Rev. William Andrews, missionary at Schenectady, 1770-1773, see.
for Munro, S. P. G. MSS. (L. C. Trans.), B3, Jan. 3, 1767; B3, No. 269; S. P. G.
Journal (L. C. Trans.), XVIII, Nov. 18, 1768, May 19, 1769, Oct. 20, 1769;
Johnson Papers, VII, 265-66, and for Andrews, Ibid., VII, 239-40, 281-83, 300-01;
Doc. Hist. of N. Y., IV, 263, 264-65, 292-93, 295-96.   Neither of these men was
of the caliber of Ogilvie and Stuart.   Nevertheless, Johnson supported and encouraged them.*

[87]*S. P. G. MSS. (L. C. Trans.), B2, No. 91, No. 92; B21, No. 22, No. 226;
S. P. G. Journal (L. C. Trans.), XVIII, Aug. 17, 1770.   Johnson Papers, VII,
516-17, 517-19, 543, 840-41.*

[88]*S. P. G. MSS. (L. C. Trans.), B2, No. 203; S. P. G. Journal (L. C. Trans.),
XXI, Jan. 19, 1776.   After the Mohawks moved to Canada in 1777, Stuart fol-
lowed in 1780, settled in Montreal and continued to preach to them once a month
until transferred to Upper Canada.   S. P. G. MSS. (L. C. Trans.), B2, No. 205.
Young says that Molly Brant, Sir William's Indian "housekeeper" was a parish-
ioner of Stuart's at Fort Hunter and later in Upper Canada.   See Ont. Hist. Soc.
Papers and Records, XXVII, 577.   For memoir of Stuart, see Doc. Hist. of N. Y.,
IV, 313-22.*

[89]*S. P. G. MSS (L. C. Trans.), B21, No. 24.   See also Ibid., B2, No. 66, No.
196; Doc. Hist. of N. Y., IV, 277; Perry, Hist. Coll. Rel. to Amer. Col. Ch. II,
450, 454.*

[90]*S. P. G. MSS. (L. C. Trans.), B2, No. 197; see Stuart's notitia parochialis, Ibid., B3, No. 7.*

". . . gratitude obliges me to acquaint the Society, that Sir William does everything in his power to render my life agreeable, and my ministry useful, . . ."[91] Stuart had difficulties with the language, and although he set about at once to learn the Mohawk tongue, he was forced for some time to use an interpreter.[92] He informed the Society that the Indians wanted books in their own language. He, therefore, started to translate some tracts for them which he hoped to have ready for the press by the next summer. Johnson, he stated, had agreed to have them printed as soon as they were ready.[93] Sir William, however, died before this was accomplished.

During these years Johnson's growing personal importance in the community was reflected in his successive and increasingly stately residences, Fort Johnson, Mount Johnson, and Johnson Hall. The last of these was part of a semi-manorial estate upon which he settled families and encouraged the growth of the village of Johnstown, close by his own residence. As part of his interest in this project, he built a church and school[94] in the village, and, in 1767, applied to the Society for the appointment of a clergyman to officiate there to make his plan complete.[95] Sir William was very definite as to the type of clergyman he wanted for his village, ". . . a Man of an affable winning Disposition, of a Middle Age, Zealous in the Discharge of his Duty, & of an exemplary life, as distant from Gloominess as from Levity."[96] He added that, although he hoped the Society could pay the salary in consideration of his expense in erecting the buildings, rather than let the plan drop, he himself, if necessary, would pay £30 per year which, with other con-

[91]*Ibid.*, B2, No. 198; S. P. G. Journal (L. C. Trans.), XIX, April 10, 1772.
[92]*S. P. G. MSS.* (L. C. Trans.), B2, No. 199, No. 200; S. P. G. Journal (L. C. Trans.), XIX, Nov. 20, 1772; XX, May 20, 1774. In 1773, his interpreter weary of confinement and regular living, had left him. Ibid., April 16, 1773. See also Ibid., XX, Oct. 15, 1773.
[93]*Stuart's tracts included an abridged history of the Bible, a "large and plain explanation" of the church catechism and some chapters out of the Gospels concerning the birth, life and crucifixion of Christ, S. P. G. MSS. (L. C. Trans.), B2, No. 200. After Johnson's death, Stuart wrote to the Society about the disposal of the MSS. The Society took over the work of having Stuart's translations checked for accuracy and finding out how many copies Stuart wanted printed. S. P. G. Journal (L. C. Trans.), XX, Dec. 16, 1774.*
[94]*In a letter to Barton written in 1766, Johnson wrote ". . . my Stone Church is finished a pretty Snug Building . . . ." Johnson Papers, V, 436.*
[95]*S. P. G. Journal (L. C. Trans.), XVII, Feb. 20, 1767. He promised to contribute toward the clergyman's salary and to furnish him with a house and glebe. He pointed out that the many Indians visiting him and living near his estate would profit greatly by the presence of a minister there. Johnson wrote to Auchmuty in November, 1776, of his hope of having a missionary for Johnstown. Johnson Papers, V, 426-29.*
[96]*S. P. G. Journal (L. C. Trans.), XVII, Feb. 20, 1767. Barton approved highly of Johnson's description of what constituted a suitable clergyman. Johnson Papers, V, 845-46.*

tributions, would bring the income up to £60. The Society agreed to appoint a missionary such as Sir William described.[97]

Johnson experienced the same difficulty and delay in obtaining a minister for Johnstown as he had in securing an incumbent for the Mohawk mission, and, therefore, much of his detailed correspondence with the New York clergy on the difficulties of securing missionaries for work in the Indian country related to Johnstown as well as to Fort Hunter.[98] In the spring of 1769 he wrote, "It is [a] matter of much concern to me to find that After building a Church & Parsonage house & being at other great Expences to forward the Establishmt of a Missionary where he is so much Wanted, I should still be without one. . . ."[99] In 1771, he still complained he could find no one for the mission at Johnstown.[100]

Of all the attempts to secure a missionary for Johnstown,[101] the one to interest Samuel Seabury is the most interesting. Seabury[102] was the Society's missionary in East and West Chester, New York. After the American Revolution, as is well known, he became the first American Episcopal bishop, in 1784. He was considered by his colleagues as the outstanding missionary in the American colonies and it is a tribute to the position which Johnson held with the Society that efforts should have been made to move Seabury to the Johnstown mission. In November, 1767, Myles Cooper,[103] speaking for the clergy as a body, in recommending him to Sir William, described him as ". . . a Man of great good Sense, of a cheerful Disposition, and has a mod-

[97]S. P. G. Journal (L. C. Trans.), XVII, Feb. 20, 1767. It is to be assumed that, with the decision to make the appointment, the Society agreed to pay the salary, but the Journal omits this item. See also Johnson Papers, V, 413-15, 436, for other correspondence on this matter. For the application of one Thomas Bateman of Boston, Lincolnshire, England, for this position see Ibid., VI, 190-92, 329-31.

[98]Ibid., VI, 291-94. In December, 1768, he wrote to Dr. Auchmuty that Mohawk Castle, Johnstown, and Schenectady were still vacant and he saw no prospect of their being speedily filled. Ibid., VI, 544. Auchmuty replied that he continued his efforts to find missionaries and schoolmasters. On this subject he noted, "I have no late Advices from the Society of any Consequence. Their Secretary I fear eats too much roast Beef & pud'in." Ibid., VI, 685-86. See a letter from Auchmuty to Johnson, January, 1768, which shows the scope of his efforts to aid Johnson, Ibid., VI, 77-79.

[99]Johnson Papers, VI, 711, 745. The Rev. Mr. Oel, still acting as a catechist to the Mohawks in 1770, believed the Indians were losing their interest in religion but hoped things would have a better aspect when a minister should arrive for the church which Sir William had built. S. P. G. Journal (L. C. Trans.), XVIII Oct. 19, 1770.

[100]Doc. Hist. of N. Y., IV, 284.

[101]For correspondence relating to these efforts see S. P. G. Journal (L. C. Trans.), XVIII, March 16, 1770; Johnson Papers, VI, 517-18, 542-44, 544-46, 745; VII, 390-91, 516-17; Doc. Hist. of N. Y., IV, 375.

[102]For a sketch of Samuel Seabury, see Dictionary of American Biography, XVI, 528-30.

[103]Myles Cooper was President of King's College in New York and a member of the S. P. G., though not one of its missionaries. See Ont. Hist. Soc. Papers and Records, XXII, 333 note.

erate Family— . . . He is the most suitable person We know of to live at Johnstown, and it is our Opinion that he would give You great Satisfaction."[104] Johnson, upon such testimony, hoped to secure him, but Seabury, after some correspondence and reflection, seems to have felt that the position was uncertain in the event of Sir William's death. Although he had the Society's permission to make the change, this and the small salary made him hesitate.[105] Auchmuty informed Johnson, in June, 1769, that Seabury ". . . is chargreened at the Salary the Society propose, which he thinks is much to small. . . . I am trying all I can to prevail upon him to pay you a Visit; . . ."[106] Seabury shortly did so and was thus able to look over the location, but Johnson was away from home at the time and the two men failed to meet. Auchmuty urged the Society to increase the salary and Seabury himself suggested joining the Mohawk mission with Johnstown in order that he might have a suitable salary. To this last, Sir William objected and evidently the Society's financial condition at the time prevented an increase in the allowance for the missionary. Thus the matter came to nothing.[107]

Finally, in 1772, Johnson reported to the Society that he had secured Mr. Richard Mosley (or Mozley) for the mission at Johnstown and had considerably enlarged the church building.[108] Mosley served there until May, 1774, when ill health forced him to leave. The mission was not refilled at the time of Johnson's death a few months later. Mosley, upon leaving, wrote to the Society that "The only thing I re-

[104]*Johnson Papers, V, 781. For Johnson's inquiries about Seabury's decision and his desire to have an interview with the missionary, see Ibid., VI, 293-94, 544, 685.*
[105]*S. P. G. MSS. (L. C. Trans.), B2, No. 159; S. P. G. Journal (L. C. Trans.), XVII, May 20, 1768; XVIII, Jan. 20, 1769. See also Johnson Papers V, 800-01 for Auchmuty's letter, of November, 1767, to Johnson in regard to Seabury. The next year in a letter to the Society, Auchmuty said that Seabury then seemed adverse to go to Johnstown, and added that he did not know how Sir William would get supplied. S. P. G. Journal (L. C. Trans.), XVIII, Jan. 20, 1769. See also Ibid., XVII, March 18, 1768.*
[106]*Johnson Papers, VII, 4. See also Ibid., VI, 456. In 1768 Seabury had thought of making a visit to Johnson. S. P. G. MSS. (L. C. Trans.), B2, No. 31; Johnson Papers, VII, 25, 53, 169.*
[107]*S. P. G. Journal (L. C. Trans.), XVIII, Oct. 20, 1769, Dec. 15, 1769; Johnson Papers, VII, 212-13, 282; Doc. Hist. of N. Y., IV, 280-81. Mr. Murray, the S. P. G. missionary at Reading, Pa., had been recommended for the place by the Pennslyvania clergy in 1768 and described as ". . . not overburdened with Zeal but is a Gentleman of good Sense & sprightly Conversation—" Johnson Papers, VI, 521. Johnson did not consider him because he had already approved of Seabury and hoped to secure him.*
[108]*It was most unusual for the Society to permit a layman to choose a missionary in this fashion and merely report his action to the Society. See S. P. G. Journal (L. C. Trans.), XIX, Dec. 18, 1772. See also Doc. Hist. of N. Y., IV, 295-96, 299. The rebuilt church was 90 feet long, had a chancel and a steeple and Sir William added an organ which cost him £100 sterling. S. P. G. MSS. (L. C. Trans.), B2, No. 94. In a letter to Barton in 1771, Johnson remarked that his church, when completed, would hold 1000 people. Doc. Hist. of N. Y. IV. 274*

grett . . . is to go from so worthy and good a man as Sir William Johnson . . . "[109]

Johnson, both as the Indian Superintendent and as the chief man of the region, had a keen interest in encouraging the Mohawk Indians at Canajoharie as well as those at Fort Hunter to maintain their interest in the English Church. To this end, he erected a chapel for them there. At first he hoped to obtain money by means of subscriptions for this purpose from the Church of England people in the colonies, especially in New York and Pennsylvania.[110] When this plan failed, he took upon himself, in 1770, the cost of the erection of the building.[111] The church was completed in the summer of 1770. Johnson asked the Rev. Harry Munro, the Society's missionary at Albany, to preach there on June 17, the church ". . . being quite finished, & they [the Indians] all returned from Hunting."[112] Sir William wished for the Society's appointment of a schoolmaster and catechist to reside constantly among the Indians at Canajoharie. This the Society agreed to and Mr. Hall, recommended from Philadelphia, was appointed in 1770. He, however, never arrived at his post, much to Johnson's disappointment,[113] which, as he wrote two years later, made the church he had built there more or less useless.[114] The next year he sent a schoolmaster there at his own expense in order to keep the Indians well disposed.[115]

One of the interesting sidelights of Sir William's interest in the spiritual state of his Indian neighbors, even before his admission to the Society, was the preparation of a new edition of the Mohawk prayer book. In this work he was assisted by his son-in-law, Daniel Claus. He also corresponded with Ogilvie and Barclay in Albany and New

[109]*S. P. G. MSS. (L. C. Trans.)*, B23, No. 427; *S. P. G. Journal (L. C. Trans.)*, XX, June 17, 1774.

[110]*Johnson Papers*, VI, 563-64; VII, 516, 518.

[111]*Ibid.*, VII, 543; *S. P. G. MSS. (L. C. Trans.)*, B21, No. 24; *S. P. G. Journal (L. C. Trans.)*, XIX, Oct. 18, 1771. The building cost £459. He wrote that he had been promised the assistance of others in erecting the church . . . But the times did not admit of it, ..." *Doc. Hist. of N. Y.*, IV, 269.

[112]*Johnson Papers*, VII, 720. For an interesting account of the sermon Munro preached there, see *S. P. G. MSS. (L. C. Trans.)*, B3, Sept. 25, 1770; *S. P. G. Journal (L. C. Trans.)*, XIX, March 15, 1771; *Johnson Papers*, VII, 962-63 note. Stuart, who took the Mohawk mission in 1771, told of preaching there in the church built by Sir William. *S. P. G. MSS (L. C. Trans.)*, B2, No. 197.

[113]*S. P. G. MSS. (L. C. Trans.)*, B21, No. 24, No. 226; *S. P. G. Journal (L. C. Trans.)*, XVIII, Aug. 17, 1770; XIX, Oct. 18, 1771. *Johnson Papers*, VIII, 257-58, Stuart reported that the Indians at Canajoharie were very anxious for a minister of their own. A native reader officiated on Sunday, and the Indians, through Stuart, asked for an allowance for him. The Society agreed to grant him £5 per year if Sir William approved. *S. P. G. Journal (L. C. Trans.)*, XX, May 20, 1774, March 17, 1775; *S. P. G. MSS. (L. C. Trans.)*, B2, No. 198.

[114]*S. P. G. Journal (L. C. Trans.)*, XIX, Dec. 18, 1772; *Johnson Papers*, VIII, 928.

[115]*S. P. G. MSS. (L. C. Trans.)*, B2, No. 94. He asked the Society for some school books. The S. P. G. agreed to send a number and inquired of him what ones were most wanted. *S. P. G. Journal (L. C. Trans.)*, XX, Feb. 18, 1774; *Kemp, Supp. of Schools, in Col. N. Y. by S. P. G.*, 227 note.

York about the work.[116] Much of his interest is revealed in a letter
he wrote to Barclay in 1763 asking as to the progress of the volume,
observing that the prayer book was ". . . much wanted, & greatly
enquired after by the Indians."[117] He hoped the new edition would
make the already Christianized Indians think favorably of the Established Church, ". . . which will have a better effect upon them than
what I see arises from their inclination to the Presbyterian as all those
Ind[s]. who are Instructed by the Dissenting Ministers, . . . have im-
bibed an air of the most Enthusiastical cant, . . ."[118] In theory and in
practice, Johnson now emphatically wished the established faith of the
British government, represented by the Society for the Propagation
of the Gospel, to be the only one promulgated among the natives. As
late in his life as February, 1774, he wrote to the Rev. Henry Caner,[119]
of Boston, that he was trying to write a short history of the Bible which
would contain a brief ". . . historical deduction of facts & incidents
in a regular & well connected order, . . ."[120] which work he thought
would be useful to the Indians.

The story of his efforts to obtain the creation of an American episcopate is worthy of additional detailed study. However, Johnson's cooperation with the colonial clergy in this agitation can only be briefly
noted here as another aspect of his relations with the Society and his
concern with religion from the standpoint of good policy. Particularly,
after his admission to the Society, he became outspoken in favor of an
American bishop. He realized, along with many of the colonial Church
of England clergy, that the growth of the Church in the colonies was
hampered by its distance from the parent institution. Moreover, he
believed a bishop in America would insure a more vigorous attention
to Indian conversion. He, therefore, offered 20,000 acres of land to
be equalled by a similar grant to be obtained by the Society from the
crown for the support of the episcopate. This offer overwhelmed the

[116]*Johnson Papers, III, 355, 363, 630. The Doc. Hist. of N. Y., IV, passim,*
has many references to Johnson's interest in the matter, the preparation of the
book, its printing in 1769, etc. See N. Y. Col. Docs., VIII, 815-17, for a long
*"note" on the translation of the Prayer Book into the Mohawk language. This
work should not be confused with the tracts translated by Stuart at Fort Hunter
which Johnson agreed to have published.*
[117]*Johnson Papers, IV, 72.*
[118]*Herbert E. Bolton, "The Mission as a Frontier Institution in the Spanish
American Colonies," American Historical Review, XXIII, pp. 42-61, October, 1917.*
[119]*Rev. Henry Caner, called the "Father of the American Clergy," was the
Society's missionary in Fairfield, Conn., and later officiated at King's Chapel in
Boston. He was outstanding among the Society's missionaries in New England.
See Pascoe, Two Hundred Years of the S. P. G. II, 853.*
[120]*Proceed. of Amer. Antiq. Soc., New Ser., VIII (1907), 400-01. He also
thanked Caner for a copy of the church service in the Mohawk tongue which the
latter had sent to him. See also Johnson Papers, VIII, 1039-40.*

Society's missionaries with gratitude.[121]   The Society directly acknowledged his offer in 1769, reporting that the Archbishop of Canterbury had presented a memorial to Lord Hillsborough[122] for advice as to the presentation of a petition to the crown for the proposed grant of lands. At that time of writing, the Society had received no reply, but hoped Johnson would send a description of the lands to be applied for.[123] The next year the Secretary of the Society wrote to Johnson saying that the Society had not progressed one step in the affair.[124]   The project came to nothing because the government failed to support it. Having difficulty enough with its new policy of imperial control after 1763, the ministry feared to ignore the protests of all the dissenting groups which objected to the introduction of the episcopate as a further insidious evidence of control.   In brief, an episcopate would cost lands and money and, in return, make enemies of large colonial groups.[125]

Not only did Johnson carry on an extensive correspondence with the Anglican clergy, but he also, as mentioned above, urged his views upon the Board of Trade and the Secretary of State for the colonies until his death in 1774.   A synopsis of his suggestions, as a British governmental official, must now be given, covering in good part the same chronological period already surveyed.

Johnson, as a government official, presented Indian conversion as an integral part of British Indian policy at the Albany Convention of 1754.[126]   At that time he urged the building of a fort in the Indian country at Ononadaga, which should be well garrisoned and supplied with a missionary.[127]   Two years later, he wrote directly to the Board of Trade, suggesting that any garrison chaplains in the Indian country should act as missionaries among the Indians in addition to their other

[121]*Johnson Papers, V, 837-39; S. P. G. MSS (L. C. Trans.), B2, No. 27. No. 29; Schneider, Samuel Johnson, I, 399, 433, 435.*

[122]*Hillsborough was Secretary of State for the Colonies from 1768 to 1772.*

[123]*Johnson Papers, VI, 746-47. Sir William sent the description in December, 1769, asking that it be omitted in the Society's publications lest it raise a hue and cry from the enemies of the Church. Ibid., VII, 290, 292.*

[124]*Ibid., VIII, 693.*

[125]*Cross, Anglican Episcopate and American Colonies, 271 note; Adams, J. T., Revolutionary New England, 201-02. 286, 359-60. Auchmuty and Johnson exchanged letters, however, which indicated that they believed that all the blame for procrastination did not lie with the government but much with the heads of the S. P. G. Auchmuty wrote "I could wish that the Bishop had a little more zeal, & were not afraid of shadows, & the Society more resolution & application in affairs that immediately concern them." Johnson Papers, VII, 309. See also Ibid., VII, 583-85, 690-92, and Young "Sir William Johnson" in Ontario Hist. Soc. Papers and Records, XXVII, 580-81.*

[126]*In 1751, Cadwalder Colden wrote to Governor Clinton of New York concerning Johnson's work among the Indians. He recognized the advantage of having missionaries among the tribes and hoped the S. P. G. would contribute in this cause to its utmost ability. He also believed the missionaries should be subject to the Superintendent of Indian Affairs. N. Y. Col. Docs., VI, 744.*

[127]*Pennsylvania Archives, 2nd. Ser., VI, 214ff. For Indian concern about religion at this Congress, see Doc. Hist. of N. Y., II, 345, 346.*

duties,[128] and again, in 1759, he repeated this advice.[129]   In 1761, he informed Lieutenant-Governor Colden of New York that the Mohawks of Fort Hunter had all met at his house ". . . and made a verry long Haraunge on the want of a Minister, . . ."[130] The Indians, he declared, believed they were now being neglected because they no longer had land to give the English.   Moreover, two Indian boys, whom he had sent to school, could be of use in instructing the other Indians. These boys the Society should encourage.[131] The Board of Trade agreed to recommend that the Society appoint missionaries in each district, to live where the Indian Superintendent should direct.[132]

In September, 1767, Johnson drew up a comprehensive review of trade and Indian affairs in the northern district, dealing with all aspects of the Indian problem, which he sent to Lord Shelburne.[133]   In this report he explained the necessity of placing missionaries and assistants with the Indians, especially with the Six Nations as the "door" to the rest, to hold them to the British interest.   These missionaries should be Church of England clergy to keep the Indians away both from the French Catholic priests and the dissenting teachers.   The latter he criticised as ". . . well meaning but gloomy people amongst us, . . ."[134] and maintained it to be unsound policy to introduce the natives to dissensions existing in the Protestant religion.   Finally, he asked that the crown support the recently formulated plan of the Society to set up missions and schools in the Mohawk country.[135].   In December, following up this report, Johnson again wrote at length to

[128]Doc. Hist. of N. Y., II, 415; N. Y. Col. Docs., VII, 42-43. In the same year, Governor Shirley of Massachusetts, at this time in close touch with Johnson, sent a sketch of a system for managing Indian affairs to the Board of Trade. He, too, urged the sending of Protestant missionaries among the Indians. Lincoln, C. H., Shirley Correpondence, II, 374; Johnson Papers, II, 410-11. See the address of the Mohawks of Canajoharie, made in 1756, asking the king to provide them with a church and minister. Doc. Hist. of N. Y., IV, 194-95.
[129]N. Y. Col. Docs., VII, 377; Doc. Hist. of N. Y., II, 455.
[130]Johnson Papers, III, 365-66.
[131]N. Y. Col. Docs., VII, 578-80.
[132]Ibid., VII, 637. The Board had been giving some attention to Indians at this time as a result of a royal command of 1763 to draw up a plan for the regulation of Indian affairs. Ibid., VII, 567. In October, 1764, Johnson sent over some "Sentiments and Remarks" on the future management of Indian affairs. He urged the appointment of good missionaries as "highly requisite." Ibid., VII, 662.
[133]Lord Shelburne from 1766 to 1768, was Secretary of State for the Southern Department, which then passed on colonial affairs, For Shelburne's interest in Indian affairs, see Alvord, C. W., The Mississippi Valley in British Politics, I, 287-88.
[134]N. Y. Col. Docs. VII, 970.
[135]Ibid. The Board of Trade Journal, December 21, 1767, noted the receipt of this report, probably transmitted to the Board by Shelburne. Illinois Historical Collections, XVI, 151.

Shelburne, urging the establishment of missionaries, for the Indians were ". . . greatly disgusted at our neglects. . . ."[136]

The hope of securing royal financial aid for the work of the Society became faint when Lord Hillsborough informed Sir William, in October, 1768, of the necessity for strict economy in all matters of government. Johnson, replying from Fort Stanwix, pointed out that economy in the Indian department lowered the Indian respect for the English, and that to neglect to send English missionaries among them on the score of retrenchment simply gave the French and Spanish added arguments in their attempts to alienate the Six Nations from adherence to the English.[137].

In 1770, Sir William faithfully reported to the home authorities a resumé of the Fort Stanwix proceedings, just as he had sent an account to the Society. In this letter he again explained the Indian attitude on the religious question. The Indians had discussed the lack of missionaries several times during the negotiations and were so incensed at this particular evidence of neglect that he encouraged them to hope soon for redress in order to end their complaints. "The Majority of Indians," he explained, " 'tis true, do not as yet request it [religious instruction], but even *they,* consider our neglecting to gratify those that are so disposed, as a further instance of our indifference and disregard."[138] He repeated that the Society, from the scarcity of clergymen or some other cause, could not procure missionaries for the salaries to which they were forced to limit themselves. However, the Iroquois Indians found that the Canadian natives, who had been enemies a short time before, were regularly supplied with religious teachers. Johnson, therefore, recommended that the crown grant some allowance for the Mohawk mission and added that, if some further provision could be made to employ others in the same work, it would materially increase the Indian ". . . reverence for the Crown, and their attachment to the British Interest."[139]. Under the circumstances, it is not

---

[136]*N. Y. Col. Docs., VII, 1002. In this same year, Johnson sent a letter to the Society in which he referred to the critical period in Indian relations and urged that the Society no longer neglect this field. Johnson Papers, VI, 26-30. Early the next year, 1768, Johnson, in a letter to Barton, said he hoped that religious instruction among the Six Nations would encourage the western tribes to embrace Christianity. Ibid., VI, 67-68.*

[137]*Doc. Hist. of N. Y., II, 520; N. Y. Col. Docs., VIII, 105.*

[138]*N. Y. Col. Docs., VIII, 226. For Johnson's proceedings with the Indians at this time, see Ibid., VIII, 237. See also Johnson Papers, VII, 875-79.*

[139]*N. Y. Col. Docs., VIII, 226. This same letter appears in Doc. Hist. of N. Y. II, 563-66. Hillsborough replied that he had laid the dispatch before the King, but he made no mention of the special request with regard to religion. Ibid. VIII, 253-54. See also a letter to the Society from Dr. Cooper and Rev. Charles Inglis, telling of a visit to Johnstown in 1770, where they were waited upon by a delegation of Indians, who asked them to second Sir William's efforts to obtain a missionary for them, pointing out their disappointment at not having a missionary when the Canadians were so gratified. S. P. G. MSS. (L. C. Trans.), B3, No. 339, S. P. G. Journal (L. C. Trans.), XVIII, Aug. 17, 1770.*

difficult to understand Johnson's impatience with the government's failure to act on a matter which he thought of vital importance in British relations with the Indians.[140] The situation was eased somewhat shortly after, when, in 1771, the Society's appointee, Rev. John Stuart, arrived.

With the approach of the American Revolutionary crisis, Sir William, from 1770 to his death, four years later, became more aggressive in his recommendations to the British government, to the Society, and to the Anglican clergy in the colonies, more particularly to the Rev. Charles Inglis, prominent Loyalist, and later, in 1787, appointed Bishop to British North America.[141] Inglis and Johnson joined forces in working out an Indian conversion plan[142] in the hope of support from the British government. In this hope, they were mistaken, for as Johnson saw in the political troubles of the period an added reason for attempting to hold the Indians, by all means, to Great Britain, so the ministry at home, overwhelmed by more immediately acute problems, let the subject of Indian work fall into the background.

This correspondence, begun in January, 1770, by Inglis, grew out of the home government appointment of a Roman Catholic missionary at £100 per year for the Indians in Nova Scotia. Surely, Inglis argued, the authorities should be willing to grant a similar sum to a Protestant clergyman for Indians who had always been faithful allies. He hoped an application from Johnson would secure this grant.[143] Sir William replied cordially and promptly. He agreed heartily that the Six Nations were entitled to superior attention from the government and that he would mention the subject, but feared economy would prevent suc-

140*The Indian attitude, of course, developed from the earlier work of the French when attachment to the government and the church were parts of the same policy. Two years after Sir William's death, Col. Guy Johnson gave a summary of Indian affairs to Lord George Germain, in which he observed that the Indians had repeatedly applied to the government for a religious establishment, and he again at that time requested that some provision be made for them. Such action, he said would strengthen their attachment to the British government. N. Y. Col. Docs., VIII, 657.*

141*Rev. Charles Inglis, who later became the first colonial bishop of Nova Scotia, was at this time the assistant to Dr. Samuel Auchmuty, rector of Trinity Church, New York. He had formerly been the S. P. G. missionary for Kent County. Delaware. For an account of the career of Inglis see John Wolfe Lydekker, The Life and Letters of Charles Inglis: His Ministry in America and Consecration as First Colonial Bishop, from 1759 to 1787. Reviewed by Frank J. Klingberg in The American Historical Review, April, 1937, pp. 558-559.*

142*The completed Inglis-Johnson plan is available in Doc. Hist. of N. Y., IV, 661-75, and in Kemp, Schools in Col. N. Y. by S. P. G., 229-32.*

143*Johnson Papers, VII, 357-59. It was precisely this situation which actuated the government. The Six Nations had been fairly loyal without many special favors. On the other hand, the Canadian Indians were inclined to be intractable and threatening. Hence the concession to them.*

cess.[144] Inglis urged the matter upon the Society, asking it to second Johnson's application to the government. He added, "As a Body, it may not be in their power to do much. But the Interest of some particular Members may be of Service."[145] The details of the plan were unfolded to Johnson with the request that he give it his attention so that it would be workable and practical. Inglis stated, in urging this point, "Your good Sense, your thorough Knowledge of Indian affairs, Your Influence & Authority with the Indians, with the Government & Society, conspire to point You out as the properest person,"[146] to bring these ". . . . Savage Natives under Subjection to the Messiah, . . ."[147]

Sir William took immediate exception to Inglis' idea, as he had in 1763 to Dr. William Smith's, that civilization of the Indians, to a partial degree, should precede Christianization.[148] He believed a plan of agricultural economy would alarm the Indians, arouse their suspicion of the whites, and, in addition, would mean the loss of their fur trade. No other way of life than hunting was agreeable to these Indians and they utterly failed to see the advantages of an agricultural civilization. Amusingly enough, as a result of his distress at the turmoil of the time, he singled out the New Englanders for attack on this score. He railed at them, asserting that with all their zeal and piety they were intent on extirpating the natives and securing advantages for themselves. Moreover, he would rather trust twenty Ottawas in a room with his plate, he said, than one Indian who had taken on some civilization of the New England type.

Johnson was convinced, in short, that the Indians could be taught religion and morality without altering their basic ways of life. As to the missionaries to be sent among the Indians, not only should they be men of exemplary lives, but they should also learn the language, be able to care for the sick, and distribute sums of money in charitable work. When a mission based on this scheme appeared to be developing successfully, schools should then be erected in which some of the Indian boys might assist. He dismissed, as mistaken, Wheelock's idea of educating Indians outside their own territory. He appreciated dissenter objection to the introduction of more Church of England clergy

[144]*Johnson Papers, VII, 391-93. Upon receiving Johnson's reply, Inglis wrote to the S. P. G. about the "popish missionary" and enclosed Johnson's letter. S. P. G. MSS. (L. C. Trans.), B2, No. 64; S. P. G. Journal (L. C. Trans.), XVIII, April 20, 1770.*

[145]*Johnson Papers, VII, 504. In this letter, Inglis blamed the scarcity of clergymen for service in America upon the publication of Blackstone's Commentaries which made legal study very easy and attractive to young men and therefore diverted them from the Church.*

[146]*Johnson Papers, VII, 505.*

[147]*Ibid., VII, 508.*

[148]*See Johnson's letter to Auchmuty in which he approved of Inglis' project and said it deserved support. He feared, however, the lukewarmness in religion of many in power would make the success of the plan uncertain. Ibid., VII, 544.*

among the Indians, recognized the problem of finding English clergymen adaptable to Indian customs and habits, but nevertheless, hoped that the government would support the plan and that a sum might be raised in England by subscription.[149]

As a result of this interest, Inglis and Dr. Cooper of King's College visited Johnson the next month to discuss details more fully and to see the Indians themselves. Upon his return, Inglis informed the Society of the scope of the plan and asked for its approval.[150] Sir William had approved of the idea and would advise in the work. Inglis understood that political troubles for the moment might divert the government's attention from the project of Indian conversion but optimistically hoped the disturbances would soon subside, and then, ". . . an extensive plan, with the Society at its Head, supported by Sir William Johnson's Influence here, & attended with the greatest Probability of Success; would not fail, I imagine, to command Notice and awake the slumbering Charity of many Christians."[151]

Inglis became an indefatigable correspondent and advocate of religious activity among the Indians. He referred to Sir William " 'as the most zealous Friend, & ablest Advocate the Church of England has in America,' "[152] asked him regarding the number of missionaries and schoolmasters needed, the number of Indians in the Six Nations, and for other statistical information. Endorsed by Sir William and the Society, the scheme would be presented to the crown. New and old arguments were to win governmental approval. The danger of the Indians falling under the influence of the Roman priests, if left without religious care from the Church of England; the commercial value of Christianized Indians who would ". . . become sober, would multiply, & be more attentive to Business";[153] and lastly, that the provisions of the colonial charters mentioned the conversion of the savages as one of the reasons for colonization.[154] All these points were carefully worked up.

In the same year, 1770, Johnson, too, wrote to the Society, outlining the main features of the plan. He suggested specifically that the Archbishop of Canterbury and the other bishops, as well as the Society as a whole, request royal acceptance of the scheme. The Society

[149]*Johnson Papers, VII*, 596-602.
[150]*Apparently the Society expressed its approbation. See a letter of Inglis to the S. P. G., Mar. 8, 1771. S. P. G. MSS (L. C. Trans.), B2, No. 66.*
[151]*Johnson Papers, VII*, 749; *S. P. G. MSS. (L. C. Trans.), B2, No. 65; S. P. G. Journal (L. C. Trans.), XVIII, Oct. 19, 1770.*
[152]*Johnson Papers, VII*, 761.
[153]*Johnson Papers, VII*, 764.
[154]*Ibid., VII, 764. He added that he thought the government had as much reason to be apprehensive of Wheelock's Indian converts as those of the Catholic missionaries, but it would not do to so inform the public. See a letter from Auchmuty to Johnson referring to the plan. Ibid., VII, 309-10.*

assured him, in reply, that it would take every opportunity of recommending the project.[155]   In the fall, Inglis wrote, full of hope, relaying a rumor that Lord Hillsborough had told Dr. Samuel Johnson, former president of King's College, that upon proper application the government would allow the quit-rents of New York for the purpose of Christianizing the Indians.   He thought Sir William the proper person to make this request.[156]   Johnson answered in November, saying he hoped the attention of the government would soon be directed to the religious desires of the Indians.   As for the quit-rents, he thought it ". . . a matter that may rather be wished for than Expected, . . ."[157]

Inglis still clung, it appears, to the idea of teaching the Indians at least a few of the arts of civilization by introducing mechanics, blacksmiths, or other artisans into their villages.   Johnson once more opposed this on the ground that anything which tended to produce a change in their present mode of life should be deferred because nothing so quickly aroused their suspicions.[158]

In March, 1771, Inglis informed the Society of his progress.   He remarked that he and Sir William had estimated that £500 per year would be sufficient to start the proposed plan.   He knew the Society could not bear the expense alone but believed the government should meet some or all of it.   Sir William would, he said, apply to the government for funds.   The funds, from whatever source obtained, however, should be controlled by the Society.[159]

Johnson, a man of action, naturally grew impatient with the slow progress.   He feared an indifferent response in England, where "This extraordinary lukewarmness in matters of this nature, may . . . in some measure be attributed to the peculiar cast of Modern politicks, . . ."[160]   Inglis had suggested sending the plan immediately upon its completion to Hillsborough.   This Sir William wished to defer until he had heard from the Secretary of State in answer to his previous re-

[155]*S. P. G. Journal (L. C. Trans.), XVIII, Aug. 17, 1770.*
[156]*Johnson Papers, VII, 963.   He also reported that the Secretary of the S. P. G. had explained the circumstances surrounding the appointment of the Catholic missionary in Nova Scotia.   Lieutenant-Governor William Franklin, a member of the S. P. G. intended, if Hillsborough permitted, to publish a vindication of the government and the Society with regard to the affair.   Ibid., VII, 964.   See Johnson on this matter in Doc. Hist. of N. Y., IV, 268.*
[157]*Ibid., IV, 268.   He added that, if Inglis could procure a statement of the annual income from the quit-rents, he would consider it further.   Writing to the Society a little later, apropos of this, Inglis remarked that the quit-rents, were so poorly paid as to amount to only £300 per year.   S. P. G. MSS. (L. C. Trans.), B2, No. 66.   He also proposed, upon Lieutenant-Governor Franklin's suggestion, that the Society apply for islands in the Delaware, not yet granted, the income to be used to further Indian conversion.   S. P. G. Journal (L. C. Trans.), XIX, Oct. 18, 1771; Doc. Hist. of N. Y., IV, 288.*
[158]*Doc. Hist. of N. Y., IV, 268.*
[159]*S. P. G. MSS. (L. C. Trans.), B2, No. 66.   This letter appears as an abstract in S. P. G. Journal (L. C. Trans.), XIX, May 17, 1771.*
[160]*Doc. Hist. of N. Y., IV, 276.*

ports on the religious grievances of the Indians.[161]   Nevertheless, rather than see the plan fail, he agreed to present a memorial to Hillsborough. Johnson added some suggestions to Inglis' list of arguments especially designed to influence the government in favor of the plan, pointing out that the setting up of religious establishments among the Indians would remove tribal jealousies and would be proof of the King's regard for them.   Moreover, to make them members of a church which taught obedience to civil authority would strengthen the allegiance of the natives to the government and it would also be an effective means of preventing the alienation of the savages by England's enemies, who continually reminded the Indians that the English took no care of their salvation.   To the Society, Inglis apologetically explained that these arguments aimed at winning over the government to the scheme were of a political sort, as he imagined those of a religious bearing would not have as much weight.[162]

From time to time Sir William analyzed the problems of Christianizing the Indians, placing the blame for failure on the English government, which lacked knowledge and understanding of Indian mental characteristics and ideas, and zeal and perseverance in this work,[163] and hence had failed to provide adequate funds.   Conversion to the Church of England, he constantly insisted, would help secure the Indians to Great Britain and counteract the efforts of the French, which danger, though not as great as formerly, was, nevertheless, still present and could only be defeated by setting up Anglican religious establishments.   The King's support of this plan would be the best security of Indian allegiance.   The capacity of the Indians to receive instruction and comprehend religion was unquestioned and their genius for imitation would lead them from the teachings of Christianity into an acceptance of civilization.   He suggested that, in place of the historical and topographical account of the natives that Inglis had meant to include, he would confine himself to a brief general sketch.[164]   This letter answers, once more, the question of Johnson's motives in supporting the Society's Indian missionary enterprises.

In August, 1771, Inglis sent Johnson the Society's abstract and added, "Providence seems to mark you out as the proper Instrument in its Hand, to civilise those poor savages, & bring them out of the Bosom of Heathen Darkness into the Fold of his blessed son; & I am confident that this will add Lustre to your memory amongst Pos-

---

[161]*Doc. Hist. of N. Y., IV, 277.*

[162]*S. P. G. MSS. (L. C. Trans.), B2, No. 67; S. P. G. Journal (L. C. Trans.), XIX, Oct. 18, 1771.*

[163]*He again commented on the superior zeal and enthusiasm of the dissenters for the cause, which was, however, marred by their "Gloomy Severity of manners," which disqualified them for the work. Doc. Hist. of N. Y., IV, 282.*

[164]*For this letter see Ibid., IV, 282-83.*

terity.[165]   He suggested obtaining the support of the newly appointed
New York Governor, Tryon, recently a successful administrator in
North Carolina. He was reported to have influence with Hillsborough
and was friendly to the Church of England.[166]   Sir William lamented
that though the conversion of the savages was mentioned in charters
and in governors' instructions, it was considered a matter of form. He
hoped for better things from Governor Tryon.[167]

Steps were immediately taken to tie Governor Tryon into the plan
by securing his endorsement.[168]   And Inglis continued to scout for
funds. If some available fund could be indicated, he thought the government would more readily assent to the project. "Your Recommendation will draw their [the ministry] attention, if any Thing can; for
it is not only my Opinion, but that of every one besides, that there is
no person whatever whose Influence is more essential to the Peace &
Welfare of America than Yours at present."[169]

A little later Johnson approved the plan, except the proposal to
introduce farmers and mechanics among the Indians. Evidently Inglis
had not yet abandoned this feature. Johnson wrote to Hillsborough,
introducing Inglis as the author of the plan[170] and Dr. Cooper as the
person who would present the memorial.[171]   Inglis promptly answered,
assuring Sir William that he had removed the objectionable sections
and stated that he had added a few more details at Colonel Guy Johnson's direction.[172]

[165]*Doc. Hist. of N. Y., IV, 285. Inglis commented on Johnson's ability to
find time to write so often amidst such a multiplicity of other business. During
this period, Bishop Lowth, in an anniversary sermon before the S. P. G., paid public
tribute to Sir William's interest and efforts. Ibid., IV, 285-86. See also Barton's
account to Sir William of the intention of the Society to carry on work in the
Mohawk country until the government should be willing to take over the expense.
He also states a rumor that something was intended to be done in the present ses-
sion by Parliament. Ibid., VIII, 182.*
[166]*Doc. Hist. of N. Y., IV, 285-86.*
[167]*Ibid., IV, 287. He suggested a map to illustrate the plan. In the finished
memorial one appears, drawn by Col. Guy Johnson. Ibid., IV, opposite p. 661.*
[168]*In October, 1771, Inglis wrote that he had laid the memorial before Tryon,
who approved it, and he thought recommended it to Hillsborough. Ibid., IV, 291.
No correspondence between Johnson and Tryon on this subject appears. In 1772,
Governor Franklin of New Jersey, in a letter to the Society, approved of the
project. S. P. G. Journal (L. C. Trans.), XIX, Oct. 23, 1772.*
[169]*Doc. Hist. of N. Y., IV, 289.*
[170]*Inglis' idea seems to have been to have Johnson appear as the author, which
arrangement seemed unwise to Sir William. Inglis told Governor Tryon and the
Society that Johnson deserved all the credit for the memorial. Doc. Hist. of N. Y.,
IV, 291-92.*
[171]*Ibid., IV, 290. For Johnson's letter to Hillsborough see Ibid., II, 572.*
[172]*Sir William had Guy Johnson return the plan to Inglis in person for these
changes. The additional details included a fuller discussion of Pontiac's affair so
that people would not have the notion that the colonists were free from the Indian
danger, and also, a hint of how much more agreeable the Indians found the Church
of England service than that of the dissenters. He also pointed out the wisdom of
trusting the conversion of the Indians to the Church of England clergy by which
their fidelity to the crown would be assured. In this same letter, Inglis gave minute
description of the outward appearance of the memorial. Ibid., IV, 291-92.*

Dr. Cooper presented the memorial sometime in 1771. W. L. Stone[173] says that the influence of Lowth, Bishop of Oxford, was brought to bear on Hillsborough, who, however, took no action on the matter, due doubtless to his other pressing colonial problems. In October, 1772, Inglis wrote to Johnson saying that, although he regretted the resignation of Hillsborough, the appointment of Lord Dartmouth might turn out for the benefit of their plan as Dartmouth was one of the most religious men in England.[174]

As the proponents of the plan feared, the Anglo-Colonial political situation diverted the attention of the government from a consideration of the memorial. From 1772 until the Revolution, the colonial clergy were increasingly concerned with their own safety, as the *Journal* of the Society shows, and therefore could not urge the conversion of the Indians very effectively. Sir William, also, found his efforts hampered by local problems and by ill health.

Johnson's relation to the Society was well stated by his friend, Thomas Barton, the Society's missionary in Lancaster, Pennsylvania, who wrote in July, 1770, to him that "The Society, I find, have turn'd their Eyes upon you, as the principal Patron of their Cause in America— They mention you in their Letters in Terms of the highest Respect; & hope, thro' your Influence & Assistance, to accomplish at last what they have so long wish'd, . . ."[175] And four years later, at the time of Johnson's death, Stuart, who as missionary to the Mohawks, represented the culmination of much of Johnson's activity with the Society, wrote home on August 9, 1774, that "The Church of England has lost a powerful and zealous protector by the death of Sir William Johnson,— his Influence was always exerted in her defence, when any opportunity offered ; . . ."[176]

---

[173]*Stone (Jr.), Johnson, II, 356-57. See also Kemp, Supp. of Schools in Col. N. Y. by S. P. G., 231; Johnson Papers, VIII, 621-23.*

[174]*For Inglis' reports to Johnson on the progress made by Cooper in bringing the matter to the attention of the ministry, see Johnson Papers, VIII, 541.*

[175]*Johnson Papers, VII, 811. A few months earlier he had spoken of Sir William using every means in his power to promote the designs of the Society. S. P. G. MSS. (L. C. Trans.), B21, No. 122. By far the most glowing account of Sir William was written by Col. Babcock, in 1773, when trying to further a scheme of his own for an Indian seminary in the Mohawk country under Johnson's sponsorship. "—Why may not Sir William be the means of introducing Learning & Religion amongst the Indians, and civilize them as well as Peter the Great did the Muscovites and altho Sr Wm like Solomon has been eminent in his Pleasures with the brown Ladies, yet he may lay the Foundation of a Building in the Mohawk Country that may be of more real use, than the very splendid Temple that Solomon built . . . ." Doc. Hist. of N. Y., IV, 304. Johnson looked coldly upon Babcock's plan. On this subject see Ibid., IV, 302-05, 305-09; Johnson Papers, VIII, 857-59, 869-70, 922-23.*

[176]*S. P. G. MSS. (L. C. Trans.), B2, No. 201; Johnson Papers, VII, 1195. In March, 1775, the clergy of New York recommended that three of Johnson's sons-in-law be made members of the Society. S. P. G. Journal (L. C. Trans.), XX, March 17, 1775. The "three sons-in-law" is an error and refers doubtless to*

This study of Johnson's cooperation with the Society illustrates the significance of the by-products of a movement. Just as Eleazar Wheelock had relatively slight success with his Indian plans, but founded a great educational institution, Dartmouth, so the S. P. G. founded Columbia University and established the educational system of New York colony. In its various efforts, it helped create and spread "The Cult of the Noble Savage" and stimulated Anglo-American evangelical interests in the protection of the backward peoples of the world against economic exploitation.

And again, this cooperation shows that often men do not understand the tides on which they sail. The Atlantic Coast, with its 2,000,-000 white men, in 1770, and with European hordes waiting to join them, was too small to contain the oncoming millions who wished to establish farm colonies in the St. Lawrence and the Mississippi Valleys. And, by a strange fate, the sturdy and self-respecting Iroquois tribes, so highly praised by Ellsworth Huntington,[177] were right on the line of march of the all water level route later followed by the Erie Canal and the New York Central Railway lines.

These Indians, as Johnson so often pointed out, could not quickly adapt themselves to a farm-colony economy. Nor could they become a part of the white man's world in the way the Negro did. The Negro has often fought with great tenacity for his tribal life in Africa, and still does, but the slave trade and slavery necessarily made him a non-tribal individual, who had to, and could, adapt himself to the white man's industry, commerce, and agriculture. The Indian could, for example, in the Hudson's Bay Region adapt himself to the white man's hunting interests but not to those of the settler, cultivating the land.

The plans for the Iroquois are particularly intriguing because an experiment that reformers rarely see in the heat of battle was performed, when a hardy race of Indians, a capable Indian governor, and a powerful missionary society tried to take a stand against the too rapid impact of the white settler in the rushing decades just before the American Revolution.

The Society and its agent, Johnson, as has been seen throughout all the stages of the European rivalry in seizing and settling these rich New York lands, tried to Christianize and protect the Indian, but also to use him as a "Warlike Christian Man" in the battle lines of the day. Indeed, Johnson himself, as is well known, carried along by the conditions of the day, helped push the Indian boundary lines west and incidentally acquired large tracts of land for his own use. And then, after his death,

Sir John, son and heir, as well as Col. Guy Johnson and Col. Daniel Claus who married Sir William's two daughters. This recommendation was doubtless an effort to keep up the connection between the Indian Superintendents and the Society.
[177]*Ellsworth Huntington, The Red Man's Continent, pp. 119-21, 158-160.*

the Iroquois Indians took the side of the British, and thereby sealed their fate as a power in the United States.   They were defeated in battle by General John Sullivan, whose Yankee soldiers spied out the land and soon returned with wives to settle in this fertile region.   In short, a large white population, doubling every 20 years, spelled the doom of the American Indian east of the Mississippi.   Neither the ingenuity and devotion of imperial representative, nor missionary ardor could protect the Red Man from the White Man's closely packed settlements.   This tragedy of the Aborigine was to be enacted so quickly that he was romanticised almost in his own time by James Fenimore Cooper and others as "the noble savage."   Inevitably, the all but insoluble Indian policy was taken over by the new American government.

In the northern and middle colonies leading Anglicans had so frequently taken the Tory side that the long attempt to found an American episcopate seemed hopeless.   However, the zeal and stamina of the S. P. G. missionaries had been such that the Episcopal Church was established on a firm foundation both in the United States and Canada immediately after the American Revolution.   As is well known, one leader, an American born Loyalist, Samuel Seabury, became the first American bishop in 1784; another leader, an Irish born Loyalist, Charles Inglis, became the first colonial bishop in 1787, with jurisdiction over British North America.

In the short view, the Society's work had seemed crushed by the Revolution; in the long view, its activities were taken over by the Americans themselves, and the Society was therefore freed to focus upon new fields in Canada, the West Indies, and other parts of the Empire.

CHAPTER IV

THE S. P. G. PROGRAM FOR NEGROES IN COLONIAL NEW YORK

THE program of the Society for the Propagation of the Gospel to search out and teach the Negro at the very opening of the eighteenth century, seems, unlike most events in perspective, more gigantic an undertaking in its difficulties and its obstacles to twentieth century appraisal than to contemporary opinion. Not only was the slave trade bringing in hundreds of slaves at a time, but the problem of their Christianization was added to that of the native people, the Indians, who were equally the charge of the early missionaries. Again, little cognizance could be taken at first of the Negro's lost African culture and therefore a bridge connecting his so different world with British civilization, comparable with the cautious procedure of a modern missionary going to Africa or the homeland of any native people, could not be attempted. For, today, the S.P.G. draws on its two centuries of accumulated experience and knowledge of native peoples, and on the voluminous literature of its colleague, the Society for the Promotion of Christian Knowledge.

The specific program of the S.P.G. for Anglican Negro Christianization, and the consequent education inevitably necessary as the slave was prepared for the sacraments of the Church, introduced an ameliorative agency between master and slave. The greater the missionary's success, the more difficult it became to regard the Negro merely as a piece of property. Sometimes clearly and again dimly, the owner realized that vital transformations were contemplated or subtly involved.

The power and drive of the S.P.G., with its semi-official standing, created a new situation in the British colonies, both continental and West Indian, and necessitated an adjustment of the clergy of all denominations, lay officials, masters and slaves to the new agency. It was clear from the beginning that the Society was not a transient visitor but a permanent resident in America, supported by British religious and humanitarian interests of great strength.

At once the vital question was brought up, did baptism free the

slave? The S.P.G., confronted by the firm economic and social realities of slavery and of the slave trade,[1] interests unshakeable during the
first three-quarters of the Society's existence, took the position that
Christianization was not emancipation and thereby significantly committed itself and the British government to a program of religious liberty for an enslaved race, rapidly increasing in numbers in the continental colonies from an estimated 60,000 in 1715 to half a million in
1775.[2] The estimates for New York are 4,000 Negroes and 27,000
whites in 1715, and 20,000 Negroes and 150,000 whites in 1771, both
races having increased about five times.[3]

The masters were able to secure endorsement of this position on
the legal effects of baptism from the law officers of the crown, and also
from colonial legislatures, so that in law the matter was clear beyond
the shadow of doubt. In practice, however, the slave owner was constantly confronted, as long as slavery existed, by the fact that baptism,
marriage, and other religious rites, convinced the Negro that he was
on the road to freedom because these elaborate white man's religious
ceremonies, recognizing the soul of a black slave on terms of equality
with that of a white free man, carried not merely religious, but civil
and economic implications, disturbing to master and slave alike. The
complete cycle of a sacramental progression from baptism to burial,
with the special training of each successive step between, including the
learning of the white man's language, might not be a legal emancipa-

---

[1] *The slave trade is reputed to have yielded a return of 24% per annum
throughout the eighteenth century and these huge profits explained the underlying
resistance in the long history of attempts at abolition during the last 150 years.
Estimates of the profits naturally vary widely but all agree that profits were huge.
Frank J. Klingberg, the Anti-Slavery Movement in England (New Haven, 1926),
p. 13, "During the last sixteen months before the trade was abolished Liverpool
alone sent out one hundred and eighty-five ships for the African trade, capable of
carrying about 50,000 slaves at a profit of over thirty per cent of the investment."
R. Coupland, The British Anti-Slavery Movement, (London, 1933), p. 38, "It
paid on the average at least 15 per cent. One slaveship alone might bring in as
much as £60,000 by a single successful voyage. It was calculated that, even if two
out of every three ventures failed, the profit might still be substantial." The
history of the slave trade has been studied as a major research project by Elizabeth Donnan, in Documents Illustrative of the History of the Slave Trade to
America, Washington, 1930-1935, four volumes. Her contribution as well as that
of Mrs. Catterall have not yet been incorporated into general historical scholarship.*

[2] *Evarts B. Greene and Virginia D. Harrington, American Population before
the Federal Census of 1790, New York, 1932, Columbia University Press, p. 4.
Helen T. Catterall, Judicial Cases Concerning American Slavery and the Negro,
IV, p. 351, gives the number of Negro slaves in 1723 as 6,171. The census of
1790 showed 21,324.*

[3] *Ibid., Greene and Harrington, p. 102.*

tion, but was, nevertheless, a participation in the white man's folk ways amounting to something like tribal adoption.

Sharp-witted defenders of slavery, such as Edward Long,[4] were never in doubt that the Christianization of the Negro was at least a first step in his eventual emancipation and that the moral weight of the slogan, "Am I not a man and a brother,"[5] widely used during the last years of the eighteenth century, would in time force judge and legislature to outlaw slavery and the slave trade by declarations that both were illegal and contrary to Christian teaching.

During the course of the eighteenth century, philosophers adopted and promoted theories reflecting this changing mood. John Locke, for example, held that "religious liberty for slaves does not in any way exempt a Negro from that civil dominion his master hath over him."[6] Somewhat later, Francis Hutcheson appeared as "the first British philosopher fully to apply to slavery the 'romantic' ethics of pity instead of the 'classical' ethics of reason."[7] Specifically, he stated,

> Strange, that in any nation where a sense of liberty prevails, where the Christian religion is professed, custom and high prospects of gain can so stupify the consciences of men, and all sense of natural justice, that they can bear such com-

[4]*Edward Long, History of Jamaica, (3 vols., London, 1774). Long was for some years judge of the vice-admiralty court in Jamaica. He returned to England in 1769 and was one of the ablest exponents of the West Indian point of view. He died in 1813.*

R. Coupland, The British Anti-Slavery Movement, pp. 28-29, (London, 1933), includes a quotation from Long in a statement presenting the average master's point of view in plantation colonies in the eighteenth century, "Surrounded by an overwhelming multitude of barbarous Negroes, most owners were convinced that a policy of 'amelioration' which aimed, not merely at protecting them from excessive cruelty, but at educating and civilizing them, was doubly bound to lead to trouble. On the one hand, the slaves would acquire new ideas, a new sense of their rights and of their power to obtain them—a process which would excite their discontent, impair their willingness to work, and culminate in a general and irresistible rebellion; on the other hand, their rise in the scale of civilization would make it increasingly difficult and finally impossible to justify the institution of slavery itself. As it was, in their primitive state, they could be and commonly were regarded as virtually disqualified by nature for the enjoyment of human rights. Edward Long, an official in Jamaica, whose well-known history of the island was published in 1774, desired that slaves should be humanely treated, but he argued at some length that they should be classed with orang-outangs as 'a different species of the same genus'."

[5]*R. Coupland, The British Anti-Slavery Movement (London, 1933), p. 94, "A cameo depicting a Negro in an attitude of entreaty had been designed by Wedgwood, the famous master-potter and an ardent abolitionist, and widely adopted for decorating snuff boxes, bracelets and hair pins."*

For an interesting recent use of the seal with its slogan see Maggs Bros., Catalogue No. 677, Cover and title page, London, 1939.

[6]*Wylie Sypher, "Hutcheson and the 'Classical Theory' of Slavery," Journal of Negro History, XXIV, No. 31, July, 1939, p. 273. Frank J. Klingberg, The Anti-Slavery Movement in England (New Haven, 1926), pp. 34-35.*

[7]*Op. cit., Journal, p. 216.*

putations made about the value of their fellow-men, and their
liberty, without abhorrence and indignation.[8]

In this study it is not intended to discuss the complicated inter-
relationship between the growth of religious freedom and civil liberty
in the white man's history, but to point out that in the case of the Negro
in the British colonial world, a quite appreciable religious liberty preceded the attainment of civil rights.

The work of the S.P.G. in the mission field, throughout this century of profound changes, enables the student to get a continuity of
record vouchsafed by few other sources.[9] The field reports of the
missionaries, from their widely separated stations, and the codifying
activities of the central control body in London tell the story of the
part played by the Society. Besides, the annual Sermons, preached
before the Society in London by distinguished men, throw appreciable
light on the mood in England, and the financial records give many items
of social history.[10]

I. IN NEW YORK CITY

The work in New York opened under promising conditions. On
April 12, 1705, the Society appointed, as catechist to the Negroes in
New York City, the justly famous Elias Neau. French born, imprisoned as a Protestant for several years, he emigrated and settled in
New York as a trader, where he determined to help the enslaved Negroes. In 1703, he had asked the Society to appoint a teacher for
them. And, in the meantime, he had spent many hours in their instruction. In 1705, he was delighted[11] to be licensed as a catechist by

[8]*Ibid., p. 279. On p. 280, Sypher states "*. . . *the modern attitude on slavery
originates in Hutcheson's humanitarian attack on Aristotle.*" *Thomas Clarkson,
History of the Abolition of the Slave Trade (London, 1808) I, pp. 49-50.*

[9]*For an illuminating survey of the S. P. G. work, see Sir Edward Midwinter,
"The Society for the Propagation of the Gospel and the Church in the American
Colonies," Historical Magazine of the Protestant Episcopal Church, IV, 67-82.
Sir Edward carries his New York account through the Revolution, quickly pre-
senting the work at each mission station for whites, Indians, and Negroes.*

[10]*The famous Sermon of Bishop Warburton before the S. P. G. in 1766 is
found in The Huntington Library, A Sermon. Preached before the Incorporated
Society for the Propagation of the Gospel in Foreign Parts; At Their Anniversary Meeting in the Parish Church of St. Mary-Le-Bow, on Friday, February
21, 1766, by the Right Reverend Father in God, William Lord Bishop of Glocester, London; Printed by E. Owen and T. Harrison in Warwick-Lane.
MDCCLXVI. The records of the Society constantly present the problems of
finance. The collection of the funds, from a widespread base, testify to the success of the Society's appeals. The disbursements were a constant problem, for
not all of the demands for help could be met.*

[11]*Neau had left his position as an elder in the French Church to conform to
the Church of England. He stated that he devotedly approved of the English
Liturgy, much of which he had learned while in the dungeons.*

the governor, Lord Cornbury, and confirmed in that position by the Society, with the approval of the bishop of London. He worked with enthusiasm and devised special methods of work. He reported that the rector of Trinity Church and commissary for New York, the Rev. William Vesey,[12]

> . . . read a note on Sunday morning in the church in the form of an exhortation to the masters and mistresses to take care to send me their slaves every Wednesday, Friday and Sunday at five o'clock in the evening to the end that I may teach them the principles of our holy religion. They sent me to the number of thirty. . . . These people come in such great numbers Sundays only. Wednesdays and Fridays there comes but eight or ten. . . . I have performed this office for the space of two months, and . . . the number of my catechists diminish instead of increasing. The inhabitants do not lay to heart their own salvation. . . . The love of pleasure and of perishing goods is so rooted in their hearts and minds that there is no room left for piety . . . impurity, blasphemy, and public adulteries are crimes which are committed openly in the sight of the world.[13]

Mr. Neau concluded his letter by saying that, although he would use his best endeavours to instruct the Negroes, he questioned, in moments of discouragement, the Society's rapid success with the slaves. Mr. Vesey had promised to cooperate by preaching sermons to his white congregation on Negro Christianization. Mr. Neau believed he, himself, would be more successful as a layman, than in orders, because this work would seem less pretentious. An early report to the Society indicates a striking initial success and its statistics are worthy

[12]*Vesey at first opposed Neau because he was in the French Church congregation, but Neau soon proved a zealous "servant of Christ in proselyting the miserable Negroes . . ." and became a constant communicant of Vesey's Church, and Vesey wrote to the Secretary that Neau was doing "great service to God and his Church." See William Vesey to John Chamberlayne, New York, November, 1705, in S. P. G. MSS. (L. C. Trans.), A2 No. CXXX.*

Edward Hyde, Lord Cornbury, was a grandson of the Earl of Clarendon of Charles II's reign and a cousin of Queen Mary and Queen Anne. He later inherited the Clarendon title. Edward Channing in his A History of the United States (New York, 1920), II, p. 436, states, "Lord Cornbury was the most discreditable governor New York ever had and also one of the firmest adherents of the Established Church in the province." He prosecuted Francis Makemie, a Presbyterian minister, for preaching without the Governor's license. Makemie was acquitted, and the New York dissenters were powerful enough to secure Cornbury's recall and thereby ended the prosecution of Protestant dissenters in New York. As the eighteenth century reached maturity, Presbyterians, due in part to the Scotch-Irish immigration, gathered strength everywhere and identified themselves in New York and elsewhere with the Independence movement. Channing, IV, 446-447.

[13]*Translation of Elias Neau to John Chamberlayne, New York, October 3, 1705, in S. P. G. MSS. (L. C. Trans.) A2, No. CXXIV.*

of reproduction here as a list of notable names in the early support of the Society's program.

Master or Mistress	Women sent	Men sent	Catechisms given	Other books
My Lord Cornbury	1 mulatress		2 catechisms	2
Mr. Vesey	2 negresses		2 do.	2.2 letters
Mr. Wm. Leaths	2 negresses	1 Indian	3 do.	3.3 do.
Mr. Abr. Wandil	1 negress		1 do.	1 do.
Mrs. Widow Keep	1 negress		1 do.	1.1 do.
Capt. Trevet	1 negress		1 do.	1.1 do.
Mr. Stanton	1 negress		1 do.	1.1 do.
Mr. Joseph Smith	1 negress		1 do.	1.1 do.
Mr. Dudelo	1 negress	1 negro	2 catechisms	2.2 letters
Mr. Crook	1 negress	1 negro	2 do.	2.2 do.
Mr. Skentour		1 negro	1 do.	2.2 do.
Mr. Mool		1 negro	1 do.	1.1 do.
Mr. Daniel Cromelin	1 negress		1 do.	1.1 do.
Mr. Welson Sheriff		1 negro	1 do.	1.1 do.
Mrs. Jourdain	1 negress		1 do.	1.1 do.
Mr. Fauconnier	1 negress	1 negro	2 do.	
Mr. de Neak		1 negro	1 do.	
Mr. Burgins		1 negro	1 do.	
Mr. George Milar		1 negro	1 do.	
Mr. Boarn Boum		1 negro	1 do.	
Mr. Abraham Keep	1 negress		1 do.	
Mr. Brodfurt	1 negress	1 negro	2 do.	
Mr. Vandam	1 negress		1 do.	
Mr. Morin	1 negress		1 do.	
Mr. Allaire	1 negress		1 do.	
Mr. Isaac Nephtaly	1 negress		1 do.	
Mr. Henry Shepherds	1 negress		1 do.	
Mr. Blockgrose	1 negress		1 do.	
Mr. Richard Laurins	1 negress		1 do.	
Col. Depatris		1 negro	1 do.	
Col. Morice		1 negro	1 do.	
Mr. Bloom	1 negress		1 do.	
Mr. Mindar	1 negress		1 do.	
Mr. John Vincent	1 negress		1 do.	
Mrs. Van Vosse		2 negros	2 do.	
Mrs. Marcomb	1 she Indian	2 Indians	2 do.	

28 Women   [18] Men   46 Books   (14)

In his letter the following month, Mr. Neau reported,

I had a good number of scholars that made me hope I should be force to bring them to church under the tower, because my room could not holt [sic] them all, which was what Mr. Vesey and I resolved to do, but instead of the numbers increasing, it has been much diminished, for the most that come on Sundays are between 12 and 20, and Wednesdays and Fridays 6, 8, or 10 . . . This city is the chief, for I dare say there is more than a thousand Negroes that are actually there, great and small, men and women, and I make no difficulty—to say that the slaves that are amongst us are more

14 *Translation of Elias Neau to John Chamberlayne, New York, October 3, 1705, in S. P. G. MSS. (L. C. Trans.) A2, No. CXXIV. The number of men is not summed up in the MSS.*

numerous than all the Indians, . . . I would say that one may
make more proselytes of the blacks than of the Indians, . . .[15]

By March 1, 1706, Neau was able to report a few new pupils;
many of his pupils were irregular in attendance; some, indeed, came but
two or three times, took the catechisms, and never returned. As often
happened elsewhere, after the first burst of enthusiasm, the real long
time difficulties appeared. He explained that he had ". . . not been
catechizing in the country, because if they that live in the city have
not time enough of whom there [are] a great many, they that live in
the country have much less."[16]   Moreover, he had heard that many
ministers were beginning to catechize the Negroes in their own parishes.

At this stage the question of the legal effects of baptism raised
its head. Mr. Neau wrote to the Society that Mr. Vesey had baptized
some Negroes, ". . . against the will and without the knowledge of
their masters, because they [the masters] fear lest by baptism they
should become temporally free."[17]   Mr. Neau joined with Mr. Vesey
in encouraging the masters in the right way of thinking, especially the
Dutch and the French, but they could not free the owners from this
fear. And accordingly, the two workers resolved

> . . . to obtain an act of assembly to confirm the right of
> the inhabitants over their slaves after baptism in the same
> manner that they had it before, for without that, they will not
> suffer them to be instructed, for fear they should be baptized
> without their knowledge. I reckon that there are in this town
> above 1000 slaves, and that if their masters would take as much
> care of their salvation as they do of the bodily health (for the
> sake of the work they do for them) I should not be able to do
> my office alone, but unhappily they seek not the kingdom of
> God and his righteousness . . . solid piety is very rare in
> this country.[18]

In November, 1706, the act was passed for which Mr. Neau had
been working, and Lord Cornbury publicly announced his approval.[19]

[15]*Translation of Elias Neau to John Chamberlayne, New York, November
15, 1705, in S. P. G. MSS. (L. C. Trans.), A2, No. CXXV.*
[16]*Translation of Elias Neau to John Chamberlayne, New York, March 1, 1706,
in S. P. G. MSS. (L. C. Trans.) A2, No. CLIX.*
[17]*Translation of Elias Neau to John Chamberlayne, New York, April 30,
1706, in S. P. G. MSS. (L. C. Trans.), A2, No. CLXVII.*
[18]*Translation of Elias Neau to John Chamberlayne, New York, April 30,
1706, in S. P. G. MSS. (L. C. Trans.), A2, No. CLXVII.*
[19]*Translation of Elias Neau to John Chamberlayne, New York, December
28, 1706, in S. P. G. MSS. (L. C. Trans.), A3, No. XVII. Mr. Neau enclosed a
copy of the Act with this letter to the Secretary.*

Mr. Neau hoped for greater success under the new legal assurances, but asked for the prayers of the Society in his undertaking because, he wrote, ". . . my career is full of difficulties and because I attack the Devil in his fort, he fails not to lay snares in my way."[20]

As expected, this legislation produced the desired effect, for, in the summer of 1707, Neau reported the number of his catechumens as "mightily augmented," so that he now had above 100. He had furnished the second story of his lodging for their use. The room, as described, was forty-eight feet long and twenty-two broad, and would hold two or three hundred students. The most inconvenient part was that Neau had to receive the Negroes after dark, because they worked all day, except on Sundays. Neau explained his plans,

> I have changed the method I took in the beginning a little, or rather changed nothing, but have added a few things as prayers and singing of psalms, that encourages both them and me, for I represent to them that God placed them in the world only for his glory; and that in praying and singing those divine praises, one doth in part obey his commands. I observe with pleasure that they strive who shall sing best. I have but 8 to 9 of those people who are baptized. The others are not at least a great many who might be for asking. I endeavour to make them comprehend the necessity of baptism, but their hearts are desperately corrupted. . . . Catechising days . . . are Wednesday, Friday, and Saturday. I would catechize them much oftener, but their masters desire me not to keep them long. I keep them always two hours in summer, but longer in winter. . . . I want 200 small catechisms of the cheapest sort . . . [and] an English psalter with the singing notes. There are none in this country. . . .[21]

A memorable picture of conditions of work and of the fortitude shown by Mr. Neau, and the slaves assembling at the end of the working day is contained in a revealing letter to the Society,

> I have the honor of sending you two copies of the act of Assembly in the months of November and December last, I hope that at least one of them is come safe to your hands, by that Sir you will perceive that they have begun to give me some encouragement in the instruction of slaves, and what has done us no harm has been, that the Dutch minister has also

[20]*Translation of Elias Neau to John Chamberlayne, New York, November 28, 1706, in S. P. G. MSS. (L. C. Trans.), A3, No. XVII.*

[21]*Translation of Elias Neau to John Chamberlayne, New York, July 24, 1707, in S. P. G. MSS. (L. C. Trans.), A3, No. CXXVIII. Neau said also that he was drawing £100 for two years' salary. He had given up most all of his business to instruct the Negroes.*

preached up the necessity of that matter, since when I have had a great number of catechumens. I would have had 'em to church to instruct them in the usual places, viz. the belfrey, but besides, that that is too little to contain them, I am moreover obliged to keep my school by candle light; because in the day time they are employed in working, neither would it be so easy for them, nor me, especially in winter, for which reason I have fitted up for them a place in the house where I live, 'tis a room up two pair of stairs of 48 foot in length and 22 in breadth. I have placed benches for them to sit on and to encourage them to come; I endeavor as much as is possible to give them an idea altogether spiritual of a Being infinitely perfect. I cause them to pray and sing psalms, reading every time each verse to them. This draws abundance of people to see and hear them. 'Tis certain Sir, that some of them appear affected with the truths of our religion. Last Sunday I had 75 of 'em men and women, but I have not above 8 or 9 that are baptized. I shall want 200 catechisms of the smallest sort that have been sent me before, divided into 13 lessons, in order to distribute from time to time. Sir, I must also inform you that I have drawn a bill of £100 upon the Treasurer at one month's sight for two years salary due the first of August, for I have not yet begun to reckon it, but from the arrival of Mr. Brooke who brought me your letter confirming me anew in the office of catechist, the time which I had begun before having been interrupted as I had the honor to write you, I count nothing for it. I don't think it necessary Sir, to tell you that I have been obliged to quit a good part of my business to the end that I might act with greater liberty in this employment, you will easily imagine it. If these people with whom I have to do were free, I should have some ease by teaching them in the daytime, but God has given me the grace to accommodate myself to all and to surmount these little difficulties. I don't begin to teach them in summer any more than in winter till sunset or till candlelighting. . . .[22]

The musical gifts of the Negro, as already mentioned, appeared early and attracted white attention. The sensitive ear of the African was apparent not merely in music, but in learning the language of their masters. The eagerness to learn new languages and new forms of song, both in contrast with the Indian's reserved habit, made a ready means of communication with the missionary and the white man's culture.[23]

Although the number of catechumens remained large during the

[22]Translation of Elias Neau to John Chamberlayne, New York, July 22, 1707, in S. P. G. MSS. (L. C. Trans.), A3, No. LXXX.
[23]For an appraisal of the Negro's linguistic capacity see Allen Walker Read "The Speech of Negroes in Colonial America," Journal of Negro History, XXIV, No. 3, July, 1939, pp. 247-258.

following year, Mr. Neau still lamented the fact that the slaves were not encouraged by their masters. Some, he said, dared not come to him at all, because, he wrote,

> . . . upon desiring the approbation of their Masters to be baptised they are either threatened to be sold to Virginia or else to be sent into the Country if they come any more to school; Good God! What sort of religion have these people for my part I can't help saying that they have none at all; but you must not believe Sir that all Masters are of this mind, only it falls out unfortunately that the Slaves of the aforesaid Masters have been the best fitted for Instruction and have had their heart touched by those truths which they know.[24]

But the difficulties inherent in the Christianization of the slaves became increasingly apparent and the cultural gap was not to be bridged in a day. Mr. Neau observed ". . . with sorrow that the knowledge they acquire makes but little impression on their hearts and indeed the corruption that reigns and which like a torrent overflows all our country, serves only to strengthen them in the unfortunate practice of vice."[25] Mr. Neau's school, in spite of obstacles, continued to progress, and after his pupils learned the catechism he took them to Mr. Vesey to be examined, then to the Church to be baptized, with free and white persons for witnesses. On Easter, 1710, two Negroes and three Negresses of his catechumens were baptized, and on Whitsunday, one Negro and two Negresses.[26] Mr. Neau reported with satisfaction that ". . . the negros who have been baptized do their best to have their children baptised also. . . . But the greatest number remain without baptism because the masters don't care. . . ."[27] However, the Frenchman's success was held up as an example to other missionaries. John Thomas of Hempstead made a spirited reply to Secretary Chamberlayne and explained the problems of a large rural parish, ending his letter with a contrast,

> Sir, I hold a very amicable correspondence with Mr. Elias Neau, whom you propose in yours as a pattern and example to us missionaries, and whom I likewise esteem a good man: but please to consider that his business is wholly with the

[24]Translation of Elias Neau to John Chamberlayne, New York, August 24, 1708, in S. P. G. MSS. (L. C. Trans.), A4, No. 68.
[25]Translation of Elias Neau to John Chamberlayne, New York, February 27, 1709, in S. P. G. MSS. (L. C. Trans.), A4, No. 121A.
[26]Translation of Elias Neau to John Chamberlayne, New York, July 5, 1710, in S. P. G. MSS. (L. C. Trans.), A5, No. CXXXIV. On the Church holy days, Mr. Neau usually distributed the small tracts sent to him by the Society.
[27]Translation of Elias Neau to John Chamberlayne, New York, October 3, 1710, in S. P. G. MSS. (L. C. Trans.), A6, No. XLIII.

slaves at New York City where they live contiguously and when they come to his house; ours, to prepare for preaching every Lord's Day twice, besides visiting and instructing the poor ignorant people of my parish, who are distantly scattered about the wilderness, overgrown with almost invincible ignorance. I appeal to the . . . Society, whether this be not employment sufficient for one man conscientiously to perform. Your zeal for the conversion of infidels is eminently glorious and charitable, but I have within my district infidels, God knows, of my colour, too many, upon whom I bend my whole force. . . .[28]

The Rev. John Bartow of West Chester, in writing on the same subject said frankly that he had ". . . lately baptized a free negro man and three children and a negro woman servant, but 'tis very rare that those people can be brought to have any true sense of the Christian religion."[29] These straightforward doubts show a spirit of free inquiry and free report, and an exchange of ideas between headquarters and field men.

In the year 1711, Mr. Neau made some interesting comparisons between the conduct of the whites and Negroes, and, incidentally, defended the slaves under his instructions well in advance of the insurrection of the following year:

> . . . It is true that I have not as many student whites as I have of them, but that is a matter of fluctuation because sometimes I have had more and at other times less. It is according to the whim of our youth, which is extremely libertine in this country, because it doesn't love spiritual things. . . . They [the masters] will come to recognize that the trouble and expense of the illustrous Society is not without fruit, because the Christian religion inspires in their slaves love and obedience to their masters and mistresses. But one responds to that that one doesn't notice any change. In this the real reason is the great number of slaves that are in the city. There is not one in ten that comes to the catechism. They are naturally libertines and those to whom they belong do not bother themselves much about their welfare so long as they serve well. Thus it is as much the fault of the masters as that of the negroes if their slaves are not good men. Furthermore the bad examples of the whites confirm the negroes only

[28]John Thomas to Secretary John Chamberlayne, Hamstead, June 12, 1709, in S. P. G. MSS. (L. C. Trans.), A5, No. IX. Mr. Thomas said the whites in his parish had degenerated into atheism and infidelity; the Indians were incapable of any Christian impression.

[29]John Bartow to John Chamberlayne, West Chester, New York, November 30, 1710, in S. P. G. MSS. (L. C. Trans.), A5, No. CLXXIX; Journal of S. P. G. (L. C. Trans.), II, April 20, 1711. Mr. Bartow asks in this letter for more Common Prayer Books and Catechisms.

too much in their impenitence and in their [undecipherable word]. I have been told that the negroes bear on their foreheads the marks of the reprobation and that their color and their condition confirms that opinion. I always cry out against the temerity that dares *fouiller* in the impenetrables of God, and furthermore I do not see that the turpitude of their crimes is more attrocious than that of the whites, because we are only to often scandalized by the horrors that the Christians commit. I know, sir, that the evil of one doesn't excuse that of the other, but at least these wretches are in some sort more excusable. I must tell you after that that Mr. [Vesey] baptized six persons the day after Christmas last, to wit two men and four women black slaves, and the day after Paque he baptized four negroes. There would be a great *moisson* to make . . . [if] the masters desired as much the welfare of their slaves as they desire the health of their bodies. I can assure you, sir, that those who were baptized had it done to them without consent of their masters and there are . . . [some] who wish me ill and many negroes come to catechism unknown to their masters. . . .[30]

The Negro uprising of 1712 is vividly described by the Rev. John Sharpe in a report to the Secretary of the Society,

Some negroe slaves here of the Nations of Carmantee and Pappa, plotted to destroy all the white, in order to obtain their freedom, and kept their conspiracy secret that there was not the least suspicion of it. . . . It was agreed to on New Year's day, the conspirators tying themselves to secrecy by sucking the blood of each others hands. And to make them invulnerable, as they believed, a free negro who pretends sorcery gave them a powder to rub on their clothes, which made them so confident that on Sunday night, April 1 [not clear on MSS], about two o'clock, . . . they set fire to a house, which alarming the town, they stood in the streets and shot down and stabbed as many as they could, till a great gun from the Fort called up the inhabitants in arms, who soon scattered them. They murdered about 8 and wounded about 12 more. . . . Some . . . in their flight shot themselves. One shot first his wife and then himself, and some who had hid themselves in town, when they went to apprehend them, cut their own throats. Many were convicted and about 18 have suffered death. This barbarous conspiracy of the negroes . . . opened the mouths of many against negroes being made Christians.[31]

[30]*Translation of Elias Neau to John Chamberlayne, n. p. [New York], n. d. [c. May, 1711], in S. P. G. MSS. (L. C. Trans.), A6, No. LXXXVII. (A rough translation only.)*
[31]*John Sharpe to [Secretary], New York, June 23, 1712, in S. P. G. MSS. (L. C. Trans.), A7, pp. 215-218. The reader should note that New Year's Day at that time was March 25th and not January 1st.*

The terror inspired by this outburst caused the usual hue and cry for a scapegoat so that Mr. Neau dared hardly appear, because his school was at first blamed as a factor in it.[32] However, only two Negroes had been pupils of his, and one only was a baptized person. Condemned on slender evidence, this slave was, after his execution, believed to have been innocent by the generality of the people.   The other catechumen was a slave of an eminent merchant, Hendrick Hooghlandt. This slave had tried for two years to gain Mr. Hooghlandt's consent to baptism, but had failed. He confessed to Mr. Sharpe that he knew of the conspiracy but was not guilty of murder in the tumult. The cry against catechizing the Negroes continued for some time, but Mr. Sharpe wrote hopefully,

> . . . and what is very observable the persons whose negroes have been found guilty are such as are declared opposers of Christianizing negroes. . . . Upon the whole the Christian religion has been much blasphemed, and the Society's pious design has been much obstructed by this bloody attempt of the negroes, I am hopeful that both shall be promoted since it appears on trial that those are innocent who have been seasoned with principles of religion and those are a small number that come to school in comparison of the many hundred that are in this place. I believe not above the tenth.[33]

Other clergy as well came to Mr. Neau's aid, notably the Rev. Thomas Barclay, conspicuous for his work with the Mohawk Indians.[34] He wrote that, although only one of Mr. Neau's proselytes was concerned in the conspiracy, the abolition of missionary work among the Negroes was being considered; even Mr. Vesey, he said, had become lukewarm.[35]

The Society's Secretary, rallying to Mr. Neau's defence, wrote,

> It is to be hoped people will conceive better things than to believe Christianity makes men worse, or that it is any sub-

[32]*A petition against Neau was started, but the Governor stood by Neau's cause and it was dropped.*

[33]*John Sharpe to [Secretary], New York, June 23, 1712, in S. P. G. MSS. (L. C. Trans.), A7, pp. 215-218.*

[34]*For an account of Barclay's success, see the foregoing chapter, "The Noble Savage as Seen by the S. P. G. Missionary in Colonial New York, 1702-1750."*

[35]*Thomas Barclay to William Taylor, New York, May 31, 1712 [Post Script], in S. P. G. MSS. (L. C. Trans.), A7, pp. 204-206. Mr. Barclay expressed the hope that the Society would encourage the Governor of New York, because he had remained faithful to Neau and his efforts.*

stantial objection against the duty of your office, or the design of the Society in endeavoring to convert infidels to true religion, which teaches men otherwise.   I hope they are before this time convinced to the contrary, and that none instructed by you were in that fact or that they ought not to draw inferences from the bad practices of one professor or rather probationer, to the prejudice of religion in general or the pious endeavours of the Society by the means in particular.[36]

Governor Hunter, a member of the Society, likewise was fully convinced of the innocence of Neau's scholars, and, in December, 1712, endorsed Mr. Neau's instruction by visiting the school, in the company of several missionaries.[37]   Two years later, in 1714, the Governor inserted a paragraph in his proclamation commending Negro instruction, and ordered all of his own slaves to go to Neau's school.[38]   The Common Council, however, made an order by which the Negroes of the city were forbidden to go along the streets without lanterns.   This order was an indirect attack on Neau's school, for it was well known that the slaves did not come to be catechized until after sunset, and frequently without their master's knowledge.   The masters were unlikely to furnish lanterns or candles for this purpose.[39]

The Rev. Thomas Barclay, in coming to Neau's defence, became sufficiently interested to begin Negro work himself.   In 1713, he reported the baptism of two Negroes, one free, and the other a slave.[40]   In a different environment at Albany, he found fewer obstacles in his way.   He had about thirty adult catechumens, five of whom had been baptized.   Barclay wrote,

The names of the baptized are, Elizabeth, the slave of Barnet Bratt citizen of Albany; Jacob the slave of Col. Killian Van Rensselaer, lord of the manor Rensselaer Wick; Brit slave of Robert Livingstone, Junior esq., Mayor of Albany, Scipio

[36]*William Taylor to Elias Neau, London, November 6, 1712, in S. P. G. MSS. (L. C. Trans.), A7, p. 277.*
[37]*Elias Neau to [Secretary], New York, December 15, 1712, in S. P. G. MSS. (L. C. Trans.), A7, pp. 226-227.*
[38]*Elias Neau and others to the Rev. Gentlemen of the Clergy Assembled in the city of New York, February 28, 1713/14 in S. P. G. MSS. (L. C. Trans.), A8, pp. 292-293.   Neau asked the clergy to thank the Governor for his endeavors.*
[39]*Translation of Elias Neau to John Chamberlayne, New York, September 8, 1713, in S. P. G. MSS. (L. C. Trans.), A8, p. (?).*
[40]*Thomas Barclay to William Taylor, Albany, April 17, 1713, in S. P. G. MSS. (L. C. Trans.), A8, p. 167.*

the slave of Peter Matthers, commandant of the garrison; and
Christiana the slave of Gerrit Van'est, citizen of Albany.[41]

Barclay catechized at his own house, on Sundays after the service,
and on Wednesday and Friday evenings. He instructed many slaves
in the Dutch language because few of them in this Dutch Community
understood English. Encouragingly he wrote to the Society,

> I am glad to acquaint the . . . Society that I find in
> these poor slaves a great forwardness to embrace the faith
> of Christ and a readiness to receive instruction . . . the
> first thing I inculcate upon them is that by being baptized
> they are not free. I am obliged with the greatest caution to
> manage this work, and I have publicly declared that I will ad·
> mit none of them into the Church by baptism till I have ob-
> tained their masters consent.   Yea, I send them home with-
> out instruction who cannot have their masters' allowance to
> come, for some masters are so ignorant and averse that by no
> entreaties can their consent be had. . . .[42]

Barclay was supported by a certain Col. Killian van Rensselaer
and his wife, who sent their slaves constantly, and publicly declared
that their Negroes were better for being instructed,[43] and from Col.
Mathews, Mr. Livingston Jr., Col. Peter Schuyler, and others. Barclay's insistence on securing the consent of the masters before he gave
instruction[44] is worthy of special mention. These prominent citizens,

[41]*Thomas Barclay to William Taylor, Albany, June 29, 1714, in S. P. G.
MSS. (L. C. Trans.), A9, p. 144.*
[42]*Thomas Barclay to William Taylor, Albany, June 29, 1714, in S. P. G.
MSS. (L. C. Trans.), A9, pp. 144-145.*
[43]*A brief history of the Van Rensselaer family can be found in a recent publication by Henry W. Farnam, (Edited by Clive Day), Chapters in the History
of Social Legislation in the United States to 1860, (Carnegie Institution of Washington, 1938), pp. 43, 44, 96. On pp. 42-43, Farnam states, "The Dutch . . .
in 1629 decided to offer manorial privileges to leaders who would establish settlements there [New Netherland]. These leaders, dignified by the term patroons,
were tempted by the offer of tracts of land. . . .*
*The only patroons who succeeded in getting any substantial advantage from
their grants . . . were the Van Rensselaers, who built up a settlement near Albany. Under the English rule the Van Rensselaers colony was converted into
'an English manor . . .' and new manors were constituted: Livingston, Cortlandt,
Fordham, Pelham . . . ."*
[44]*Thomas Barclay to William Taylor, Albany, June 29, 1714, in S. P. G.
MSS. (L. C. Trans.), A9, pp. 145-146; Journal of S. P. G. (L. C. Trans.) III,
January 21, 1714/15. His only opposition was from a Major Mindet Schuyler
and his brother-in-law, Peter Vandressen, minister of the Dutch Congregation at
Albany. He declared that Schuyler bore no good will to the Society, and Vandressen was a novice sent over from Amsterdam, and he was ". . . both ignorant
of the constitution of his own or our Church, . . . and has obstructed my labors
not only of late but while I labored among the Mohawk Indians."*

following the example of the clergy in sending their own slaves, gave their stamp of approval in establishing new customs.

Another fellow-missionary, the Rev. Daniel Bondet,[45] stationed at New Rochelle from 1709 to 1722, was struck by the fact that a number of the Negroes in the town had learned the principles of the Christian religion by listening to the family service. He encouraged these slaves, by assigning them seats in his Church. At catechizing time, he questioned them as well as the white candidates. On Whitsunday, 1715, he baptized a Negro mother and her daughter,[46] and two years later he admitted two carefully instructed Negroes to Communion.[47]

In New York City, Neau, not in orders, could not baptize his catechumens; and, in December, 1715, he charged Vesey with refusing to baptize an eighteen-year-old mulatto girl, even though she had a letter from her mistress desiring that she be baptized. The mistress thereupon sent a note to the chaplain of the fort who catechized and baptized the girl. Continuing the controversy, Neau charged that Mr. Vesey, doubtless alarmed by the Negro uprising, had not read in church the Governor's proclamation against vice and immorality, because one clause encouraged the instruction of the Negroes. Since Mr. Vesey was not a missionary of the Society, but was appointed by the bishop of London, the matter of his conduct was evaded by it.[48] The Society instead decided to investigate Neau's business activities, for it regarded trading as open to question. And accordingly, Neau, despite his successful work, was discharged with the allowance of a year's salary.[49] He at once wrote to the Society and enclosed a certificate signed by Governor Hunter and several clergy of the province giving a good account of his services, and, after careful consideration, he was vindicated and reinstated as catechist.[50] In 1719, as evidence of the cooperation of prominent people, Neau sent to the Society a list of the catechumen slaves who came constantly to his school since

[45]*Daniel Bondet had formerly been a French minister. He was driven out of France, ordained by the bishop of London, and was employed for a time by the New England Company.*

[46]*Daniel Bondet to [Secretary], New Rochelle, July 22, 1715, in Journal of S. P. G. (L. C. Trans.), III, February 3, 1715/16.*

[47]*Daniel Bondet to [Secretary], New Rochelle, November 12, 1717, in Journal of S. P. G. (L. C. Trans.), III, October 24, 1718.*

[48]*Abstract of letters from Elias Neau to [Secretary], New York, December 6, 1715, in Journal of S. P. G. (L. C. Trans.), III, June 15, 1716, and September 21, 1716.*

[49]*Journal of the S. P. G. (L. C. Trans.), III, March 7, 1717/18. However, the Society delivered a memorial to the archbishop of Canterbury stating that Neau's dismissal had been made for the purpose of reducing expenses. See Journal of S. P. G. (L. C. Trans.), III, September 19, 1718.*

[50]*Journal of S. P. G. (L. C. Trans.), IV, March 20, 1718/1719.*

his reinstatement.[51] The list includes several free blacks and therefore gives a hint of the amazingly complicated relationships inevitable in a slave society. This inter-relationship of slave, freedman, Indian, free and slave, has been made a subject of special study by the Department

Masters and Mistresses Names	Negro Men Their Ages by Guess		Negro Women Their Ages by Guess				Negro Boys Negro Girls
Collo Depeyter	1	45 yrs	2	50 yrs / 35			the negro man Bap. & Com.t
Capt. Isaac Depeyter	1	30 yrs					he is baptized Anthony
Mr. Jacob Vinross	3	30 / 25 yrs / 20	1	50 yrs			the men bap. Jephty, Robert, & John
Mr. Dl Cromelin	1	24 yrs			1		
Mr. Vandham	1	30 yrs	2	40 yrs / 30	1		the women & boy bap. Susanah Lillie, & Jacob.
Mr. Philip Scuyler			1	25 yrs			a communicant
Mr. Glaves			1	35	1		both baptized
Mrs. Rattray			2	45 / 24			both commts Mary: Sarah
Mrs. Narett			1	22			baptized Annah
Mr. Hardinbourg	1	20 yrs					baptized Cesar
Mary black free woman			1	45			baptized
Aigar Do			1	40			baptized
Mr. Th: Robert	1	25					baptized
Magdalin free woman			1	25			baptized
Mr. Catale	1	26	1	25			baptized
Mr. Minville	1	35	1	50			woman baptized
Cornt Depetyr	1	30					baptized
Mr. Vanhorn	1	30					
Andr: Franccan	1	30					
Dr. Dupey	2	30 / 28	2	25 / 40			One man baptized
Abrah. Vanghorn	2	45 / 30					one communicant
Mr. Bone	2	28 / 30					both baptized
Mr. Rindell	1	26					communicant
Mr. Alexn Moore			1	22			
Mr. Sim. Souman			1	30			baptized
Mr. Harrison					1		
Mrs. Droyer			1	25			
Mr. Wright	2	35:30					baptized John & George
Mr. Drick de Neack	2	30:27					baptized John & Oliver
Mr. John Read	1	30					
Annah free black woman			1	45			
Mr. Conrads Comfort	1	22					
Mr. Bachan						1	
Mr. Gerrd Vanhorn			1	35			
Mr. Edd Elsward			12	25			baptized Dorothy
Mr. Bayeur	1	40	1	35	2	1	all baptized
Mr. Renehett					1		
Mrs. Marit					1	1	
Mr. Abrah. Evans					1		
Madm Ingoldshoes	1	28					
Mr. Governoua						2	

[51] *A list of the Negroes taught by Mr. Neau, December 23, 1719, inclosed in Elias Neau to David Humphreys, New York, January 22, 1720, in S. P. G. MSS. (L. C. Trans.), A14, pp. 141-143. These are in addition to the white apprentices, boys and girls.*

of History of the Carnegie Institution in a monumental five volume work.[52]

The Society had asked Neau to take his students to church for catechizing, but he replied that the church was not large enough even for the whites, and furthermore, many of the slaves were bashful, because, as yet, they pronounced the English language very poorly.[53] In 1720, he reported that two of his Negroes had received the holy communion, and five had been baptized by Mr. Vesey.[54] In June, 1721, Neau reported steady progress,

> . . . I have caused eight of my catechumens to be baptized: four at Christmas, 2 negro men and two negro women, and 4 in Whitsunday week . . . by the consent of their masters, which they gived by a note they wrote to the Rev. Mr. Veesy, and he baptized them in the Church before the whole congregation. My school is numerous, yet there is but few who will go [to] the catechism of Mr. Huddleston in the Sunday at church for the reason I've told you last year. . . . I spare nothing to encourage them poor miserable slaves to learn them the way to be saved. A ship from Madagsor hath brought 120 of them since three weeks. The number doth increase daily and the spiritual harvest would be great if the glory of God was earnestly seeked by our white people.[55]

Masters and Mistresses Names	Negro Men Their Ages by Guess		Negro Women Their Ages by Guess		Negro Boys	Negro Girls
Mrs. Bloom				1		
Mr. Derick Defort			1	1		
Mr. Amillton	1	28				
Mr. Henry Lane	2	30:24				
Cornet: Vanhorn	1	20				
Jacobus Courland	1	35				
Aldolph Phillips	1	40				
Dr Couling			1	35		
Mr. Congrove			1	30		
Mrs. Dekey			1	40		
Mr. Vanderhill	1	24	1			
Mr. John Roswell						1
Mr. Jer: Reading	1	27				
Dec. 23: 1719	37		28	12	8	Elias Neau S:

[52]Helen Tunnicliff Catterall (Editor), Judicial Cases Concerning American Slavery and the Negro (Washington, 1926-1937), 5 volumes, published by the Carnegie Institution of Washington. Volumes IV and V, brought out after Mrs. Catterall's death, were completed by James J. Hayden.

[53]Translation of Elias Neau to David Humphreys, New York. January 22, 1720, in S. P. G. MSS. (L. C. Trans.), A14, pp. 110-111.

[54]Translation of Elias Neau to [Secretary], New York, November 20, 1720, in Journal of S. P. G. (L. C. Trans.), IV, April 21, 1721. The baptized included two men and three women; Neau was preparing others for baptism on Christmas.

[55]Elias Neau to David Humphreys, New York, June 22, 1721, in S. P. G. MSS. (L. C. Trans.), A15, pp. 95-96; Journal of S. P. G. (L. C. Trans.), IV, June 15, 1722.

The problem of supplying the Negroes with simple religious literature constantly engaged the attention of the Society and its field workers. In 1722, Mr. Neau asked for Church catechisms with the alphabet in them, because, he said, several Negroes learned to read and rehearse the Church catechism at home, which was also a means for the white children of the Dutch and French to learn the catechism.[56] That same year, death brought Mr. Neau's activities to a close. His devotion to religious and charitable work was shown by his bequest of a considerable part of his estate.[57]

Mr. Vesey asked the Society to appoint some one in priest's orders in Neau's place. In that way, Vesey would have some one to assist him in instructing the children, and the newcomer could function in all religious services.[58] The churchwardens and vestry of Trinity Church also petitioned the Society for an ordained catechist to replace Neau, urging that by the assistance of a man in orders, the Society would, ". . . exceedingly advance the honor . . . of our holy Church . . . at this critical juncture when the dissenters here have united their forces, and by the encouragement and liberal contributions from abroad, have been enabled to raise two meeting houses and support ministers. . . . "[59]

The Rev. William Huddleston, who had been catechizing slaves and apprentices on Sunday afternoons under Mr. Vesey's direction,[60] asked for Neau's position, saying that "Swarms of negroes come about my door and asking if I would be pleased to teach them and build on Mr. Neau's foundation. Mr. Neau upon his death had begged me

[56]*Elias Neau to [Secretary], New York, May 22, 1722, in Journal of S. P. G. (L. C. Trans.), IV, February 15, 1722/1723. Neau also reported in this letter the baptisms of an Indian woman, and a mulatto woman; both had frequented his school.*

[57]*Trinity Church received 20£, rector of Trinity Church 25£, and several ministers welcomed substantial legacies. William Huddleston to David Humphreys, New York, Nov. 24, 1722, in S. P. G. MSS. (L. C. Trans.), A16, pp. 213-214.*

[58]*Mr. Vesey said he had been officiating 24 years, and was in declining age and health, and his increasingly heavy burdens of parochial duties were more than he could do efficiently. See William Vesey to David Humphreys, New York, October 4, 1722, in S. P. G. MSS. (L. C. Trans.), A16, 209-210.*

[59]*Minister, churchwardens, and vestry [of Trinity Church] to David Humphreys, New York, December 18, 1722, in S. P. G. MSS. (L. C. Trans.), A16, pp. 229-230. Which faith the dissenters belonged to was not mentioned, but Neau had earlier said his enemies included "Arians, Socinians, Quakers, deists." See Neau to David Humphreys, New York, April 2, 1722, in S. P. G. MSS. (L. C. Trans.), A16, p. 196.*

[60]*William Huddleston to David Humphreys, New York, July 29, 1721, in S. P. G. MSS. (L. C. Trans.), A15, p. 98; Journal of S. P. G. (L. C. Trans.), IV, June 10, 1722. Mr. Huddleston said he usually catechized about 100 a Sunday, and his wife was a great help to him in this work.*

to do the same."[61] Although Huddleston was permitted to take over these duties for a year,[62] the work was given to the Rev. James Wetmore.[63] However, Huddleston was appointed as Negro catechist in the parish under Mr. Vesey, instead of being supported by the Society.[64] He remained faithful to his task until his death, in 1726. Never appointed by the Society, it nevertheless gave his widow, Sarah Huddleston, £50 as a reward for her husband's services.[65]

Mr. Wetmore was warmly welcomed in New York. For his support, in addition to the Society's allowance, he reported that,

> . . . a subscription was promoted for one year which amounts to 71£ in New York money. I assist the Rev. Mr. Vesey in his parochial work and attend catechizing every Wednesday, Friday, and Sunday evening at my own house besides in the church every Sunday before evening service. I have sometimes near 200 children and servants to instruct whom I teach the Church catechism and commonly add some practical discourse suitable to their capacities joined with some devotions.[66]

But within two years after his arrival the usual ebb and flow appeared, and he complained that his catechumens were very few; the masters chose to instruct the Negroes at home, rather than let them venture into companies together. Following this argument, he was of the opinion that a missionary was not as necessary in New York as in other parts of the country where, he declared, ". . . people are wholly destitute." Mr. Wetmore also found it too expensive in New York, and asked for a transfer to Rye, New York.[67]

The Society, upon receipt of this letter, appointed Mr. Wetmore to Rye, but asked him to explain his intimation that a catechist was no longer needed in New York. He complained that his energies were needlessly dissipated so that on Sundays, he read prayers in the morn-

[61]*William Huddleston to David Humphreys, New York, November 24, 1722, in S. P. G. MSS. (L. C. Trans.), A16, pp. 213-214; same idea presented in a letter written by Huddleston Dec. 18, 1722, in ibid., A. 16, p. 228.*
[62]*William Huddleston to David Humphreys, New York, June 27, 1723, in S. P. G. MSS. (L. C. Trans.), A17, pp. 233-234. Huddleston wrote that he had been teaching the Negroes in the steeple every Sunday afternoon, and before and after the sermon at his own house, until he received further orders.*
[63]*Journal of S. P. G. (L. C. Trans.), IV, December 20, 1723.*
[64]*William Vesey to David Humphreys, New York, November 8, 1725, in S. P. G. MSS. (L. C. Trans.), B1, No. 85.*
[65]*Journal of S. P. G. (L. C. Trans.), V. April 15, 1726.*
[66]*James Wetmore to David Humphreys, New York, November 7, 1724, in S. P. G. MSS. (L. C. Trans.), A18, pp. 202-203; Journal of S. P. G. (L. C. Trans.), V. February 19, 1724/[1725]; see also a letter from Mr. Vesey to the Society thanking the members for Wetmore's appointment, November 6, 1724, in Journal of S. P. G. (L. C. Trans.), V, February 19, 1724 [1725].*
[67]*James Wetmore to David Humphreys, New York, June 24, 1726, in S. P. G. MSS. (L. C. Trans.), A19, p. 396.*

ing, catechized at noon, preached in the afternoon, catechized again in the evening.   In addition, he instructed his Negroes on Wednesday and Friday nights, gave catechisms to the poor whites and Negroes, and invited them to attend catechetical lectures.   Mr. Wetmore then explained,

> As to the negroes, they are not *sui juris* and I believe many of their masters are in fault, but most of them are so vicious that people don't care to trust them in companies together, and some have under pretense of going to catechizing taken opportunity to [be] absent from their masters service many days, so that when I discoursed with some they have told me they chose to instruct their servants at home. . . . I continued my instructions at eight o'clock Friday evenings, the first winter, in hopes of gaining a company, but was disappointed.   Before spring I had not more than two or three negroes that attended.[68]

Nevertheless, the officials of Trinity Church were not discouraged, but wrote the Society for another catechist.   They asked the Society

> . . . to appoint another catechist with the usual salary to officiate in this place, here being about one thousand and four hundred Indian and negro slaves, and the number daily increasing by births and importations from Guinea, and other parts.   A considerable number of these negroes, by the Society's charity, have already been instructed in the principles of Christianity, have received holy baptism, are communicants of our Church, and frequently approach the altar.   We doubt not but the Society has received from Mr. Neau, their former catechist, repeated accounts of the great success of his mission.   And since Mr. Wetmore's appointment, we have with great pleasure observed on Sundays, upwards of an hundred English children and negro servants attending him in the Church and their Catechetical instruction being ended, singing Psalms and praising God with great Devotion.
> The Honorable Society at all times and more especially of late has most zealously patronized the cause of these poor infidels, who otherwise might still have remained ignorant of the True God and the only way to happiness; and their great charity dispensed among them here, having already produced such blessed efforts, must raise them an extraordinary joy at present, will be a vast accession to their future happiness and increase their rewards of glory in another world.   We could say much more on this occasion, but this we hope will be sufficient to guard them against any attempts to persuade them to turn their bounty another way and induce them to believe,

[68]*James Wetmore to David Humphreys, West Chester, December 3, 1726, in S. P. G. MSS. (L. C. Trans.), B1, No. 72.*

that the office of a catechist here, is of as great an importance as ever, and that his salary is as well and charitably bestowed, as any missionary in all these parts.[69]

Mr. Vesey supported this request and recommended the appointment of the Rev. Thomas Colgan, and arranged for continued support,

> I am sensible what endeavors have been used to divert the current of the Society's bounty another way, but I trust that no solicitations will ever pre [vail] on that Venerable Body to withhold from the poor slaves of this city the means of catechetical instruction which their great charity has for so many years been vouchsafed to them. For sure I am that the Society cannot do a greater charity to these poor infidels, than to employ a person on purpose to instruct them to in the principles of religion, who I fear would otherwise remain ignorant of the true God, and the only way to happiness. . . . The number of slaves . . . already amounting to near one thousand five hundred souls, which are redeemed by . . . the Society's charitable assistance. . . . The only imaginable objection against it, is that some Masters are not so forward as they should be to command their slaves duely to catechist.[70]

The Society appointed the Rev. Mr. Colgan in December, 1726,[71] and the following May he reported that his catechumens numbered only fifty, mostly white, but he expected an increased attendance of slaves, and asked for prayer books and Church catechisms to distribute among them.[72] In December, 1728, he reported his black students as numbering sixty, and the adults among them had "a pretty good knowledge of the principles of the Christian religion." He had baptized men, women, and children, and those who could read attended public service.[73] The masters, he believed, were becoming more compliant, careful, and desirous of having their Negroes educated. In 1731, the Rev. Thomas Colgan was transferred to Jamaica, Long Island, and next year his New York position as catechist was filled by the Rev.

[69]*Rector, Churchwardens and Vestry of Trinity Church to [Secretary], New York, July 5, 1726, in S. P. G. MSS. (L. C. Trans.), B1, No. 73. The qualifications for the new catechist included a good, clear voice, pious character, education and orders.*
[70]*William Vesey to David Humphreys, December 20, 1726, New York, in S. P. G. MSS. (L. C. Trans.), A19, pp. 421-422. The success of Neau and Huddleston is stressed in this letter.*
[71]*Journal of S. P. G. (L. C. Trans.), V, December 16, 1726.*
[72]*Thomas Colgan to David Humphreys, New York, May 10, 1727, in S. P. G. MSS. (L. C. Trans.), A20, p. 186.*
[73]*Thomas Colgan to David Humphreys, New York, December 23, 1728, in S. P. G. MSS. (L. C. Trans.), A21, p. 376. Colgan again asked for Prayer Books for those who could read.*

Richard Charlton.[74] Mr. Charlton explained that in the summer season he had a large number of catechumens, but, in the winter, the severity of the weather reduced attendance.   However, he was able to report eighteen Negroes baptized, six of them adults, from April 23, 1732, to April 23, 1733.[75] This number rose to thirty-four from April 20, 1735, to April 20, 1736.[76] The Negroes naturally were learning slowly. He asked for common prayer books with the new version of Psalms, some catechisms with explanations for those Negroes who could read. Many Negroes could repeat the Church catechism from memory, ". . . and give a tollerable acc^t of the Lord's Supper."[77] Mr. Charlton wrote in 1739,

> The great numb^r of Negroes here, belonging to Mas^{rs} of different persuasions, and I am sorry to say of many, so negligent of their instruction, will I doubt not, tho' of a different colour yet having precious & immortal souls, be always look'd upon as true objects of ye Charity. I for my part wth the assistance of God will do what in me lies to promote their Salvation. . . .[78]

Beginning in the following year, 1740, Mr. Charlton's records noted that his Negro catechumens, who had been remiss, were more diligent in their attendance, and were improving surprisingly. Some masters supported his activities, a change due in part to public and private exhortations. Mr. Charlton wrote to Secretary Philip Bearcroft,

> I am now training up more y^n 20 Negroe children in the way of religion, and i am instructing near an equal number of Adults in the Christian faith, who as they are qualified are admitted to baptism. Some of ye former have been recev^d into ye Church when Infants: but alas! if we shod rest there, they might have the form wth out ever acknowledging the power of Godliness.
> Since ye year of my appointment for New York, 20th of Aprill 1732 there have been 198 Negroes bap: 24 of wch were Adults. And since the 20th of October Last to ye 20th of

[74]*Richard Charlton had asked for the position in 1731 but was not appointed immediately. See Charlton to [Secretary], June 6, 1731, in Journal of S. P. G. (L. C. Trans.), V, November 19, 1731.*

[75]*Richard Charlton to [Secretary], New York, June 5, 1733, in Journal of S. P. G. (L. C. Trans.), VI, March 15, 1733/[1734].*

[76]*Richard Charlton to [Secretary], New York, December 13, 1736, in Journal of S. P. G. (L. C. Trans.), VII, May 20, 1737; S. P. G. MSS. (L. C. Trans.), A26, p. 311.*

[77]*Richard Charlton to [Philip Bearcroft], New York, December 3, 1739, in S. P. G. MSS. (L. C. Trans.), B7, pt. II, p. 103.*

[78]*Ibid.*

Apr^ll 1740, 16 Negro children and Six Adults were baptised and there are now 6 Negro Com^ts.[79]

In March, 1740, Mr. Charlton reported that he read, after divine service on Fridays, a short lecture upon part of the Church catechism, and afterwards examined the catechumens out of Lewis' *Exposition of the Church Catechism.* The vestry of Trinity Church, to encourage the undertaking, had reprinted between 200 and 300 of the catechisms. The student of these Anglican records gains the impression that much was required of the Negroes, in the way of attendance, instruction and attainment, and that superficial work was discouraged.

It should be noted that the missionary was equipped both as schoolmaster and catechist with the considerable literature provided for the purpose, the origin of the great volume of tracts which provided the lower classes with dramatic and solid reading in the Victorian period. Every missionary appointed by the S.P.G. was given not only a "Mission Library," but small books and tracts for distribution among the whites, Negroes, and Indians. The catechists often asked for Bibles, common prayer books, Church catechisms and the expositions on the catechism, also books such as the homilies, expositions on the articles, and spelling books. Sometimes the translation of these books was required either for the Dutch, French, or Indian language, according to the racial backgrounds of the inhabitants.[80]   Under this

[79]*Richard Charlton to [Philip Bearcroft], New York, July 15, 1740, in S. P. G. MSS. (L. C. Trans.), B7, P. II, p. 106. In addition to the Negroes, many white children and servants attended catechism.*

[80]*The books most commonly called for by the Society's workers among the heathen were: (1) Thomas Wilson (Bishop of Sodor and Man), The Knowledge and Practice of Christianity made easy to the meanest capacities: or an Essay towards an Instruction for the Indians, which will be of use to such Christians as have not well considered the meaning of the Religion they profess . . . London, 1741, (Huntington Library); (2) Bishop Gibson, Three Addresses on the Instruction of the Negroes (1727), which includes an address to the Christians in England to promote Negro instruction, another to the Masters and Mistresses in the plantations, and one to the Society's missionaries; (3) Lewis, Exposition of the Church Catechism, was the favorite explanation of the Catechism for students, although others could be found in the missionaries' libraries, such as The Church-Catechism broke into short Questions, Worthington's Scripture Catechism, Dr. Woodward's Short Catechism, with an Explanation of diverse hard Words, New Method of Catechizing, and Bishop Gloucester on the Catechism; (4) The Whole Duty of Man by Way of Question and Answer; (5) Dyche's spelling books; (6) and a never ending request for Bibles, Common Prayers, Catechisms, and Hornbooks.   From 1702 to 1741, ten thousand Bibles and Common Prayers, and a hundred thousand small Tracts were distributed by the Society. See the statement made in 1741 by Bishop Secker, in C. F. Pascoe, Two Hundred Years of the S. P. G., I, p. 8; for a list of books distributed and translations of the Bible, Catechism, Liturgy, etc., see ibid., pp. 798-816a. A list of books found in a missionary's library can be found in a letter from R. Maule to John Chamberlayne, Charleston, S. C., November 28, 1707, in S. P. G. MSS. (L. C. Trans.), A3, No. CLXXXV, also see a list of books available for the Society's schools in William Webb Kemp, Support of Schools in Colonial New York, pp.*

regime of ample literature and instruction, Mr. Charlton emphasized that the spiritual knowledge of some of his Negroes, was such ". . . as might make many white people (who have had more happy opportunities of instruction) blush, were they present at their examination."[81]

Mr. Vesey praised Mr. Charlton in several letters to the Society, saying that Charlton was ". . . very Diligent in his Business and takes Effectual Care that the Society's Bounty towards him Shall not be ill Bestowed."[82] And Mr. Charlton, in turn, wrote to the Society that his Negroes not only improved in knowledge but also reduced it to practice, which was remarkable because there was at this time, as might well be expected, much "immorality" among the black men.[83] From November 11, 1740, to June 18, 1741, he baptized five adult Negroes and thirteen children,[84] and from June to October 26, 1741, seventeen more were baptized.[85] He hoped that by Christmas, 1741, five or six more Negroes would be qualified for baptism and added,

> The Num[r] of my Friday Catechumens exceed 90, and y[t] of the Negroes is above 70: and I do believe it wold [sic] have been greater by this time, had not that wicked plott (w[ch] no doubt y[u] have heard of) been set on foot here— Whence it had it's rise I will not presume to say; but this I can't help declaring, y[t] Mr. Whitefield's letter to the people of Maryland . . . gave great countenance to it, and I am Satisfied, y[t] whoever carefully reads it will join in opinion wth me: not that I sho'd think Mr. Whitefield to be so extreamly wicked as to promote destruction of this City, wth it's inhabitants: but the misfortune was y[t] imprudence & indiscretion directed his pen, when he wrote that letter. . . .[86]

24-25; and for translations of the Bible into the Mohawk language see David Humphreys, Historical Account of the Society for the Propagation of the Gospel, (1730) pp. 302-303.

[81]Richard Charlton to [Philip Bearcroft], New York, November 11, 1740, in S. P. G. MSS. (L. C. Trans.), B7, pt. II, p. 107; Journal of S. P. G. (L. C. Trans.), VIII, March 20, 1740/1741.

[82]William Vesey to [Secretary], New York, December 1, 1739, in S. P. G. MSS. (L. C. Trans.), B7, Pt. II, p. 71; see also ibid., Journal of S. P. G. (L. C. Trans.), VIII, April 18, 1740, and August 17, 1739.

[83]Richard Charlton to Philip Bearcroft, New York, June 18, 1741, in S. P. G. MSS. (L. C. Trans.), B9, No. 61; Journal of S. P. G. (L. C. Trans.), VIII, October 16, 1741.

[84]Ibid.

[85]Richard Charlton to Philip Bearcroft, New York, October 30, 1741, in S. P. G. MSS. (L. C. Trans.), B9, No. 62.

[86]Richard Charlton to Philip Bearcroft, New York, October 30, 1741. in S. P. G. MSS. (L. C. Trans.), B9, No. 62; Rev. John Gillies, Memoirs of the Late Rev. George Whitefield, revised by Aaron C. Seymour (N. Y. 1835), II, p. 454. No doubt the letter Charlton speaks of was the one Gillies mentions as written on April 18, 1740. He states (p. 454), "This day [April 18, 1740] was published Mr. Whitefield's letter to the Inhabitants of Maryland, Virginia, North and South Carolina, about their abuse of the poor negroes."

Mr. Charlton's baptisms continued at a steady pace; nine, between October, 1741, and March, 1742,[87] ten, between March and September,[88] thirteen during the next half year,[89] and three were admitted to communion.[90] Besides, the catechumens were improving in spiritual knowledge, and the common prayer books were inducing several of them to learn to read. Charlton asked for more prayer books, catechisms, and the bishop of Man's essay.

This heartening success temporarily ceased during 1743 and 1744, because of the illness of Mr. Charlton.[91] By March, 1744, he had sufficiently recovered to baptize fourteen Negroes that year, sixteen the next year, when three were admitted to communion.[92] However, the load was too heavy, and, in 1745, he induced Mr. Joseph Hildreth to assist him. Hildreth early reported forty white children in his school besides twelve Negroes.[93] In 1746, his slave attendance had increased to fifteen evening scholars sent him by their masters. These he taught to read the Bible and to sing psalm tunes.[94] He believed that psalm singing, after catechizing, was a reading aid as well as valuable in enabling the slaves to join and identify themselves with the regular worship. A "pious spirit" combined with an "apparent earnest attention" gave Mr. Charlton the prospect of a "hopeful harvest."[95] The Negroes, held in slavery, often recently from Africa, in process of learning the English language, and faced with the problems of adapting themselves into the white man's social order, could not always live up to missionary expectancy. And the hard work told on the missionaries. Mr. Charlton became ill again, in 1746,[96] and asked to be transferred to Staten

[87]*Richard Charlton to Philip Bearcroft, New York, March 26, 1742, in S. P. G. MSS. (L. C. Trans.), B10, No. 67. Two of the Negroes were adults.*
[88]*Ibid., September 30, 1742, B10, No. 68.*
[89]*Ibid., March 28, 1743, B11, No. 146.*
[90]*Ibid., September 30, 1742, B10, No. 68.*
[91]*Mr. Charlton was struck by a fever which kept him confined for five weeks. He wrote that his Negroes showed a deep concern for him. See Charlton to Philip Beaxcroft, New York, September 30, 1743, in S. P. G. MSS. (L. C. Trans.), B11, No. 147.*
[92]*Richard Charlton to [Secretary], New York, September 30, 1745, in S. P. G. MSS. (L. C. Trans.), B14, p. 104.*
[93]*Joseph Hildreth to [Secretary], New York, November 21, 1745, in S. P. G. MSS. (L. C. Trans.), B13, No. 221; Journal of S. P. G. (L. C. Trans.), X, March 21, 1745/1746.*
[94]*Joseph Hildreth to [Secretary], New York, March 29, 1745/46 in Journal of S. P. G. (L. C. Trans.), X, September 19, 1746. Mr. Hildreth asked for an addition to his salary of £10 per year. Five pounds additional was granted.*
[95]*Richard Charlton to [Philip Bearcroft], New York, July 14, 1746, in S. P. G. MSS. (L. C. Trans.), B14, p. 103.*
[96]*Richard Charlton to Philip Bearcroft, New York, September 29, 1746, in S. P. G. MSS. (L. C. Trans.), B14, p. 107. Mr. Charlton wrote, "To my great misfortune I have been greatly afflicted with an exquisite pain in the Small of my back (where the grand seat of pains was in my late disorder) but yet thank God I can in some measure relieve it by sitting."*

Island to the position formerly held by the Rev. Richard Caner, who had died of smallpox.[97] This request was granted.[98]

On July 1, 1747, the Rev. Samuel Auchmuty petitioned the Society for the position of catechist at New York,[99] was accepted, and arrived in New York, in January, 1748, where he found the slaves well instructed. In August, he wrote to the Society,

> This is . . . to inform you y^t I now constantly every Friday read a Lecture, after wch I Catechise ye Children; the Slaves not being able to attend on any Day but Sunday. It's with the greatest pleasure, y^t I can now acquaint you, y^t several of my black Catechumens make no small proficiency in the Christian Religion, & y^t the Number of y^m increases. I have baptized since my arrival here Five full grown Blacks, & at least Thirty Infants, & have now several Adults preparing, themselves for Baptism. . . .[100]

Mr. Hildreth continued his instructions under Auchmuty's supervision and reported a class of twenty Negroes, whom he taught in the evenings. Besides his school he stated, there were ". . . 1 Lattin, 1 French, 1 Dutch, & 8 English schools in New York."[101] A new school house was built by the parishioners of New York for the teacher,[102] but the year after its completion, it was completely destroyed by fire.[103]

Two years later, in 1750, Mr. Auchmuty reported his success,

> Since my last [December 1749] I have baptized about twenty-five negro infants, and eight adults, and can with truth assure you that my black catechumens daily increase, and seem to be fonder of becoming Christians than they were when I first came among them. I must also acquaint you that the Masters of the slaves in this place have also become more desirous than they used to be, to have their servants baptized,

[97] *Richard Charlton to Philip Bearcroft, New York, December 17, 1746, in* S. P. G. MSS. (L. C. Trans.), B14, p. 109.

[98] *Journal of S. P. G. (L. C. Trans.), X, March 20, 1746/1747.*

[99] *Samuel Auchmuty to* [Secretary], *London, July 1, 1747, in Journal of S. P. G. (L. C. Trans.), X, July 17, 1747. Mr. Auchmuty was born in Boston, educated at Harvard, and ordained by the bishop of London in 1747. He was the son of Robert Auchmuty, Judge of the Court of Admiralty at Boston.*

[100] *Samuel Auchmuty to Philip Bearcroft, New York, August 22, 1748, in* S. P. G. MSS. (L. C. Trans.), B16, No. 59; Journal of S. P. G. (L. C. Trans.), XI, November 18, 1748.

[101] *Joseph Hildreth to Philip Bearcroft, New York, March 26, 1748, in S. P. G. MSS. (L. C. Trans.), B16, No. 44; see also Journal of S. P. G. (L. C. Trans.), XI, July 15, 1748.*

[102] *Samuel Auchmuty to Philip Bearcroft, New York, December 30, 1749, in* S. P. G. MSS. (L. C. Trans.), B17, No. 116; Journal of S. P. G. (L. C. Trans.), XI, March 16, 1749/1750.

[103] *Joseph Hildreth to* [Secretary], *New York, April 6, 1750, in Journal of S. P. G. (L. C. Trans.), XI, July 20, 1750.*

and instructed in the principles of our most holy religion. I, for my part, shall do whatever I can to promote Christianity among them. . . .[104]

The much needed school was rebuilt, thirty black scholars[105] usually attended, and Mr. Hildreth taught psalm tunes to at least twenty Negroes every evening.[106]

In October, 1751, Mr. Auchmuty again reviewed his work in a report, stating,

> Agreeable to my inclination, as well as my duty, I now readily embrace this opportunity of acquainting you with the present state of my black catechumens. The number of those who are arrived to manhood are not so numerous as those who are about the age of fourteen or under. Most of the former (to the number of forty or more) are well acquainted with the principles of our most Holy Religion, and a good number of them, I have the pleasure to see, lead lives agreeable thereto. Some few of them are communicants. The latter seem to promise well, being pretty well acquainted with their catechism, owing in a great measure to the care and piety of their respective masters and mistresses. I constantly attend both great and small, every Lord's Day unless unavoidable prevented, and not only heard them repeat their catechism, but also I endeavour to make them sensible of the true meaning of every question, which naturally opens and discovers to them the Christian scheme, and the Duty and Obligation they are under to live as Christians. Besides catechizing the blacks, I have attending at the same time a number of white children, seldom less than sixty or seventy, which with my black catechumens make up a congregation of one hundred and thirty, sometimes more. . . . I have now two negro adults preparing themselves for the Communion, and I trust in God, before long, will be worth[y] communicants. From the second of October 1750, (the date of my letter in the last abstracts) to the second of October 1751, I have baptized sixteen black adults, all well instructed in the principles of our most Holy Religion and constant attendants on Divine Service and catechizing. Also thirty-nine black infants.[107]

104*Samuel Auchmuty to [Philip Bearcroft], New York, October 2, 1750, in S. P. G. MSS. (L. C. Trans.), B18, No. 98; Journal of S. P. G. (L. C. Trans.), XI, January 18, 1750/1751.*

105*Samuel Auchmuty to Philip Bearcroft, New York, December 28, 1750, in S. P. G. MSS. (L. C. Trans.), B18, No. 99. Mr. Auchmuty stated that he had no place to teach school except in the Church.*

106*Joseph Hildreth to Philip Bearcroft, New York, March 28, 1751, in S. P. G. MSS. (L. C. Trans.), B19, No. 68; see also B19, No. 70; B20, No. 58 (April 10, 1752); and B20, No. 59 (October 28, 1752).*

107*Samuel Auchmuty to Philip Bearcroft, New York, October 2, 1751, in S. P. G. MSS. (L. C. Trans.), B20, No. 52; Journal of S. P. G. (L. C. Trans.), XII, February 21, 1752.*

During the winter of 1751-1752, his black catechumens suffered the usual seasonal decline, intensified by the missionary's illness.[108] In the following year, 1753, his black scholars numbered sixty, and from July, 1752, to January, 1753, twenty-four children and six adults were baptized,[109] and in the first six months of 1753, fifty Negro infants, and twelve adults were baptized.[110] The black catechumens had been divided by Mr. Auchmuty into two classes, one of which learned Lewis' *Exposition,* and the other the Catechism itself. Many of the Negroes could read very well, and attended divine service regularly and used their prayer books.[111] His baptisms from January, 1756, to July, 1759, included one hundred and thirty-four children and seven adults.[112] Mr. Auchmuty was pleased with his Negroes' piety and intelligence. He wrote to the Society, on January 2, 1762, in this optimistic vein,

> In my last, I acquainted you that I had two black catechumens preparing themselves to receive the Sacrament of the Lord's Supper; Since which, with great satisfaction, I have admitted them to the Holy Table; their characters being unexceptionable, and their knowledge of our most holy religion, and their duty, very considerable for people of their colour. They read well. I have also admited a negro man to the communion, that was recommended to me, after finding his character and proficiency in the principles of our most holy religion, joined with an eager desire to fulfill the injunction of our blessed redeemer, such as I could wish or expect. The good pleasure these blacks afford me, is still augmented by the prospect I have of soon admitting two more to the Table of the Lord. They are two women of unexceptionable character, at present under instruction, read well, are very desirous of tasting the heavenly feast.
>
> Since the date of my last, I have baptized 25 negro children and three adults, and have three more under my care preparing for baptism.[113]

[108]*Samuel Auchmuty to Philip Bearcroft, New York, March 26, 1752, in S. P. G. MSS. (L. C. Trans.), B20, No. 56; Journal of S. P. G. (L. C. Trans.), XII, July 17, 1752. Auchmuty had a severe cold which kept him from his duties for several weeks.*

[109]*Samuel Auchmuty to [Secretary], January 6, 1753, in Journal of S. P. G. (L. C. Trans.), XII, April 19, 1753.*

[110]*Ibid., November 23, 1753, in Journal of S. P. G. (L. C. Trans.), XII, February 15, 1754.*

[111]*Samuel Auchmuty to [Secretary], New York, July 3, 1756, in Journal of S. P. G. (L. C. Trans.), XIII, December 17, 1756.*

[112]*From January, 1756, to July, 1756, 35 children and one adult were baptized; from July to December, 1756, 25 children and one adult baptized; from December, 1756, to June, 1757, 36 children and 2 adults baptized, and from July, 1758, to July, 1759, 38 children and three adults were baptized, also one mulatto woman slave was admitted to communion.*

[113]*Samuel Auchmuty to Philip Bearcroft, New York, January 2, 1762, in S. P. G. MSS. (L. C. Trans.), B2, No. 3.*

These religious and educational activities, the modern equivalent of evening schools for working people, were carried on as voluntary enterprises. The teachers had no powers of compulsion and the pupils were usually living in a state of slavery.

In September, 1760, the educational facilities in New York City were enlarged through the establishment of a Negro school by the Bray Associates.[114] "The most significant result," as stated by William Webb Kemp in his *Support of Schools in Colonial New York by the S.P.G.,* "was the division of the instruction between this new enterprise and the catechist. Thereafter the Negro catechumens were assembled for the usual service and catechetical exercises. To the school was assigned the work related to lay instruction."[115] Mr. Auchmuty described his relation with the new Negro school to Secretary Bearcroft,

> . . . I have had a considerable addition of young catechumens from our negro school.
> This school was begun at the desire and expence of the Associates of the late Dr. Bray. It was opened on the 22[d] day of September, 1760, and in a little better than four months was completely full, and so continues to this day. The number is limited to thirty; though double that number, at least, have requested to be admitted. The necessity and usefulness of such a school, being already seen, by many pious owners of young slaves. Prompted by duty and inclination, and requested by the Associates, I frequently visit the school, hear the scholars read, say their prayers, and catechise, and give them such instruction and advice, as they require. Besides this I order them to attend my lectures constantly on the Lord's Day, and catechise them and the adults together, by which means, I hope, as they grow up, to perfect them in the great and important doctrines of our most holy religion, and to lead them, by the blessing of God, upon my poor endeavors, to happiness hereafter, I must confess I can't help being very sanguine in my expectation from this little flock, as they are early instructed in their duty to God and man. They have already made a very considerable progress in sewing, knitting, reading, etc., and will I make no doubt, with proper management, and care, answer the truly pious designs of the worthy Associates.[116]

[114]*Edgar Legare Pennington, Thomas Bray's Associates and Their Work Among the Negroes (Proceedings of the American Antiquarian Society, October, 1938, New Series, vol. 48, part 2, pp. 381-396.) Dr. Pennington traces the work done for the Negro in Colonial New York from 1704 to the outbreak of the Revolutionary War.*

[115]*William Webb Kemp, The Support of Schools in Colonial New York by the S. P. G., p. 253.*

[116]*Samuel Auchmuty to Philip Bearcroft, New York, September 19, 1761, in S. P. G. MSS. (L. C. Trans.), B2, No. 2; Journal of S. P. G. (L. C. Trans), XV, January 15, 1762.*

Moreover, the Negroes, in Mr. Auchmuty's charge were making progress. Between sixty and seventy were in constant attendance. Even those who could not read paid strict attention to his lectures on the catechism. During a sixteen month period, he had admitted three adults to communion and baptized nine adults and ninety-nine children.[117]

Mr. Auchmuty, from time to time, reported progress,

> My number of black catechumens is increased, and many of them are serious, well-disposed people and communicants. By all that I can learn they are in general exemplary in their conduct and behaviour. It affords me no small pleasure to reflect that not one single black that has been admitted by me to the Holy Communion, has turned out bad; or been in any shape, a disgrace to our holy profession.
>
> Since my last I have baptized four adults, after previous instruction; and thirty-five infants. I have also admitted one man, and one woman to the Holy Communion. There are two more preparing for that sacred ordinance.[118]

Mr. Auchmuty's success pointed him out for clerical advancement, and, when Dr. Henry Barclay, rector of Trinity Church, died in August, 1764, he was chosen by the Vestry to fill the vacancy, and resigned as Negro catechist. The Rev. Charles Inglis, missionary at Dover, Delaware (1759-1765), was chosen as his assistant.[119] The work of catechizing the Negroes was given temporarily to Mr. Ogilvie.[120] Concurrently, the Negro school of the Bray associates was thriving, constantly aided by the Society's catechist. The school in Mr. Auchmuty's opinion, would always need inspection and supervision. Constant pressure on masters and slaves was necessary to keep the work

[117]*Samuel Auchmuty to Daniel Burton, New York, June 29, 1762, in S. P. G. MSS. (L. C. Trans.), B2, No. 4; ibid., March 30, 1763, B2, No. 5.*

[118]*Samuel Auchmuty to Daniel Burton, New York, March 29, 1764, in S. P. G. MSS. (L. C. Trans.), B2, No. 6a; Journal of S. P. G. (L. C. Trans.), XVI, July 20, 1764.*

[119]*Samuel Auchmuty to Daniel Burton, New York, September 10, 1764, in S. P. G. MSS. (L. C. Trans.), B2, No. 8; Journal of S. P. G. (L. C. Trans.), XVI, November 16, 1764. Charles Inglis was missionary for Dover 1759-1765, Rector of Trinity Church, New York, 1777-1783, and in 1787 went to Nova Scotia as the first colonial bishop. For an excellent study of the Rev. Mr. Inglis see John Wolfe Lydekker, Life and Letters of Charles Inglis.*

[120]*Samuel Auchmuty to Daniel Burton, New York, April 13, 1765, in S. P. G. MSS. (L. C. Trans.), B2, No. 9. Although the MSS. spells the temporary catechist's name as Ogilive, and does not give his Christian name, no doubt this is the Rev. John Ogilvie, S. P. G. missionary to the Albany and Fort Hunter Indians, 1749-1762. In 1759, he went as chaplain to the Royal American Regiment in the British expedition to Niagara. In 1763, Ogilvie was appointed senior assistant curate to Dr. Auchmuty at Trinity Church, New York. See John Wolfe Lydekker, Life and Letters of Charles Inglis, pp. 72 (footnote 3), 91.*

going. Trinity Church, in debt for the large sum of £10,000, could as yet give no adequate local aid.[121]   The Society reluctantly, after several pleas, agreed to contribute £10 per annum.[122]   Mr. Joseph Hildreth, already familiar with the work, as he had been schoolmaster for several years, was appointed.[123]   Mr. Auchmuty asked for Bibles, prayer books, and tracts, the only texts for the use of the slaves.   It is difficult for the modern reader to visualize the school of the mid-eighteenth century when the rich equipment of texts, maps, carefully devised curricula for the use of skilled teachers was largely unknown. He wrote gratefully to the Society,

> You will be so good as to return my sincere thanks to the Society for appointing a catechist to the poor Negroes in this city, whose hearts are filled with gratitude upon the occasion.   The Catechist has entered upon his office.   I have attended him, and have classed them in such a manner as will render his business easy to himself, and useful to the catechumens.   The numbers that attend exceed two hundred.   I will have a complete list made out, of their names, etc., with a list also of the communicants and send them to you by the first good opportunity.   You may be assured that I have their eternal interest so much at heart that I shall visit them almost every Sunday.   If prevented by other avocations, I will take care that one of my assistants supply my place.[124]

Mr. Hildreth explained his methods to the Society,

> As to my negro catechumens, about a hundred adults be [sides] children give constant attention every Sunday evening after Church, they behave with the utmost decency, and are fond of instruction.   Each of the ministers have visited this little Society, and favoured them with a lecture; but the duty of this Parish is so great that it can but seldom be expected from them.   However, in order to forward their instruction as much as possible, I am going through Dr. Bray's catechetical lectures; as they are short I can read one each evening (in absence of the minister) after catechise, and so conclude with

[121]*Samuel Auchmuty to Daniel Burton, New York, April 13, 1765, in S. P. G. MSS. (L. C. Trans.), B2, No. 9; Journal of S. P. G. (L. C. Trans.), XVI, July 19, 1765.*

[122]*Samuel Auchmuty to Daniel Burton, New York, January 30, 1770, in S. P. G. MSS. (L. C. Trans.), B2, No. 35; see also ibid., August 16, 1770, B2, No. 37.   Mr. Auchmuty said his and his assistant's duties were too numerous to include the instruction of the Negroes.*

[123]*Ibid., April 25, 1771, B2, No. 39.*

[124]*Samuel Auchmuty to Daniel Burton, New York, April 25, 1771, in S. P. G. MSS. (L. C. Trans.), B2, No. 39; Journal of S. P. G. (L. C. Trans.), XIX, July 19, 1771.*

the post Communion Prayers, general thanksgiving, and *singing* a Psalm.[125]

In 1773, Hildreth's catechumens numbered about 100, who attended the schoolroom on Sunday evenings and behaved "with utmost decency and attention." He, like his predecessor, formed two classes, one to learn Lewis' *Exposition* and the other the Church catechism. He usually read one of Archbishop Secker's lectures to the Negroes and concluded with prayers and the singing of a psalm.[126] The catechumens, he felt, were sincere Christians, but, by 1776, his catechumens were diminishing, due of course to the upheaval of the American Revolution. He told sadly of the shutting of the Church after the Declaration of Independence, of the Loyalists leaving the city to prevent their arrest, and the burning of part of the city causing the loss of ". . . our ancient, beautiful Parish Church, the Parsonage, and schoolhouse. So rapid and violent were the flames that nothing could be saved out of either."[127] To New York City, as to other parts of the colonies, ideas and institutions had come and adapted themselves, so that the War, with its destructive effects, produced merely temporary interruptions in Negro Christianization and education.

II. In Towns and Rural Areas

Turning now to towns and rural areas and their beginnings earlier in the century, it is to be remembered that the Society was giving close attention to Negro education outside of New York City. Missionary and schoolmaster were active in the smaller communities of the colony. As early as 1722, Mr. Charles Taylor, of Richmond County, wrote to the Society,

> I presume by these to inform you that I have kept school last year in the south precinct of this county and taught 48 scholars and 6 negros. The most of them I teach to write and cipher. I teach all of them the Church catechism with the explanation thereof and to bear a part in the public worship. I have taught several of them upon account of the venerable Society's bounty without any other consideration and upon the same account I keep night school for teaching of negros and of such as cannot be spared from their work in the daytime.

[125]*Joseph Hildreth to Daniel Burton, New York, October 17, 1772, in S. P. G. MSS. (L. C. Trans.), B3, No. 168; Journal of S. P. G. (L. C. Trans.), XIX, December 18, 1772.*
[126]*Joseph Hildreth to Richard Hind, New York, November 7, 1773, in S. P. G. MSS. (L. C. Trans.), B3, No. 169.*
[127]*Joseph Hildreth to Richard Hind, New York, October 6, 1776, in S. P. G. MSS. (L. C. Trans.), B3, No. 171.*

Therefore I make bold to draw for 15 £ sterling as the bounty which the venerable Society is pleased now yearly to bestow for instructing of the poor youth upon this island.[128]

Throughout the century, specific instructions were sent to the missionaries, as to the education of the Negroes, of which a letter written by Secretary David Humphreys, on July 30, 1725, is a forceful example,

It has been intimated to the Society that proper care hath not been taken to instruct in the Christian religion and baptize the negroes in the plantations in America. The Society being desirous so good a work should be promoted as far as possible by them, and apprehending that their missionaries may have some negroes themselves, have directed me to acquaint them, that they do require all their missionaries who have any negroes or other slaves of their own to instruct them in the principles of the Christian religion and to baptize them as soon as they are sufficiently instructed and are willing to receive baptism. You will please, sir, to take notice of this particular direction of the Society and also encourage and advise your parishioners who may have negroes to let them be instructed and baptized. The Society have reprinted a sermon preached before them on this head, some copies of which you will receive herewith to be distributed among your parishioners.[129]

The New York missionaries, as did those in the other colonies, noted and made careful replies as to the condition in their respective parishes. And besides, they were often convinced that the Society did not understand the obstacles of Christianizing Negroes in slavery. The Rev. John Bartow analyzed his situation in Westchester clearly, saying,

. . . return the Society my humble thanks [for books sent] begging leave to answer that I cannot be very zealous to baptize slaves because I know they will not or cannot live up to the Christian covenant in one notorious instant at least, viz. matrimony, for they marry after their heathen way and divorce and take others as often as they please, and Christian baptism cannot [be consistent] with adultery, and should we marry them I fear they would do the same unless there were a law

[128]Charles Taylor to David Humphreys, Richmond county, New York, March 8, 1722, in S. P. G. MSS. (L. C. Trans.), A16, pp. 216-217; see also ibid., A17, p. 220. The statements made in this letter were certified by the minister in the county.

[129]David Humphreys to all missionaries, London, July 30, 1725, in S. P. G. MSS. (L. C. Trans.), A19, p. 113. A comprehensive analysis of the humanitarian and other ideas contained in the Annual Sermons preached before the Society is presented at length in Chapter I and elsewhere. The Sermon was often printed with the Abstracts of Proceedings for the previous year, and, an almost complete file of these valuable works beginning in 1701, can be found in the Huntington Library, and the Library of Congress.

to restrain. But against our marrying them the masters will
object and say it is not lawful to part man and wife, and
how can we sell one of them? This will be a hard obligation upon us to sell both to our detriment. I never knew but
one couple that were married by the Society's missionary,
Mr. Brooks, and afterwards their master George Willocks
of Amboy, had occasion to sell one and because he would not
part man and wife, he sent both to be sold at York, and soon
after the man ran away and forever foresook his wife.

My negro man who was baptized by me and can read
English had got a trick of marrying slaves with the office in
the Common Prayer Book, and I forbade him because it was
a desecration of the Holy rite. This shows that they are ambitious of being as free, but I fear their freedom would be
unsafe and dangerous as well as very chargeable to the inhabitants.

I do assure the Society I have been and am willing and
ready to baptise such slaves as confess the faith and desire
baptism as also instruct and inform any that come to me, but
to follow them about my parish I have neither will nor ability.
Our Churches are open in time of Divine Service and no pro-
hibition to them to come in. . . .[130]

The Rev. William Vesey acknowledged the frequent instructions
from the Society and with other missionaries stated that he heartily
wished the masters would comply with the Society's pious designs as
regards the Negroes, but a great many Negroes in New York never
even came near the catechist or missionaries, although they pursued
their offices with the utmost care and diligence.[131]

One of the most penetrating letters again analyzing the problem
of Negro Christianization from the standpoint of the Anglican, was
written by the Rev. Robert Jenney,[132] stationed at Rye and Hempstead.
It is worth quoting at length, as illustrative of the careful details furnished in the reports:

It has always been my practice to use all proper motives
I can think of, to bring my own negro slaves to a regular
practice of the moral duties, in which most of their colour
are very loose, but without which I cannot conceive that they
have any title to Church membership, nor consequently to bap-

130John Bartow to David Humphreys, Westchester, November 15, 1725, in
S. P. G. MSS. (L. C. Trans.), B1, No. 81. See also H. T. Catterall, (Ed.), Judicial Cases Concerning American Slavery and the Negro, Indices, see "Christianization."
131William Vesey to David Humphreys, New York, November 18, 1725, in
S. P. G. MSS. (L. C. Trans.), B1 No. 79.
132Robert Jenney later became the bishop of London's commissary in Pennsylvania and rector of Christ Church, Philadelphia. He had been an S. P. G.
missionary in Philadelphia before coming to New York. Mr. Jenney died on
January 5, 1762.

tism.   My negroes are two adults and one child; of which
adults one is a young man, the other a woman, mother to the
child.   Her husband lives in the city of New York by whom
she has had four children, of which only one lives now.   These
I oblige constantly to be present at our family devotion; and
the two adults to attend public service of the Church by turns,
and to take the child along with them, as often as the weather
is sufficiently moderate for her tender age to bear.   This I do try
whether good influence our own and the practice of others will
have upon them, to bring them not only to the knowledge,
but also the practise of religious duties.   But all this together
with my private instruction in the family, have not had so
good success as to influence me to give them the benefit of
baptism as yet, but as to the children of unbelieving parents,
I have always been of opinion that they ought to be baptized,
provided their masters and mistresses will engage for them,
which is my practice in my family.   My negro woman's first
child was baptized by Mr. Poyer and died about seven months
after; the second and fourth died suddenly when I was from
home so as to prevent their being baptised.   The surviving one
it was always and is yet my design to have baptised, whenso-
ever any clergyman passes this way; for because my wife and
I stand sureties, I think it not so regular to perform the office myself.

I am so particular in relation to my own family that the
Venerable Society may be satisfied, that I have not been altogether negligent in my duty in this particular, which gives me
the satisfaction to believe that, whosoever the informer may
be, he had no eye to me in his information against the missionaries of the neglect of their duty to instruct and baptise
their negro and Indian slaves.

As to my parish, there are very few slaves in it, and the
people generally so poor that they are not able to purchase
any; and amongst the few that we have, I know of no more
than two (both men) that are baptized; one an old man belonging to the estate of Coll. Heathcote, deceased; the other a
middle aged man belonging to a miller [may be Miller] in this
town, both of them sober, honest men, who as far as I can
learn do live up to their profession.   In those that have negroes I find little or no disposition to have them baptized;
but on the contrary an aversion to it, in some, and in most
an indifference.   Some are so profane as to say that they do
not think that baptism will be of any service to them, and there
are many that think it does them hurt by giving them better
notions of themselves than is consistent with their state of
slavery and their duty to their masters.   And not withstanding
the unreasonableness of this notion, yet all that I or any man
can say against it will not prevail upon them to remit anything of their obstinacy in defending an opinion which they
think can be evidently proven by experience.   And this af-

fair is still the harder to be managed, because our best people have either no slave at all, or not above one or two at the most. Those therefore with whom I am generally to treat upon this subject having (if any) a very superficial sense of the obligation to religious duties, are not easily influenced by arguments drawn from religious topics.

But after all, as no negroes or other slaves have offered themselves for baptism since I have been engaged in this parish, yet if any should, I cannot but profess that I find myself entangled in two considerable difficulties; the first relating to their sureties; there are scarce any masters or mistresses, if they are willing that their slaves be baptised, that will be prevailed with to engage for them as their sureties, much less will Christian freeman engage for slaves and whether or not it would be proper to accept of those who are not masters of themselves as sureties for others I leave to the determination of my superiors, for my part I cannot but help thinking it improper, though I confess it is practiced in these parts, so that we the ministers are entangled in this inevitable dilemma; either we must refuse baptism to slaves that deserve it; and this is uncharitable, or accept the surety of slaves for slaves, which most of us think improper.

The other difficulty relates to their marriages, arising from their irregularities therein, and some circumstances which make it almost impossible that they can be joined together till death parts them. Their irregularities arise from an opinion, almost natural to them, that they can change their wives upon every disgust. And if any of them are weaned from that wicked custom, yet it is not marrying free from difficulties and inconveniences, whether they are both in the same or different families. If Christian persons live together as man and wife without marriage, they live in fornication, and if they are married they must not be parted, for whom God hath joined together let No man put assunder. Hence it will follow that if both parties are in the same family the Master lies under an obligation either to keep both or sell both, let his necessities be ever so pressing, which often obliges men to sell one when the other cannot be spared. And if they are in different families (as is most usual) then the removal of one of the family to a different part of the country at some considerable distance is a parting of man and wife. This is the case with my negro woman, and I find it a very difficult thing, almost impossible, to keep them faithful at any considerable distance from one another.[133]

[133]Robert Jenney to David Humphreys, Rye, November 19, 1725, in S. P. G. MSS. (L. C. Trans.), B1, No. 78. As Mrs. Catterall pointed out in her volumes, marriage under slavery, at least in its early stages, could not take place legally, and the judicial complexities that arose were almost infinite in their variety. While the S. P. G. worked for baptism and communion as first objectives, the other sacraments would eventually follow, including that of marriage. In short, Christianization was a many headed enemy of slavery. One opinion given by Mrs.

Jenney concludes by saying that he does not mention these difficulties as reasons or excuses for his small success in coping with the problem but that the Society might note the facts and advise him.

When Mr. Jenney was transferred to Hempstead, his new parish contained many Negroes.[134]   In May, 1727, he reported the baptism of one Negro infant, owned by himself, and the admittance of a Negro slave to communion.[135]   Yet Mr. Jenney found the Negroes so scattered that it was all but impossible to instruct them.   At Oyster Bay, where he preached every third Sunday, he recommended the appointment of Mr. Daniel Denton as schoolmaster.[136]   The latter reported within a year that he had taught three Negroes to read and repeat the Church catechism.[137]

A further rapid roll of other centers of Negro work, outside of New York City, shows that S. P. G. determination and methods of procedure were yielding results, whatever the obstacles.   Each parish is to be regarded as an experiment station in which tests of the Negro's ability and willingness to learn to read, write, and understand the fundamentals of Christian practice were made; the cooperation of the masters was to be gained, as well as that of other leaders of opinion; all were witness to the fact that the Negro had won the right to religious instruction. The reports went back to London where the trustees of the Society were themselves receiving a liberal education through this research into

Catterall must suffice, IV, 46-47, December, 1767, from the Maryland records: "I adopt the rule of the civil law . . . that slaves are incapable of marriage, . . . slaves are bound by our animal laws generally, yet we do not consider them as objects of such laws as relate to the commerce between the sexes. A slave has never maintained an action against the violator of his bed. A slave is not admonished for incontinence, or punished for fornication or adultery; never prosecuted for bigamy or petty treason, for killing a husband, being a slave. . . . In consequence of my opinion, that slaves are incapable of civil marriage, I consider A. and C. in the light of bastards, and therefore conclude that the lands of A. are escheatable, . . . A. and C. had no civil capacities to take by purchase, or to take or transmit by descent, whilst in their original state of slavery." When gradual emancipation became the policy of the British Anti-Slavery party and of the British government in 1823 and 1824, the legalization and protection of marriage and the prevention, in the sale of slaves, of the separation of husband and wife, and of infant children from the mother, were adopted as a program. See Frank J. Klingberg, The Anti-Slavery Movement in England (New Haven, 1926), pp. 213-214.

[134]*The number of Negroes and slaves totaled 116 men, 76 women, 76 boys, and 51 girls. And in Oyster Bay, where Mr. Jenney preached off and on, there were 41 men, 27 women, 17 boys, and 26 girls. See Robert Jenney to David Humphreys, Hempsted, June 27, 1728, in S. P. G. MSS. (L. C. Trans.), A21, p. 343.*

[135]*Robert Jenney to David Humphreys, Hempsted, May 1, 1727, in S. P. G. MSS. (L. C. Trans.), A20, p. 183. The slave had been baptized years before by Mr. Thomas and had all along been known for piety and honesty.*

[136]*Robert Jenney to [Secretary], Hempsted, July 21, 1726, in Journal of S. P. G. (L. C. Trans.), V, September 16, 1726. Mr. Denton's salary was £10 per year.*

[137]*Daniel Denton to David Humphreys, Oyster Bay, October 17, 1728, in S. P. G. MSS. (L. C. Trans.), A21, p. 363.*

the problems of and results from this directed contact with "native peoples."

Another worker, the Rev. Thomas Standard, of Brookhaven, Long Island, was as discouraged by the difficulties of Negro instruction under slavery as was Mr. Jenney. He replied, too, to David Humphrey's exhortation that the masters were adverse to education of any kind, largely on account of the insurrection which occurred 14 years before in New York City in 1712.[138] Furthermore, he stated, he

> . . . had almost forgot one thing which however is of great moment in this case, and it is this, that few of them are capable of being instructed. I have now two negroes . . . one of which is a girl of about nine years . . . whom I have had above a twelve month, and have during that time several times attempted to teach her to read, but cannot yet make her to know her alphabet, nor have all the endeavours hitherto used with her, which have not been inconsiderable, been sufficient to make her to number ten, tho' she was born in this country. Nor can a fellow that is at least 20 whom I have lately bought, tho' he hath been seven years in this country count up that number. . . .
>
> I have in obedience . . . publicly exhorted those that have negroes to instruct them . . . and have offered my assistance therein, but . . . with little success.[139]

Statements from other parishes regarding Negro instruction were more encouraging. In 1733, the schoolmaster at Oyster Bay, Thomas Keble, reported thirty scholars, four of whom were Negroes, another instance of teaching white and black together. Mr. Keble taught the Negroes without pay, because they were poor. The schoolmaster wrote ". . . I think I answer best the Honourable Society's design, if I have a regard to those who are not able to pay me."[140] In the following year, Mr. Keble's school increased to thirty-one children. The curriculum included reading, writing, arithmetic, and the Church Catechism.[141] He taught the poor whites gratis, his school flourished,

[138]*Thomas Standard to David Humphreys, Brookhaven, Long Island, October, 1726, in S. P. G. MSS. (L. C. Trans.), A19, pp. 404-405. This letter in good part repeats the points in Jenney's letter (Nov. 19, 1725), which states the difficulties encountered in Negro conversion.*
[139]*Thomas Standard to David Humphreys, W. Chester, New York, November 5, 1729, in S. P. G. MSS. (L. C. Trans.), B1, No. 50.*
[140]*Thomas Keble to David Humphreys, Oyster Bay, November 5, 1733, in S. P. G. MSS. (L. C. Trans.), B1, No. 10; Journal of S. P. G. (L. C. Trans.), VI, February 15, 1733/[1734].*
[141]*Thomas Keble to David Humphreys, Oyster Bay, November 5, 1734, in S. P. G. MSS. (L. C. Trans.), A25, p. 39; Journal of S. P. G. (L. C. Trans.), VI, January 17, 1734/[1735].*

with an enrollment of thirty-seven[142] in 1735, at which level it remained during the next decade. The Negro enrollments, however, were small.[143]

Another schoolmaster, Mr. Edward Davies of Southampton, on the island of Nassau, mentioned that he was teaching all the Negroes and Indians that were "inclinable to come." He taught at night because the masters kept the slaves at work during the day.[144] His difficulties were recounted in a letter of November 12, 1734,

> The number of negroes and Indians I instructed last winter from October to the middle of March were from ten to twenty, and some times more, as they could spare them, and as the weather would admit, they living a great distance from the school. (Please to note) I am obliged to teach them in the night, that is from sunset to nine o'clock in the night, they being confined all the day to their labour. Neither can they come any other time in the year, but in the winter, their Masters confining them close to labour.
>
> I have with a great deal of difficulty and pains, learned some to spell, some to read, and some to write. Most are grown to mens years. I am now preparing to instruct them, this winter, and hope to make . . . a greater progress than last, they having some notion of their books now, but the last year very few of them knew anything.[145]

Another worker, the Rev. William Harrison, missionary at Staten Island, taught the Negroes after the Sunday service, along with this other work, and baptized, in November, 1735, two adult Negroes and three Negro children.[146]

In comparing the Negro's capacity with other immigration groups, and considering his status as a slave, and the illiteracy of the age among white men in the colonies and in England, the response of the

[142]Thomas Keble to [Secretary], Oyster Bay, New York, November 24, 1735, in Journal of S. P. G. (L. C. Trans.), VII, April 16, 1736.

[143]Thomas Keble to [Philip Bearcroft], Oyster Bay, June 23, 1744, in S. P. G. MSS. (L. C. Trans.), B13, p. 322; Journal of S. P. G. (L. C. Trans.), IX, January 18, 1744/1745.

[144]Edward Davies to David Humphreys, Southampton, November 6, 1733, in S. P. G. MSS. (L. C. Trans.), B1, No. 9. Mr. Davies requested stitched catechisms, Lewis's exposition of the catechism, and Dyche's spelling books.

[145]Edward Davies to David Humphreys, Southton, [sic], New York, November 12, 1734, in S. P. G. MSS. (L. C. Trans.), A25, p. 49; see also the certificate of Mr. Davies' teaching in A25, p. 77.

[146]William Harrison to [Secretary], Staten Island, November 20, 1735, in Journal of S. P. G. (L. C. Trans.), VII, April 16, 1736.

slaves is surprising.[147]   In 1742, this parish of Staten Island had a population of about 1,540 whites and 349 Negroes.[148]   Mr. Harrison's successor, the Rev. Jonathan Arnold, baptized between four and ten Negroes annually.[149]   A Mr. Charles Taylor aided him as a schoolmaster, giving instruction to Negroes and whites in the same school.[150] Mr. Arnold, in turn, was succeeded by the Rev. Richard Charlton, who remained in this mission for thirty years, from 1747 to 1777.   An enthusiastic worker, in his first letter he reported the baptism of nine infant and six adult Negroes, in addition to accepting two communicants.[151]   About two years later, in September, 1749, he reported the baptism of five Negro children, the regular examination of twenty Negro catechumens immediately after prayers on Sundays, followed by a catechetical lecture on Sunday afternoons.   Here, as elsewhere, when given a fair chance, the slaves learned rapidly.   Many of them could repeat the Catechism from memory, and some could give a "tolerable exposition" of several of its parts.[152]   During the winter, however, Mr. Charlton was obliged to discontinue his instruction on account of bad weather, bad roads, and long distances, which kept the Negroes away. The schoolteacher, however, Mr. Nicholas Barrington, instructed those

[147]*Two studies on Negro education may be of comparative value, one of which was the Codrington enterprise of the S. P. G. in Barbados, a pioneering Protestant experiment, beginning in 1710 and carried on into our own time; and the other, an interdenominational activity based on The Lady Mico Charity. See two articles by Frank J. Klingberg, "British Humanitarianism at Codrington" in Journal of Negro History, XXIII, No. 4, October, 1938, pp. 451-486, and "The Lady Mico' Charity Schools in the British West Indies, 1835-1842" in ibid., XXIV, No. 3, July, 1939, pp. 291-344.   See also M. G. Jones, The Charity School Movement; A Study of Eighteenth Century Puritanism in Action, Cambridge, England, The University Press, 446 pp., 1938.*

[148]*Jonathan Arnold to Philip Bearcroft, Staten Island, June 18, 1742, in S. P. G. MSS. (L. C. Trans.), B10, No. 81; Journal of S. P. G. (L. C. Trans.), IX, December 17, 1742.*

[149]*In November, 1742, Arnold reported the baptism of six Negroes; in July, 1743, ten Negroes were baptized; November, 1743, two more were baptized, and in 1744, the same number is recorded. See letters of Jonathan Arnold to Secretary, Staten Island, November 10, 1742, in Journal of S. P. G. (L. C. Trans.), IX, April 15, 1745; ibid., July 19, 1743, in IX, October 21, 1743, in IX, October 21, 1743; ibid., November 1, 1743, in IX, May 18, 1744; ibid., March 25, 1743/44, in IX, September 21, 1744; S. P. G. MSS. (L. C. Trans.), B11, Nos. 148, 149, and B13, p. 304.*

[150]*Charles Taylor passed away on May 27, 1742, and was succeeded by Mr. Andrew Wright, see Petition of the Minister, Church Wardens, & Vestrymen of St. Andrew's Parish to the Society, Staten Island, New York, June 5, 1742, in S. P. G. MSS. (L. C. Trans.), B10, No. 83. For the work of Taylor in Richmond County see S. P. G. MSS. (L. C. Trans.), B3, Pt. II, p. 150.*

[151]*Richard Charlton to Philip Bearcroft, New York, March 26, 1747, in S. P. G. MSS. (L. C. Trans.), B15, fo. 77 (duplicate); Journal of S. P. G. (L. C. Trans.), X, August 21, 1747.*

[152]*Richard Charlton to [Secretary], Staten Island, September 30, 1749, in Journal of S. P. G. (L. C. Trans.), December 15, 1749.*

Negroes who could go to his home, so that those receiving instruction varied from about nine to twenty according to the season.[153]

Mr. Charlton's methods of religious instruction and the resultant success brought constant and uniform results. On Sundays in spring and summer he examined two groups of catechumens, one out of Lewis's *Exposition of the Church Catechism* in the presence of the congregation immediately after the sermon in the forenoon, and the other in the afternoon, combining the Negroes and whites, to whom he gave a lecture.[154]   In September, 1751, he wrote to the Secretary,

> I have great satisfaction in informing the Venerable Society that my catechumens improve in spiritual knowledge, and I find that amongst others, who do not answer, their serious behavior has produced most happy effects, a spirit of devotion prevailing in general amongst them.
>
> My negro catechumens have exceeded my expectation: and unless God had been pleased in an extraordinary manner to bless our endeavors, I could not have hoped for so plentiful an harvest.
>
> Since my last I have admitted three of 'em, after full instruction, to baptism, and have several more who now stand candidates for that Holy Ordinance.[155]

Mr. Charlton found that the plain explanation of the Catechism which he gave the Negroes suited the uncultivated minds of some whites.[156]   The Society's work among white colonists cannot be entered upon here, but it may be stated, in passing, that illiteracy was the common lot of many poor people both in Great Britain and the United States until well into the nineteenth century. At times smallpox crippled Charlton's activities.[157]   In 1760, there were 300 cases on the Island, among them, Mr. Price, the schoolmaster.[158]   Mr. Charlton reported that,

[153]*Richard Charlton to [Secretary], Staten Island, March 26, 1750, in S. P. G. MSS. (L. C. Trans.), B18, No. 115; Journal of S. P. G. (L. C. Trans.), XI, July 20, 1750; Nicholas Barrington to [Secretary], Staten Island, New York, March 26, 1750, in Journal of S. P. G. (L. C. Trans.), XI, September 21, 1750. In 1752, the number of Negroes remained the same, see Barrington to Philip Bearcroft, Staten Island, March 31, 1752, in S. P. G. MSS. (L. C. Trans.), B20, No. 72; Journal of S. P. G. (L. C. Trans.), October 20, 1752.*

[154]*Richard Charlton to [Philip Bearcroft], Staten Island, September 30, 1750, in S. P. G. MSS. (L. C. Trans.), B18, No. 116; Journal of S. P. G. (L. C. Trans.), XI, February 15, 1750/1751.*

[155]*Richard Charlton to Philip Bearcroft, Staten Island, September 30, 1751, in S. P. G. MSS. (L. C. Trans.), B19, No. 86.*

[156]*Richard Charlton to [Secretary], Staten Island, New York, October 11, 1753, in Journal of S. P. G. (L. C. Trans.), XII, January 18, 1754.*

[157]*In the judgment of Mr. Charlton long interruptions were unfortunate, as many of the Negroes had poor memories and forgot from month to month.*

[158]*Richard Charlton to Philip Bearcroft, Staten Island, April 10, 1760, in S. P. G. MSS. (L. C. Trans.), B3, No. 60. Almost every inhabitant had been ill, this of course thinned his congregation.*

Since my last of the 10th April, we have, the 13th ultimo, lost the inoffensive and diligent Mr. Price. The want of his assistance for the present season will be a sensible loss to my catechumens, especially the negros, whose improvements in psalmody must meet with a considerable check and what is yet worse, I have it not in my power to pitch upon one of suitable morals and capacity, that I can recommend to the venerable Society as his successor. I have used my best endeavors to find out John Watts, lately a schoolmaster of good behavior and knowledge in psalmody in this island, whom necessity has drove to go as clerk to a sutler towards Oswego. Were I sure of the honorable Society's appointment and his acceptance, I should not doubt, with God's assistance, of success in the blessed work I have in hand. . . .

I humbly hope, considering circumstances, that my request will not be deemed improper by that Venerable body, which is, that they will be pleased to grant me leave to pitch upon a person to succeed Mr. Price as their schoolmaster in this island.[159]

Even with an increase in salary, the new teacher was hard to find and to keep. A present day note was struck when Charlton wrote, ". . . it must be a great misfortune to the employed that when the expenses of living increase, salaries do not on proportion rise."[160] No sooner had Mr. Watts been appointed than the Society received the following news from Charlton,

Did you truely know my situation I am convinced you would pity me. I have, blessed be God, a prospect of doing good; but alas! I am not equal to the task. Mr. Watts whom I recommended to succeed Mr. Price, and with whose assistance I formed the pleasing hopes of the desired success, has deserted me and now my catechumens must suffer not only in the part preparative to my instruction, but in the psalmody also, a part I cannot come up to. I have requested the worthy president of our college, Dr. Johnson, in his tour to New England to make inquiry for a proper person, and I hope he may be able to effect what is not in my power to obtain.[161]

[159]*Richard Charlton to Philip Bearcroft, Staten Island, June 21, 1760, in S. P. G. MSS. (L. C. Trans.), B3, No. 61; Journal of S. P. G. (L. C. Trans.), XV, November 21, 1760.*
[160]*Richard Charlton to Philip Bearcroft, Staten Island, December 13, 1760, in S. P. G. MSS. (L. C. Trans.), B3, No. 62. The salary was increased £5 per year, see Journal of S. P. G. (L. C. Trans.), XV, February 19, 1762.*
[161]*Richard Charlton to Philip Bearcroft, Staten Island, April 2, 1761, in S. P. G. MSS. (L. C. Trans.), B3, No. 63. Dr. Samuel Johnson (1696-1772) had been a missionary for the Society at Stratford, Connecticut, for 32 years (1723-1754) prior to taking up his duties as president of King's College (later Columbia University). Dr. Johnson was a close friend of Dean Berkeley, the English idealist philosopher, and spread the Berkeleian theories throughout the New England colonies. At the same time, Johnson was leading the Church of England*

In 1763, after a two year vacancy and much searching for the proper person, a Mr. Tunis Egberts[162] was appointed, a man of character and the necessary musical ability. He continued with Mr. Charlton for over ten years. Ten years later, Mr. Charlton explained that he encouraged competition and had succeeded in producing "a noble emulation among his Catechumens." He had prevailed upon five men and five women to read an epistle out of the prayer book after services. Many of his congregation could not read and he strove to teach the rising generation in this manner. In order to interest them, the best performers were to be rewarded with prayer books, and he asked the Society for more books.[163] Mr. Tunis Egberts, in 1765, wrote to Daniel Burton,

> My earnest endeavor is a conscientious discharge of my duty. Every Sunday afternoon when church is over, I teach a number of the Rev. Mr. Charlton's catechumens to sing psalms and do my best to prepare them for his lectures. I hope, as he told me he would shortly write that he will so acquaint the honorable Society of my diligency.[164]

An important parish in New York was Hempstead. Here, in 1725, the Rev. Robert Jenney, formerly stationed at Rye, began to work. In 1731, he reported the baptism of nine Negroes, five children and four adults.[165] The usual requests for religious aids followed. Jenney wanted prayer books for the Negroes as well as the whites, for many Negroes in his parish could read, use them in divine service.[166] Mr. Jenney's baptisms of Negroes averaged two or three annually from 1735 to 1739. In 1740 ten baptisms of Negro children set a record.[167]

Thomas Temple, the schoolmaster at Hempstead, began his work

movement in the northern colonies; he desired to see bishops in the colonies, and took active part in the agitation. See F. B. Chandler, The Life of Samuel Johnson (1805); E. E. Beardsley, Life and Correspondence of Samuel Johnson (1874), and Herbert and Carol Schneider, Samuel Johnson, President of King's College: His Career and Writing (4 volumes; 1929).

[162]*See a petition of the parishioners to Charlton, April 15, 1763, in S. P. G. MSS. (L. C. Trans.), B3, No. 72; also B3, No. 70.*

[163]*Richard Charlton to [Secretary], Staten Island, New York, October 15, 1773, in Journal of S. P. G. (L. C. Trans.), XX, December 17, 1773.*

[164]*Tunis Egberts to Daniel Burton, Staten Island, April 2, 1765, in S. P. G. MSS. (L. C. Trans.), B3, No. 77.*

[165]*Robert Jenney to [Secretary], Hempsted, Long Island, July 10, 1731, in Journal of S. P. G. (L. C. Trans.), V, December 17, 1731; S. P. G. MSS. (L. C. Trans.), A23, p. 334. Mr. Jenney enclosed in this letter a letter from the people of Oyster Bay, complaining that Mr. Denton, the schoolmaster there, kept a tavern and brewhouse instead of teaching school.. Denton was removed.*

[166]*Robert Jenney to [Secretary], Hempsted, July 30, 1735, in Journal of S. P. G. (L. C. Trans.), VII, April 16, 1736.*

[167]*Robert Jenney to [Secretary], Hempsted, April 21, 1740, in S. P. G. MSS. (L. C. Trans.), B7, Pt. II, p. 121; Journal of S. P. G. (L. C. Trans.), VIII, September 19, 1740.*

in June, 1741, and, during that summer, he had twenty-six pupils, including four Negroes.[168]   Mr. Temple, in his report to the Society, inadvertently emphasized the difficulty of securing well-trained teachers,

> . . . this Last Winter At Night School I Taught four Negroes men and one Indian boy with Some others to the the [sic] Number of Ten and this Spring I have Done My Endiver to Seek out for those Children that theire parients are Very poor which I teach Six and Two Negroes Children and One Man and my Number in all his Twenty but I Expect More for they Come daily and Still as it tis my daily prayers for that honorable body of C[harity] humbly begging your prayers that God would give me wisdom and knowledged that I May teach Those which are Committed to my [task] to know god and Jesus Christ one thing more I Crave and that his that I may have the Benefit of the late Bishop fleetwood Sarmon preached in the Year 1711 Concerning ye Instructon of Negroes and the present Lord Bishop of London Sermon in the Year 1727 for they are Some here that say that a Negro hath no soul and I shall take abundance of pains to read them amongst them and theire is some Negroe that would learn their Catechism and I did get them from the Rev. Mr. Charlton and I have Distri[buted] of them Abroad among them.[169]

During the two following years, 1743,[170] and 1744, Temple taught none "but of poor white children."[171]

In 1742, during Mr. Temple's tenure as schoolmaster, the Rev. Samuel Seabury, Senior, was appointed missionary at Hempstead. He reported several Negro baptisms, two, in March, 1744; four adults, in October, 1744; five children, in March, 1746; one in September of the same year.[172]   Seabury asked for copies of the "Reasonable Communicant," common prayer books, and catechisms with questions and

[168]*Thomas Temple to Philip Bearcroft, Hempsted, December 14, 1741, in S. P. G. MSS. (L. C. Trans.), B10, No. 90. He also had taught one Indian to read his Testament.*

[169]*Thomas Temple to [Philip Bearcroft], Hempsted, May 17, 1742, in S. P. G. MSS. (L. C. Trans.), B10, No. 91; Journal of S. P. G. (L. C. Trans.), IX, September 17, 1742; William Fleetwood (Bishop of St. Asaph), Sermon preached before S. P. G. in St. Mary Le Bow, February, 1711, pp. 1-34. (Huntington Library.) This Sermon was preached to urge further conversion of Negro slaves. Bishop Fleetwood refuted at length the then common belief that baptism would make slaves free, and states, p. 21, "If therefore it be lawful in our Country, to have or keep any slave at all, it is equally lawful to have or keep them so, tho they are Christians." See Chapter I and Book II.*

[170]*Thomas Temple to [Philip Bearcroft], Hempsted, Long Island, January 1, 1743, in S. P. G. MSS. (L. C. Trans.), B13, p. 244.*

[171]*Ibid., June 16, 1774, in B13, p. 246.*

[172]*See letters of Samuel Seabury to Secretary, Hempsted, March 25, 1743/1744 in Journal of S. P. G. (L. C. Trans.), IX, September 21, 1744; October 15, 1744, in X, April 19, 1745; March 26, 1745/46, in XII, October 17, 1746; September 3, 1746, in X, March 20, 1746/47; also S. P. G. MSS. (L. C. Trans.), B13, p. 237, and B14, p. 132.*

answers, which he thought would be of great use in the instruction of the Negroes. Negro baptisms were made at Hempstead up to the time of the elder Seabury's death in 1764.[173] His church grew in the presence of many enemies—sectaries and infidels. Originally in charge of Huntington, ten miles from Hempstead, he later gave that work to his son, Samuel Seabury (later Bishop Seabury) whom the Society appointed as catechist with a salary of £10 per year.[174] After Seabury's death, the Hempstead mission was placed in the care of the Rev. Leonard Cutting, who continued the Negro work.[175]

As a foundation for discussion and the formation of opinion, it mattered little whether few or many slaves were in the class for instruction. The practice was for the missionary, on entering upon his duties, to invite the masters and mistresses of plantations to send their slaves to him for instruction, to include his own, if he had slaves, to furnish the masters with letters of instruction from the Society, and other literature. It might be said that the missionary publicly featured the progress of the slave in catechism before the congregation. This quiet routine set people thinking. Sources of opposition to slavery developed sufficient strength so that in the decades after the Revolution, the general view that slavery was an evil came to be the attitude of the better planters, even in the South.[176]

Again returning to an earlier time to survey the Society's Negro work at Rye, in 1726, the Rev. James Wetmore found one hundred Negroes in that parish, with the usual encouragement from London and discouragement from the masters.[177]   In this parish, the slaves

[173]*One Negro adult was baptized in 1748, two children in 1750, and another adult in 1753. See Samuel Seabury to Secretary, Hempsted, [December, 1748] in Journal of S. P. G. (L. C. Trans.), XI, February 17, 1748/1749; April 18, 1753, in XII, September 21, 1753; see also S. P. G. MSS. (L. C. Trans.), B18, Nos. 112, 113.*

[174]*Samuel Seabury to [Secretary], Hempsted, September 30, 1748, in Journal of S. P. G. (L. C. Trans.), XI, February 17, 1748/1749.*

[175]*Leonard Cutting's baptisms were: one adult in 1768, two, in 1771, one, in 1774, one in 1776, one child and one adult woman, in 1777. See Leonard Cutting to Secretary, Hempsted, December 28, 1768, in S. P. G. MSS. (L. C. Trans.), B2, No. 144; January 5, 1771, in B2, No. 147; January 8, 1774, in B2, No. 149; January 9, 1777, in B2, No. 150; January 6, 1777, in B2, No. 152.*

[176]*Religious cooperation in reform activities was of course never broken. Many examples are found in A. H. Abel and F. J. Klingberg (Eds.) A Side-Light on Anglo-American Relations, 1839-1858 (1927).*

[177]*The Bishops, in their annual Sermons before the Society, were constantly asking for the support of Negro work in the colonies. The Lord Bishop of Oxford, Thomas Secker, in his Sermon preached before the S. P. G. in St. Mary-le-Bow, February 20, 1741, (London, 1741), (Huntington Library), pointed out the necessity for Negro instruction, and added a reprimand to the masters of slaves, p. 8, "For it is not to be expected that Masters, too commonly negligent of Christianity themselves, will take much Pains to teach it to their Slaves: whom even the better Part of them are in a great measure habituated to consider as they do their Cattle, merely with a view to the Profit ensuing from them." Chapter I and Book II.*

that belonged to Quaker masters were not allowed any instruction. Some Presbyterians would allow their servants to be taught, but were unwilling they should be baptised. "And those of the church are not much better, so that there is but one negro in the parish baptized."[178] In 1729, for example, the baptism of two Negro children[179] and one Negro slave was reported by Wetmore and four Negroes were under instruction.[180]

In 1733, Mr. Wetmore requested the Society to appoint Mr. Flint Dwight catechist for the parish of Rye, with liberty to teach school in such parts of the parish where he should find the prospect of doing service, and that he be ordered ". . . to take particular pains in instructing and catechizing the negroes as well as the white children."[181] Mr. Dwight taught both white and Negro children after evening service with lessons from the Creed, Lord's Prayer, and Ten Commandments, and such other instruction as he was "capable of giving and they of receiving."[182]   Together Wetmore and Dwight, as the *Notitia Parochialis* shows, prepared from two to four Negroes for baptism in some years and at times as many as eight or ten, successes showing that the Christianization of the Negro was duly in process, in miniature but impressive form, before the eyes of the parish.   Mr. Wetmore often complained of the difficulty of getting exact information for his *Notitia Parochialis*.   His Notitia for July, 1738, found in *Journal* of S. P. G. (L. C. Trans.), VIII, April 13, 1739, contained the following items of information concerning Rye:

Number of inhabitants	2382
Number of baptized (Estimated)	759
Number of adults baptized this last half year	5
Actual communicants	46
Those who profess themselves of the Church	762
Dissenters of all sorts	1044
Baptists	none
Heathen and infidels	736
Converts	120

Mr. Wetmore continued at Rye until 1760, his Negro baptisms

[178]*James Wetmore to David Humphreys, Rye, February 20, 1727/1728 in* S. P. G. MSS. (L. C. Trans.), A20, pp. 218-219. *He had two of his own Negroes baptized but sold them out of the parish before 1728.*
[179]*James Wetmore to David Humphreys, Hempsted, September 8, 1729, in* S. P. G. MSS. (L. C. Trans.), B1, No. 55.
[180]*Ibid., Rye, July 21, 1729, in* S. P. G. MSS. (L. C. Trans.), B1, No. 59.
[181]*James Wetmore to David Humphreys, Rye, New York, August 20, 1733, in* S. P. G. MSS. (L. C. Trans.), B1, No. 21.
[182]*Flint Dwight to David Humphreys, Rye, New York, November 12, 1735, in* S. P. G. MSS. (L. C. Trans.), A26, p. 75.

averaging between eight and ten yearly,[183] his records showing the growth of the community. In 1741, Mr. Purdy, schoolmaster at Rye, reported fifty-one children in daily attendance, of whom twenty-seven had been baptized in the Church of England. Twenty-two had dissenting parents. Two Negroes were enrolled,[184] and in later years, the Negro enrollments varied in this school, one being enrolled in 1762 and in 1764.[185] While the Negro work was limited, dissenters were constantly becoming members of the Anglican Church. Even among the Negroes baptisms were reported with surprising regularity. It may be noted that even dissenting parents seized the opportunity to send their children for instruction by the Anglican missionary, usually the best educated man in the community.

The Rev. Ephraim Avery, appointed to Rye in 1766, baptized eight black infants and two adults, in 1767;[186] two infants and two adults, in 1768;[187] and six infants, in 1769,[188] continuing his work with Negroes and whites throughout the years until his retirement in 1776.[189]

[183]For example, in 1740-1741, he baptized four negro children, and one Negro adult; and in May, 1742, his notitia parochialis showed three adults baptized, and two children; in October, 1745, three Negro children and one adult Negro were baptized; in March, 1748, two adult Negroes were baptized; and in April, 1749, only one Negro adult was baptized. See the following letters of James Wetmore to the Secretary, Rye, New York, September 28, 1741, in Journal of S. P. G. (L. C. Trans.), VIII, January 15, 1741/1742. This year he also baptized 65 white children and five aduts; May 1, 1742, in S. P. G. MSS. (L. C. Trans.), B10, No. 104. The complete record showed 2,500 inhabitants, 12 Indians, 100 Negroes, and 1,000 whites (not baptized); October 1, 1745, in Journal of S. P. G. (L. C. Trans.), April 18, 1746; S. P. G. MSS. (L. C. Trans.), B13, p. 266; March 26, 1748, S. P. G. MSS. (L. C. Trans.), B16, No. 43; Journal of S. P. G. (L. C. Trans.), X1, July 15, 1748; April 12, 1749, in S. P. G. MSS. (L. C. Trans.), B17, No. 99. The complete record for this year showed 4,000 inhabitants, 2,500 baptized, actual communicants 51, and heathen and infidels, 100.

Pennsylvania soon outgrew New York in population and remained ahead throughout the eighteenth century, although in later years New York began to overtake it. Estimates for 1755, and 1775 are Pennsylvania, 220,000 and 300,000; New York, 55,000 and 200,000. In 1765, New York, 100,000.

[184]Mr. Purdy to [Secretary], New York, November 6, 1741, in Journal of S. P. G. (L. C. Trans.), VIII, February 19, 1741/1742.

[185]Timothy Wetmore to Daniel Burton, Rye, May 25, 1762, in S. P. G. MSS. (L. C. Trans.), B3, No. 216; September 17, 1764, in B3, No. 224; June 30, 1763, in B3, No. 222. He taught six hours daily, his scholars numbered 63, 24 baptized in the Church, and 38 born of dissenting parents. His brother James Wetmore, had been helping him for a year, and Timothy had given his whole salary to James.

[186]Ephraim Avery to Daniel Burton, Rye, September 29, 1767, in S. P. G. MSS. (L. C. Trans.), B3, No. 233.

[187]Ibid., September 29, 1768, in B3, No. 234.

[188]Ibid., May 2, 1769, in Journal of S. P. G. (L. C. Trans.), XVIII, July 21, 1769.

[189]Ephraim Avery gave little account of his parish except baptisms. Between May, 1769, and May, 1771, he baptized seven black infants and two black adults. The following year, four more black infants and one adult were baptized; in 1773, five more children; and in 1774 Avery wrote his last report which recorded four black and thirty-three white infant baptisms, and four white adults. See Ephraim Avery to Daniel Burton, Rye, May 1, 1771, in S. P. G. MSS. (L. C. Trans.), B3,

The concern of the clergy for the Negro formed here as everywhere an intangible wedge of humanitarian protection between slavery unalleviated, and a degree of amelioration. Mr. Thomas Bradbury Chandler was the Society's catechist in the neighboring towns of North Castle and Bedford, with a salary of £10 per year with an arrangement that it be doubled by the inhabitants.[190]

In 1759, Mr. Wetmore reported that Mr. St. George Talbot, of New York, had granted him £600 New York money, from which he was to receive a life income and thereafter that sum was to be used to purchase a glebe for the support of the Society's missionary at Rye. In addition, in the terms of his will he provided £400 for the same purpose, and £1000 to the Society for providing a salary for a minister at North Castle and Bedford, for the use of schools in Rye, North Castle, and Bedford, and for clothing poor children.[191]

Himself devout, Mr. Talbot provided for the religious education of his slaves. A Negro girl of 11 years and a Negro boy of 6 years had responded so well that he proposed to give them freedom and to make some financial provision for them. The manumission of slaves by Talbot illustrates the fact that emancipation was a difficult economic process. The slave, in order to be free in fact, needed definite training so that he could count on some security as a wage earner or a farmer. At Mr. Wetmore's suggestion Talbot was made a member of the Society, thanked for the £600 already given and for the favors yet to come.[192]

A few years later, in 1763, Mr. Talbot surveyed religious conditions in nearby regions for the Society, and suggested that it might be able to increase its mission without additional expense by withdrawing the salaries of missionaries in flourishing and wealthy parishes, making them self-supporting, and applying funds elsewhere. He specifically recommended that the catechists for the Negroes in New York and Philadelphia should be supported from local funds raised in these two prosperous cities.[193]

No. 239. Mr. Avery said he transmitted his baptisms for 2 years, instead of one, as evidently his other letters had miscarried. In this interval, 86 white children and 15 adults had been baptized; ibid., May 1, 1772, in B3, No. 240. Also baptized were 54 white infants and 1 adult; ibid., November 1, 1773, in B3, No. 241. Also baptized were 90 white infants and 6 adults; September 6, 1774, in Journal of S. P. G. (L. C. Trans.), XX, January 19, 1775.

[190]*Journal of S. P. G. (L. C. Trans.), X, May 15, 1747.*

[191]*James Wetmore to [Secretary], Rye, April 7, 1759, in Journal of S. P. G. (L. C. Trans.), XIV, October 19, 1759. In this letter, Wetmore suggested that the Society make Mr. Talbot one of its members.*

[192]*James Wetmore to [Secretary], Rye, April 7, 1759, in Journal of S. P. G. (L. C. Trans.), XIV, October 19, 1759.*

[193]*Mr. St. George Talbot to [Secretary], Barn Island, New York, July 1, 1763, in Journal of S. P. G. (L. C. Trans.), XVI, October 28, 1763.*

The minutiae of baptisms in this colony must be read as a part of the S. P. G. program from its organization to the emancipation of the slaves in the British empire in 1834. The Society committed itself to the steady and unwavering conviction that baptism was not manumission or emancipation, but a recognition of the Negro as a human being, even though technically in slavery. It is interesting to note that this stability is in contrast with judicial decisions and legislative enactments which varied from time to time and place to place.[194] This conservatism enabled the Society to carry on its work under conditions where slavery was universal and the Negro in overwhelming majority as in its major enterprises at Codrington College in Barbados. The Society's middle of the road policy which allowed it to operate successfully in a wide variety of social conditions, also exposed it to the extremists among the planters on the one hand, and the advanced emancipators on the other who sarcastically at times addressed the trustees of the Society as the "honorable body of slaveholders." But by way of contrast with the Society's firm and steadfast program and practice were the varied decisions of the judiciary in Great Britain which recognized freedom in the British Isles and slavery in the West Indies, so that a Negro, free in England, was a runaway slave if he returned to the West Indies.[195] In the United States, a century later the Federal Fugitive Slave Law provided for compulsory return to slavery. Even in colonial days, as a number of the documents in this paper show, the mood for freedom, both in theory and actual practice, was developing. Towards this drift, in many posts and centers of its work, the S. P. G. made intangible and specific contributions by bringing into the open the inconsistent and inhuman restrictions put upon the slave in regard to the difficulties of marriage, the separation of children from parents, as well as by present-

[194]*For information on the variety of judicial decisions concerning Negro and Indian slavery, in the English Colonies from the beginning to 1875, including pertinent decisions in England, see Helen T. Catterall, Vols. I to V. It may be pointed out that former French and Spanish regions would be involved and therefore light is thrown on the attitude of all religious bodies, including the Roman Catholic. The multitude of complications deal with importations of slaves into this or that state, the migrations of free Negroes, the relations of husbands to wives whom they owned or to wives owned by others, and of white fathers to their slave children, with cases involving the distribution of estates, and the difficulties as to whether slaves were real or personal property, with the practices of giving little Negroes to children, of hiring out adults, of letting them hire themselves out and lay up money, with escapes to Canada, to Ohio, with cases of kidnapping, runaways, permitted temporary residences in free states, church cases, cases of crime and punishment. Vol. I, iv, v.*

[195]*As to the present slavery legislation in England, see Anti-Slavery Reporter and Aborigines Friend, July, 1939, p. 56—"It was not generally known that our forbears so framed their legislation that any British subject committing any act of slavery in any part of the world is deemed to have committed the act within the county of London, and is therefore open to arrest on his return to British territory."*

ing his abilities of every sort, particularly his capacity to take a place in the parish as "a man and brother."[196]

The activity of the Rev. Peter Stouppe of New Rochelle, goes back to the first quarter of the century. In August, 1726, he reported a list of baptisms made with the consent of the masters. Ten Negroes, six of them children, were prepared by parents, owners and the missionary. The four adults knew the Lord's Prayer, the Creed, and the Ten Commandments, and besides were able to give a good verbal account of the Christian faith.[197] Out of about 78 Negroes he reported from three to seven baptisms from time to time and a constant Negro church attendance. He assured the Society that the Negroes would always have a share in his assistance, ". . . as far as will be necessary to make them good and religious persons, without the least prejudice to the rest of my flock."[198] During the long period from 1726 to 1760, Mr. Stouppe's baptisms at New Rochelle kept a steady pace.[199] This watchful observation of the Negro, directed from London, relieved the black man in some degree from the fate of mere property under the unnoticed management of the owner. The Church in a sense claimed a part of the slave. Stouppe confined his letters mainly to the records of his baptisms which, of course, included reports of white baptisms as well. The usual number of Negro baptisms was between one and three, representing a steady, quiet pursuit of the Society regime.[200]

[196]*Dr. Carter G. Woodson, in his studies, has pointed out that the seasoning of the Negroes was an education in skills necessary for agricultural and domestic work. His, The African Background Outlined (1936), has two excellent chapters on "The Education of the Negro," and "The Religious Development of the Negro."*

[197]*Peter Stouppe to David Humphreys, New Rochelle, August 20, 1726, in S. P. G. MSS. (L. C. Trans.), A19, pp. 397-398.*

[198]*Peter Stouppe to David Humphreys, New Rochelle, December 11, 1727, in S. P. G. MSS. (L. C. Trans.), A20, p. 204. In June, 1730, Mr. Stouppe recorded the baptism of six Negro children and one adult, and in December of the same year several more, and in 1731 three slaves. See letters from Peter Stouppe to David Humphreys, New Rochelle, New York. June 19, 1727, in S. P. G. MSS. (L. C. Trans.), A20, p. 189; June 5, 1730, in A23, p. 63; December 29, 1730, in A21, p. 92; December 22, 1731, in A23, p. 35.*

[199]*A few reports taken at random will illustrate. Three black children were baptized on Easter, 1733, five on the following Easter, two in December, 1735, five in June, 1736, four in June, 1737, and six in 1740. See letters of Peter Stouppe to David Humphreys, New Rochelle, April 7, 1733, in S. P. G. MSS. (L. C. Trans.), B1, No. 40; June 7, 1734, in A25, p. 13; see also July 30, 1734, in A25, p. 26; December 2, 1735, in A26, p. 95; June 1, 1736, in A26, p. 270; June 10, 1737, in Journal of S. P. G. (L. C. Trans), VII, April 21, 1738; November 9, 1748; in ibid., VIII, February 20, 1740/1741.*

[200]*From May 22, to November 12, 1741, one black child was baptized; from January to June, 1743, three black children were baptized; from April to November, 1744, the same number were baptized, and in June, 1745, the number increased to five black children, and one Negro woman. From 1747 to 1750, the baptisms ran as follows: six children, between July, 1747, and April, 1748; the same from October, 1748, to May 1, 1749; eight from May to November, 1749, and four from November, 1749, to June, 1750. Mr. Stouppe's Negro baptisms*

Despite heavy enlistments for the French and Indian War, Stouppe reported in 1758, that his congregation was "orderly and peaceable."[201] His successor at New Rochelle, the Rev. Michael Houdin, was equally successful in his Negro work,[202] reporting seventeen Negro baptisms in 1764.[203]

As was to be expected, life on the new frontiers was difficult and dangerous. Hard work was the standard assignment and disease took a steady toll of young and old. In Jamaica, the Long Island mission, for example, the first worker of the Society, the Rev. Patrick Gordon died with a fever in 1702, the year of his arrival. His successor, the Rev. James Honyman, a Scotsman,[204] was in 1705 transferred to Rhode Island, the first resident S. P. G. Missionary in that colony.[205] The third man in the Jamaica station, the Rev. William Urquhart, although "very diligent in his Mission and well respected by all the Members of the Church,"[206] lived only a few years after his appointment in 1704.[207] The hazards of the Atlantic Sea voyages to secure ordination and the hardships of pioneering were matters of constant comment and arguments for a resident bishop. However, the Jamaica parish grew in importance. The Rev. Thomas Colgan, appointed in 1732, not only showed an interest in Negro work, but brought his parish into a thriv-

were five in 1751, seven in 1752; six in 1756; five in June, 1758; seven in November, 1758. See letters of Peter Stouppe to Secretary, New Rochelle, New York, November 12, 1741, Journal of S. P. G. (L. C. Trans.), IX, April 9, 1742; June 15, 1743, in S. P. G. MSS. (L. C. Trans.), B11, No. 142; Journal of S. P. G. (L. C. Trans.), IX, September 16, 1743. He also reported the baptism of ten white children and 66 communicants; November 15, 1744, in Journal of S. P. G. (L. C. Trans.), X, April 19, 1745; S. P. G. MSS. (L. C. Trans.), B13, p. 250; June 5, 1745, in S. P. G. MSS. (L. C. Trans.), B13, p. 251; Journal of S. P. G. (L. C. Trans.), X, November 15, 1745. In this letter Stouppe asks leave to go to Switzerland and spend his last days with his relatives. The Society granted this request but evidently Stouppe changed his mind, as he continued letters from New Rochelle. April 15, 1748, in S. P. G. MSS. (L. C. Trans.), B16, No. 45. May 1, 1749, in S. P. G. MSS. (L. C. Trans.), B17, No. 100; November 25, 1749, in B18, No. 124; June 8, 1750, in B18, No. 123; June 10, 1751, in S. P. G. MSS. (L. C. Trans.), B19, No. 89; May 10, 1752, in B20, No. 75; June 10, 1756, in Journal of S. P. G. (L. C. Trans.), XIII, December 17, 1756; June 5, 1758, in XIV, November 17, 1758; November 28, 1758, in XIV, March 16, 1759.

[201]*Peter Stouppe to Philip Bearcroft, New Rochelle, November 28, 1758, in Journal of S. P. G. (L. C. Trans.), XIV, March 16, 1759.*

[202]*Michael Houdin to [Secretary], New Rochelle, April 17, 1764, in Journal of S. P. G. (L. C. Trans.), XVI, July 20, 1764. Three white adults of the same family were also baptized. The father was a convert from the Church of Rome and the mother from the Anabaptists. For the best extant account of Houdin's career, see J. W. Lydekker's biography in Historical Magazine, V. (1936), 312-324.*

[203]*Ibid., October 23, 1764, in XVI, January 25, 1765.*

[204]*Journal of S. P. G. (L. C. Trans.), I, March 19, 1702/1703.*

[205]*Ibid., April 21, 1704. S. P. G. Digest, p. 853.*

[206]*David Humphreys, Historical Account of the Incorporated Society for the Propagation of the Gospel, p. 226. (London, 1730.) Humphreys gives an invaluable account of the Society's work in all the colonies up to 1725.*

[207]*Journal of S. P. G. (L. C. Trans.), I, February 4, 1703/1704.*

ing condition.[208]   During one twelve month period, he baptized five Negroes.   A little later, he recorded ten Negro baptisms.   Three were baptized in 1751; eighteen, in 1752; and six, in 1753.[209]   These baptisms show that, despite the usual pioneer difficulties, the education of blacks, poor whites, and masters was going forward, according to the Society's pattern of experiment.   In 1760, Mr. Seabury lamented the very slight increase in the number of his church members, attributing the slow growth to philosophical deism, which, he believed, brought indifference to religion in his parish, with reduction in regular church attendance. The records, however, show a steady baptism of white men as well as of Negroes and a development of this religious community.[210]   Sea-

[208]*Thomas Colgan reported four Negro baptisms in 1743, three adults between September, 1743, and March, 1744, two from March to September, 1744. See the letters of Thomas Colgan to [Philip Bearcroft] Jamaica, Long Island, September 29, 1743, in S. P. G. MSS. (L. C. Trans.), B11, No. 135 [?] Journal of S. P. G. (L. C. Trans.), IX, March 16, 1743/1744. Other items in this 'Notitia parochialis" were*

Number of Inhabitants	*about 1,500*
Number of baptized in last half year	*25*
Number of adults baptized last half year	*4 negroes*
	5 whites
Number of Heathens and Infidels	*a few Indians*

See also the letter of March 26, 1744, in S. P. G. MSS. (L. C. Trans.) B13, pp. 228-229, 232.

[209]*Thomas Colgan to Philip Bearcroft, Jamaica, March 25, 1751, in S. P. G. MSS. (L. C. Trans.), B19, No. 88; March 25, 1752, in Journal of S. P. G. (L. C. Trans.), XII, November 17, 1752; March 26, 1753, in ibid., XII, October 19, 1753; March 25, 1752, in ibid., XII, November 17, 1752.*

[210]*However a few Negroes continued to be baptized, one adult in March, 1759, one again in October with three infants; three children in March, 1760; one adult and one child in October, 1760; one infant and five adults in March, 1761; three children and one man in September, 1761; one adult and three children in March, 1762; five children in October, 1764; three children and one adult in April, 1765; one adult and four children in October, 1765. In South Side the same year he baptized four white children, one Negro adult, and five negro children, the' slaves of William Nicol. In April, 1766, he reported three Negro children baptized, and one adult; three children in October, 1766. In 1767, Seabury was transferred to East and West Chester, and recorded four children's baptisms in December, 1767, and for the next eight years, his Negro baptisms continued between three and six. See the letters of Samuel Seabury, Jr., to Secretary, Jamaica, March 28, 1760, in Journal of S. P. G. (L. C. Trans.), XV, November 21, 1760; March 28, 1759, in XIV, November 16, 1759; October 10, 1759, in XIV, June 20, 1760; March 28, 1760, in S. P. G. MSS. (L. C. Trans.), B2, No. 155; Oct. 26, 1760, in B2, No. 156; March 26, 1761, in B2, No. 157; September 30, 1761, in B2, No. 158; March 26, 1762, in B2, No. 197; October 6, 1764, in B1, No. 18; April 8, 1765, in B2, No. 165; October 1, 1765, in B2, No. 167; April 8, 1765, in S. P. G. MSS. (L. C. Trans.), B2, No. 165; April 17, 1766, in B2, No. 169; October 7, 1766, in B2, No. 170; Westchester, December 28, 1767, in B2, No. 172; baptisms in 1769 were six, four in 1770, five in 1771, two in 1772, and four in 1775. See S. P. G. MSS. (L. C. Trans.), B2, Nos. 175, 178, 179, 181-183, 185, 188. Mr. Seabury when stationed in West Chester 1766-1776, recorded several black baptisms. In 1771, three infants and two adults were baptized; in 1772, two children were baptized; in 1773, ten; and in 1774, two children. See Samuel Seabury to [Secretary] Westchester, April 8, 1771, in Journal of S. P. G. (L. C. Trans.), XIX, July 19, 1771; March 28, 1772, in XIX, October 23, 1772; October 6, 1773, in XX, March 18, 1774; October 5, 1774, XX, January 19, 1775.*

bury's reference to deism illustrates the migration of the intellectual concepts of the time across the Atlantic, and the interest in them.   The weapons used by the Anglicans were such fiery and masterly sermons as that of Bishop Warburton in 1766, in which he surveyed the duty of Christian man to "savage natives", and encompassed an evaluation of the whole range of 18th century ideas.   He delivered an especial blast against those who postponed the Negro's reward to heaven, while exploiting him here, and failing to prepare him for heaven.

The Rev. Samuel Seabury, Jr., Colgan's successor in Jamaica, had been catechist at Huntington, Long Island, from 1748 to 1752.   He held the Jamaica mission from 1757-1765, and was transferred to East and West Chester for the years 1766 to 1776. On the Tory side during the American Revolution he was, nevertheless, elected bishop of Connecticut, in 1783, and was consecrated by the Scottish bishops at Aberdeen, on November 14, 1784.   His attention to regular Negro care is shown in his reports of baptisms and religious instruction.[211]

A missionary for Philipsburg, the Rev. Harry Munro, arrived on May 20, 1765, after an eight weeks' passage from London,[212] and at once taking up the special charges of the Society, was able to report within half a year, the baptism of twenty-three white and four black children, and six black adults, out of a total of 1,500 inhabitants.   In attendance, he soon had twenty-one white and six Negro catechumens.[213] In July, 1766, he wrote,

> I have baptized nine white children, four black children, and two black adults. . . . My black catechumens being fewer in number are instructed in Church every Sunday, after evening prayer; and I can, with pleasure, assure the Society that my labours, in this useful part of my duty, are attended with success.
> The remarkable proficiency of my young catechumens, and the great desire the negros have of learning, give me great hopes that God will bless my endeavours, and make me an instrument of advancing his glory.[214]

[211]*From January to Michaelmas, 1757, Seabury baptized two Negro children, and in the following year one child was baptized and he had two negro adults under instruction. See Samuel Seabury to [Secretary] Jamaica, October 2, 1757, in Journal of S. P. G. (L. C. Trans.), XIV, June 16, 1758; ibid., March 28, 1758, in XIV, November 17, 1758.*

[212]*Harry Munro to Daniel Burton, Phillipsburg, New York, June 8, 1765, in S. P. G. MSS. (L. C. Trans.), B3, No. 258.*

[213]*Harry Munro to the Society, Philipsborough, April 28, 1766, in S. P. G. MSS. (L. C. Trans.), B3, No. 260 [belongs to No. 259—dated February 1, 1766]; Journal of S. P. G. (L. C. Trans.), XVII, July 18, 1766.*

[214]*Harry Munro to Daniel Burton, Albany, July 12, 1766, in S. P. G. MSS. (L. C. Trans.), B3, No. 267. Although this letter and others up to June, 1767, are dated at Albany, Munro held the Philipsburg station until 1767.*

And again in December, 1766, he explained his work,

> In the summer season, I read prayers and preach twice every Sunday, catechizing the children regularly after the second session in the evening, and the negros after divine service is ended. My success in this respect is very visible. I have now upwards of fifty catechumens, who can say our Church catechism extremely well.[215]

And, a little later,

> The black children and adults are catechized every Sunday evening. . . . My catechumens are fifty in number, viz., thirty-three white children, and seventeen blacks. Baptized since my last account, forty-seven, viz, thirty-two white children, seven black children, and eight black adults, whom I have previously instructed in our church catechism and the nature of the baptismal covenant.
>
> These poor negros are very fond of my instructions, and seem to be extremely thankful for my care and attention to their spiritual concerns. Many of them can answer every question in the catechism properly and distinctly; and against next Whitsunday, I hope, some of them, who are now preparing, shall be found worthy to be admitted to Holy Communion.[216]

In spite of these successes, on account of a controversy with a leading parish member, he asked to be transferred to Albany where he began his work in 1768.[217]

At the Albany mission the major part of the work of the S. P. G. was with the Indians,[218] but the Rev. John Beasley[219] pleaded the cause of the Negroes and asked to be given a salary as catechist.

He wrote,

> I perceive by your letter that the Society [have not come] to any resolution of fixing a salary at Albany, but intend to

[215]*Harry Munro to Daniel Burton, New York, December 26, 1766, in S. P. G. MSS. (L. C. Trans.), B3, No. 262; Journal of S. P. G. (L. C. Trans.), XVII. April 10, 1767.*

[216]*Harry Munro to Daniel Burton, Albany, January 3, 1767, in S. P. G. MSS. (L. C. Trans.), B3, No. 268.*

[217]*Harry Munro to [Secretary], Philipsburg, June 26, 1767, in Journal of S. P. G. (L. C. Trans.), XVII, October 16, 1767.*

[218]*For a detailed study of the Society's work with the Indians in New York, see Chapter II, p. 49. and Chapter III, p. 87.*

[219]*Sometimes spelled Beazley or Beazly.*

employ the money arising by that fund for the instruction of
the negroes where they are most numerous; if the Honourable
Society [were] but acquainted of the vast number of ignorant negroes that [are] amongst us, and during the summer
months yearly more [brought] hither to be sold.   I humbly
conceive they would think it very necess[ary] as well as a
charitable work to establish a catechist in Albany [where]
there is more than 300 inhabitants in this city, and by a modest
computation there can't be less than 400 negroes and their
N[umber] must unavoidably increase, since there is yearly such
[vast numbers] of them imported in this province; wherefore
should the [Society] condescend to fix a salary upon me for
such service, I doubt [not it] would answer the end of so
charitable a work. . . .
    Since my last there have been [eight] negroes baptized
here 6 adults and 2 children.[220]

The Society agreed to send him ten pounds gratuity, but informed
him that it could not establish a Negro catechist at Albany nor at any
other place.[221] Additional pleas brought the same response.[222]

The Rev. John Ogilvie, the missionary in Albany from 1749-1762,
whose work with the Indians at Fort Hunter was outstanding, found
many Negroes in Albany desirious of instruction.   To encourage them
he catechized them on Sundays, after service in the afternoons.   In
1750, he baptized two Negro children,[223] and in June, 1752, Ogilvie
wrote of his church in Albany,

As to the Church of Albany, no great alteration, only that
I've received five persons to the communion and baptized 22
white and 4 black children, who had passed thro' a regular
course of catechetical instruction, and brought a certificate of
their good behavior from their masters.   The good people of
the Church in this place which was very much fallen to decay;
and by the generous contribution of his excellency Governour
Clinton and the Honourable Council, and most of the principal inhabitants of Albany, have erected a handsome steeple
and purchased a very good bell, and other ornaments of the

    [220]John Beasley to David Humphreys, Albany, November 20, [1733], in S.
P. G. MSS. (L. C. Trans.), B1, No. 6; Journal of S. P. G. (L. C. Trans.), VI,
April 19, 1734. (N. B. Words in brackets supplied because original manuscript
torn.)
    For details on the Slave Trade, see Elizabeth Donnan's volumes, referred to
above, Note 1.
    [221]Journal of S. P. G. (L. C. Trans.), VI, April 19, 1734.
    [222]John Beazley to David Humphreys, Albany, June 15, 1734, in S. P. G.
MSS. (L. C. Trans.), A25, p. 19; Journal of S. P. G. (L. C. Trans.), VI, Oc-
tober 18, 1734.
    [223]John Ogilvie to [Philip Bearcroft], Albany, July 27, 1750, in S. P. G. MSS.
(L. C. Trans.), B18, Nos. 102-103.

Church, so that the public offices of religion are attended with circumstances of dignity and solemnity.[224]

In Albany and in Schenectady, Ogilvie baptized from February, 1759, to February, 1760, 104 white children and fifteen Negroes.[225] A hint of the cooperation he had gained from the masters is given in the certificate of good behavior from the master indicating that he had committed the master to join him in the observation of the parish work for Negroes. When the Rev. Mr. Munro came to Albany, in 1768, as stated above, he found the Negroes eager for religious instruction and the masters cooperative. He baptized eighteen adult Negroes, whom he had previously instructed in the Christian faith. He reported,

> These and some more blacks I constantly catechise every Sunday, after evening prayer; and can with great pleasure inform the Society that there is a visible change and reformation among these poor negros. I have had no complaints of immorality since they were baptized; nor has any proved a scandal to his Holy profession; and the daily petitions I receive from their masters, requesting me to baptize more, is, I humbly think, a plain argument in their favour.
>
> I have lately admitted a negro man to the Holy Communion, after due instruction, and enquiring particularly into his morals, I have also, since my appointment to this mission, baptized two white adults; one of them a convert from the Anabaptists, the other a woman detained a prisoner for many years among the Indians.[226]

By 1772, Mr. Munro had instructed and baptized more than fifty Negroes, and six of them had been admitted to Holy Communion.[227] Next year, he stated, "Divine service is duely and punctually performed twice every Sunday, and the children and negros catechized, as in my last account."[228]

Returning to an earlier time, 1743, and surveying another place, the Rev. Isaac Browne, of Brookhaven, reported success in his work

[224]*John Ogilvie to Philip Bearcroft, Albany, June 29, 1752, in S. P. G. MSS. (L C. Trans.), B20, Nos. 55-56.*
[225]*John Ogilvie to [Philip Bearcroft], Albany, May 20, 1760, in S. P. G. MSS. (L. C. Trans.), B2, No. 106.*
[226]*Harry Munro to Daniel Burton, Albany, July 20, 1771, in S. P. G. MSS. (L. C. Trans.), B3, No. 272; Journal of S. P. G. (L. C. Trans.), XIX, November 15, 1771.*
[227]*Harry Munro to Daniel Burton, Albany, August 12, 1772, in S. P. G. MSS. (L. C. Trans.), B3, No. 273; Journal of S. P. G. (L. C. Trans.), XIX, December 18, 1772. Munro stated that Governor Tryon had made the Church a generous donation to repair the windows.*
[228]*Harry Munro to Richard Hind, Albany, October 20, 1773, in S. P. G. MSS. (L. C. Trans.), B3, No. 274.*

with Negroes and Indians and threw interesting side lights on conditions in his parish.[229]

> Of Heathens and Infidels—Those who were lately call'd Heathens, Seem many of them now to be a Miraculous compound of Paganism and Methodism—Some of the Indians & Negroes come often to Church, and I take all the pains I can with them in private as I have Opportunity.

He found the Lord Bishop of Man's essay on the instruction of the Indian, a valuable guide for Negroes, Whites and Indians.[230] He occasionally visited neighboring communities, Crab Meadow for one, where he carried on his religious work.[231]

The Church of England, a pioneer in many a new community, often began in a small way and the early missionary frontiersman is as interesting and as important as fur trader and first settler. The early scattered settlers asked for and accepted the church and the school, two institutions helpful in preventing a return of barbarism. The many sided efforts of the missionary must be kept in mind as each new religious center is mentioned in rapid survey. The Rev. Thomas Standard, missionary at West Chester for many years, 1726-1760, reported an occasional Negro baptism[232] and his successor, the Rev. John Milner, found the masters cooperative. In 1763, one master requested the baptism of ten black infants and promised to see them instructed. As a sampling, from the records, fifteen Negroes were baptized by Milner in 1761, ten in 1762, and five in 1764.[233]

At another mission, New Windsor, the Rev. Hezekiah Watkins baptized a Negro adult in 1746, who appeared "to have a right sense

[229]*Isaac Browne to Philip Bearcroft, Brookhaven, March 25, 1743, in S. P. G. MSS. (L. C. Trans.), B11, No. 138. Feeling between religious bodies often ran high, and the same observation is true of politics.*

[230]*Isaac Browne to Philip Bearcroft, Brookhaven, September 25, 1743, in S. P. G. MSS. (L. C. Trans.), B11, No. 140.*

[231]*Isaac Browne to [Philip Bearcroft], Brookhaven, March 26, 1744, in S. P. G. MSS. (L. C. Trans.), B13, p. 279, Journal of S. P. G. (L. C. Trans.), IX, September 21, 1744. Crab Meadow had a population of 100 and a third of the inhabitants had never seen a church in their lifetime.*

[232]*Thomas Standard to Philip Bearcroft, [Westchester], New York, October [25?], 1745, in S. P. G. MSS. (L. C. Trans.), B13, p. 226. Other items in the "Notitia Parochialis" included:*

No. of inhabitants	*Not known*
No. of baptized (past year)	*29*
Adults baptized	*One, a negro*
Communicants of Church of England	*20*
Heathens and Infidels	*(Negroes—considerable*
	(Indians—few

[233]*John Milner to [Secretary] West Chester, New York, December 10, 1763, in Journal of S. P. G. (L. C. Trans.), XVI, July 20, 1764.*

of the Christian religion," and in 1747, one adult Negro Man and two children were baptized.[234] The following year he had "worn out his health" with his duties. By way of summary he stated, in 1754, that he had, in the last five years, baptized in all 275 white children and five black ones, ten white and five black adults.[235] And again six years later in 1760, he related from his new station at Newburgh that he had

> heard that several of our ships from these parts have been taken by the enemy, perhaps my last letters are not come to hand, therefore, I would observe to you, that from June 29, 1759, to November 18, 1760, I have baptized 81 white children and 4 black children. . . .[236]

His success at Newburgh with whites and Negroes up to 1759 is revealed in a total of 612 baptisms, with favorable reports in the succeeding years.[237] In 1771, from Huntington, the Rev. James Greaton commented on Negro conduct at religious services,

> My hearers behave with the greatest decency at public worship;—among whom are a number of negros (between 30 and 40), the masters of which come to church. The rest belong to Dissenters who are actuated with so much charity as by no means to forbid their attendance. The negroes behaviour is highly meritorious and many of them are really Patterns of Goodness. Some of them read *well*, and accurately perform the responses of the Church, and one is a

[234]*See letters of Hezekiah Watkins to [Secretary], New Windsor, New York, March 26, 1746, in Journal of S. P. G. (L. C. Trans.), X, June 19, 1747; May 6, 1747, in S. P. G. MSS. (L. C. Trans.), B15, fo. 84; November 3, 1747, in B15, fol. 101; October 6, 1748, in S. P. G. MSS. (L. C. Trans.), B6, No. 52; Journal of S. P. G. (L. C. Trans.), XI, April 21, 1749.*

[235]*Hezekiah Watkins to [Secretary], New Windsor, May 5, 1754, in Journal of S. P. G. (L. C. Trans.), XII, December 20, 1754.*

[236]*Hezekiah Watkins to Philip Bearcroft, Newburgh, November 18, 1760, in S. P. G. MSS. (L. C. Trans.), B3, No. 300; Journal of S. P. G. (L. C. Trans.), XV, April 17, 1761.*

[237]*From the time of Mr. Hezekiah Watkins' letter of November 17, 1757, to the one of June 20, 1759, he baptized 81 whites and five blacks, which made the whole number baptized since the beginning of his work in Newburgh 612. Mr. Watkin's Negro baptisms were four from June 29, 1759, to November 18, 1760; two from June 24, 1761, to May 5, 1762; three from July 30, 1763, to November 2, 1763; and two in October, 1764. See letters of Hezekiah Watkins to Philip Bearcroft, Newburgh, June 29, 1757, in S. P. G. MSS. (L. C. Trans.), B3, 299; Journal of S. P. G. (L. C. Trans.), XIV, May 16, 1760; November 18, 1760, in Journal of S. P. G. (L. C. Trans.), XV, April 17, 1761; May 5, 1762, in S. P. G. MSS. (L. C. Trans.), B3, No. 303. Total number Watkins had baptized in Newburgh given as 767. July 30, 1763, in B3, No. 306. He also baptized a white woman who "had been educated in Quaker principles," and 19 white children; October 30, 1764, in B3, No. 308.*

member in full communion—am in hopes that there will be further addition of them.[238]

And in 1768, from Poughkeepsie, the Rev. John Beardsley reported steady progress with white men and Negroes up to the American Revolution.[239] And not far away, at Schenectady, during the years 1770-1773, the Rev. William Andrews[240] baptized three Negroes in 1771.[241] The next year he wrote, "Since the 30th of June last I have baptized 1 white and 24 black children; married 4 couples; buried 7; and have 43 communicants; and also 16 catechumens."[242] An interesting item was inserted in his letter of March 25, 1773, when he said his congregation, by means of a lottery, had just finished a wooden steeple on the Church.[243] In 1773, he reported the baptism of two black infants along with fifty-nine white children and four adults.[244]

In 1773, at Johnstown, the Rev. Richard Mosley, explained that he had a group of New England dissenters in his parish, early emissaries of those millions of men who later spread across the continent, but that Sir William Johnson labored as much as possible to forward religion in this newly settled place. Mosley baptized twenty-three black adults in May, 1773,[245] and seventeen in October, 1773.[246]

[238]*James Greaton to Daniel Burton, Huntington, New York. January 23, 1771, in S. P. G. MSS. (L. C. Trans.), B3, No. 147; Journal of S. P. G. (L. C. Trans.), XIX, May 17, 1771.*

[239]*John Beardsley in October, 1768, reported four black infant baptisms and three black adult ones, one Negro child was baptized in 1771, and his church was in "a tolerable good state." This continued into 1772 and 1773, and in April, 1774, he baptized two black infants. One was also baptized in 1775 but in his report for 1775 there was no mention of Negroes baptized. See letters of John Beardsley to [Secretary], Poughkeepsie, New York, October 10, 1768, in Journal of S. P. G. (L. C. Trans.), XVIII, January 20, 1769; April 26, 1771, in XIX, July 19, 1771; S. P. G. MSS. (L. C. Trans.), B3, No. 33, April 26, 1774, in S. P. G. MSS. (L. C. Trans.), B3, No. 35; Journal of S. P. G. (L. C. Trans.), XX, August 19, 1774; April 26, 1775, in S. P. G. MSS. (L. C. Trans.), B3, No. 36; October 26, 1775, in B3, No. 37.*

[240]*This William Andrews is not to be confused with the man by the same name who worked with the Indians in the Albany parish from 1712-1719.*

[241]*William Andrews to [Secretary], Schonectady June 30, 1771, in Journal of S. P. G. (L. C. Trans.), XIX, October 18, 1771. In this letter, he also mentioned the attendance of the Dutch at his services.*

[242]*William Andrews to Daniel Burton, Schenectady, June 30, 1772, in S. P. G. MSS. (L. C. Trans.), B3, No. 10, Journal of S. P. G. (L. C. Trans.), XIX, December 18, 1772.*

[243]*William Andrews to [Secretary], March 25, 1773, in Journal of S. P. G. (L. C. Trans.), XIX, September 17, 1773. Two Negro baptisms were also recorded in this letter.*

[244]*John Beardsley to Richard Hind, Poughkeepsie, New York, October 26, 1773, in S. P. G. MSS. (L. C. Trans.), B3, No. 34; Journal of S. P. G. (L. C. Trans.), XX, January 21, 1774.*

[245]*Richard Mosley to [Secretary], Johnstown, New York, May 19, 1773, in Journal of S. P. G. (L. C. Trans.), XIX, September 17, 1773.*

[246]*Ibid., October 22, 1773, in XX, January 21, 1774; S. P. G. MSS. (L. C. Trans.), B4, No. 297.*

Although New York was not the most populous colony, its strategic importance was so great that New York City became British Headquarters in 1776, and remained in British hands until the final evacuation in 1783.   Center of the Tory concentration of population during this time, it was the city of refuge for men such as Samuel Seabury and Charles Inglis.   Even before the fighting began, the colony had many loyalists, was sharply divided in opinion, and for a decade or more had been the center of a pamphlet war in which S. P. G. missionaries entered heartily, including the two men just mentioned.   With such divisions and consequent bitterness, the temporary abandonment of most Anglican religious activity was inevitable.[247]   No man of William White's prominence appeared in New York as in Pennsylvania on the patriot side.   A quick roll call of those who were active in S. P. G. and their fate in the maelstrom of the Revolution cycle will show how the storm affected several of the parishes.

III. EFFECTS OF THE WAR OF INDEPENDENCE

The American Revolution produced a crisis in the affairs of the Society in the thirteen colonies.   The S. P. G. clergy, bound by a special oath to the king, were naturally marked out for persecution. The Rev. Luke Babcock of the Philipsburg station, 1771-1777, was taken prisoner in 1776 and dismissed while ill, in February, 1777.

Mr. C. F. Pascoe, in *Two Hundred Years of S. P. G.* writes,

> According to Dr. Inglis and others, the Rev. E. Avery of Rye was "murdered by the rebels" in a most barbarous manner, on Nov. 3, 1776, "for not praying for the Congress," "his body having been shot thro', his throat cut, and his corpse thrown into the public highway," but Dr. Seabury seemed to impute his death to insanity occasioned by the losses he had sustained.[248]

Dr. Samuel Seabury, in March, 1770, observed that the Church people, considered as a body, had conducted themselves in these times of violence so as to do honor to the Church, and it would be remem-

---

[247] *In New York, the Anglican versus dissenter controversy went back to the days of Elias Neau and Lord Cornbury. Accustomed to a minority position, the Anglican leaders were intelligent, resourceful, and courageous, and fought on terms of equality with men such as Alexander Hamilton and Thomas Paine. Cowards had been eliminated and men such as Samuel Seabury and Charles Inglis had come to the front. The New York story has been told from the standpoint of Charles Inglis by John Wolfe Lydekker in his The Life and Letters of Charles Inglis (London, 1936); and the fate of the New York S. P. G. Library, as well as the effect of political controversy and warfare, has been presented by Austin Keep in his History of the New York Society Library, with an Introductory Chapter on Libraries in Colonial New York, 1698-1776 (New York, 1908.)*

[248] C. F. Pascoe, *Two Hundred Years of the S. P. G.*, I, p. 75. For Dr. Inglis' letter see *Journal of S. P. G. (L. C. Trans.)*, XXI, January 17, 1777.

bered many years with approbation.[249] Treated with kindness at first, in 1775, he wrote that he had been forced to retire for a few days to escape the threatened vengeance of the rebels. Extreme language flew back and forth. The charge against the clergy was that they, in conjunction with the Society and the British ministry, had laid a plan for enslaving America. Seabury declared that those who raised this charge did not believe it themselves, but only used it to arouse popular fury.[250] The same year Seabury was carried a prisoner to Connecticut because he was a leading loyalist pamphleteer, offensive to the "Sons of Liberty". On his release several months later, he returned to New York where he received daily insults from the Patriot army. After the Declaration of Independence had been made, rather than not pray for the king, he shut his church. Yet none of his parishioners did for him or the church any harm. He wrote, in 1778, that the general position of the clergy in New England was that they could perform every duty of their office unmolested except public service in the church.[251]

The Rev. Leonard Cutting, of Hempstead, wrote, in 1777, that his church had fared better than might have been expected. After the Declaration of Independence, he was obliged to shut his church up for some time, until after the arrival of the king's troops, when his work continued, and he reported the baptism of 25 white and one Negro child, five adults and one Negro girl.[252] He also conducted services at Oyster Bay, but under the circumstances, he questioned the possibility of the continued existence of the Anglican Church.[253] In 1783, he reported that the church at Oyster Bay had been totally stripped, nothing was left except the shell and that was considerably damaged.[254]

West Chester, Staten Island, and other parishes were suffering from frequent incursions of the Patriots and some of the residents had to flee to New York or to Long Island.[255] The Rev. Joshua Bloomer, of Jamaica, reported his mission was greatly distressed on account of the loyal sentiments of his people.[256] The Rev. Richard Charlton, of Staten Island, indicated that in the midst of the present distractions, the people

[249]*Samuel Seabury to [Secretary], East and West Chester, March 29, 1770, in Journal of S. P. G. (L. C. Trans.), XVIII, August 17, 1770.*

[250]*Samuel Seabury to [Secretary], East and West Chester, New York, May 30, 1775, in Journal of S. P. G. (L. C. Trans.), September 15, 1775.*

[251]*Samuel Seabury to [Secretary], West Chester, January 20, 1778, in Journal of S. P. G. (L. C. Trans.), XXI, April 10, 1778.*

[252]*Leonard Cutting to [Secretary], Hempsted, New York, January 6, 1777, in Journal of S. P. G. (L. C. Trans.), XXI, March 21, 1777.*

[253]*Leonard Cutting to [Secretary], Hempsted, July 1, 1778, in Journal of S. P. G. (L. C. Trans.), XXI, October 16, 1778.*

[254]*Ibid., XXIII, II, July 28, 1783.*

[255]*Journal of S. P. G. (L. C. Trans.), XXII, September 6, 1780.*

[256]*Joshua Bloomer to [Secretary], Jamaica, February 7, 1776, in Journal of S. P. G. (L. C. Trans.), XXI, May 17, 1776.*

of his island had remained steadfast in their loyalty, and had no connection with Congresses and Committees.[257]

The Rev. Epenetus Townsend, of Salem, assured the Society of his constancy in performing his duties and he had not had, in September, 1775, any decrease in numbers.[258] The Rev. John Sayre, of Huntington, could not give as favorable a report. He had tried to instruct the Negroes but found it of little use in a time of war and confusion.[259]

The Rev. John Doty, of Schenectady, stuck to his post from 1775 to 1778, kept up his catechetical lectures for slaves and baptized several Negroes, but he was finally forced to flee to Canada, where he was appointed a chaplain.[260]

The Rev. Gideon Bostwick, of Great Barrington, was repeatedly admonished by the committee of correspondence to omit prayers for the king in the church service. When he refused to omit any part of the service, he was informed that he continued his defiance at his own peril.[261]

Mr. Hildreth, schoolmaster, thanked the Society for some books for his school; for due to the non-importation agreements, not a prayer book could be bought in the city of New York.[262] In 1776, when his school house was burned down, he took a vacant house and collected a few scholars, including one or two Negroes.[263]

As early as 1774, Dr. Samuel Auchmuty wrote that he would like to say much on the subject of the rebellion, but through prudence, he would observe only that had the government established an American bishopric twenty years earlier, these circumstances, in his judgment, never would have arisen.[264] New York City was in great confusion, and the churches in the neighboring colonies were taken over by the patriots, the missionaries jailed, or sent into the back country.[265]

[257]*Richard Charlton to [Secretary], Staten Island, New York, April 24, and October 13, 1775, in Journal of S. P. G. (L. C. Trans.), XXI, January 19, 1776.*
[258]*Epenetus Townsend to [Secretary], Salem, September 29, 1775, in Journal of S. P. G. (L. C. Trans.), XXI, July 19, 1776.*
[259]*John Sayre to [Secretary], New York, January 30, 1778, in Journal of S. P. G. (L. C. Trans.), XXI, April 10, 1778.*
[260]*John Doty to [Secretary], Montreal, May 30, 1778, in Journal of S. P. G. (L. C. Trans.), XXI, October 16, 1778. For Doty's biography, see J. W. Lydekker, Historical Magazine, VII. (1938), pp. 287-300.*
[261]*Gideon Bostwick to [Secretary], Great Barrington, New York, June 28, 1775, in Journal of S. P. G. (L. C. Trans.), November 17, 1775.*
[262]*Joseph Hildreth to [Secretary], New York, October 16, 1770, in Journal of S. P. G. (L. C. Trans.), XVIII, December 21, 1770.*
[263]*Joseph Hildreth to [Secretary], New York, October 6, 1776, in Journal of S. P. G. (L. C. Trans.), XXI, January 17, 1777.*
[264]*Samuel Auchmuty to [Secretary], New York, September 12, 1774, in Journal of S. P. G. (L. C. Trans.), XX, January 19, 1775; the Government was also criticised by Dr. Jonathan Shipley (Bishop of St. Asaph) in his Sermon before the S. P. G. on February 19, 1773, pp. 1-20. (Huntington Library.)*
[265]*Ibid., November 20, 1776, in XXI, January 17, 1777.*

A good description of the Revolution from the missionary's point of view was given by the Rev. Charles Inglis in a letter, dated October 31, 1776. He stated that all the Society's missionaries and other clergy of the Church in the New England provinces had proved themselves faithful subjects, had used their utmost power to oppose any spirit of disaffection, and had avoided politics, but this very silence gave offense. After the Declaration of Independence, the clergy were greatly embarrassed, for, to officiate publicly and not pray for the king was against their oath and conscience, but to do so was to bring on themselves inevitable destruction. Therefore, most of the ministers had shut up their churches and had removed to points of safety. Inglis told of an interesting encounter with General Washington. On Washington's entrance to New York, he requested Inglis to omit the king's prayers. Inglis replied that it was in his power to shut up the churches, but not to make the clergy depart from their duty. He was permitted to continue in spite of threats and insults, and, after the Declaration of Independence, he ceased to preach but remained in the city to visit the sick and perform other parochial duties. He had, at the risk of his life, answered *Common Sense*. The reply was seized and burned by the "Sons of Liberty." However, he later had it brought out in Philadelphia. Inglis believed that the Church had lost none of its members by the rebellion.[266] Yet the following year, 1777, he said the parish of New York was practically bankrupt, and asked for aid from England. All the missionaries were being persecuted.[267] In 1778, he reported the war was threatening the extinction of the Church of England in America. Besides, almost all the conscientious clergy of the South had gone to England or taken refuge in New York to avoid imprisonment or taking the oath of allegiance.[268]

In 1778, Mr. Inglis asked for a catechist for the Negroes, but was refused on account of insufficient funds. All of the New York clergy, he stated, were within the king's lines except Messrs. Doty, Munro and Stuart.[269] Many loyalists, during and immediately following the Revolution, fled to various parts of the Empire. Many went to Canada, a few to New Brunswick and Nova Scotia, and others to the Bermudas and West Indies. They were sought out and welcomed by the resi-

---

[266]*Charles Inglis to [Secretary], New York, October 31, 1776, in Journal of S. P. G. (L. C. Trans.), XXI, January 17, 1777, pp. 126-132; John Wolfe Lydekker, Life and Letters of Charles Inglis, pp. 156-171.*
    It is to be noted that Inglis was within the British lines from the capture of New York by the Howes in 1776 until its evacuation in 1783, when he left with Sir Guy Carleton's departing troops. Not always on the scene, the different missionaries could not at times report as eye witnesses.
[267]*Charles Inglis to [Secretary], New York, November 10, 1777, in Journal of S. P. G. (L. C. Trans.), XXI, February 20, 1778.*
[268]*Ibid., October 24, 1778, in XXI, December 18, 1778.*

dent missionaries of the Society. The education and Christianization work of the Society thus emigrated to these other colonies of the empire.

The frequent references in this paper to the sacrament (rite) of baptism must not be interpreted in a narrow sense but must be regarded throughout as synonymous with Christianization. Christianization in turn must be regarded as having large social significance, involving as it did the transference of European civilization to the Negro by teaching him the English language and thus handing him the key to the white man's culture. In New York at least, public opinion, legislative enactment, and judicial decision were moving in the direction of the Negro's freedom and the recognition of his civil rights. Steps were forward, not backward, and it is obvious from the body of evidence presented in this paper that the S. P. G. played a leading part in securing the Negro's religious freedom, a prelude to his civil and political rights.

The complete achievement of the S. P. G. in New York, which includes the founding of Columbia University and a major part in establishing the educational system of the Commonwealth, is beyond the scope of this study.[270]

The Society's force cannot be assessed at any one place, or even at one period of time. Exerted now for nearly two and one-half centuries, the continuity of effort, the accumulation of experience, made the Anglican effort a world power of weight. In the eighteenth century the exchange of personnel was as remarkable as the exchange of ideas. Christian Frederick Post went from the Pennsylvania frontier to the Mosquito Shore, others from the colonies to the West Indies and to Africa. In the elusive but always fascinating might-have-beens, the question may be asked, except for the separation of the thirteen colonies, would not the momentum have brought emancipation to America as a member of empire in 1830's without the bloody 1860's and the loss of a million dead?

However interesting this speculation may be, the attainment of political independence with its salvage of much of the British heritage by American born men is matched by a similar development in the American Episcopal Church. Americans such as Samuel Seabury and William White were able to found this new independent American

[269]*Charles Inglis to [Secretary], New York, May 1, 1778, in Journal of S. P. G. (L. C. Trans.), XXI, June 19, 1778. The Connecticut clergy were not allowed to leave their province.*

[270]*See William Webb Kemp, The Support of Schools in Colonial New York by the Society for the Propagation of the Gospel in Foreign Parts (New York, 1913).*

Church in the creation of which the S. P. G. had played a notable part. In brief, political separation did not break religious and cultural contacts, but these heritages, among dissenters as well as Anglicans, were saved and incorporated in the new nation and the new American churches. The making of the Church's constitution, the admission of the laity directly into the legislative councils of the Church, the whole process by which the first offspring of the Church of England set itself up as a "free church in a free state," the principle of the separation of church and state as the chief contribution of American Christianity to the world, are among the developments which have been traced in penetrating studies in the Constitution Number of the *Historical Magazine*, September, 1939.[271] The Episcopal Church met its peculiarly difficult problems with resourcefulness. Under wise leadership, as the nation grew, the Church established itself in all parts of the country as a vital force in American life.

Returning to the main theme of this presentation, the Anglican contributions to humane interest in the Negro were weighty, long sustained, based on first hand experience, fully recorded in the mass of S. P. G. records, and like other initial and small scale beginnings of reform, grew in scope from generation to generation. Intellectual history, elusive and intangible, suggests that ideas, like water, go underground, and reappear later and at unexpected distances from the point of absorption. The later phases of British and American anti-slavery opinion, which are beyond the scope of this discussion, indicate the existence of an earlier eighteenth century attitude or mood on which positive humanitarian action could be based. The Annual Sermons preached before the Society in London throughout the eighteenth century by distinguished leaders of public opinion, Bishops Fleetwood, Butler, Berkeley, Shipley, Secker, Warburton, kept the idea of humanitarianism towards native people before the British governing class of which these notable men were themselves members. Their philosophical speculation and Christian idealism were accompanied by the laboratory field work of the Society's numerous agents in the New World. The clergy and parishes of Great Britain, constantly informed and solicited for funds, formed an active part in this enterprise, which, during the century, kept London and the frontier, bishop and "savage native", in unbroken communication.

[271]*Historical Magazine of the Protestant Episcopal Church, VIII, No. 3, September, 1939. This number includes, "The Colonial Background and Preparation," by Edgar Legare Pennington: "The State or Diocesan Conventions of the Critical Post-War Period," by Walter Herbert Stowe; "The Interstate or General Conventions of 1784, 1785, 1786, and 1789," by William Wilson Manross; "Constitutional Developments Since 1789," by Percy V. Norwood.*

CONCLUSION

The fate of the Indian programs, revealed in Chapters I, II, and III, is clearer to our times than it was to the bishops and officials of the Society in the eighteenth century. Not even Sir William Johnson, in reality the super-chief of the Iroquois Indians, was able to foresee the grinding impacts of imperial rivalries in which these tribes, as migratory buffer states, were thrown first against the French and then against the Americans. These rivalries and the white man's land hunger overwhelmed these Indians, and crippled the work of the Society among them, even though it continued in Canada.

In Chapter IV, the stark realities of the slave trade and of slavery are presented as the obstacles. The profits of the trade were enormous and Africa was raided wholesale to furnish the Americas with a labour supply. Today, approximately one-tenth of the people of the United States are of African origin; and, in the long view, the greater success of the S. P. G. was not with the vanishing American race, but with the inrushing one. The Negro of the United States became a Christian, adopted the white man's language and civilization and yet remained appreciably of his own race. The Indian continued aloof from the white man; the Negro joined in the white man's mastery of the continent.

To gauge the shift of opinion in the course of the century, one may, from the convenient pinnacle of 1775, note that the S. P. G. program for the Negro had evolved gradually from its position at the opening of the century, that Christianization and education were its prime objectives, and that baptism was not emancipation. The program, which the conservative planters had at first considered dan-gerous and revolutionary in its invasion of their property rights, was, in the early nineteenth century, beginning to be regarded as reactionary by the anti-slavery forces. The Society's activities had doubtless helped create a public opinion that outran its own program. From the beginning, the movement was largely clerical, but it appealed to laymen and received lay funds such as the Codrington estate, and it constantly enlisted laymen in its work. By the eighth and ninth decades of the eighteenth century the Society had the parallel help of dissenting churches and of independent men: reformers, like Granville Sharp, lawyers, like Lord Mansfield, and Edmund Burke, author of a famous Slave Code. Sir William Johnson was perhaps the greatest of these able laymen won by the Society. They brought to it a weight of opinion, practical sagacity, and the layman's tools of judicial decision, legislative enactment, and orders in council. The work of the Society throughout the first three quarters of the century, and after 1775, was characterized by a union of high idealism with practical realism, the first represented by an unflagging pressure to accomplish its ends, despite the difficulties which were anticipated from the beginning. The earliest sermons and missionary letters show no false optimism or fallacy as to the ease of exchanging native *mores* for those of British civilization. The realism showed itself in the Society's adaptability to the economic and social stress and strain of an aggressive, commercial England, and of frontier case work with the Indian native and the Negro, captured, transported and enslaved in the colonies. If emancipation had been the first cry, missionary work for the Negro would have remained an idle London dream.

The American Revolution produced an hiatus in the activities of the Society in this country during the transfer of its work to American hands, and consequently in its records as well. The dwindling of the records, however, did not mean that the movement had stopped, but rather that the work was being taken over by the colonists themselves as they set up their states. From the beginning, the program of the S. P. G. had been to build each parish into self-sufficiency. Such a far-sighted policy in the early decades of the eighteenth century, before the Revolution could have been anticipated, was in large measure responsible for the fact that the church and the principles established by the missionaries were able to survive the intense anti-British sentiment of its latter decades. Had the missionaries confined themselves entirely to a more rigid ecclesiastical program, disregarding the humanitarian aspects of their work concerned with education as well as Christianization, with libraries as well as liturgies, the Revolution might well have all but liquidated the church in the Northern and Middle Colonies.

Even without the Revolution, which abruptly hurried the transfer of British controlled activities into American hands, the Society expected in time to withdraw from New York entirely, placing under local control all the parishes, as soon as each community could assume the financial support. In the province of South Carolina, for instance, this transfer of the Society's work was made before the Revolution by an Assembly provision of £100 sterling for each rector, after which the missionaries were withdrawn. The work among the Iroquois Indians also, although more definitely imperial in character, would eventually have been assigned to American officials and missionaries, as Indian affairs were taken over by Canada.

In Pennsylvania, by way of further comparison, the transfer of the Society's work to Americans can be followed in the career of Bishop William White (1748-1836), who chose the Patriot side and served as chaplain to various Congresses. Overlapping in length of service the career of John Marshall, he was an outstanding representative of the rising American nationalism and was as important in establishing the Episcopal Church in Pennsylvania and in America, as Franklin was in creating that state and the nation. What the Society for the Propagation of the Gospel had founded, White protected and extended throughout the whole country. For example, during his long career he consecrated more than twenty-five bishops.

Returning to New York for a final statement, the Society in this province, had so thoroughly grounded its work, that any temporary interruption of the parochial functions of the clergy did not prevent the resumption of the Society's work by Americans themselves after Independence. As has been noted, King's College became Columbia College; the educational work in the state was largely built on former S. P. G. foundations; libraries were rebuilt; Trinity Parish became a great institution; old parishes grew and new ones were founded. Under the leadership of American Episcopal bishops the Church participated in the dynamic development of the nation.

In Great Britain, as well as in the colonial empire, the never-ending intensity of the S. P. G. drive suggests an historical revision of the Anglican Church. Has the eighteenth century been seen too much through nineteenth century eyes? And are the overwhelming enthusiastic statements in favor of the eighteenth century British constitution to be regarded as propaganda? Or did both State and Church serve the needs of men well, despite inequalities in both?

The many movements which resulted from or produced the eighteenth century mood acted together. The separate studies of the specialist tend to become too separate, and, to avoid "narrows" in the river of social change, all the humanitarian currents and forces of the century may be thought of as the struggle for the reorganization of a civilized social life, with the economist, the legislator, the churchman, the reformer, the poet, the satirist, each working in many related "causes" for the change of social conditions. This study may throw some light upon the forces, which, by producing social evolutions, have repeatedly prevented violent revolution, when conditions seemed ripe for it, as at the time of the French Revolution.

The S. P. G., with its wide contact with the people of the British Isles, and with the native peoples in the colonies, provides a convenient yardstick for the measure of humanitarian achievement in the economic and social order of that day, and affords sufficient evidence on which to base some conclusions as to the creation and transit of religious and humanitarian ideas. The Society emerges as a major factor, creative in its ideology of a new social conscience, and yet prosaically practical in putting into effect actual measures and techniques for the humane handling of native peoples, particularly in the experiment for Indians under Sir William Johnson, and for schooling of Negroes in New York and at Codrington. The strategy in demanding support and co-operation from vested interests which opposed humanitarian principles, and in showing that profits and the civilization of the labourers might be developed in ratio to each other, was both bold and well sustained.

The growth of the British empire in the eighteenth century in commerce, in plantations, and in white settlements, is well known. The accompanying development of Anglican humanitarianism as an ameliorative and civilizing agency, not hitherto analyzed and assessed, is presented in the preceding pages, through the study of the activities of the S. P. G. in Great Britain and in colonial New York, as a contribution to the understanding of Anglo-American relations in the eighteenth century.

BOOK TWO

———

THREE NOTABLE S. P. G. SERMONS

FOREWORD

The function and the significance of the annual sermon in the program of the S. P. G. have been discussed in Chapter I with selected excerpts. For the benefit of the reader, the following sermons are reproduced in full in order to reveal the intellectual and moral state of the times and the trend of events and of humanitarian thought.

The form of the eighteenth century sermon is well illustrated in each of the three sermons chosen. Bishop Fleetwood has about six pages of theological argument characteristic of sermons of the age. Biblical grounds established, the sermon is so incisive, clear cut, and vigorous, that it was used for over one hundred years and has not lost its power today. Its emphasis is on Negro Christianization and Education.

Bishop Secker appeals to the common sense of his countrymen by pointing out that religious work among Whites, Indians, and Negroes is not only a religious duty but sound imperial policy. He breathes confidence in ultimate success and, as a Christian, he deems failure impossible.

Bishop Warburton, speaking after the French and Indian War, calls for the support of the white colonist, the protection and civilization of the Indian, and the abolition of the slave trade. He indicts the slave system in striking terms: "The infamous traffic for slaves, directly infringes both divine and human Law. *Nature* created Man, free: and *Grace* invites him to assert his freedom."

A
SERMON

PREACHED BEFORE THE

SOCIETY

FOR THE

PROPAGATION OF THE GOSPEL

IN

FOREIGN PARTS,

AT THE PARISH CHURCH OF

ST. MARY-LE-BOW,

ON FRIDAY THE 16TH OF FEBRUARY, 17 $\frac{10.}{11}$

Being the Day of their Anniversary Meeting.

By the Right Reverend Father in God,
WILLIAM Lord Bishop of St. ASAPH.

LONDON,
Printed and Sold by *Joseph Downing* in *Bartholomew-Close*
near *West-Smithfield*, 1711.

At a General Meeting of The Society for the Propagation of the Gospel in Foreign Parts,
Friday, February 16. 1710-11.

AGREED, That the Thanks of this Society be given to the Lord Bishop of St. Asaph, for his Excellent Sermon preach'd this Day in the Church of St. *Mary-le-Bow:* And that his Lordship be desired to Print the same.

John Chamberlayne, Secretary.

ACTS XXVI. v. 18.

To open their Eyes, and to turn them from Darkness to Light, and from the Power of Satan unto God; that they may receive forgiveness of Sins, and an Inheritance among them which are sanctified by Faith that is in me.

St. *Paul* is in this Chapter giving an Account of his Conversion, to King *Agrippa, Festus,* and a numerous Audience of Attendants, *Jews* and *Romans*; and amongst other things he tells them, that *Jesus Christ,* who appeared to him, told him he would deliver him from the People, *i. e.* the *Jews,* and from the *Gentiles,* to whom he was now sending him. The Errand he now sent him on, was this, expressed in the Words of the Text; *to open,* &c. In which Words we have, *First,* a Description of the State the *Gentile World* was then in; their Eyes were *shut,* they lived in *Darkness,* and under *the Power of Satan. Secondly,* The change that *Christianity* was to make in them; it was *to open their Eyes, to turn them from Darkness to Light and from the Power of Satan unto God. Thirdly,* The end of this Conversion, that by *Faith in Christ* they might receive *forgiveness of their Sins* here, and an *Inheritance* hereafter in Heaven *among the Saints,* or *them which are Sanctified.*

First, Here is a Description of the State and Condition the *Gentile World* was then in, expressed by *Blindness* and *Darkness,* as the most comfortless, so the most hazardous Estate of Life; and by being *under the Power and Dominion of Satan,* the declared Enemy of God and Man; the great Usurper of God's Honour, and a great Tyrant over all his Vassals. These Expressions are all of them Figurative, and put to shew how deplorably sunk the World was, in Worship and in Practice; plung'd into all Idolatry, and into all sort of Wickedness, into which they fell, *being blinded in their Understanding. Their Idols* (saith the Psalmist, 135.) *are Silver and Gold, the Work of Men's Hands; they have Eyes, and see not; Ears, and hear not; Noses have they, and smell not: They that make them are like unto them, and so are all such as put their Trust in them.* The Man who discerns not the Vanity of Idols, is as *blind,* with respect to Reason, which is the Eye of the Soul, as the Idol itself is, which seeth not, tho' it look as if it could. And as for Sin, it is every where represented as a State of *Blindness,* and all its Works are accounted *Works of Darkness,* as well because Men cannot fall into them, before they have extinguish'd *the Light* that God hath placed in them to guide and direct their Steps;

as also because they are generally ashamed of them, and seek Concealment and Obscurity; and because they lead to Misery and Punishment, which the Scriptures call a place of *outer Darkness.*

The Power of Satan implies, 1. The *Idolatry* in which the World was then, and long before held; all Worship besides that of the true God, terminating in Him, who is therefore call'd *the God of this World.* 2. The Power and Possession he had in, and over Mens Bodies, to afflict and torment them with Diseases and strange Sufferings; which God for some secret Purposes, but especially for the greater Manifestation of the Power and Glory of His Son *Jesus Christ,* permitted those bad Spirits to exercise in greater Degree and Measure, *about,* and *at* the time of *Christ's* appearing in the Flesh, and for about Two Hundred Years *after,* than ever He did before or since. And 3. it implies (and that most commonly in Scripture) *the Power and Dominion of Sin;* *Satan* being in some sort the proper Author of Sin, the first Sinner himself, and the first Seducer of his Fellow-Angels; the first tempter of Mankind to Sin, the great encourager of it ever since, and the designed Executioner of God's Vengeance on it in the World of Misery to come. For these Reasons, all Sin is in a manner referr'd to *Him,* as to its first *Principle;* and all Sinners are call'd *his Children,* *his Subjects,* and *his Servants*: Not that he is indeed a *Father,* a *Prince,* and *Master* of the World, (as some too easily conclude from these and such Expressions) but because they *do his Works,* they follow *his Example,* and *imitate* this apostate Spirit, in his Wickedness and Disobedience; and are therefore said to be *under his Power and Dominion* as well when they follow the wicked Devices of their *own* Hearts, as when they are actually led by *his Suggestions,* and truly tempted by him.

From this Ignorance of the true God, from this Blindness of their Understanding, from these Works of Darkness, and from this Power of Satan; the *Apostles,* as the *Ministers* of Christ, were to deliver the *Gentile-World*: Which was the *Second* thing I was to speak to; for so saith *Christ* himself: *I send thee to open their Eyes, to turn them from Darkness to Light, and from the Power of Satan unto God,* i. e. Christianity was to overthrow Idolatry, root out the Worship of many Gods, and to reform the wicked World in all Instances: It was first to introduce the Worship of one, and the true God into the World, and then to conform the Reason and Manners of it, to his Will, to engage Men to live with one another, like Children of the same common Father, and Subjects of the same Prince, and Servants of the same Master. These were the two great things that Christianity was to do, to convince the World that there was but one God, and that the way to please Him, was to live well with one another, to do Justice, shew Mercy, live Virtuously, and discharge Honestly the Duties of our natural, and our civil Relation.

Our *Saviour* preaching to, and living with the *Jews,* who were now free from all Idolatry, does not often take notice of this great End of his coming, to let them know there was but one God: But the *Apostles,* who were to go into the *Gentile-World,* are full of this Doctrine, and always insist upon this Article. They must indeed, as they did evermore begin with it; for *Christianity* supposes it, and without that Bottom cannot stand. Reveal'd Religion pretends to be the Will of God declared to Mankind; but if there be more Gods than One, then there may be more Revelations, and contrary to this that is now brought: And a Man may be as much obliged to receive them, as this, and that in the end comes to nothing; for contrary Obligations, if equal, void each other, and leave Men at their Liberty. One may see, by all the Writings of the *Apostles,* and by all the *Apologies* of Old, in Behalf of Christians, and their Faith, that nothing was to be done with the *Gentiles,* till they believed there was but *One God.* This also made good Way for the Reception of that pure Morality, that Christ commanded to be taught: for, as the idolatrous Worship of the *Gentiles* was generally accompanied with Rites, either *cruel* or *obscene;* so the returning to the Worship of the true God, abolish'd naturally those bad Customs. And as Men think they ought to endeavour to resemble, as well as they can, the God they worship; so by having God represented to them, just and true, holy, merciful, and good, they would naturally conform their Manners to those Notions. Which is one Reason why the *Christian* Morality exceeds all others; because the *Christian* Revelation discovers a more excellent and perfect supream Being, than any other Institution or Religion.

These Discoveries of the true God, who is so holy, just, and pure a Being, and of the way of worshiping Him acceptably, by addressing to Him in, and through the Mediation of his *Blessed Son,* together with the absolute Necessity of leaving all our Sins, and of endeavouring to be holy, just, and true, and merciful our selves, as he enables us to be.—These Things, I say, are implied in *Opening the Eyes of the Gentiles, and turning them from Darkness to Light, and from the Power of Satan unto God.*

To live in *Ignorance* and *Error* is no uneasy State, because no Condition of the Mind is any farther Evil than it is apprehended so; and whilst Men are ignorant of the Truth, they feel no real want of it; nor can they well desire it, whilst they do not know they have it not. But to live under *the Power of Satan,* i. e. under *the Dominion of Sin,* is really grievous and uneasy, a Thing that reasonable Men do truly suffer under, and complain of. They find themselves vex'd and disquieted with their own Passions, and are neither at Rest under the Importunity of many of their Desires, nor yet with their Indulgence and Satisfaction: They feel a Sort of War within themselves, betwixt their Appetites, which are tumultuous and disorderly, and their Reason, which would fain restrain them; And altho' they know not naturally how *to deny themselves,* yet they are secretly convinced they *should and ought,* are pleas'd when they *can and do,* and griev'd and asham'd of their Weakness when they *yield.* Thus far the Reason and natural Conscience of some Men have carried them, without the Aid of Revelation: And therefore wise and reasonable Men would be glad to be deliver'd from this Bondage they are under, to their own corrupt Affections, considering them as *troublesome,* tho' not *sinful,* and to be redeemed to such a noble Liberty, as Reason tells them they might and should enjoy. But when, moreover, they consider, that their disorderly Affections do not only shew them to be *weak* and *imperfect* Creatures, but by yielding to them, make them *false, unjust, cruel, impure* and *mischievous,* and consequently odious in the Sight of God, and obnoxious to his Anger, and what Vengeance may be justly due to those Offences —When they consider this, they find their Sins not only *burthensome,* but *hazardous,* and such as give them *Fear* as well as *Trouble.*

From this Fear and from this Hazard, Christ's Religion only can deliver Men; that is, the End of their Conversion, *that they may receive Forgiveness of Sins,* which is the *Third Thing* to be spoken to.

By *Forgiveness of Sins,* is properly meant the Remission of that Punishment that is due to Sin; for, if Sin were not punishable, it were not to be forgiven: And look what Apprehension People have of their Danger; just so they value their Deliverance, and Escape: And therefore forgiveness of Sins, is a Matter of infinitely greater Consequence with *Christians,* than it could be with the *Gentiles,* or seems to have been with the common *Jews;* because the *Christian* Revelation opens a much sadder Scene of Misery to wicked and impenitent People, than common Reason could discover to the *Gentile,* or the *Law and Prophets* did to the *Jews,* at least with any clearness: *The Wrath of God is now Reveal'd against all Unrighteousness,* and the Effect of it, is endless Punishment, in Pains most exquisite: Deliverance from which, is now included in *the Forgiveness of Sins:* And so St. *Paul* saith, 1 Thes. 1. 10. That *Jesus delivereth us from the Wrath to come.* And Heb. 2. 14. *From him who hath the Power of Death,* i. e. *the Devil.* There is no way of discovering the Mercy and Goodness of God, in sending His Son to die for the forgiveness of Sins, like shewing the astonishing Danger to which those Sins had certainly expos'd us; and whoever will truly understand, in order truly to value *Christ's Redemption,* must first consider the *Captivity* in which He lay, the *Chains* He was laden with, the *Darkness* in which He sat, and the *Punishment* to which He was reserved. Consider what that Saviour and Redeemer saith himself, Matth. 25. 41. *Depart from Me, ye Cursed, into everlasting Fire, prepared for the Devil and his Angels*: And ver. 46. *These shall go away into Everlasting Punishment, but the Righteous into Life Eternal.* Consider what St. *Paul* says, 2 Thes. 1. 7. *When the Lord shall be revealed from Heaven with his mighty Angels in flaming Fire, taking Vengeance on them that know not God, and obey not the Gospel of our Lord Jesus Christ, who shall be punished with everlasting Destruction.* Let us find as many *Figures* as we will, in these and such like Passages, the *Truth* must needs be, that the Punishment assign'd to wicked and impenitent People, in the other World, will certainly be great and endless; which shows us also what the Mercy is, of having our Sins forgiven; and what a mighty Saviour and Deliverer *Christ* was, who was, as the Angel said, *to save us from our Sins.*

But the Goodness of God is like Himself, Infinite. He does not only save us from our Sins, but *crowneth us with Mercy and loving Kindness.* The Design of sending Christ into the World to live and die for us, was not only that we might thereby receive *the forgiveness of Sins,* but also *an Inheritance among the Saints,* or them which are Sanctified: *Whom He will Justify, them He will also Glorify.* It is with Men, we see, one thing to *Pardon,* and another to *Reward*; but with God it is the same; they whose Sins shall be forgiven, shall also be Inheritors of everlasting Happiness. The Reason of that is, that the Purpose of God was, that Man continuing Innocent and in Obedience, was to be for ever Happy, and nothing but Sin could possibly defeat this gracious Purpose, and put him under God's Displeasure; but Sin intervening did it; the Mischief therefore had been endless and irreparable, had not God in his boundless Mercy, sent His Son to die for the Forgiveness of our Sins: So saith St. *Paul,* 2 Cor. 5. 20. *For he hath made Him to be Sin for us,* (i. e. He dealt with Him, as if He had been a Sinner) *who knew no Sin, that we might be made the Righteousness of God in Him.* The only thing therefore that cast Man out of God's Favor, being thus removed and taken away, He became Reconciled to God, received again into His Favour, and returned, as it were, to his former State of Happiness. These means of Grace brought back with them, the hopes of Glory which were lost by Sin.

I have not, I see, been able, within the Compass I have taken, to speak to the Words of *the Text,* with near that Clearness and that

Fulness which they very well deserve. I chose them upon THIS OCCASION, because they contain in them, the short, but very lively Description, as well of the sad Estate and Condition of the *Gentiles,* with respect to the Worship of the true God, the Knowledge of *Jesus Christ,* their Vassalage to *Satan,* and their Slavery under *Sin;* as also of the Remedies that God in his boundless Goodness hath provided for these Evils, *Faith* in His Son, *Repentance* of their Sins, and *Obedience* to His Laws; together with the inestimable Favours, Privileges, and Mercies that attend the Conversion of them to Christianity, *forgiveness of Sins,* and *an Inheritance among the Saints,* in everlasting Happiness.

For these Reasons it was, that I chose these Words to speak to; and because the Application of them to our *present Meeting* is so easie and so proper. For if the end of my appearing here be (as I think it is) to excite the *Zeal* of every one that hears me, to contribute all that in them lies to the Advancement of the Kingdom of Christ, *the Propagation of the Gospel in Foreign Parts*: What single Motive can I name, what Argument or Reason can I bring to effect this End, that is not properly reducible to some of these forementioned Heads? The World with which we are concern'd, still *sits in Darkness and the shadow of Death*: The People as *ignorant,* as *vicious,* and *idolatrous* as then: The Gospel brings as *glad Tidings of Peace and Salvation* to These, as Those: Their Wants are much the same, so are the Remedies. And if the *Mission* be not now so *Personal* and immediate as St. *Paul's* in this Case was, from *Christ* himself; yet I am sure the *Mission* is so *general,* and the *Command* so binding, that I believe it would be hard for any single Christian in the World, to find himself exempted from complying with it, according to the measure and degree of his Abilities and Opportunities. *Go,* saith our Lord, *and make Disciples in all Nations, Baptizing them in the Name of the Father, and of the Son, and of the Holy Ghost: Teaching them to observe all Things, whatsoever I have commanded you: And lo! I am with you alway, even unto the End of the World.* The Work is to last as long as there is Occasion; and tho' it be put into the Hands of his Apostles, and all that shall succeed them to the World's End, in all the necessary Parts of their Ministration, and such as are peculiar to their Office; yet does the Reason of the Command oblige all *other* Christians to be as Serviceable, Useful, and Instrumental to the fulfilling it, as they are able. No Christian is exempted from contributing to the best of his Power, to the spreading and enlarging the Kingdome of Christ, *the giving Him the Heathen for His Inheritance, and the utmost parts of the Earth for His Possession*: Not that every *Christian* or every *Church-Man* is hereby oblig'd to leave his Country to convert the Infidels, but that such be sent, to whom such Work is proper, and encouraged and assisted in their Undertakings, with all the Advantages and Powers, that *Governments* are able to afford them; and that all private *Christians* forward and assist them by all the Means and Methods they are masters of, doing whatever in them lies towards a Work of such unspeakable Compassion and true Charity.

Now taking this for granted, that all *Christians,* both by the Nature and *Reason* of the Thing, as well as *Christ's Command,* stand obliged to contribute to the bringing the whole World to the Knowledge and Faith of *Christ,* as they have Opportunity and Abilities of doing it—Taking this for granted, it will be very hard to find Excuses for those *Christian Governments,* or those private *Christians,* who are not content barely to pass by, and neglect the Opportunities of bringing many thousand Souls to Christ, who died to save them all; but who really discourage such as, animated with true and godly Zeal, would undertake that godly Work.

That I may not lose my self in Generals, nor be encumbered with too many Particulars, I will at this time, with your Patience, consider only the Case of such, as will not permit their Slaves to be instructed in the Faith of Christ, and brought to Baptism: A thing so common in all our *Plantations* abroad, that I have reason to doubt, whether there be any Exception of any People *of ours,* who cause their Slaves to be Baptized. What do these People think of *Christ?* What of their *Slaves?* What of *themselves?* What do they think of *Christ?* That He who came from Heaven, to purchase to Himself a Church, with his own precious Blood, should sit contented, and behold with unconcern, those who profess themselves his Servants, excluding from its Gates those who would gladly enter if they might, and exercising no less Cruelty to their Souls (as far as they are able) than to their Bodies? One may ask with Indignation indeed, what such People think of *Christ?* But 'tis more proper to say, they think not at all of Him: For if they would consider Him in any Quality or Capacity whatever, as *Saviour, Law-giver, Head of His Church,* or *Judge,* they would no more venture to lay an Impediment in any one's way to Conversion, than they would throw themselves into the Fire deliberately. It would be as hard for them, to give an Account of what they think of those unhappy *Creatures,* whom they use thus cruelly: They see them equally the Workmanship of God, with themselves; endued with the same Faculties, and intellectual Powers; Bodies of the same Flesh and Blood, and Souls as certainly immortal: These People were made to be as Happy as themselves, and are as capable of being so; and however hard their Condition be in this World, with respect to their Captivity and Subjection, they were to be as Just and Honest, as Chast and Virtuous, as Godly and Religious as themselves: They were bought with the same Price, purchased with the same Blood of Christ, their common Saviour and Redeemer; and in order to all this, they were to have the Means of Salvation put into their Hands, they were to be instructed in the Faith of *Christ,* to have the Terms and Conditions fairly offered and proposed to them. Let any of these cruel Masters tell us, what part of all these Blessings were not intended for their unhappy Slaves by God, purchased for them by the Blood of Christ, and which they are not equally capable of enjoying with themselves? What Account then, will these Masters give of *themselves,* who are the Occasion and the Instruments of bringing these unhappy People, from a Country where the *Name of Christ* is never heard, or call'd upon, into a Country where *Christians* govern all, and *Christ* is call'd their *Lord and Master,* and yet will not permit these Slaves to be Instructed, and become the Servants of this heavenly *Master?* Who bring them, as it were, into Sight of *the Waters of Life,* and then with-hold them from receiving any Benefit from them! They hope, 'tis likely, *God* will be Merciful to these unhappy Creatures, tho' *they* themselves will not be so: Their Hope is good; but they have Reason to fear God may deny that Mercy to themselves, which they deny to others: And no Man living can assign a better and more justifiable Cause, for God's with-holding Mercy from a *Christian,* than that *Christian's* with-holding the Mercy of *Christianity* from an *Unbeliever.* If these Men ever read the Scriptures, and meet with such a Question as this—*Lord, are there few that be Saved?* What a strange puzzle must they be at to make an Answer? I for my own particular part, hinder, as much as possibly I can, some Fifty or an Hundred, it may be many more, from being Saved. I can be certain only of the Salvation of *Christians,* and therefore am my self a *Christian:* I know it is impossible for any one to become a *Christian,* without being instructed in the Knowledge of Christ, and being afterwards *baptized* with Water, in the manner and form prescribed by Christ himself; and I know I hinder all these People that are under me, from being Instructed and Baptized; go on—Therefore I know I hinder them, as much as in me lies, from being *Saved.* I dare not for all the World renounce to my own Baptism: I would not venture my own Salvation on God's unpromised, unrevealed Mercy, without the being made a *Christian,* as I should; but yet I have nothing to depend upon, but that unpromised Mercy for these poor Creatures; and now, 'tis in my Power to seal that Mercy to them certainly, by Means and Instruments of God's own Appointment, and yet refuse to do it. The Scriptures will read strangely with such Practices as these; and a *Christian* hindring others from becoming *Christians,* must needs be a strange Creature, even to himself, when he considers.

To these and other heavy Objections that lye to this inhumane Practice, there are but two or three poor Pretences that must answer, which I will now consider in a few Words. The *First* is, that were their Slaves *Christians,* they would immediately, upon their Baptism, become *Free.* The *Second* is, that were their Slaves *Christians,* and still continue Slaves, yet they should be oblig'd to treat them with more Humanity and Mercy, than the nature and necessity of their Service would admit of, to make their Masters Gainers. And the *Third* is much of the same kind, that were their Slaves *Christians,* they could not sell them, it being Unlawful, they say, *to sell Christians.*

To the *First* of these Pretences, namely—That should they suffer their Slaves to be Baptized, they would immediately become Free— We may Answer, that were this true, the Mischief of it would be no greater in our *Plantations* abroad, than it is at home, where there is no such thing as *Slavery,* but all our Work is done by *hired* Servants; for good Wages and good Usage will always invite Servants, even to the hardest Labours: And if this would not turn to a good Account, 'twere better the World should pay much dearer for the Pleasures and Conveniences those Places afford, than purchase them so cheaply at the expence of so much Misery, such Cruelty and hard Treatment of Men, as good as our selves, and at the hazard of their Souls. But allowing this would be some Inconvenience to the Civil Government, with respect to Trade, is there any Question, whether the Blessing of God upon their Piety and good Designs in furtherance of his Glory, in the Salvation of Mens Souls, would make an ample Compensation for all the Inconveniences and Loss it might sustain, by making their Slaves, or letting them be made *Christians?* But after all, what considering Man would run the hazard of being under God's Displeasure, by hindring others from becoming Christians, for all the Profit, Honour, and Advantage in the World? But *Secondly,* there is no fear of losing the Service and Profit of their Slaves, by letting them become *Christians:* Their Avarice and Cruelty are grounded on a certain Mistake: They are neither prohibited by the Laws of *God,* nor those of the *Land,* from keeping *Christian Slaves;* their Slaves are no more at Liberty after they are Baptized, than they were before. There were People in St. *Paul's* time, that imagined they were freed from all former Engagements, by becoming *Christians;* but St. *Paul* tells them, this was not the meaning of *Christian Liberty;* the Liberty wherewith *Christ* had made them Free, was Freedom from their Sins, Freedom from the Fears of Death, and everlasting Misery, and not from any State of Life, in which they had either voluntarily engaged themselves, or were fallen into through their Misfortune. *Let every Man* (says He, 1

Cor. *7.20.*) *abide in the same Calling, wherein he was called*. Let every Man know, that his being called to the Faith of Christ, does not exempt him from continuing in the same State of Life he was before; it makes no alteration of his Condition in this World; the Liberty of Christianity is entirely Spiritual. *Art thou called, being a Servant? care not for it; but if thou mayst be made free, use it rather.* Art thou Baptized and made a Christian, being a Slave? mind it not; be not much concerned at it; but if thou canst obtain thy Liberty, by fair and honest Means, *use it rather,* take the Opportunity: If Liberty comes legally, or by the favour of thy Patron, accept of it by all Means; thou mayst thereby be better enabled to serve God, when thou are at thine own Disposal. *Brethren, let every one wherein he is called, therein abide with God.* In a Word, the *Law of Christ* made no changes of this Nature, but left Men under all the Obligations and Engagements that it found them, with respect to *Liberty* or *Bondage*: Nor do *the Laws of the Land* hinder People from being Slaves when they become *Christians.* Christianity has so long prevailed in these Parts of the World, that there are no Advantages or Privileges now peculiar to it, to distinguish it from any other Sect or Party; and therefore whatever Liberties the Laws indulge to us, they do it to us as *English-Men,* and not as *Christians.* If therefore it be lawful in our Country, to have or keep any Slaves at all, it is equally lawful to have or keep them so, tho' they are *Christians*: The Laws do not distinctly favour *Christianity* in this Point: And if they should see fit to do it here *at home,* where there is no Occasion for such Slaves, what need were there yet of doing it *abroad,* where there is great Occasion for them? And supposing *Christianity* did (by the favour of Laws, and by the Indulgence of Princes) immediately emancipate and free all Slaves receiving Baptism, yet since it would be so much, either to the Dishonour of God, the Prejudice of Christ's Religion, or to the prejudice of Trade and Civil Government at home; who could despair of obtaining Laws, to reconcile these Interests, in an Age so free and fruitful of Laws as ours is? I would not have any one's Zeal for Religion (much less my own) so far outrun their Judgment in these matters, as to cause them to forget that we are a People who live and maintain our selves by *Trade;* and that if *Trade* be lost, or overmuch discouraged, we are a ruined Nation; and shall our selves in time become as very *Slaves,* as those I am speaking of, tho' in another kind: I would not therefore be understood, in what I have already said, or in what I am to say farther, to plead for any other Liberties or Privileges, than what are reconcileable with Trade, and the Nation's Interest, tho' a little perhaps abated.

But this, I say, is a Mistake common to Masters and to Servants, and occasions the latter to seek for Baptism purely for the sake of Liberty, without Regard to the true unspeakable Advantages of Christianity; and occasions the former to hinder them, by all Means, from being Baptized, for fear of losing their Service; and with as little regard to the Spiritual Privileges, which they thereby with-hold from those unhappy People: Whereas if both were undeceived, the Masters would be no losers, and the Servants the greatest gainers in the World.

The *Second* Pretence is this, That should their Slaves continue Slaves after their Baptism, yet they should be oblig'd to use them with *less Rigour,* than the nature and necessity of their Service will admit, if their Masters must be Gainers by them. This indeed is somewhat for the Honour of *Christ's Religion,* that it commands the Exercise of all Compassion, Kindness, and good Nature towards *Christians;* but this, I think, is common to most Religions with it, which equally favour their particular Professors; and *Christianity* distinguishes it self from them, by commanding Mercy and Compassion to be shewn to *all the World* alike, without respect to Sect or Party, unless where there is an unavoidable Occasion of Preference. We are commanded to follow His Example, *who is rich in Mercy towards all,* whether *Jew* or *Gentile, Bond* or *Free.* Should some Necessity compel us to deal hardly with either *Jew* or *Christian;* our Love to *Christ,* and Honour to *His Name,* would soon determine where the Hardship were to fall; but where there is no occasion for any Preference, the *Christian* Religion does as strongly and certainly oblige to shew Mercy and Compassion to *Jews* and *Gentiles,* as to *Christians.* The Commands of *Christ* do certainly bind us to pity all Mankind, to do to all Men, indistinctly, all the good we can, and not to *Christians* only; for that would be to fall into the Partiality of the *Jews,* who would only shew Kindness to *Jews,* which Christ himself reproves, and condemns as a straitness and narrowness of Mind, and falling very short of His extensive Charity: So that to deal more rigorously with an *Infidel* than with a *Christian,* is to compliment our Saviour with Disobedience; to do some Honor to His *Name,* which He would have us pay to His *Nature,* in shewing Kindness to our Fellow Creatures: It is therefore a great Mistake at the bottom, to think themselves at Liberty, to treat a *Savage,* and an *Infidel,* with Inhumanity and Rigour; but 'tis a strangely cruel and most wicked Absurdity that is built on this Mistake: I may not use a *Christian* Unmercifully, therefore I will not let this *Savage* be a Christian, for I fear I may not use him afterwards unmercifully. What a Mockery would it be, to pretend that I cannot

relieve a Man, because he is not qualified for my Charity, when I
know at the same time, that I hinder him from being qualified,
least I should find my self obliged to relieve him? What is this, but
to hinder him, as much as in you lies, from being happy *for ever,*
for fear he should be a little more at Ease in *this Life?* Be true to
your Religion, and go through with it; it obliges you to shew all Pity
and good Nature, even to the *Bodies* of your Slaves; and then when that
is settled and believed, you will find your selves disposed to shew all
Mercy to their *Souls;* since the best Reason you can find for being
cruel to their Souls, is fetch'd from the Fears of being afterwards
disabled from being cruel to their Bodies. Were one talking to good
Christians on this Subject, we should only need to say to them—
Here is an Opportunity of being merciful both to the Souls and
Bodies of your fellow Creatures, for whom *Christ* died, as well as you,
and both whose Soul and Blood He will require at your Hands at the
last Day, as far as you were instrumental in Tormenting the one,
without Occasion and most just Necessity; and in hindring the other
from coming to the Knowledge and Faith in *Christ,* that was to
save it.

The *Third* and last Pretence, is built upon the same Bottom, *i. e.*
that of Interest: For, since they bought their Slaves for Money, they
should be Losers by permitting them to be made Christians, since
after that, they could not part with them for Money; it being, they
say, Unlawful to sell *Christians.*

Away with all these Honours, that are so hurtful to our Lord! I
dare engage He parts most freely with them: He well remembers,
how he who betrayed Him, gave Him first *a Kiss*; and could never
since endure, that a seeming Respect should do Him Mischief, and
debar Him of a real Advantage. A *Christian* must not, it seems, be
Sold; but then he shall not be a *Christian,* because he may not afterwards be Sold. This is too like to—*Hail King of the Jews,* and Buffet-
ting Him, *bowing the Knee before Him,* and then Spitting at Him.
If *Christ* might be the Advocate for these poor People, He would consent, He would intreat they might be Sold, condemn'd to Bonds, to
Stripes, Imprisonment, and Death, rather than live the Slaves of Sin,
and Unbelievers, the freest and most arbitrary Princes of their Country. He was Himself both Sold and Bound, and loves a virtuous and
religious Slave, rather the better for his Chains or Clogg. Let but
the Soul be free from Sin, and the Hands clean from all Unrighteousness, and He regards not how the Body is encumbered with its Weights,
nor how those Hands are worn with Bonds and Labours.

But after all, 'tis far from certain, that the Laws forbid a *Chris-*

tian to be Sold: If Men had truly a Propriety in their Slaves before they were Baptized, and could dispose of them as they do of other Goods and Chattel for Money, or its worth, I dare be positive the *Laws of Christ* will not deprive them of this Property; and I am very sure the *Laws of the Kingdom* take not away the Right of such a Sale, upon receiving a Baptism, if it were justifiable before.

But did the Laws indeed pretend, in a sort, to honor *Christ's Religion,* it could be no hard matter to convince our Lawgivers, how prejudicial all such Favours were to Christianity; and to desire them no longer to honour *Christians* already, with such Privileges as put a Stop to the Propagation, and farther growth of *Christianity;* but let the Christians (as was said above) be Sold, and Bound, and Scourged, condemn'd to Bonds and Imprisonment, to endure all Hardships and Disgrace, *and to enter into Heaven, Blind, and Halt, and Maimed,* rather than having two Eyes, and Hands and Feet entire, to perish Miserably. That is the Sum of all I have been saying, (and which may shame one to recount) that were these Reasons and Pretences, for with-holding Baptism from our Slaves in our *Plantations* abroad, justifiable and true, they ought to be removed: And all that can consider seriously these Things, will certainly consent, nay, and be glad, that Slaves, tho' *Christians,* might be Bought and Sold, and used like Slaves, rather than still be Bought and Sold, and used like Slaves, and not permitted to be *Christians.* And one may wonder how a *Christian Government* can look upon it self as unconcern'd in this Affair; and only consider these unhappy Wretches, as Creatures that save the Kingdom the Charge of transporting Horses, and Beasts of Carriage, for the *Islands* Service, without reflecting on their Shape and Form, and intellectual Powers, and without looking up to *Christ* their common Master, the Saviour and Redeemer of us all.

This unconcernedness of the Publick it is, most probably, that encourages a great many private People at home amongst our selves to keepe these *Africans,* or *Indians,* in their native Ignorance and Blindness, and to continue them *Infidels* in the midst of a *Christian Kingdom.* These People ought to think what answer they will make to *Christ,* when He shall ask them, why they would not help to increase His Kingdom, and to make their fellow Creatures as Happy, as they hoped themselves to be, by being *called by His Name?* Such Questions will be asked them, with Severity enough, and will require a better Answer than, I fear, the subtillest Christian in the World can make: And therefore, sure, it were better to prevent them by removing the Occasion.

Thus I have done with the *single Case,* that I proposed to consider at this Time. The Excellent Labours of my *Honoured Brethren,* who have gone before me, in this Exercise, have truly made it almost necessary for me, to confine my self to some such single Subject: They have, with so much Learning, Piety and Prudence, and so discreet a Zeal, handled all the general Heads; that whether I should have tried to shew the Excellency and Usefulness of such an *Institution and Society,* as ours is: The general Obligations all *Christians,* and in particular, *all in holy Orders,* lye under, to promote this Charitable Work of bringing Souls to Christ; or whether I should have ventured to prescribe and lay down *Rules* for the conducting our selves and others in this Affair; or have proposed some proper *Means,* for the better carrying on this great Design; or should have spent my Time in returning Thanks and Praise to God, for the Grace He hath given to those who, all along, have shewn an Exemplary truly Christian Fervency, in promoting, and contributing to this good Work; or in Encouraging, Exhorting, and Persuading others to the like: Whatever of this kind I should have undertaken, my best Endeavours had, I find, been happily superseded.

But that which chiefly inclined me to speak to this particular Case, at this Time, was—That it is really, now, *our own Case;* a thing, in which we are all of us here, that belong to *this Society,* so personally concerned, that it behooves us, every one of us, to think of it. We are now, by the Munificence of a truly *Honourable Gentleman* [Colonel Christopher Codrington], our selves become the *Patrons* of at least *Three Hundred Slaves,* who are to Cultivate, and be Maintain'd upon the *two Plantations* he hath left to *this Society,* for the promoting Learning and Religion.

The Name of this our *Noble Benefactor* will certainly be held, by *this Religious Corporation,* in everlasting Honour and Remembrance. And tho' the constant good Effects of this his Bounty, will speak his Praises to Posterity; yet some good Hand, I hope, will sooner pay due Honours to his Memory, and recommend his great Example to such as shall be found able, in some Degree, to follow it. For, give me leave to assure you, (you that know it not) that after all that has been done, *the Issues, and the necessary Charges of the Society, do double, very near, the certain and the settled Yearly Income of it,* and that too, but just as certain and as settled as the Life of Man: And therefore it requires that *others* also, like this our good *Araunah,* should give *as a King.* I see, and cannot but adore, the gracious Hand of God, in thus supplying our Necessities, by casual unexpected Charitable Benefactions: Nor have we any Reason to distrust the Continuance of His Goodness, whilst we sincerely seek His Glory, and the Good of Mankind. But He Himself, who, for a Season, bid the *Ravens* feed the *Prophet,* and then commanded a *Widow Woman* to sustain him, (her self the while sustain'd by Miracle) 1 *Kings* 17. 4, *&c.* yet, *after,* left him to subsist, as others did, by common Providence, and usual humane Methods—But I forget my self—The thing I was to say, was this, or something like it; That if all the Slaves throughout *America,* and every *Island* in those Seas, were to continue Infidels for ever, *yet ours alone must needs be Christians*: We must instruct them in the Faith of Christ, bring them to Baptism, and put them in the way that leads to everlasting Life. This will be preaching *by Example,* the most effectual way of recommending Doctrines, to a hard and unbelieving World, blinded by Interest, and other Prepossessions.

And this, it may be, will weigh more, and operate better, with those who are concerned, than the Example both of *French* and *Spaniards* will, who all along have brought their Slaves to Baptism. Who could endure so absurd and wounding a Reproach objected with Cause, as this—That *those poor Men,* the Profit of whose never-ceasing Labours is bestowed by a *Christian Gentleman,* on a *Society* erected and established by a *Christian King,* (of ever glorious Memory) to propagate *the Christian Faith,* should not themselves be suffered to be *Christians?* How would that merciful Command of God, in Deut. 25. 4. rise up in Judgment and condemn us all—*Thou shalt not muzzle the Mouth of the Ox, that treadeth out the Corn,* i. e. Thou shalt not starve the Creature, whilst he is preparing Bread to feed his Master. *That Text,* I undertake to say, shall never be applied to *this Society,* with any manner of Reproach. The *Servants* of *this Society* shall be, assuredly, the *Lord's Free-Men,* whatever else their Condition shall be in this World; and yet, I hope, even *that* will be changed a good deal for the better: They must be *Christians,* and they will be treated too as such, *i. e.* with all the Mercy and good Nature that can well be shown, consistently with their continuing *Useful* and *Laborious* Servants, which certainly are things that may be tolerably reconciled. And yet, with all the warmest Wishes and Desires that a zealous Heart can have, to see this matter take Effect, it will be very difficult for a considering Man, not to conclude, it must, and ought to be, *a Work of Time, and the maturest Counsels*: It will require, and will employ the ablest

Heads we have, and Men of the most comprehensive Views amongst *this great Society,* to find out such *a Blessed Medium.* And to their best Deliberation, Circumspection, utmost Caution and Discretion, but most especially to God's Blessing, it is that we must leave it; to whom be ascribed, as is most due, all Honour, Glory, Praise and Dominion, now and for ever.

A
SERMON

PREACHED BEFORE THE

INCORPORATED SOCIETY

FOR THE

PROPAGATION OF THE GOSPEL

IN FOREIGN PARTS;

AT THEIR

ANNIVERSARY MEETING

IN THE

PARISH-CHURCH OF ST. MARY-LE-BOW,

ON FRIDAY, FEBRUARY 20, 1740-1.

BY

THOMAS, LORD BISHOP OF OXFORD.

LONDON:

Printed for J. and H. Pemberton, at the *Golden Buck*
against St. *Dunstan's* Church in *Fleetstreet*. 1741.

At the Anniversary Meeting of the Society for the Propagation of the Gospel in Foreign Parts, *in the* Vestry-Room *of St.* Mary-le-Bow, *on* Friday *the* 20th *Day of* February, 1740-41.

Agreed, That the Thanks of the SOCIETY be given to the Right Reverend the Lord Bishop of *Oxford,* for his Sermon preached this Day before the SOCIETY; and that his Lordship be desired to Print the same.

Philip Bearcroft, Secretary.

Mark VI. 34.

And Jesus, when he came out, saw much people; and was moved with compassion towards them, because they were as sheep not having a shepherd: and he began to teach them many things.

THIS Passage of the Evangelist expresses in so strong and engaging a manner, the benevolent Temper of our blessed Lord, and his tender Regard to the spiritual Wants of Men, that it cannot fail of exciting the same Disposition in Us: especially if we consider, that the View, which he is here described to have had, of their destitute Condition, not only induced him *to teach them* Himself *many things* concerning *the Kingdom of God;*[a] but caused that most serious Reflexion, and Exhortation, *The Harvest truly is plenteous, but the Labourers are few; pray ye therefore the Lord of the Harvest, that he will send forth Labourers into his Harvest:*[b] immediately after which He sent forth *his twelve Disciples* to preach the Gospel;[c] as he did the *Seventy* at another time, on the very same Motive, mentioned by another Evangelist in the very same words:[d] thus opening the Way, by his previous Care of *the lost Sheep of the House of Israel,*[e] for uniting us all into *one Fold under one Shepherd.*[f]

To carry on the great Work which he began, of directing Mankind to present and future Happiness, is the End of this Society: incorporated by a Prince, to whom Religion and Liberty will have eternal Obligations; and established, first for the Support of Christianity in our Colonies and Factories abroad, then for the Propagation of it amongst the Heathens intermixed with them, and bordering upon them; but taking its Name from the remoter and more extensive Part of the Design.

Every possible Reason required our Predecessors in this excellent Undertaking to begin with inspecting the State of the *English* Plantations in *America*. And nothing could be more applicable to them on that Occasion, than the Words of the Text: *They saw much People, and were moved with Compassion towards them; because they were as Sheep not having a Shepherd.* The first *European* Inhabitants there, being private Adventurers, neither numerous, nor rich, nor certain

[a]*Luk. ix. 11.*
[b]*Matth. ix. 36-38.*
[c]*Matth. x. i.*
[d]*Luk. x. 1, 2.*
[e]*Matth. x. 6.*
[f]*John x. 16.*

of Success, nor unanimous in Belief, established in several Provinces
no Form whatever of publick Worship and Instruction. Too many of
them carried but little Sense of Christianity abroad with them: A
great Part of the rest suffer'd it to wear out gradually: and their
Children grew of course to have yet less than they: till in some
Countries there were scarce any Footsteps of it left, beyond the mere
Name. No Teacher was known, no Religious Assembly held; the
Lord's Day distinguished only by more general Dissoluteness; the
Sacrament of Baptism not administered for near twenty Years together, nor that of the Lord's Supper for near sixty, amongst many
thousands of People, who did not deny the Obligation of these Duties,
but lived notwithstanding in a stupid Neglect of them. Such was the
State of things in more of our Colonies than one: and where it was
a little better, it was however lamentably bad. Some Persons appear
very desirous of seeing, what sort of Creatures Men would be, without
the Knowledge of God. Here a sufficient Trial was made of this:
and it shewed to an unhappy Degree of Certainty, that they would
be wicked, and dissolute, and brutal in every Respect, and return in
a few Generations to entire Barbarism. Possibly, indeed, they might
have been delivered from this Evil, by that of Popery; which always
taking Advantage of Ignorance and Profaneness, had already begun to
spread: and dreadful was the Alternative of one or the other. In
these Circumstances the poor Inhabitants made, from all Parts, the
most affecting Representations of their deplorable Condition: the
Truth of which was but too fully confirmed by their respective Governors, and the Persons of principal Note in each Province. There
could not be worthier Objects of Regard, than such Complainants.
And if they who remained insensible did not deserve pity so much,
they wanted it still more. The Society therefore, in Proportion to their
own Ability, and the Need of each Place, first sent over Missionaries,
to perform the Offices of Religion amongst them; then Schoolmasters,
to instruct their Children in the Principles of it: who, after *enduring
much Contradiction of Sinners*,[g] and going through a great Variety
of Labours and Difficulties; have, through the Blessing of God, made
a remarkable Change in the Face of Things, and laid a noble Groundwork, of what, we hope, will every Day be carrying on towards Per-
fection. But at present much remains to be done. Multitudes continue,
as before, in a thoughtless Disregard to almost every Part of Christianity: and Multitudes also are daily petitioning for Help: which
to some we cannot give at all; and to others so little, that they have
Divine Service only once in many Weeks; and several Districts of

[g]*Heb. xii. 3.*

sixty, seventy and eighty Miles long, have but one Minister to officiate in each of them.

The next Object of the Society's Concern, were the poor Negroes. These unhappy Wretches learn, in their Native Country, the grossest Idolatry, and the most savage Dispositions: and then are sold to the best Purchaser: sometimes by their Enemies, who would else put them to Death; sometimes by their nearest Friends, who are either unable or unwilling to maintain them. Their Condition in our Colonies, though it cannot well be worse than it would have been at home, is yet nearly as hard as possible: their Servitude most laborious, their Punishments most severe. And thus many thousands of them spend their whole Days, one Generation after another, undergoing with reluctant Minds continual Toil in this World, and comforted with no Hopes of Reward in a better. For it is not to be expected, that Masters, too commonly negligent of Christianity themselves, will take much Pains to teach it their Slaves: whom even the better Part of them are in a great measure habituated to consider, as they do their Cattle, merely with a View to the Profit arising from them. Not a few therefore have openly opposed their Instruction, from an Imagination, now indeed proved and acknowledged to be groundless, that Baptism would entitle them to Freedom. Others, by obliging them to work on Sundays to provide themselves Necessaries, leave them neither Time to learn Religion in it, nor any Prospect of being able to subsist, if once the Duty of resting on that Day become Part of their Belief. And some, it may be feared, have been averse to their becoming Christians, because, after that, no Pretence will remain for not treating them like Men. When these Obstacles are added to the Fondness they have for their old Heathenish Rites, and the strong Prejudices they must have against Teachers from among those, whom they serve so unwillingly; it cannot be wondered, if the Progress made in their Conversion prove but slow. After some Experience of this, Catechists were appointed in two Places, by way of Trial, for Their Instruction alone: whose Success, where it was least, hath not been inconsiderable; and so great in the Plantation belonging to the Society, that out of two hundred and thirty, at least seventy are now Believers in Christ. And there is lately an Improvement to this Scheme begun to be executed, by qualifying and employing young Negroes, prudently chosen, to teach their Countrymen: from which, in the Opinion of the best Judges, we may reasonably promise ourselves, that this miserable *People,* the Generality of whom have hitherto *sat in Darkness, will see great Light.*[h]

[h]*Matth. iv. 16.*

There still remains another Branch of the Society's Care, the *Indians* bordering on our Settlements. These consist of various Nations, valuable for some of their Qualities, but immersed in the vilest Superstitions, and engaged in almost perpetual Wars against each other, which they prosecute with Barbarities unheard of amongst the rest of Mankind: implacable in their Resentments, when once provoked; boundless in their Intemperance, when they have Opportunities for it, and at such Times mischievous in the highest Degree: impatient of Labour, to procure themselves the common Conveniencies of Life; inhumanely negligent of Persons in Years; and, if Accounts of such Things may be credited, not scrupling to kill and eat their nearest Relations, when the long Expeditions they make, for hunting or against Enemies, have reduced them to Straits. Now these poor Creatures also, diligent Endeavours have been used to enlighten and reclaim, on such Occasions, and by such Methods, as were least suspicious. For without due Precautions, Harm would be done, instead of Good, where natural Jealousy is so industriously fomented by an artful Neighbour. And after all Precautions, it cannot be an easy Work, to convert Nations, whose Manners are so uncultivated; whose Languages are so different, so hard to learn, and so little adapted to the Doctrines of Religion; with whom we scarce ever contract Affinities; and who seldom continue long enough in the same Place, to let any good Impressions fix into Habits. Yet notwithstanding these Difficulties, which frustrated formerly a very expensive Attempt, another hath been made of late; and, through the Blessing of God, hath so reformed and improved the Morals together with the Notions of one Indian Tribe,* that we cannot but hope the rest will be induced, by seeing their Happiness, to follow their Example.

You have now heard in brief the State of our Colonies, with respect to our Religion. And were the Prospect of farther success much smaller than it is; yet our Rule would be, to do our Duty, and leave the Event to Heaven. Persons of unwilling or desponding Minds may easily find Arguments to prove every good Design unpromising, or even impracticable. But the natural Dictate of Piety and Virtue is, to try. And the express Command of our blessed Lord is, that *the Gospel be preached to every Creature.*[i] Nor is only the Offer of Instruction to Heathens, but the Continuance of it for ever amongst Christians, the Will of Him, who, as *he gave some, Apostles and Evangelists;* gave *some* also, *Pastors and Teachers, for the perfecting of the Saints, and the edifying of his Body.*[k] By endeavouring to our

*The Mohawks.
[i]*Mark xvi. 15.*
[k]*Ephes. iv. 11, 12.*

Power that these things be done; we shall pay Obedience to his Authority, and imitate his Example: we shall give a Proof to our own Hearts, that we are indeed his Disciples; and convince the World, that Zeal for Religion is not yet extinguished: we shall habituate ourselves to the most amiable of Virtues, Goodwill to Mankind in the most important of their Interests: we shall serve the Purposes of Providence; which have their Accomplishment, *whether Men will hear, or whether they will forbear:*[1] and how much soever we may *labour in vain* with respect to others; *yet our Judgment will be with the Lord, and our Work with our God.*[m]

But the same God hath promised, that his Truth shall finally prevail upon Earth. And though we cannot say, at what Time or by what Degrees this Promise shall be fulfilled; yet we have room to hope, that every sincere Endeavour is all along contributing something towards its Completion. The good Seed, which appears to lie dead for a while, will spring up in its Season: That which seems to shoot weakly at first, will gain Strength insensibly, through the favourable Influences of Heaven; and *the Grain of Mustard-seed, become a Tree.*[n] Thus have these Colonies themselves grown: thus hath Christianity grown from its Beginning, both in other Places, and in them also: nor have we any reason to doubt its going on to do so still. In less than forty Years, under many Discouragements, and with an Income very disproportionate to the Vastness of the Undertaking, a great deal hath been done: though little notice may have been taken of it, by Persons unattentive to these things, or backward to acknowledge them. Near a hundred Churches have been built: above ten thousand Bibles and Common-Prayers, above a hundred thousand other pious Tracts distributed: great Multitudes, upon the whole, of Negroes and *Indians* brought over to the Christian Faith: many numerous Congregations have been set up, which now support the Worship of God at their own Expence, where it was not known before: and seventy Persons are constantly employed, at the Expence of the Society, in the farther Service of the Gospel. All this, we grant, makes but a small Appearance, in a Tract of Land, extending sixteen hundred Miles. But it is an encouraging Specimen, however, of what longer Time and more liberal Assistance may effect.

Both the Hopes and the Means of supporting Christianity amongst our own People there, are just the same as here at home. And though the Negroes and *Indians* are prejudiced against it, and but poorly qualified, in comparison, to judge of the Evidence of it; yet they and all

[1]*Ezek. ii. 5.*
[m]*Esai. xlix. 5.*
[n]*Matt. xiii. 31, 32.*

Men *have the Work of the Law written in their Hearts, their Consciences also bearing witness.*[o] They may be convicted but too easily of transgressing evident Duties of Nature: and when once they see their need of Repentance and Pardon, they will gladly receive the Gospel of Christ, of which these two are the distinguishing Articles. It will appear in itself infinitely preferable to what they have believed hitherto. The Teachers of it will appear, both from their superior Knowledge and good Lives, worthy of Credit. The Professors of it around them, will bear a Testimony to it, in some respects the stronger, for their being often condemned by it. And if such Arguments do not amount, after all, to the highest Evidence, they afford however very rational Motives of Assent, especially to Persons capable of no farther Information: and were these Motives weaker than they are, yet the Grace of God producing by them so powerful an Effect on the Minds of Men, we undoubtedly approve ourselves, by proposing them, His Ministers for the Happiness of our Fellow-Creatures; and may justly be *confident, that he who hath begun a good Work in them, will perform it*[p] perfectly.

But perhaps not our Success, but the Use and Benefit of it, will be called in question. Now of this, we apprehend, there is abundant Proof. The bare Profession and outward Appearance of such a Religion as the Christian is, if taught in any tolerable Purity, must have some right Influence: and the Body of a People cannot go the utmost Lengths in Wickedness, whilst that Appearance subsists. What Lengths they would go in time, if it were lost, as we have not experienced, we are not apt to consider. But a little Reflexion on the Number and Strength of human Passions, and the Abilities we have of finding Means to gratify them, would give us a high Value of whatever hath any peculiar Force to restrain them. The one Institution of a Day of holy Rest, is not only, under prudent Regulations, a great Refreshment to the Bulk of Mankind; but greatly tends to civilize them also, by uniting Neighborhoods in formed Assemblies, to acknowledge their common Dependance on God, and Relation to each other, with Hearts disengaged from selfish Attentions, and open to friendly Regards. Nor is it possible, be they ever so negligent Hearers of publick Worship and Instruction, but considerable Impressions, at least general ones, must remain upon their Minds. And most evidently the Impressions of Religion dispose Men to every Thing productive of common Good: To Justice and Veracity and the Reverence of an Oath, without which the Intercourse of Man with Man is not a Moment safe: to Faithful-

[o] *Rom. ii. 15.*
[p] *1 Phil. i. 6.*

ness, Duty and Love in the several Relations of Life, publick and private: to Mildness, Charity and Compassion in their whole Behaviour: to Sobriety and Industry, the Pillars of national Wealth and Greatness: and to that joyful Hope of a better World, which is our truest Direction, and firmest Support, in every Stage of our Journey through This. Many more Persons will be thus influenced in various Degrees, than are usually observed: for a regular, inoffensive Behaviour affords little Matter of Speculation and Discourse. And though still the Generality may be bad; yet, if left to themselves, they would certainly have been worse. Every body owns, that a wrong Belief hath great Power to deprave Men's Morals. Surely then a right one must have some Power to reform them. And if not so much as might be wished; this is no more an argument against the Usefulness of Religion, than of Reason: but a strong Argument, why Both should be cultivated to the utmost; and carefully applied to so important a Purpose. If our Colonies had not experienced great Evils from the Decay of Christianity amongst them; they would never have petitioned us so earnestly for Instruction in it, as they have done. And if they had not experienced great Good from the Restoration of it, that Earnestness would never have continued, as it doth, to this Day.

Nor will our Compliance with their Request be a Benefit only to Them, but to this Nation also. If They are dishonest and profligate; every single Person here, who hath Concerns with them, will be in Danger of suffering by it. If they consume their Wealth and their Time in Vices and Follies; their Trade will be gained over, from Them and Us, by our Rivals and Adversaries. And if the Ties of a Religion, binding Men so strongly to *be subject for Conscience Sake,*[q] are loosened from off their Minds, which may some time or another need every Tie, that can keep them attached to us; it will much facilitate their becoming Adversaries themselves. And we shall well deserve their revolting from Us, if we take no care of their obeying God. But on the contrary, as Christian Principles will teach them Dutifulness and Loyalty; so receiving from hence the support of those Principles, will recommend us to their Gratitude; hoping for the Continuance of that Support, will create some Dependance in point of Interest; and agreeing in the same Faith and Worship with us, will be an everlasting Motive to civil Unity also.

But another common Benefit of propagating Christianity in our Colonies is, that thus we shall hinder Corruptions of Christianity from prevailing there, and sharing with Profaneness a divided Empire over the Land. If no authorized Teachers are sent, some Inducement or

[q]*Rom. xiii. 5.*

another will raise voluntary ones from time to time: and very possibly the less reasonable their Doctrine is, the more it may be hearken'd to. For Sentiments of Religion, as for want of due Cultivation they quite wear out of some Minds; so in others they degenerate into Superstition or Enthusiasm. And accordingly many pernicious Errors, besides the above-mentioned capital one of Popery, took early Root in these Provinces; nor are they yet extirpated, perhaps in part newly revived: Some, dissolving the Obligations of moral Duties: Some, destroying the inward Peace of very pious and good Persons, and making Life gloomy and uncomfortable: Some, leading Men to ascribe every Folly or Wickedness that possesses the Fancy to Divine inspiration: Some, inconsistent with our present happy Establishment: and others, destructive of the Safety of all Governments whatever, by forbidding to contribute any kind of Assistance to the publick Defence against Enemies: on which Notion the Representatives of the Province of *Pensylvania* have acted this last Summer.[r] Now let it only be consider'd, how fatal a more general Belief of some of these Doctrines must have been there at present; indeed how very unhappy the Belief of any of them must be at all times; and the Importance of supporting Instructors in true Religion, were it only for a standing Guard against the worldly Inconveniences of false Religion, will evidently appear very great.

[r]*See a printed Collection of Messages, Answers, Addresses, &c. the Substance of which is as follows. The Quakers, having applied themselves with great Industry to obtain an uncommon Majority in the Assembly, though they are not above one third of the People in Number, refused to make any Provision of Necessaries for the Troops to be raised in that Province, as being a thing repugnant to their Religious Principles, though his Majesty had notified under his Sign Manual, that he expected it from them. Soon after this they adjourned for above five Weeks; though the Governor made strong Instances to the contrary, setting forth, That as the new Levies were in want of every thing, even Houses to cover their Heads, He was hourly apprehensive of their committing some Disorders. And being called together again by him in about a Fortnight, instead of raising any Money, they made a Complaint, that many of their Servants had been inlisted; and demanded the Restitution of them. The Governor answer'd, that they might easily have prevented this Inconvenience, and might still easily remedy it by Methods which he pointed out to them; that he had done what he could to relieve them, and would continue to do so; but that forcing out of his Majesty's Troops at once all the Servants in them, would be unreasonable and unjust, very detrimental to the Service, and very dangerous to the publick Peace. Yet notwithstanding these Representations, and though Mr. Penn one of their Proprietors, many Merchants and other Inhabitants of Philadelphia, and the Council of the Province, concurred with the Governor, and pressed them earnestly to answer his Majesty's Expectations, they came at length to this Resolution only: That 3000 l. of their current Money be paid for the King's Use; provided that all the Servants inlisted in the Province, whom they had computed at 300, and valued at 10 l. each, be first returned to their respective Masters, free of all Charges; and such Assurances given, as three Persons, named in the Resolution, should think fitting, that the said Servants are returned, and that no Servants be inlisted for the future. These being the Conditions on which the Money was given, it will not be wonder'd at, that when the last Advices came from thence, no Part of it had been paid.*

But let us now think, what Good must follow from extending this Instruction to the poor Negroes also. The Servitude and hard Labour they undergo, be it as justifiable as it can, surely requires, that we should make them all the Amends in our Power: and the Danger, into which they have brought our Colonies more than once, demands the greatest Care to compose and soften their vindictive and sullen Spirits. Now there can be nothing contrived on Purpose, more likely to effect this, than Belief of the Gospel: which not only forbids in general, both doing and *recompensing Evil*;[s] but commands in particular *as many as are Servants under the Yoke, to count their Masters worthy of all Honour,*[t] *and be subject to them with all Fear, not only to the good and gentle, but also to the froward; for this is thank-worthy, if a Man for Conscience towards God endure Grief, suffering wrongfully:*[u] *to do Service with good Will, as to the Lord, and not to Men; knowing that whatever good any Man doth, the same he shall receive of the Lord, whether he be bond or free.*[w] The Tendency of such Doctrine must be, to make their Tempers milder, and their Lives happier. And no Imagination can be suggested to them, of any worldly Exemptions or Privileges arising from their Profession of it. For as human Authority hath granted them none, so the Scripture, far from making any Alteration in Civil Rights, expresly directs, that *every Man abide in the Condition wherein he is called,* with great Indifference of Mind concerning outward Circumstances:[x] and the only Rule it prescribes for Servants of the same Religion with their Masters, is, *not to despise them because they are Brethren; but do them Service the rather.*[y] Nor hath Experience at all shewn the Behaviour of such, in the present Case, to be different from what Reason would lead us to expect. On the contrary, in a great Rebellion of the Negroes at *New York* only two of those who had received any Instruction, and only one who had been baptized, was so much as suspected of being guilty; and he was afterwards acknowledged to be innocent: but the deepest in the Conspiracy were the Slaves of those Persons, who had opposed the most warmly all Endeavours for their Conversion. It may therefore be depended on, that Success in these Endeavours will both be a Security, and every Way an Advantage, to their Proprietors. And if it doth procure the poor Wretches themselves a little more kind Usage, they will then be fitter to receive it: and at present, as much as can be safely allowed them, is but their due. The Apostle's Injunction was

[s]*Rom. xii. 17.*
[t]*1 Tim. vi. 1.*
[u]*1 Peter ii. 18, 19.*
[w]*Ephes. vi. 7, 8.*
[x]*1 Cor. vii. 20-24.*
[y]*1 Tim. vi. 2.*

made not only for Slaves, but for Heathen Slaves: *Masters, give to your Servants that which is just and equal: knowing that ye also have a Master in Heaven:*[z] *neither is there respect of Persons with him.*[a] And if their becoming Christians will help, as it certainly will, to obtain them such Treatment; putting together their Condition and their Numbers, there are but few Things, which, even, on that Account, common Humanity more obliges us to attempt.

Then as to the Influence of Christianity on the *Indians*: it must undoubtedly restrain their mutual Barbarities, which it doth not appear what else will, and dispose them to a settled and orderly Life. By means of this, they will come to enjoy the Benefit of Agriculture, and of all the Arts that are useful in Society: they will of consequence grow happier and more numerous: and as they will become at the same time more harmless too; it would be both an immoral and a false Policy, to envy them these Advantages. They have yielded up to us a considerable Part of their Country: and it is but common Gratitude, to shew them the Way of living comfortably in the rest. We have introduced amongst them both Diseases and Vices, which have destroyed great Numbers of them: Surely it is fit we should communicate something good to them. It may be feared they are hitherto the worse for their Knowledge of Us: but they will certainly be the better for the Knowledge of our Religion. And the more they are prejudiced against it by the Wickedness of its Professors, the more need there is to lay before them in a full Light the Excellency of its Precepts: and to convince them, that there are Persons, who not only believe, but practise them. Nor should it be forgotten, that every single *Indian,* whom we make a Christian, we make a Friend and Ally at the same time; both against the remaining Heathen, and a much more dangerous Neighbour, from whose Instigations almost all that we have suffered by them is allowed to have come.

But the temporal Advantages of propagating Christianity are infinitely the least. If we allow but the Truth of natural Religion, we must admit the future, as well as present, Happiness of Mankind to depend on preserving and diffusing the Knowledge of that Religion. And there is neither Instance nor Prospect of either of these Things being attempted by any other Method, than that of preaching the Gospel: of which the Doctrines and Duties of Nature make so large a Part. If therefore it be of Importance, that the People in our Colonies should worship the Maker of Heaven and Earth, and believe Virtue to be his Law; that the *Negroes* and *Indians* should *be turned from Idols,*

[z]*Col. iv. 1.*
[a]*Ephes. vi. 9.*

to serve the living and true God;[b] and that all should know, there will be a Recompence hereafter to the Just and to the Unjust: whoever deserves the Name of Deist in a good Sense, whoever is indeed an Enemy to Superstition, and a Friend to Mankind, will rejoice to have that Faith carefully taught amongst them, by which alone they will learn these momentous Truths; to have it *told among the Heathen, that the Lord is King, and that he shall judge the People righteously.*[c]

But if *the Gospel of Christ,* besides comprehending the System of Natural Religion, be, by virtue of its own peculiar Doctrines, *the Power of God unto Salvation:*[d] then every possible Motive concurs, for being zealous in spreading it throughout the Earth. Revelation indeed neither obliges nor permits us to pass a hard Sentence on those, who have never had it proposed with sufficient Evidence. *To their own Master they stand or fall:*[e] and of them only, *to whom much is given, shall much be required.*[f] *For if there be first a willing Mind, it is accepted according to that a Man hath, and not according to that he hath not.*[ff] But still, as *all Men have sinned, and come short of the Glory of God,*[g] and there is but one *Name under Heaven whereby they can be saved;* as Christianity is inexpressibly more efficacious for the Restoration of Mankind, than unassisted Reason; as our only Assurance, either of receiving a future Reward or escaping future Punishment, must arise from Scripture; and we have no Intimation in it, of any Person's enjoying that *Life and Immortality, which Jesus Christ hath brought to Light,*[h] but such as believe in him: these Considerations, without limiting at all the free Mercies of God, cannot but shew us the great Superiority of our own Condition, and make us ask, with great Sollicitude concerning others: *How then shall they believe in Him, of whom they have not heard? And how shall they hear, without a Preacher? And how shall they preach, except they be sent?*[i] Our blessed Lord hath instructed his Followers, to preserve his Gospel in Purity, where it is; and communicate it, where it is not. By their faithful Discharge of these Duties formerly, we ourselves were *deliver'd from the Bondage of* Heathenism *into the glorious Liberty of the Children of God.*[k] It now belongs to Us, in our Turn, to *strengthen our Brethren,*[l] and *call them that are afar off:*[m] and where shall we find proper Objects of our Care and Zeal?

[b]*1 Thess. i. 9.*
[c]*Psal. xcvi. 10.*
[d]*Rom. i. 16.*
[e]*Rom. iv. 14.*
[f]*Luke xii. 48.*
[ff]*2 Cor. viii. 12.*
[g]*Rom. iii. 23.*
[h]*2 Tim. 1. 10.*
[i]*Rom. x. 14, 15.*
[k]*Rom. viii. 21.*
[l]*Luke xxii. 32.*
[m]*Acts ii. 39.*

Perhaps it will be said, They ought to maintain their own Teachers. But this cannot be expected from the Heathen, who are insensible of their Want of them: nor from those of our own People, who are too like Heathen, and have not the Sense of it which they ought. Such as have, do maintain their Teachers, where they are able. For there are very indigent Parts, as well as very opulent. Some whole Provinces have no Assistance at all from us. And in most Places we are only joint Contributors. As soon as ever there is room for it, they will be left to build by themselves on the Foundation laid: and the Society will go on to new Work. Enquiries are constantly made, what each Congregation can do: and Missionaries have been with-drawn, till they will do it. For we are not only desirous, but under a Necessity of being as frugal as possible, by the daily Increase of Petitions for Help.

But some will object farther, that all the Assistance we can give Christianity, is too much wanted in our own Country, to admit of any Schemes for propagating it in foreign ones. And would to God these Persons would ask themselves, whether they are indeed desirous of removing the Objection they make; or only argue against this and that Way of doing Good, to save the Expence of doing it in any Way. A true and judicious Zeal will carefully avoid raising an Opposition between two Charities; which is a much surer Method of hurting the One, than serving the Other: whereas with this Precaution, a first scarce ever suffers considerably, if at all, by setting up a second; but Men's Hearts are enlarged to contribute to both. Every single Member of the *Society for promoting Christian Knowledge* at home, was originally incorporated into Ours for spreading it abroad. That Society is at this Day promoting the same Knowledge in the East, as well as here; whilst We are doing it in the West. Many of us belong to Both: and promise ourselves a larger Share of the Blessing of God in Each, for neglecting Neither. In these Nations great Provision is made already, and greater we hope will daily be made, for offering Salvation to Mankind. They who will reject it after all, must do so, and take the Consequences. But let Us, *in nothing terrified by our Adversaries, strive together for the Faith of the Gospel*:[n] and not only sustain a Defensive War, but shew, that attacking the Dominions of our Lord and Master shall increase our Zeal to extend them. Our Colonies receive from hence a great deal of what is bad. We send them our Malefactors: we send them our immoral and irreligious Customs: we send them our infidel and profligate Books. Surely we ought to do some Good, where we do so much Harm. And consider, to whom

[n]*Phil. i, 27, 28.*

is it done? To our Countrymen, and Fellow-Subjects: distant indeed
from us in Situation, but closely connected by the strongest Ties. To
Them; to their Servants and Neighbours it is, that we are imparting
Happiness; and possibly securing it to ourselves or our Posterity there,
if God should permit us at home to suffer what we deserve.

Now this unquestionably right Design cannot be carried on, but
under the Direction of a regular Society. For without it, small Benefactions could not be applied at all: and large ones must be applied
separately, to great Disadvantage: no uniform Influence could be
preserved, no settled Information had; nor any of that Experience
gained, which results from long and extensive Acquaintance with the
State of Things. What sort of Persons they are who compose this
Society, will appear from the printed List. None of them receive any
temporal Advantage from being Members of it. They are all obliged
to subscribe a yearly Contribution to the good Work they undertake.
A considerable Number of the Chief of them constantly attend upon
it. And they will admit with Pleasure every serious Christian, who
offers himself, and is qualified to assist in it. Their standing Rules are
publickly known, allowed to be good, and faithfully observed. They
give the World a yearly account of their Success, with an Abstract
of their Receipts and Disbursements. They deliver yearly the Particulars of them to the Lord Chancellor and two chief Justices. And
they have proceeded from the Beginning to this Day with great Unan-
imity in all their Affairs.

It hath been pretended indeed, that immoral and negligent Men
are employed as Missionaries. And to say that this hath never once
happen'd, would be going too far. But that it hath frequently happen'd,
or ever for want of due Care, is utterly false. Strict Examination is
made at first into the Characters of all that are offer'd; strict Enquiry
into their Behaviour afterwards: and exact Accounts required from
them twice a Year, of what Duty they do, and what Progress they
make. The most earnest Requests, the most solemn Adjurations are
sent, that all who can, would give any useful Intelligence relating to
them: and great Regard is always paid to such Intelligence: yet
very few Complaints are brought in, either from good Will or bad. Too
many, it must be owned, of desperate Fortunes and Characters, who
are or pretend to be in holy Orders, transport themselves into *America,*
and behave there as it may be expected they will. But we have no
Concern with any, whose Names are not seen in the publick List of
Persons receiving Salaries from us. And the larger the Number is of
vicious Clergymen, who go thither of their own Accord; the more is

the need of sending as many worthy ones as possible, to correct their Influence.

Were there room indeed for making larger Allowances, more Persons of great Abilities might be had. Were there better Opportunities for a learned Education abroad, more of the Natives of our Colonies would be fitted for the Work: which they would undertake with many Advantages above such as go from hence. And had they Bishops there, these Persons might be ordained without the Inconveniencies of a long Voyage: Vacancies might be supplied in much less Time: the primitive and most useful Appointment of Confirmation might be restored; and an orderly Discipline exercised in the Churches. Nor would such an Establishment encroach at all on the present Rights of the Civil Government in our Colonies; or bring their Dependance into any Degree of that Danger, which some Persons profess to apprehend so strongly on this Occasion, who would make no manner of Scruple about doing other things much more likely to destroy it: who are not terrified in the least, that such Numbers there reject the Episcopal Order entirely: nor perhaps would be greatly alarmed, were ever so many to reject Religion itself: though evidently in Proportion as either is thrown off, all Dependance produced by it ceases of course. To this equally pious and harmless Design, two great Prelates,* now deceased, gave a thousand Pounds each: and a Lady, incomparably more eminent for her Virtues, than her Quality,† bequeathed the Sum of five hundred Pounds last Year to the same Purpose: which God incline the Hearts of all, in whose Power it is, to promote as it deserves! But in the mean time, let it not be imagined, that the Difficulties we labour under are too heavy to be overcome. Difficulties are Arguments for nothing, but more Zeal and more Liberality. For if we stop, till we have every thing that might be wished, When shall we go on?

Another Objection to the Conduct of the Society is, that they have sent Missionaries to some Places, in which there were already Christian Assemblies established and supported. But in one Sort of these Assemblies, there is no Christian Ministry, no Celebration of the Sacrament of the Gospel. In another, Infants are denied the Sacrament of Baptism. And in the least exceptionable, there are several Things, which the Consciences of many, we apprehend with great Reason, cannot acquiesce in; who were not therefore to be left destitute of publick Worship: especially as our Charter was granted, in express Terms, for *the Maintenance of an Orthodox Clergy in those Parts.* And the Members of this Church, I am sorry to say it, lying under peculiar

---

Archbishop Tenison, and Sir Jonathan Trelawney, Bishop of Winchester.
†*Lady Elizabeth Hastings.*

Burdens in one considerable Province,* which other Professors of Christianity do not, though equally Dissenters from the Majority there; they seem of Right entitled to some peculiar Assistance in return. We have obtruded the Service of the Church of *England* no where: we have settled no Clergyman any where, without the Inhabitants requesting it, and contributing to it: we have sent no Successor upon a Vacancy, without their renewing that Request. But if the Provision, which we have made for the People of our own Communion, hath proved instrumental at the same time to bring others over into it: we hope there is very far from being any Harm done. Indeed Unity of Profession amongst ourselves, effected by Methods of Peace and Charity, will greatly recommend our Religion to the Infidels: who else may be tempted to continue as they are, for want of knowing with whom to join.

We acknowledge it, whoever is taught Christianity by our Care, will be taught it as professed in the Church established here by Law. There can be no Teaching at all, but in some particular Form. We think our own the best. Every body thinks it far from the worst. At least our Converts will have the Bible put into their Hands, to judge for Themselves. And Which is righter, that Heathens and Persons of no Religion should continue what they are, or become what we would make them? The Society we are engaged in, is the only one for this Purpose. And were it now to be erected, instead of having subsisted so long: not a single Step could be taken on any other footing than this; that the smaller Part of those who wished well to it, must be concluded by the greater.

So good a Design therefore being so properly executed; the Expences, which must attend it, ought to be supplied. *The Lord hath ordained, that they who preach the Gospel, should live of the Gospel.*° And there is the same Reason, the same Necessity indeed, that the Missionaries in *America* should have due Provision made for them, as that the Apostles should at first, or the Ministers of our Parishes now. And if Persons of Character, being at Liberty, as they are, to exercise their Function elsewhere, are willing to undertake such an Employment as this, at such a Distance, on so small an Allowance as they receive from the Society: they ought surely to have it raised for them very chear-

In New England They are rated to the Support of what the Independents, who are the greater Part of that People, call, though without Right, the Established Church. And the Goods of many have been seized, or their Bodies imprisoned, for Non-payment. The Anabaptists, on their Petition, were exempted from paying this Rate; and the Quaker, without petitioning: but the Petition of the Members of our Church was rejected.

°1 Cor. ix. 14.

fully, and *be counted worthy of double Honour,*[p] in the Sense of Recompence as well as Esteem, if it could be paid them.

But perhaps it will be said, Supporting Designs of this Nature is the Clergy's Business: let Them take care of it. And so, God be thanked, we do: and so, I hope in God, we shall, whether we are helped in it more or less; in such manner, as both to keep pace with the Unwilling. We desire not to boast, and we need not to be ashamed, of the Proportion which we contributé. But we may notwithstanding do very well to increase it. For there is so much expected of us, and we are so greatly concerned to answer every reasonable Expectation to the utmost; that if any of our Order have omitted taking sufficient Notice of a Charity so immediately related to their Profession, it is their Duty on many Accounts, to make full Compensation to it without Delay. It is indeed our Duty, on every Occasion, at all Times, but especially in an Age when no Part of our Conduct will be interpreted favourably, to avoid all Appearance, either of preferring *Riches in this World before being rich in good Works,*[q] or of *loving Pleasures more than God.*[r] St. *Paul took Wages of* some *Churches to do* others *Service.*[s] Let Us, out of the Wages which We take, do all the Service we can to the Church of God; and *distribute* largely *to the Necessities of the Saints,*[t] particularly their spiritual ones.

But is the Support of this Design incumbent on the Clergy alone? Did not the Laiety originally maintain the Apostles in their Travels? And ought they not still to be equally zealous, *that the Word of the Lord may have free Course, and be glorified?*[u] Do they not know, how very inconsiderable the Benefices of far the greatest Part of the Clergy are; what Hospitality is required of the rest of us; and how large Demands are continually made upon us for Charities of various Kinds: to the Poor of our Parishes and Neighbourhoods, of our Brethren, their Widows and Orphans; to every pious and compassionate Use, publick or private? And are they not sensible also, that were We ever so deficient, this excuses not Them: that every Man's Duty is, not to guard against doing more Good than comes to his Share, but to do willingly what he can; and that each one's Reward shall be in Proportion to his Work?

Whoever therefore finds himself disposed to make Objections, let him examine, what is at the bottom of them: Whether it be not really Disregard to Religion, or Want of Humanity; some groundless

[p] *1 Tim. v. 17.*
[q] *1 Tim. vi. 17, 18.*
[r] *2 Tim. iii. 4.*
[s] *2 Cor. xi. 8.*
[t] *Rom. xii. 13.*
[u] *2 Thess. iii. 1.*

Prejudice, or some wrong Attachment to Self-Interest or Self-Gratification. If so, let him first plant the Gospel in his own Heart: and all his Pleas against contributing to the Propagation of it, will soon vanish.

Every Man's Charities indeed ought to be left to his own Choice. But so many, even of those who are bountiful in other Ways, neglect pious Uses almost entirely, that good Persons have both Opportunity and Reason for allotting to These a large Proportion of their Beneficence. And amongst these, as That now under Consideration is of too extensive a Nature to be thoroughly comprehended by every one, and at too great a Distance to make any strong Impression on the Generality of the World; they who do form just Conceptions of it, should, in proportion to the Smallness of their Number, be the more liberal to it: as in truth there is need. The only certain Income we have, is a Trifle: not sixty Pounds a Year. The voluntary Subscriptions, tho' they are ten times greater, are not a fifth Part of the annual Expence. Hitherto therefore almost all hath depended on occasional Gifts: which, after sinking much lower than they were formerly, for some few Years increased again. On this Encouragement, the Society, importuned continually for new Missionaries, with an Earnestness which nothing but Necessity could justify resisting, made a great Addition to their Number. And had the Contributions of this last Year risen much above the preceding ones, it had been but too easy to have disposed of them all. But on the contrary, though one noble Benefaction, of a thousand Pounds, hath been given,† to be employed for the Conversion of the Negroes; yet those to the other Parts of our Design have fallen very short: and a heavy Debt hath been of consequence incurred. This may possibly reduce us to ask Assistance, in a Method, which, though authorized, we have seldom made use of: being desirous that *he who sheweth Mercy*, might appear to do it *with Chearfulness*,ʷ and not constrained by Sollicitations. But in whatever manner Application is made to Persons, we trust the same God, who hath provided for us wonderfully thus long, will now also dispose their Hearts to consider, that on Them it depends, whether such a Design, so far advanced, through so many Difficulties, shall be carried on still, and gain ground continually, as it easily may; or whether it shall fall back, and sink into Nothing, with very little Hope of being ever revived: That he will move wise Men to think, what the publick Interest requires of them; and benevolent Persons, to regard the private Happiness of their Fellow-Creatures: true Christians, to support and enlarge the Kingdom of their Master with Zeal; true Protestants, to silence effectually the Boasts and Re-

†*By Mr. Batt of Hampshire.*
ʷ*Rom. xii. 8.*

proaches of the *Romanists* on this Head; and all true Friends of our Religious Establishment, to endeavour, that it may gain as honourable a Pre-eminence as possible, over the rest of the Reformed Churches, in so good a Work.

Persons in plentiful Circumstances, and perhaps at a loss for Ways in which they may give Alms, will here find one undoubtedly proper Way. And Persons in Arrear to Religion and Charity, have an excellent Opportunity offer'd them, of paying the Debt. They who plead the multitude of other Expences, might, a very great Part of them, by withdrawing but a little of what they ought from their Luxury and Vanity, qualify themselves for Liberalities, which will turn hereafter to a much better Account. And such as make the Increase of Taxes their Excuse, ought to consider, that as Providence hath brought that Increase upon us, by permitting us to suffer so much from our Enemies, in that Part of the World, where we have done so little for God; espousing His Cause is the likeliest Method of deriving a Blessing on our Own: and if we neglect it, whatever may befall us there, we must impute to ourselves. We enjoy very great Advantages from thence: the Government, large Revenues; the Nation in general, a most beneficial Trade; every one of us, something or another, useful or agreeable in Life. It is therefore our common Concern, both to do Good where we have received it; and to do it in such manner, as may best secure our continuing to receive it. But they more especially, who are now raising Fortunes by Commerce with our *American* Settlements, or who possess acquired or hereditary Estates, of which that Commerce laid the Foundation, they should think often, how much hath accrued to them from the Produce of these Colonies, the Country of these *Indians,* the Labour of these Negroes; and reflect very seriously, what Returns, possibly Justice, at least Gratitude, and in, many Cases Prudence also, as well as Piety, direct them to make.

Some perhaps may approve one Part of this Undertaking beyond the rest: and whatever they give, will be applied, if they desire it, to that alone. Some may be unwilling to let their Benefactions appear: and such may with Ease transmit them privately: the Donation will be acknowledged, the Donor unknown. But though Charity given in secret, from a Principle of Humanity, be laudable in the highest Degree; yet when the Motive is Fear of Ridicule or Censure from a Profane Age, this argues a Weakness of Mind, very dangerous to those who are influenced by it, and very prejudicial to Religion: which cannot have a more seasonable Service done it, than if all Persons indeed, especially of Rank and Influence, who inwardly wish well to it, would openly patronize the several Designs formed to promote it.

The Design now before us, both deserves and requires a general Co-operation, to produce its complete Effect: That they who are able, should contribute to it, in proportion to their Ability; and they who are not, speak well of it, and pray for it: that we of the Society should be vigilant and active, prudent and impartial in our Administration: that Persons in Authority abroad should countenance and protect the Work; for in their Power it is, to forward or obstruct it very greatly: that the People in general there, should not only be willing to let all under them and around them *partake of the Grace of Life,*[x] but earnestly invite them to it, *with Meekness of Wisdom,* and by the most prevalent of Arguments, *a good Conversation.*[y] But beyond the rest it is necessary for every one concerned in the immediate Execution of the Design, always to remember, that bad as it is in other Teachers of the Gospel to behave in a manner unworthy of their Profession, it will be yet worse in Them, if they take an uncommon Character upon themselves, only to dishonour it; and *compass Sea and Land,*[z] with no other Effect, than to make *God's Name be blasphemed amongst the Gentiles:*[a] that They ought with peculiar Diligence to *follow Righteousness, Faith, Charity, Peace;*[b] *holding fast the faithful Word, as they have been taught, that they may be able, by sound Doctrine, both to exhort and convince the Gainsayers;*[c] that they ought to *be instant, in season, out of season; to watch, endure Afflictions, and make full Proof of their Ministry,*[d] *shewing themselves in all things Patterns of good Works.*[e]

These then are our several Duties: and great will be our Reward for performing them. Let us all therefore, each in his Station, *arise and be doing: and the Lord be with us.*[f]

[x]*1 Pet. iii. 7.*
[y]*James iii. 13.*
[z]*Matth. xxiii. 15.*
[a]*Rom. ii. 24.*
[b]*2 Tim. ii. 22.*
[c]*Tit. i. 9.*
[d]*2 Tim. iv. 2, 5.*
[e]*Tit. ii. 7.*
[f]*1 Chr. xxii. 16.*

A
SERMON

PREACHED BEFORE THE

INCORPORATED SOCIETY

FOR THE

PROPAGATION OF THE GOSPEL

IN FOREIGN PARTS;

AT THEIR

ANNIVERSARY MEETING

IN THE

PARISH-CHURCH OF ST. MARY-LE-BOW,

ON FRIDAY, FEBRUARY 21, 1766.

By the Right Reverend Father in GOD,
WILLIAM Lord Bishop of GLOCESTER.

LONDON:
Printed by E. OWEN and T. HARRISON in
Warwick-Lane.

MDCCLXVI.

At the Anniversary Meeting of the Society for the
Propagation of the Gospel in Foreign Parts,
in the Vestry-Room *of St.* Mary-le-Bow, *on*
Friday, *the 21st Day of* February, 1766.

AGREED, that the Thanks of the SOCIETY
be given to the Right Reverend the Lord Bishop
of *Glocester*, for his Sermon preached this Day before the SOCIETY; and that his Lordship be desired to deliver a Copy of the same to the SO-
CIETY to be Printed.

Daniel Burton, Secretary.

REV. OF ST. JOHN, CH. X. VER. 11.

And he said unto me, Thou must prophecy AGAIN, *before many Peoples, and Nations, and tongues, and Kings.*

The great Commission intrusted, by our divine Master to his Disciples, was to *go and teach all Nations, baptizing them in the name of the Father, and of the Son, and of the Holy Ghost*; and we know how faithfully they discharged their trust: these latter ages of extended Commerce having discovered, by the most evident marks and traces of their footsteps, that there was no Region, how remote soever, of the then known World, into which these Missionaries of Christ did not carry *the glad tidings of the Gospel.*

But there was a *New World* to be disclosed, another Hemisphere to be explored;—reserved, indeed, for the daring search of modern Adventurers through the tractless immense of the great Atlantic Ocean.

And for this Orphaned World the holy Spirit made the like charitable provision, in his *Revelations* to St. John; where the future fortunes of the Church, from its humble Cradle to its consummation in glory, are foretold in a regular series of enigmatical representations. Amongst these Prophetic visions, the Apostle sees *a mighty angel descend from Heaven; a rain-bow surrounding his head; his face like the Sun, and his feet as pillars of fire.** In this graphical representation of the Son of God, cloathed in all the pomp and majesty of his Father, his *attitude* is most observable; *His* RIGHT FOOT WAS ON THE SEA, *and his left on the Earth* :† An attitude most expressive of his ready Providence, addressed to unveil, in the fullness of time, this NEW WORLD so long concealed in the bosom of the Deep; and pointing out to his Church the religious use to be made of this discovery, namely, the compleating of the Commission delivered to his followers. For the Angel having *sworn* (as denoting the *revelation* to be a matter of high importance) and intimated (by the words, *there shall be time no longer,* i. e. the consideration of time is not to be taken in*) that the Subject was of a distant period; he addresses himself to St. John, who here represents the *Church,* in the words of my text—*Thou must Prophecy* AGAIN *before many Peoples, and Nations, and tongues, and Kings.*—As much as to say, "The Church hath been faithfull in her great Trust, in all things that have been hitherto in her power to discharge. But a time

**Ver. 1.*
†*Ver. 2.*
**Oti chronos oun esai eti. v. 6.*

will come, when this mighty labour, so successfully undergone, in the conversion of the *Old World,* must be repeated in the *New.* For the Church must PROPHECY AGAIN, or preach the Gospel for the *second time* to many new discovered People and Nations." *To Prophecy,* signifying here what it commonly does in many Places of the New Testament, to preach the glad tidings of the Gospel.

Hence it appears, that the Church's obligation to preach the Gospel to the *new World* when discovered, is not simply a mere act of Charity, but the discharge of an indispensable duty.

The providential Discovery was at length made; and though, in itself replete with all the seeds of temporal and spirituall Blessings, was yet most horribly perverted: For as in the *Old* world so in the *New,* the Devil stepped in to take the first fruits of Creation and Renovation, due only to the all-bounteous Author. While, under the mask of the Gospel (if Popery may be said ever to have worn that Mask) the Natives of *South America* were murdered by millions because they had more Gold than they knew how to use; and the Savages of the *North* driven from their kindred Woods and Marshes, because they differed from their Invaders in the mode of cultivating their Lands: And neither One nor the Other deemed to have a right to any thing because they were Pagans and Barbarians. The honour of being made acquainted with *Civil Life* and *Christian rites,* was reserved for a more favoured People, discovered about the same time, on the most remote Coasts of Africa; whose shores and inlands were made desert to enrich the Planters of the *new World.* And honoured they were, if becoming the Supporters of Civil Life could make them so.

Indeed, by that time, the Inhabitants of this *new World* were in so fair a train towards total extirpation, God raised up his chosen Instruments in the *old* to restore Christianity to its Gospel health and purity, then labouring in its last pangs under popish tyranny and superstition. For the Gospel was of necessity to be restored before it could be *preached* AGAIN. And the *obligation* to preach it was to be seen before it could be performed. The REFORMATION OF RELIGION opened again these living Sources: And then it was that the Sense of my Text became evident; and that the Church first addressed itself to this undertaking. Nor was this the only benefit. The Church of Rome, in order to support its shaken usurpation, was obliged, in this, as in other regulations of its abuses, to vie with us in the discharge of this *second Mission,* in which our venerable Corporation has borne so distinguished a Share.

I am but little acquainted with the history of its pious Establishment; but I reasonably suppose it to have been founded in obedience to this SECOND CALL: and, consequently, that the peculiar objects of its exalted Charity were the barbarous Americans, so long lain hid *in the Shadow of Death.*

I. Our Colonies, indeed, opened the Door to this spiritual Enterprize; and were, in reason, to be paid for their pains, with some portion of the heavenly Manna; not so much in relief of their own wants, as for the wants of their Posterity. For our Colonies were formed and were first peopled by religious and conscientious men; who, made uneasy at home by their intolerant Brethren, left the *Old World,* to enjoy, in peace, that first and chief prerogative of Man, *the free worship of God according to his own Conscience*: At one time, PURITANS driven over by the Episcopal Church; at another, CHURCHMEN forced thither by the Presbyterian Faction; just as the revolutions of State threw the civil power into one or the other hand. For it must be remembered (though to the opprobrium of humanity) that, of all the errors of that Antichristian Church from which the GOSPELLERS were, with derision, expelled, this most abominable of all, PERSECUTION FOR OPINIONS, stuck the fastest; and after having tarnished the splendor of almost every Protestant Community, in its turn, was the latest, and with most difficulty shaken off.

Now, amongst the general *Wants* of new Colonies, composed of such kind of Men, RELIGION is rarely one. Of this our Colonists carried over a sound and ample Cargo; sufficient for themselves and their Posterity: and might therefore have been safely left to live upon their own stock.

So that had this been all, our important Mission had not stopped at the Door, but only taken advantage of its opening, to address ourselves directly to the *Gentiles.*

But though the zeal of the first Colonists, rekindled by this inforced and violent motion round the Globe, kept Religion alive and active, yet their Poverty disabled them from providing spiritual fuel to the vital flame; I mean, provision for A PREACHING MINISTRY. Insomuch, that without the pious aid of their Mother-Country, this new Christian Common-wealth had been, as the Roman historian expresses it of the imperial City in it's Cradle, *Res unius AEtatis.* Against this danger, a timely aid was to be provided. And the Founders of our Society not being *Fanatics,* would not intrust the care to *Fanatics*: a People always ready, yet never fitted for one of these spiritual Enterprizes; but forward to go out upon a *second call,* as naked and pennyless as those holy men, who, with the large viaticum of Miracles, went out upon the *first.* It was thought fit therefore to assign a decent maintenance for these late labourers in the Lord's Vineyard; who, having *stood all the Day idle,* were called, at the *last hour,* to their work. To this the Charter of Incorporation alludes; where, speaking of the purpose of the Society to appoint Missionaries to the Colonies, it adds—*which, by the reason of their poverty, are destitute and unprovided of a MAIN-* TENANCE *for Ministers, and the public worship of God.*

This purpose hath been hitherto soberly pursued: our Missionaries to America having carefully avoided the Conduct of those of *Rome,* into the *Levant*; whose principal design hath ever been to reduce the distressed Churches of *Greece* and *Asia* to a submission to the Papal-Tyranny.

Yet notwithstanding so sage and decent a conduct, certain of the Colonies, where the Established Church is *Presbyterian,* and still in its antient spirit of PURITY, have taken offence at the Mission exercised in their quarters, though only for the service of the dispersed Members of the *Episcopal* Church, residing amongst them.

Such a behaviour in a People, where wealth and Civil Faction, have, as usual, inflamed religious zeal, is sufficient to remind us of that crisis, when the Disciples of *Jesus* are directed *to shake off the dust of their feet* for a testimony against the rejecters of their Charity.

Nor would such a Secession lead us from the great purpose of the SOCIETY. For though a Mission to the Colonies was first in the execution, yet, as appears from what hath been said, it was only secondary in the capital purpose.

Here, then, we might well leave these factious People to themselves, did not a miserable circumstance still call for our rejected Charity: I mean, the spreading GENTILISM in the Colonies themselves. Not a brutal ignorance of God, as amongst the savage Natives; but a blasphemous contempt of his holy Dispensations, amongst our *Philosophic Colonists.* The Origine of which folly was, however, no more than this—

The rich product of the Plantations soon supplied the Colonists with all the *conveniencies of life.* And men are no sooner at their ease, than they are ready addressed to pleasure. So that the second venture of our Colonists was for the *luxuries of life*: amongst which, the Commodity called FREETHINKING was carefully consigned to them, as that which would give a relish and seasoning to all the rest. For in this close union of Sense and Reason in our Nature, the Man is at unrest, till each part be properly accommodated. While the body is content with a temperate enjoyment of its appropriated good, the mind finds its pleasure in the pursuit of Knowledge, and in the practice of Virtue. But when the Body plunges into the luxury of sense, the mind will extravagate through all the whimsies of a viciated Imagination. And these corporeal and intellectual Vices, supporting one another, the ravages they make of humanity are not to be controlled.

Thus it came to pass, that the very People, whose Fathers were driven for Conscience-sake into *the waste and howling Wilderness,* are now as ready to laugh at that Bible, esteemed by their Fathers the most precious relict of their ruined Fortunes, as at their Ruffs and Collarbands.

Now, against this outrageous Folly (the sure prognostic of a ruined People) the dearest Charity requires us to oppose all our spiritual endeavours, before we go on upon the great Duty to which we are summoned in my text.

II. And this brings me to the second point I proposed to consider, *Our Mission to the Gentiles.* And here, in entering on the subject, it may not be unuseful to observe the advantages which *Popery* hath over the *Reformed,* in training up their Labourers to this Harvest. For we should be unjust to ROME not to acknowledge their *zeal* to be equal to that of other Churches, in displaying the Christian Banner throughout the habitable world.

To see their advantages in a true light, we should reflect upon the proper qualifications of one of these *Soldiers of Christ*—What he is disposed to do, and what he is ready to suffer, in this religious warfare, amongst *Heathens,* whether civilized or barbarous—He must have an ardent zeal and unwearied diligence; Appetites subdued to all the distresses of want, and a Mind superior to all the terrors of death.

Now, these qualities and habits, their several *Orders of Religious,* from whence their Missionaries are taken, very early labour to inculcate. One quality is more deeply implanted by *this* Order, another by *that*; and the most necessary and essential are formed in *all*: thus every monastic Institution kindles and keeps alive that exalted charity, a Selfe-sacrifice for the salvation of souls.

The JESUITES subdue the Will by the severe discipline of blind Obedience;—to stand wherever they are placed, and to run wherever they are bid. The CARTHUSIANS subdue the Appetites by a tedious course of bodily labours and mortifying abstinences: and the Order called THE CONGREGATION OF ST. PAUL, subdues the whole man: For, in a sense as peculiar to them as to their holy Patron, they *die dayly*; the observance of their whole rule consisting in one continued meditation on that *King of Terrors.*

Nor is this all. The several *Orders,* like Workmen who travel separately on the various parts of the same Machine, each of them to be sent to the Master-Artist to be put into its destined place, where, by a proper combination, all are fitted for their peculiar use; the *Orders,*

I say, send their Subjects, thus prepared, to the *College* DE PROPA-GANDA FIDE, to receive their last finishing, and first motion, by instruction in the Languages, the Manners and the Customs of the barbarous Nations, to whose conversion they are appointed and addressed. And indeed without so long and regular a preparation, it is not in Nature, but in Grace only, for any man chearfully, and, at the same time, soberly to undergo all the accumulated distresses, ever ready to overwhelm a faithful Missionary.

For want of these advantages, a Protestant Society, like ours, hath been too frequently obliged to take up with subjects from amongst men of ruined fortunes; such, whose impotency of mind have shewn them to be unable to bear either Poverty or Riches.—Or else from amongst warm-headed Zealots, totally unfit for every sober and important work.

And, indeed, when we consider the greatness of our wants in this kind, we should be tempted to wish for a COLLEGE, destined for the supplial of a sufficient number of able Missionaries in constant succession, brought up, from their early youth, in such a discipline as may be judged best fitted for such a service. And here it may not be impertinent to observe, that should the Governors of that famous UNIVERSITY, to which a munificent Benefactor hath bequeathed a large estate for the erection of a NEW COLLEGE, be at a loss to execute his intention in such a manner as may give new vigour to the decayed Spirit of Learning and Religion, they may find in a COLLEGE DE PROPAGANDA FIDE an establishment which would interfere with no other, and would give additional sanctity to them all.

Having premised thus much, I come to what I proposed to consider, *Our Mission to the Gentiles*; for we must, in obedience to the Command, *Prophesy* AGAIN *before many Peoples and Nations*;—to Barbarians *bond and free*. These latter, the Aborigines of the Country, Savages without Law or Religion, are the principal Objects of our Charity. Their *temporal,* as well as *spiritual,* condition calls loudly for our assistance; and more especially, as *civilizing* will be found a necessary step to *conversion.*

The benevolent Spirit of Antiquity, which set their Heroes and Law-givers on reforming the barbarous manners of their savage Neighbours, and communicating to them the blessings of CIVIL-LIFE, as divine as it appears, hath been yet outdone in the Charity of these later times, which sends Missionaries amongst the wild inhabitants of the new World, with the greater blessing of the Gospel. But the constant ill success of this glorious undertaking, hath been long matter of grief to all good men. Something therefore must needs be much amiss to defeat a purpose which Grace and Nature conspire to advance. And, if we enquire carefully into it, we shall find it to be this, *preaching to savage and brutal Men*. For the GOSPEL, plain and simple as it is, and fitted in its nature for what it was designed to effect, requires an intellect above that of a Savage to apprehend. Nor is it at all to the dishonour of our holy Faith, that such men must be taught a previous Lesson, and first of all instructed in the *emollient arts of life*. And it is not one of the least benefits of SOCIETY that, at the time it teaches us to improve every bodily accommodation, it enlarges and enlightens the faculties of the mind, by the exercise which the mind undergoes in improving those accommodations.

For want of this preparation, it hath commonly happened, that when, by the indefatigable labour of the Missionary, numbers of these Savages have been baptized into the Faith, such Converts have never long preserved, nor were they able to propagate amongst their Tribes, the *Christianity* they had been taught; but successive Missions have found that the work was ever to begin anew.

From whence we conclude, that they set out at the wrong end; for, to make the Gospel *understood,* much more to propagate and perpetuate it, these Barbarians should have been first taught the *civil arts of life*. And, indeed, to civilize a savage People is, in itself, a work of such exalted charity, that to find it neglected, when a further and far nobler end than the *arts of life* may be procured by it, is matter of infinite astonishment.

We justly censure the Popish Missionaries for their ill-directed zeal in propagating a *Commentitious Gospel,* for pure and genuine Christianity. But then we must be so fair to confess that, in the preparatory part of their Mission, their conduct and address has been so humane and rational, as to be well worthy of our imitation. Nor need this give scandal to any good Protestant. Our great Master himself hath recommended to the *Children of light* the Example of the *Children of this World,* because, says he, *these are wiser in their generation*; that is, they are more skilful than the *Children of light* in adapting MEANS TO ENDS.

This learned audience easily understands that, by the *Children of this World,* I mean the JESUITES: they are emphatically so. Now these men have, both in South and North America, successfully practised the method I here presume to recommend: which is, first of all, to CIVILIZE the subjects of our Mission. The steps they took to effect this great purpose were no less judicious than the project itself was noble and benevolent. They began with teaching the Savages the Art of AGRICULTURE; of all the civil arts, the most essential, as it soonest reduces men from a roving wandering life into settled habitations, the first entrance into the Social State. The Provinces of *Paraguy* and the Island of *California* do, for this blessing, proclaim them the Benefactors of Mankind. And had they but taught the eternal Gospel in its *purity,* at the time they taught the transitory arts of life in their *integrity,* they would have deserved all the praise, and much of the Power they there aspired to.

But in all this affair, the awful Justice of Providence on the Instruments, is no less conspicuous than his Blessings on the Work; which, when considered together, will afford an useful Lesson to Mankind.

This SOCIETY OF JESUS, as it is too well known, had, from their very first establishment, in direct opposition to the professed end of their institution, and in defiance of the sacred name they had assumed, immerged themselves in the worst part of civil intrigues; and in so flagicious a manner, that there is hardly a Court in Christendom, (into most of which they had insinuated themselves) where they have not left manifest traces of their Machiavelian Politics, in seditions and assassinations, sanctified and supported on the two main pillars of their system, *relaxed Morals* and *Papal Omnipotency.*

At length, after rioting in these disorders for a century and an half, they conceived, either out of humanity or avarice, the noble project of civilizing the inland Inhabitants of South America; whom, the Spaniards and Portuguese on the east and west, had, by their diabolic treatment, rendered so outrageous against their Persecutors, that the fiercest beasts of prey were a more desirable neighbourhood.

In this condition the Missionary Jesuites found these persecuted Indians: and, for the ease and safety (as they pretended) of the Christian Colonies on each side, they sat upon the desperate project of taming them to humanity: which at length indeed, they effected; though with infinite labour and prodigious slaughter of the brethren of the Order.

However, the attempt succeeded: and the Jesuites, out of these wild and rabid tribes, founded so equal and powerful a republic, as by their virtues to disgrace the neighbouring Colonies, and by their Policy to give umbrage to the two Catholic Monarchs, to whom those Colonies belong.

For the FATHERS, now Fathers indeed, and worthy of their name, the *Fathers of a People,* seeing the morals of the surrounding Colonies incurably corrupt, pretended they could find no other possible means of securing the infant virtue of their new establishments, from the contagion of Spanish and Portuguese manners, than by a total exclusion of all commerce and communication between them.

This served for a reason to the two Monarchs (whose sovereignty over Paraguy the Fathers acknowledged) to take to themselves the fruits of that Sovereignty, now become a morsel delicious enough to excite a regal appetite.

They therefore entered into a kind of partition-Treaty to share Paraguy between them; a Treaty which is likely to end in the ruin of this long envied and detested Order. Indignant Providence seeming to have decreed, as a lesson to mankind, that while, for the sake of Humanity, this glorious work should be preserved, that yet for the sake of divine Justice, these unworthy instruments, who with impunity had so long wantoned in civil mischief, and confounded and insulted all things sacred and prophane, should at length fall by their first and only virtuous purpose.

But we, who have God and the Monarch on our side, have nothing of this dreadful Catastrophe to fear. On the contrary, we have every thing to encourage us in this arduous task; which is now rendered more promising and easy, by the large dominions lately acceded to the British empire in America: Our entrance into the heart of these barbarous Nations being now no longer interrupted and traversed by the frauds, the false insinuations, and the malicious Tales of our European Rivals.

The *spiritual* benefits arising from the labour of *civilizing* are many and substantial. As the matter stands at present with us, busied only in our Gospel-Mission, the Savages observing in us (and they have sense enough to observe, that the Europeans keep many things from them, which it would be useful to them to know) the Savages, I say, observing in us a total disregard of their temporal interests, will with difficulty be brought to think, the other matters, pressed upon them, of much importance, or their Teachers greatly in earnest. But when they have been first of all so sensibly obliged, as, by our means, to be redeemed from the miseries of a brutal life, and set at ease by the *security* and *accommodations* of Society, they will naturally give a grateful and serious attention to their Benefactors, instructing them in sublimer *Truths,* and directing them to still more substantial *happiness.* In a word, of mortal enemies, ever addressed to ravage and desolate the extremities of our Colonies, we shall make them our cordial Friends, ready to embrace a Peace, not forced upon them by the terror of our arms or feigned with the allurements of treacherous Presents, but immoveably established by gratitude and love, and further supported by the mutual advantages of HONEST COMMERCE.

But alas! We are yet far from this glorious Term of our labours. The hindrances have been many—Partly from the *qualities* of the Missionaries, and in part from the *rapacious pursuits* of our Colonists.

Of the Missionaries, some have been overheated with that Fanaticism which disposes men to an utter contempt of *worldly things*: So that, instead of teaching the Savages the benefits of Social Life, and recommending civil manners to their roving Tribes, they are much rather inclined to throw aside their *own,* and accommodate themselves with the dried skins and parched Corn of the Natives.   Others of a cooler turn and lower form of Superstition took it into their heads, that the *Vices* of improved life (as they may be now gathered, full-blown, amongst the Colonists) would more indispose the Americans to the *precepts* of the Gospel than their present state of brutality can incapacitate them from apprehending the *doctrines* of it: and therefore, on the whole, have thought it best to keep their Converts shut out from the advantages of so dangerous a Society.

But, without question, the persevering in this fatal neglect, is chiefly owing to the false and inhumane Policy of the Colonists.   A policy common to them all, which makes them despise and set at nought even the horrors of a *Savage War*, for the sake of an unequal Traffic between the *improved* and *unimproved* gifts of all-bounteous Nature.

From the *Free Savages* I now come (the last point I propose to consider) to the *Savages in bonds.*

By these I mean the vast Multitudes yearly stolen from the Opposite Continent, and sacrificed by the Colonists to their great Idol, the GOD OF GAIN.   But what then, say these sincere Worshippers of Mammon, they are our own Property, which we offer up.   Gracious God! to talk (as in herds of Cattle) of Property in rational Creatures! Creatures endowed with all our Faculties, possessing all our qualities but that of colour; our BRETHREN both by Nature and Grace, shocks all the feelings of humanity, and the dictates of common sense.   But, alas! what is there in the infinite *abuses* of Society which does not shock them!   Yet nothing is more certain in itself, and apparent to all, than that the infamous traffic for Slaves, directly infringes both divine and human Law.   *Nature* created Man, free: and *Grace* invites him to assert his freedom.

In excuse of this violation, it hath been pretended, That though, indeed, these miserable Outcasts of humanity be torn from their homes and native Country by fraud and violence, yet they thereby became the happier, and their condition the more eligible.   But who are You, who pretend to judge of another Man's *happiness?* that State, which each man, under the guidance of his Maker, forms for himself; and not one Man for another.   To know what constitutes mine or your Happiness, is the sole prerogative of Him who created us, and cast us in so various and different Moulds.   Did your Slaves ever complain to you of their *unhappiness* amidst their native woods and desarts? or, rather, let me ask, did they ever cease complaining of their condition under you their Lordly Masters? where they see, indeed, the accommodations of Civil life, but see them all pass to others, themselves unbenefitted by them. Be so gracious then, ye petty tyrants over human freedom, to let your Slaves judge for themselves, what it is which makes their own *happiness*. And then see whether they do not place it in the *Return* to their own Country, rather than in the contemplation of your grandeur, of which, their misery makes so large a part. A *Return* so passionately longed for, that despairing of happiness *here,* that is, of escaping the Chains of their Cruel Task-masters, they console themselves with feigning it to be the gracious reward of Heaven in their *future State*; which I do not find their haughty Masters have as yet concerned themselves to invade. The less hardy indeed wait for this felicity till overwearied Nature sets them free; but the more resolved have recourse even to self-violence, to force a speedier passage.

But it will be still urged, that though what is called human *happiness* be of so fantastic a nature, that each man's imagination creates it for himself, yet human *misery* is more substantial and uniform throughout all the tribes of Mankind. Now, from the worst of human Miseries the savage Africans, by these forced emigrations, are entirely secured, such as the being perpetually hunted down like beasts of prey or profit, by their more savage and powerful Neighbours.—In truth, a blessed change! —from being *hunted* to being *caught.* But who are they that have set on foot this general HUNTING. Are they not these very civilized violaters of humanity, themselves? who tempt the weak appetites, and provoke the wild passions of the fiercer Savages to prey upon the rest. However, in favour of an *established* enormity, it is fit that nothing that can be said should be omitted. Something, it must be owned, may be alledged, (indeed not much) that the TRADING IN MEN is very ancient. It was the staple Commodity of the most early times: for, as the Poet says,

> Proud Nimrod first the bloody chase began,
> A mighty Hunter, and his prey was MAN.

Now, to bring this matter home to ourselves. We of this Corporation, by the ceaseless change and alienation of Property, are become the innocent partakers of the fruits of this iniquitous trafit. We have had bequeathed unto us, in trust for the Propagation of the Gospel, by a very worthy Benefactor, *a Plantation stocked with Slaves.* A Legacy, perhaps, intended as a kind of compensation for these violations of the Laws of nature and humanity. And, if so, I am very certain it will fully answer the pious intention of the Donor. God, out of this

Evil, having (according to the gracious way of his Providence) made us the honoured Instruments of producing *Good.*

The *cruelty* of certain Planters, with respect to the temporal accommodations of these poor Wretches, and the *irreligious negligence* with regard to their spiritual, is become a general Scandal.

Now this singular Legacy will enable us to redress both the inhumanity and impiety of their conduct, within the limits of our own property. But this is the least part of our advantages. What is of infinite more importance is the EXAMPLE we shall be able to hold out to the Colonies at large, sufficient to invite or shame all tyrannous Masters to a more compassionate treatment of their fellow-creatures and brethren.

It would be impiety to suspect that the Society will not persevere in making this use of so fortunate a circumstance, as their *duty* more particularly exacts it, and as their *means* of all kinds enable them to do it most effectually.

To conclude, you see, my brethren, how faithfully this incorporated Society have hitherto laboured to discharge their Trust.

I have ventured to hint at what appears to me the *best means* of perfecting our Work; and have set before you, though far unable to do it to advantage, the encouragements we have to prosecute those *means,* in the performance of this indispensable duty—to *Prophecy* AGAIN *before many Peoples, and Nations, and Tongues, and Kings.*

P. S.

Since the printing this, a pamphlet has been published, intitled, *A Brief Narrative of the Indian Charity-School in Connecticut, New England;* in which is *a Letter from the Indians of Onohoquage* to the Directors of this Charity, curious enough, on many accounts, to be here transcribed.

Lake Utsage, July 31, 1765.

BRETHREN,

We were informed by our Messenger that we sent to you last Spring, (*Gwedelhes,* or *Peter Agwirondongwas*) that you would not only assist us by sending us Ministers to teach us Christianity, but also that you would assist us in setting up Husbandry, by sending a Number of white People to live with us; who, when they come, should build us Mills, teach us Husbandry, and furnish us with Tools for Husbandry, &c.

We greatly rejoiced at hearing of it, and expected them this Spring, but are disappointed; at which we are very sorry: But we hope that we may yet receive them, and should much rejoice in it, should you send them to us.

We would have you understand, Brethren, that we have no Thoughts of selling our Land to any that come to live among us. For if we should sell a little Land to any, by and by they would want to buy a little more, and so our Land would go by Inches, till we should have none to live upon.—Yet as those that come to instruct us must live, we have no Objections against their improving as much Land as they please; yet the Land shall remain ours.

We have, Brethren, never petitioned to you yet for any to assist us, but only those that come with GOD'S *News* (*i. e.* the Gospel;) yet, as you have offered to assist us likewise in teaching us Husbandry, we greatly rejoice in it, and think that they should go together, the one as well as the other, and that we want Instruction in both. Brethren, we send our kindest Love to you, and remain your Brethren.

Isaac Dakayenensere.
Adam Waoonwanoron.

BOOK THREE

A SELECT BIBLIOGRAPHY

BIBLIOGRAPHICAL NOTE

This bibliography includes those materials, primary and secondary, actually used in the preparation of the volume. And, with a very few exceptions, no work not mentioned in the text or the notes is listed. Obvious works of reference, such as the *Dictionary of National Biography,* are omitted. The items have been arranged for practical usefulness and no logical classification has been attempted.

MANUSCRIPTS

This Study is based primarily on the manuscript materials in the Library of Congress and on the sources available in the Public Record Office, the British Museum, and the Huntington Library. On October 16, 1936, Dr. J. Franklin Jameson, then Chief of the Manuscript Division of the Library of Congress, wrote: " . . . We have here handwritten copies or photographic reproductions . . . of all the Journals of the Society named, down to 1783, and of all the correspondence that came to it from America, down to that date, and in some cases a little beyond. You will find a fairly full description of the material in the archives of the Society, so far as known in 1907, in the appropriate pages (pp. 332-333) of Andrew and Davenport's *Guide to the Manuscript Material for the History of the United States to 1783, in the British Museum, in Minor London Archives, etc.* (Washington, Carnegie Institution, 1908). By 1928, however, when the Library of Congress began its large-scale enterprise of photographic copying from European archives, portions of the archives of the S. P. G. which Miss Davenport reported as not available for examination for 1907, were duly arranged and made accessible. What with the hand-written transcripts made in an earlier time and the photographic work done by us in London in 1928 and 1929, our understanding is that we have copies of everything there that relates to the colonies now embraced in the United States." The above statement was confirmed by Dr. St. George L. Sioussat, Chief of the Division, in a letter of July 19, 1938.

The footnote references throughout indicate the documents used and, in some instances, the Library where they were consulted.

ACCOUNTS, COLLECTIONS AND DIGESTS

In addition to the Annual Sermons and the Abstracts of Proceedings, the Society published other documents of value to its members at home and abroad, and an extensive literature for the use of its missionaries and teachers. The effort to furnish its agents with small libraries and to found larger libraries in key cities in the Colonies is in itself an interesting story, as is White Kennett's plan of 1714 to establish a great London library of use to the members of the Society and to the members of the Board of Trade and Plantations, for example. His initial success foreshadowed the possibility of building up a great international library on European expansion. Accounts and Digests, of which a few examples are cited below, inevitably shade into histories and no clear-cut division can be made. Only a few suggestive items are listed below:

Charter granted to the Society for the Propagation of the Gospel in Foreign Parts, the 16th of June, 1701 (London, 1702). 4 p. (Huntington Library).

An Account of the Propagation of the Gospel in Foreign Parts. What the Society established in England by Royal Charter hath done since their incorporation June the 16th, 1701, in Her Majesty's Plantations, Colonies, Factories . . . (London, 1704). 4 p. (Huntington Library).

An Account of the Society for Propagation of the Gospel in Foreign Parts established by the Royal Charter of King William III. With their proceedings and success, and hopes of continued progress under the happy reign of . . . Queen Anne (London, 1706). 97 p. (Huntington Library).

A Collection of Papers, Printed by Order of the Society for the Propagation of the Gospel in Foreign Parts, viz. the Charter, the Request, etc. The Qualifications of Missionaries. Instructions for the Clergy. Instructions for Schoolmasters. Prayers for the Charity Schools (London, 1706). 45 p. (Huntington Library).

A Collection of Papers, Printed by Order of the Society for the Propagation of the Gospel in Foreign Parts, viz. the Charter. The Request, etc. The Qualifications of Missionaries. Instructions for the Clergy. Instructions for Schoolmasters. Prayers for the Charity Schools. Standing Orders of the Society. List of Members. Missionary's Library (London, 1712). 66 p. (Huntington Library).

KENNETT, WHITE, BISHOP OF PETERBOROUGH,
Bibliothecae americanae primordia. An attempt towards laying the foundation of an American library, in several books, papers, writings, humbly given to the the Society for the Propagation of the Gospel in Foreign Parts, for the perpetual use and benefit of their Members, their Missionaries, Friends, Correspondents, and others concerned in the good design of planting and promoting Christianity within Her Majesties Colonies and Plantations in the West Indies. (London, 1713 i. e. 1714) 112 p. The greater part of the library of 300 volumes was lost, but the remainder, together with some other S. P. G. books was advertised for sale by Sotheby, Williamson, and Hodge in 1917. (Huntington Library).

A Collection of papers printed by order of the Society for the Propagation of the Gospel in Foreign Parts (London, 1741). 51 p. (Huntington Library).

PRATT, THE REV. JOSIAH,
  Propaganda: Being an Abstract of the Designs and Proceedings of the Society for the Propagation of the Gospel in Foreign Parts (London, 1819). 202 p.
Work in the Colonies: some account of the missionary operations of the Church of England in connection with the Society for the Propagation of the Gospel in Foreign Parts (London, 1865). 374 p. (Huntington Library).
PASCOE, CHARLES FREDERICK (compiler),
  Classified Digest of the records of the Society for the Propagation of the Gospel in Foreign Parts, 1701-1892 (London, 1893). 980 p. (Huntington Library).

SERMONS

According to the rules of the S. P. G., the Annual Sermons were delivered in February at the Anniversary Meetings in the Parish Church of St. Mary-le-Bow. The change in England to the Gregorian Calendar, in 1752, must be borne in mind. Bishop Ashe, for example, according to our present-day calendar, did not deliver his Sermon in 1714 as given on the title page but in February of 1715.

Indispensable for the scholar is a recent volume, F. M. Powicke, Charles Johnson, and W. J. Harte, *Handbook of British Chronology* (London, The Royal Historical Society, 1939). This work gives information about "Reckonings of Time and the Beginning of the Year": "Saints' Days and Festivals Used in Dating"; and "Legal Chronology". It also lists the Archbishops and Bishops of England, Scotland, Wales, and Ireland with dates of consecration, accession, and death or translation, from the very beginning to the present time. Invaluable bibliographical information is available in the volume, and nearly half of the 424 pages are assigned to ecclesiastical matters.

The Huntington Library has a practically complete file of the Annual Sermons, and its collection of Sermons and Abstracts of Proceedings was used. The Sermons cited in this book are arranged alphabetically by author, with the exception of the first three. These three, moreover, have their titles copied in full. Slight variations in title do not justify continued repetition. A list of the men who delivered the Sermons is given in Pascoe, Charles F., *Two Hundred Years of the S. P. G.* (2 vols., London, 1901), II, pp. 833-835.

FLEETWOOD, WILLIAM,
  A Sermon Preached before the Society for the Propagation of the Gospel in Foreign Parts, At the Parish Church of St. Mary-le-Bow, On Friday the 16th of February, 1710/11. Being the Day of their Anniversary Meeting. By the Right Reverend Father in God, William Lord Bishop of St. Asaph. London, Printed and Sold by *Joseph Downing* in *Bartholomew-Close* near *West Smithfield*, 1711.

SECKER, THOMAS,

> *A Sermon Preached before the Incorporated Society for the Propagation of the Gospel in Foreign Parts; at their Anniversary Meeting in the Parish-Church of St. Mary-le-Bow, on Friday, February 20, 1740-1.* By Thomas Lord Bishop of Oxford. London: Printed for J. and H. Pemberton, at the *Golden Buck* against St. *Dunstan's* Church in *Fleetstreet.* 1741.

WARBURTON, WILLIAM,

> *A Sermon Preached before the Incorporated Society for the Propagation of the Gospel in Foreign Parts; at their Anniversary Meeting in the Parish Church of St. Mary-le-Bow, on Friday, February 21, 1766.* By the Right Reverend Father in God, William Lord Bishop of Glocester [Gloucester]. London: Printed by E. Owen and T. Harrison in Warwick-Lane. MDCCLXVI.

ASHE, ST. GEORGE, Bishop of Clogher (1714/15).

BARRINGTON, SHUTE, Bishop of Llandaff (1775).

BEARCROFT, PHILIP, Secretary of the Society (1744/45).

BENSON, MARTIN, Bishop of Gloucester (1739/40).

BERKELEY, GEORGE, Dean of Londonderry (1731/32).

BEVERIDGE, WILLIAM, Bishop of St. Asaph (1706/07).

BURNET, GILBERT, Bishop of Sarum (1703/4).

BUTLER, JOSEPH, Bishop of Bristol (1738/39).

CHANDLER, EDWARD, Bishop of Coventry and Lichfield (1718/19).

CLAGGETT, NICHOLAS, Bishop of St. David's (1736/37).

CLEAVER, WILLIAM, Bishop of Chester (1794).

CORNWALLIS, FREDERICK, Bishop of Lichfield and Coventry (1756).

DAWES, SIR WILLIAM, Bishop of Chester (1708/9).

DRUMMOND, ROBERT, Bishop of St. Asaph (1754).

EGERTON, HENRY, Bishop of Hereford (1728/29).

ELLIS, ANTHONY, Bishop of St. David's (1759).

GREEN, JOHN, Bishop of Lincoln (1768).

GREEN, THOMAS, Bishop of Ely (1723/24).

HALIFAX, SAMUEL, Bishop of Gloucester (1789).

HARE, FRANCIS, Bishop of Chichester (1734/35).

HAYLEY, THOMAS, Canon Residentiary of Chichester, and Chaplain in Ordinary to His Majesty (1716/17).

HERRING, THOMAS, Bishop of Bangor (1737/8).

HORSLEY, SAMUEL, Bishop of Rochester (1795).

JOHNSON, JAMES, Bishop of Glo[u]cester (1758).

LAW, EDMUND, Bishop of Carlisle (1774).

LENG, JOHN, Bishop of Norwich (1726/27).

LISLE, SAMUEL, Bishop of St. Asaph (1747/48).

LOWTH, ROBERT, Bishop of Oxford (1771).

LYNCH, JOHN, Dean of Canterbury (1735/36).

MADDOX, ISSAC, Dean of Wells, and Clerk of the Closet to the Queen (1733/34).

MANNERS-SUTTON, CHARLES, Bishop ot Norwich (1797).

PORTEUS, BEILBY, Bishop of Chester (1783).

SHERLOCK, THOMAS, Dean of Chichester (1715/16).

SHIPLEY, JONATHAN, Bishop of St. Asaph (1773).

STANHOPE, GEORGE, Dean of Canterbury, and Chaplain in Ordinary to Her Majesty (1713/14)

STANLEY, WILLIAM, Dean of St. Asaph (1707/8).

STEBBING, HENRY, Chancellor of Sarum (1741/42).

THURLOW, THOMAS, Bishop of Lincoln (1786).

TOMLINE, SIR GEORGE—PRETYMAN, Bishop of Lincoln (1792).

TREVOR, RICHARD, Bishop of St. David's (1749/50).

TRIMNELL, CHARLES, Bishop of Norwich (1709/10).

VAN MILDERT, WILLIAM, Bishop of Llandaff (1822).

WARREN, JOHN, Bishop of Bangor (1787).

WAUGH, JOHN, Dean of Gloucester and Chaplain in Ordinary to His Majesty (1722/23).

WILCOCKS, JOSEPH, Bishop of Gloucester (1725/26).

WILLIAMS, JOHN, Bishop of Chichester (1705/06).

WILLIS, RICHARD, Dean of Lincoln (1701/02).

WYNNE, JOHN, Bishop of St. Asaph (1724/25).

YONGE, PHILIP, Bishop of Norwich (1765).

Twelve Anniversary Sermons Preached Before the Society for the Propagation of the Gospel in Foreign Parts (London, 1845). Included in this edition are the Sermons by Willis, Williams, Beveridge, Berkeley, Butler, Secker, Bearcroft, Warburton, Lowth, Porteus, Horsley, and Van Mildert.

COOKE, JOHN,
The Preachers Assistant (after the Manner of Mr. Letsome) (2 vols., Oxford, 1783). (Yale University Library).

BOOKS AND MONOGRAPHS

ABEL, ANNIE HELOISE AND KLINGBERG, FRANK J.,
A Side-Light on Anglo-American Relations, 1839-1858, Furnished by the Correspondence of Lewis Tappan and Others with the British and Foreign Anti-Slavery Society (Washington, 1927).

ADAMS, JAMES TRUSLOW,
Revolutionary New England, 1691-1776 (Boston, 1923).

ALVORD, CLARENCE WALWORTH,
The Mississippi Valley in British Politics; a Study of the trade, land speculation, and experiments in imperialism culminating in the American Revolution (Cleveland, 1917).

ANDERSON, JAMES STUART MURRAY,
The History of the Church of England in the Colonies and Foreign Dependencies of the British Empire (3 vols., second edition, London, 1856). (Huntington Library).

ANDREWS, CHARLES MCLEAN,
The Colonial Period of American History (4 vols., New Haven, 1934-1938).

ANDREWS, CHARLES MCLEAN,
"Materials in British Archives for American Colonial History," *American Historical Review*, X, No. 2, pp. 325-350, January, 1905.

BEARDSLEY, EBEN EDWARDS,
Life and Correspondence of Samuel Johnson, D. D., missionary of the Church of England in Connecticut, and first president of King's College, New York (New York, 1874).

BENEZET, ANTHONY,
   A Serious Address to the Rulers of America on the inconsistency of their conduct respecting slavery, forming a contrast between the encroachments of England on American liberty and American injustice in tolerating slavery (Trenton, 1783). (Huntington Library).

BENEZET, ANTHONY,
   Some Account of the Behavior and Sentiments of a number of well disposed Indians, mostly of the Minusing Tribe (Manuscript, 1761). (Huntington Library).

BLAND, A. E., BROWN, P. A., TAWNEY, R. H.,
   English Economic History: Select Documents (London, 1924).

BOLTON, HERBERT EUGENE,
   "The Mission as a Frontier Institution in the Spanish American Colonies," *American Historical Review*, XXIII, pp. 42-61, October, 1917.

[BURKE, EDMUND],
   The Works of the Right Honourable Edmund Burke (16 volumes, a new edition, London, 1822, 1826, 1827).

[BUTLER, JOSEPH],
   "The Analogy of Religion, 1736-1936, Joseph Butler's Achievement," London, *Times Literary Supplement*, No. 1784, pp. 305-306, April 11, 1936.

CATTERALL, MRS. HELEN TUNNICLIFF [MRS. RALPH C. H. CATTERALL],
   Judicial Cases Concerning American Slavery and the Negro (5 vols., Washington, 1926-1937). (Volumes IV and V, brought out after Mrs. Catterall's death, were completed by James J. Hayden). Publication number 374 of the Carnegie Institution of Washington, Division of Historical Research. "The compilation has been brought to a close, in each state, at the end of the year 1875." [Preface, Volume I].

CHANDLER, T. B.,
   The Life of Samuel Johnson, D. D. (New York, 1805).

CHANNING, EDWARD,
   A History of the United States (6 vols., New York, 1905-1925) Covers American History from the beginning through the Civil War.

CLARK, SAMUEL ADAMS,
   The Episcopal church in the American colonies. The history of St. John's church, Elizabeth town, New Jersey, from the year 1703 to the present time. Compiled from original documents, the manuscript records, and letters of the missionaries of the Society for propagation of the gospel in foreign parts, and from other sources (Philadelphia and New York, 1857).

CLARKSON, THOMAS,
   The History of the Rise, Progress, and Accomplishment of the Abolition of the African Slave-Trade by the British Parliament (2 vols., London, 1808).

Collections of the Illinois State Historical Society Library (Vol. 1, Springfield, Illinois, 1903).

COUPLAND, REGINALD,
   The British Anti-Slavery Movement (London, 1933).

CROSS, ARTHUR LYON,
   The Anglican Episcopate and the American Colonies (New York, 1902 and Cambridge, Massachusetts, 1924).

CURTI, MERLE,
"The Great Mr. Locke, America's Philosopher, 1783-1861," *Huntington Library Bulletin*, No. 11, pp. 109-151, April, 1937.

DAVIES, GODFREY,
"English Political Sermons, 1603-1640," *Huntington Library Quarterly*, III, No. 1, pp. 1-22, October, 1939.

DIX, MORGAN,
A History of the Parish of Trinity Church in the City of New York, Compiled by order of the corporation (4 vols. New York, 1898-1906). Covers the period from the beginning to around 1860.

DONNAN, ELIZABETH,
Documents Illustrative of the History of the Slave Trade to America (4 vols., Washington, 1930-1935). Publication 409 of the Carnegie Institution of Washington, Division of Historical Research.

ELIOT, THOMAS STEARNS,
Selected Essays, 1917-1932 (New York, 1932).

FAIRCHILD, HOXIE NEALE,
The Noble Savage, A Study in Romantic Naturalism (New York, 1928).

FARNAM, HENRY WALCOTT,
Chapters in the History of Social Legislation in the United States to 1860 (Washington, 1938). Publication 488 of the Carnegie Institution.

GIBSON, EDMUND, Bishop of London,
Three Addresses on the Instruction of the Negroes (London, 1727). (1) "An Address to Serious Christians among ourselves, to Assist the Society for Propagating the Gospel, in carrying on the Work of Instructing the Negroes in our Plantations abroad." (2) "Letter to the Masters and Mistresses of Families in the English Plantations abroad; Exhorting them to encourage and promote the Instruction of their Negroes in the Christian Faith." (3) "Letter to the Missionaries in the English Plantations; exhorting them to give their Assistance towards the Instruction of the Negroes of their Several Parishes, in the Christian Faith."

GILLIES, JOHN
Memoirs of the Late Rev. George Whitefield, revised by Aaron C. Seymour (New York, 1835).

GOODWIN, MARY F.,
"Christianizing and Educating the Negro in Colonial Virginia," *Historical Magazine of the Protestant Episcopal Church*, I, No. 3, pp. 143-152, September, 1932.

GREENE, EVARTS BOUTELLE AND HARRINGTON, VIRGINIA D.,
American Population before the Federal Census of 1790 (New York, 1932).

GREENE, EVARTS BOUTELL,
"The Anglican Outlook on the American Colonies in the Early Eighteenth Century," *American Historical Review*, XX, No. 1, pp. 64-85, October, 1914.

HAILEY, WILLIAM MALCOLM, LORD,
An African Survey: A Study of Problems Arising in Africa south of the Sahara (London, 1938). "The Survey does not . . . include Ethiopia and other Italian possessions, or the Anglo-Egyptian Sudan . . . [or] Zanzibar and Madagascar." [p. xxi].

HALDANE, RICHARD BURDON, LORD,
"Higher Nationality; A study in Law and Ethics," *International Conciliation* IV, No. 72, and also in the *London Times,* September 2, 1913, pp. 7-8. An Address Delivered before the American Bar Association at Montreal, September 1, 1913.

HARRIS, SIR JOHN,
"Address entitled 'The Tasks before Us' delivered before the Centenary Meeting of the Anti-Slavery and Aborigines Protection Society, London, Monday, April 24, 1939," *The Anti-Slavery Reporter and Aborigines' Friend,* Ser. V., volume 29, No. 2, pp. 55-57, July, 1939.

HARTLEY, LODWICK C.,
William Cowper, Humanitarian (Chapel Hill, North Carolina, 1938).

HAWKINS, ERNEST,
Historical notices of the missions of the Church of England in the North American colonies, previous to the independence of the United States: chiefly from the mss. documents of the Society for the Propagation of the Gospel in Foreign Parts (London, 1845).

HAWKS, FRANCIS LISTER, AND PERRY, WILLIAM STEVENS,
Documentary History of the Protestant Episcopal Church in the United States of America, containing numerous hitherto unpublished documents concerning the Church in Connecticut (2 vols., New York, 1863-64).

HENSON, THE RT. REV. HENSLEY, Bishop of Durham,
Selected English Sermons, Sixteenth to Nineteenth Centuries (London, 1939).

HOLT, RAYMOND VINCENT,
The Unitarian Contribution to Social Progress in England (London, 1938).

HUMPHREYS, DAVID,
An Historical Account of the Incorporated Society for the Propagation of the Gospel in Foreign Parts. Containing their Foundation, Proceedings, and the Success of their Missionaries in the British Colonies to the year 1728. (London, 1730).

HUNTINGTON, ELLSWORTH,
The Red Man's Continent, A Chronicle of Aboriginal America (New Haven, 1919). Volume I of the Chronicles of America Series, Allen Johnson, editor.

JONES, MARY G.,
The Charity School Movement: a Study of Eighteenth Century Puritanism in Action (Cambridge, England, 1938).

KEEP, AUSTIN BAXTER,
History of the New York Society Library, with an Introductory Chapter on Libraries in Colonial New York, 1698-1776 (New York, 1908).

KEMP, WILLIAM WEBB,
The Support of Schools in Colonial New York by the Society for the Propagation of the Gospel in Foreign Parts (New York, 1913).

KLINGBERG, FRANK J.,
Anti-Slavery Movement in England, A Study in English Humanitarianism (New Haven, 1926).

KLINGBERG, FRANK J.,
"British Humanitarianism at Codrington," *Journal of Negro History*, XXIII, No. 4, pp. 451-486, October, 1938.

KLINGBERG, FRANK J.,
"The Lady Mico Charity Schools in the British West Indies, 1835-1842," *Journal of Negro History*, XXIV, No. 3, pp. 291-344, July, 1939.

KLINGBERG, FRANK J.,
"The Indian Frontier in South Carolina as Seen by the S. P. G. Missionary," *Journal of Southern History*, V. No. 4, pp. 479-500, November, 1939.

KLINGBERG, FRANK J.,
Old Sherry: Portrait of a Virginia Family (Richmond, 1938).

KNOX, WILLIAM,
Three tracts respecting the conversion and instruction of the free Indians and negro slaves in the colonies (London, 1768).

LASCELLES, E. C. P.,
Granville Sharp, and the Freedom of Slaves in England (London, 1928).

LEWIS, W. S. AND WILLIAMS, RALPH M.,
Private Charity in England 1747-1757 (New Haven, 1938).

LINCOLN, CHARLES HENRY,
Correspondence of William Shirley, Governor of Massachusetts and Military Commander in America, 1731-1760 (2 vols., New York, 1912).

LINN, JOHN B., AND EGLE, WILLIAM H.,
Pennsylvania Archives (Second ser. Harrisburg, 1896).

LONG, EDWARD,
History of Jamaica: or General Survey of the Ancient and Modern State of that Island: with reflections on its situation, settlements, inhabitants, climate, products, commerce, laws, and government (3 vols., London, 1774).

LYDEKKER, JOHN WOLFE,
The Life and Letters of Charles Inglis: His Ministry in America and Consecration as First Colonial Bishop, from 1759-1787 (London, 1936).

MANROSS, WILLIAM WILSON,
"The Interstate Meetings and General Conventions of 1784, 1785, 1786, and 1789," *Historical Magazine of the Protestant Episcopal Church*, VIII, No. 3, pp. 257-280, September 1939.

MARAIS, JOHANNES STEPHANUS,
The Cape Coloured People, 1652-1936 (London, 1939).

McCALLUM, JAMES DOW,
The Letters of Eleazor Wheelock's Indians, Edited from the Originals (Hanover, New Hampshire, 1932).

McILWAIN, CHARLES H.,
An Abridgement of the Indian affairs Contained in four-folio volumes, transacted in the colony of New York, from the year 1678 to the year 1751, by Peter Wraxall (Cambridge, Massachusetts, 1915).

MEAD, EDWIN D.,
Old South Leaflets, General Series (200 nos., Boston, 1888-1909).

MIDWINTER, SIR EDWARD,
"The Society for the Propagation of the Gospel and the Church in the American Colonies," *Historical Magazine of the Protestant Episcopal Church*, IV, No. 2, pp. 67-115, June, 1935.

MOSSNER, EARNEST CAMPBELL,
Bishop Butler and the Age of Reason, A Study in the History of Thought (New York, 1936).

NEWCOMBE, ALFRED W.,
"The Appointment and Instruction of S. P. G. Missionaries," *Church History* V, No. 4, pp. 340-358, December, 1936.

NORWOOD, PERCY VARNEY,
"Constitutional Developments since 1789," *Historical Magazine of the Protestant Episcopal Church*, VIII, No. 3, pp. 282-303, September, 1939.

O'CALLAGHAN, EDMUND BAILEY,
Documents Relative to the Colonial History of the State of New York (15 vols., Albany, 1853-1857).

O'CALLAGHAN, EDMUND BAILEY,
The Documentary History of the State of New York (4 vols., Albany, 1849-1851).

OLIVER, DAVID DICKSON,
The Society for the Propagation of the Gospel in the provinces of North Carolina (Raleigh, 1910).

OSGOOD, HERBERT,
The American Colonies in the Eighteenth Century (4 vols., New York, 1924-25).

PALMER, ROBERT R.,
"The French Jesuits in the Age of Enlightenment," *The American Historical Review*, XLV, No. 1, pp. 44-58, October, 1939.

PASCOE, CHARLES FREDERICK,
Two Hundred Years of the S. P. G., An Historical Account of the Society for the Propagation of the Gospel in Foreign Parts 1701-1900 (2 vols., London, 1901). Based on a Digest of the Society's Records.

PENNINGTON, EDGAR LEGARE,
Thomas Bray's Associates and their Work among the Negroes (Worcester, 1939).

PENNINGTON, EDGAR LEGARE,
"Colonial Clergy Conventions," *Historical Magazine of the Protestant Episcopal Church*, VIII, No. 3, pp. 178-218, September, 1939.

PENNINGTON, EDGAR LEGARE,
Apostle of New Jersey, John Talbot, 1645-1729 (Philadelphia, 1938).

PERRY, WILLIAM STEVENS,
The History of the American Episcopal Church 1587-1883 (2 vols., Boston, 1885).

PERRY, WILLIAM STEVENS,
Historical Collections Relating to the American Colonial Church (5 vols., Hartford, 1870-1878). Documents relate to Virginia, Pennsylvania, Massachusetts, Maryland, and Delaware.

PITMAN, FRANK WESLEY,
The Development of the British West Indies 1700-1763 (New Haven, 1917).

POUND, ARTHUR, AND DAY, RICHARD E.,
  Johnson of the Mohawks, A Biography of Sir William Johnson, Irish immigrant, Mohawk War Chief, American Soldier, Empire Builder (New York, 1930).

RAGATZ, LOWELL JOSEPH,
  A Guide for the Study of British Caribbean History 1763-1834, Including the Abolition and Emancipation Movements (Washington, 1932).

READ, ALLEN WALKER,
  "The Speech of Negroes in Colonial America," *Journal of Negro History*, XXIV, No. 3, pp. 247-258, July, 1939.

SCHNEIDER, HERBERT AND CAROL,
  Samuel Johnson, President of King's College, his Career and Writings (4 vols., New York, 1929).

[SHIPLEY, JONATHAN],
  "A Georgian Prelate, Jonathan Shipley and His Friends," (London), *Times Literary Supplement*, No. 1851, pp. 533-534, July 24, 1937.

SHELLING, RICHARD I.,
  "Benjamin Franklin and the Dr. Bray Associates," *Pennsylvania Magazine of History and Biography*, LXIII No. 3, pp. 282-293, July 1939.

SMITH, DR. WILLIAM,
  A Discourse Concerning the Conversion of the Heathen Americans, and the Final Propagation of Christianity and the Sciences to the Ends of the Earth. (2 parts, Philadelphia, 1760).

STONE, WILLIAM LEETE,
  Life of Joseph Brant (2 vols., Albany, 1865; first edition, 1838).

STONE, WILLIAM LEETE (JR.),
  The Life and Times of Sir William Johnson, Bart (2 vols., Albany, 1865).

STOWE, WALTER HERBERT,
  "State or Diocesan Conventions of the War and Post-War Periods," *Historical Magazine of the Protestant Episcopal Church*, VIII, No. 3, pp. 220-250, September, 1939.

SULLIVAN, JAMES, FLICK, ALEXANDER C., LAUBER, ALMON W.,
  The Papers of Sir William Johnson (9 vols., Albany, 1921-1939).

SYKES, NORMAN,
  Church and State in the Eighteenth Century (Cambridge, England, 1934).

SYKES, NORMAN,
  Edmund Gibson: Bishop of London, 1669-1748, A Study in Politics and Religion in the Eighteenth Century (London, 1926).

SYKES, NORMAN,
  "The Church," in *Johnson's England* (2 vols., Oxford, 1933), I, pp. 15-38.

SYPHER, WYLIE,
  "Hutcheson and the 'Classical Theory' of Slavery," *Journal of Negro History,* XXIV, No. 3, pp. 263-280, July, 1939.

THOMPSON, THOMAS,
  An Account of two Missionary Voyages by the Appointment of the S. P. G., the one to New Jersey in North America: the other from America to the coast of Guiney. London, Printed for Benjamin Dod, 1758. (Huntington

Library). Through the cooperation of Walter Herbert Stowe, rector of Christ Church, New Brunswick, Rutgers University Library, Sir Edward Midwinter of the S. P. G., and J. W. Lydekker, Archivist of the S. P. G., this work was reprinted in facsimile with introduction and notes in 1937 by the S. P. C. K. for the S. P. G.

THIRLWALL, JOHN CONNOP (JR.),
Connop Thirlwall, Historian and Theologian (London, 1936).

TINKER, CHAUNCEY BREWSTER,
Nature's Simple Plan, A Phase of Radical Thought in the Mid-Eighteenth Century (Princeton, 1922).

TRAPPES-LOMAX, MICHAEL ROGER,
Bishop Challoner, a biographical study derived from Dr. Edwin Burton's The Life and Times of Bishop Challoner (London and New York, 1936).

WEARMOUTH, ROBERT FEATHERSTONE,
Methodism and the Working Class Movements of England 1800-1850 (London, 1937).

WERTENBAKER, THOMAS JEFFERSON,
The Founding of American Civilization, the Middle Colonies (New York and London, 1938).

WHITNEY, LOIS,
"English Primitive Theories of Epic Origins," Modern Philology, XXI, No. 4, pp. 337-378, May, 1924.

WILD, JOHN DANIEL,
George Berkeley: A Study of His Life and Philosophy (Cambridge, Massachusetts, 1936).

WILLIAMS, BASIL,
The Whig Supremacy, 1714-1760 (Oxford, 1939).

WILSON, THOMAS, (Bishop of Sodor and Man),
The Knowledge and Practice of Christianity Made Easy to the Meanest Capacities: or an Essay towards an Instruction for the Indians, which will be of use to such Christians as have not well considered the meaning of the religion they profess. In several short and plain dialogues. Together with directions and prayers. . . . The second edition with additions: and corrected throughout (London, 1741). 271 pp. (Huntington Library).

WOODFORDE, JAMES,
The Diary of a Country Parson, The Reverend James Woodforde (5 vols., London, 1924-1931). Edited by John Beresford. The Diary covers the years 1758-1802.

WOODSON, CARTER,
The African Background Outlined (Washington, 1936).

WOODSON, CARTER,
"Snatching Learning in Forbidden Fields," The Negro History Bulletin, III, No. 2, p. 21, November, 1939.

WOODSON, CARTER,
"Educating the Negro before the General Emancipation," The Negro History Bulletin, III, No. 2, pp. 17-19, November, 1939.

WOODWARD, E. L.,
The Age of Reform, 1815-1870 (Oxford, 1938).

WYNDHAM, HUGH ARCHIBALD,
The Atlantic and Slavery (London, 1935).

YOUNG, A. H.,
"Reverend John Ogilvie, D. D. An Army Chaplain at Fort Niagara and Montreal, 1759-1760," Ontario Historical Society *Papers and Records*, XXII, pp. 296-337, 1925.

YOUNG, A. H.,
"Sir William Johnson, Bart., an appreciation, 1715-1774," Ontario Historical Society *Papers and Records*, XXVII, pp. 575-582, 1931.

BOOK FOUR

GENERAL INDEX

GENERAL INDEX[1]

The Christianization and the education of Negroes and Indians are the chief topics throughout the book. The headings listed below are intended to guide the reader to important materials and to ideas stated or implied, rather than to cover the complete store of information. The major divisions are listed in the Table of Contents.

A.

Abel, Annie H., 166n, 257.

Aberdeen, Scotland, 174.

Aborigines, see Barbarians.

Abraham, an Indian sachem, 80, 90, 91.

Abstracts of the Proceedings of the S. P. G., 9, 13, 154n.

Adams, James Truslow, 109n, 257.

Africa, 9, 29n, 46, 146, 185; capture of Negroes in, 39, 187, 217, 247; conditions in America compared with, 34, 39, 217; culture of, 121; Philip Quaque, native missionary in, 50.

Africans, participate in slave trade, 217, 247.

Aigar, a free Negro woman, 137n.

Albany, New York, 51, 53, 54, 56, 58, 60, 60n, 61, 61n, 63, 64, 64n, 67, 68, 70, 71, 72, 73, 73n, 74, 75, 75n, 77n, 78, 79, 83, 83n, 84, 84n, 85, 89n, 96n, 102, 103n, 107, 134, 135, 135n, 151n, 174n, 175, 176, 177.

Allaire, Mr., a slave owner, 126.

Alleyne, Abel, manager of Codrington estates, in Barbados, 20n.

Allies, Indians as, of Dutch, see Dutch; of English, see English; of French, see French; of Spaniards, see Spaniards.

Alvord, C. W., 110n, 257.

Amboy, New Jersey, 155.

America, 121, 154; destiny of, 40, 43, 44; growing nationalism of, 189; Negro contribution to, 5; wealth of, 27, 41, 42, 43, 240. See also American culture, Colonies, New World, White colonists.

[1]For this Index I am indebted to Helen Livingston and Florence Cook Fast.

American Acta Sanctorium, vii.

American Antiquarian Society Proceedings, 150.

American Bar Association, 3n.

American bishopric, 4, 183. see also American episcopate.

American colonies, see Colonies.

American culture, Anglicanism in middle class environment of, 4; clash with native cultures, 49, 246;

—S. P. G. contributions to, King's college (Columbia university), see King's college; libraries furnished, viii, 14, 32n; printed matter distributed, 13, 17, 29, 32n, 54, 58, 61, 144, 144n, 145, 219. see also Colleges, Instruction, New World, Schools, White colonists.

American Episcopal Church, see Episcopal Church.

American episcopate, efforts for, 108, 109, 109n, 120, 183; founded in 1780's, 4. see also Diocesan convention, Episcopal Church.

American Historical Review, vii, 13n, 50n, 84n, 89n.

American Revolution, viii, 40, 124n, 153, 166, 174, 180, 188, 189; Anglicanism revived after, 5n; Negro school destroyed by burning during, 183; opposition to an American bishop prior to, 4;

—S. P. G. in, 181-186; missionaries remain loyal during, see Missionaries; reorganization of, 4, 45, 46, 85, 185, 188, 189; see also, Tories, Loyalists, Declaration of Independence.

Amherst, Jeffery, General, 82.

Amillton, Mr., a slave owner, 138n.

Amsterdam, Holland, 135n.

Anabaptists, 172n, 177, 229n. see also

—of whites, 168n, 169n, 171, 172n, 173n, 174, 175, 176, 177, 179n, 180, 182.

Baptists, 167, *see also* Anabaptists.

Bachan, Mr., a slave owner, 137n.

Barbados, the, 14, 20n, 21, 161n, 170.

Barbarians, 242, 243, 246, *see also* Heathen, INDIANS, Native peoples, Noble savage.

Barclay, Henry, missionary to Albany, Fort Hunter, the Mohawks, and rector of Trinity church, New York City, 73, 74, 74n, 75, 75n, 76, 77, 77n, 78, 79, 83n, 151; and Sir William Johnson, 91, 91n, 92, 92n, 96, 96n, 102n, 107, 108.

Barclay, Thomas, missionary to Albany and Schenectady, 58, 59, 59n, 60, 60n, 61, 61n, 62, 63, 64, 70, 71, 71n, 72, 73, 74, 133, 133n, 134, 135, 135n.

Barn Island, New York, 169n.

Barrington, Nicholas, 161, 162.

Barrington, Shute, bishop of Llandaff, sermon of, 21, 39n, 41n, 256.

Barton, Thomas, missionary to Lancaster, Pennsylvania, 39n; and Sir William Johnson, 95, 95n, 96n, 97n, 99n, 102, 103, 104n, 106n, 111n, 117n, 118, 118n.

Bartow, John, missionary to Westchester, 131, 131n, 154, 155.

Bearcroft, Philip, secretary of the S. P. G., 31n, 214; sermon of, 31, 31n, 32, 32n, 33, 33n, 256.

Beardsley, Eben E., 95n, 164n, 257.

Beardsley, John, missionary to Dutchess county and Poughkeepsie, 180, 180n.

Beasley, (also Beazley, and Beazly), John, a catechist for the Negroes, 175, 175n, 176.

Becket, William, 20n.

Bedford, New York, 169.

Bellomont, Richard Coote, Lord, Governor of New York, 62.

Benezet, Anthony, 48n, 258.

Bennett (or Bennet), Cornelius, catechist to the Mohawks, 101, 102.

Benson, Martin, bishop of Gloucester, sermon of, 26, 27, 28, 256.

Beresford, John, editor, 7n, 12n.

Berkeley, George, dean of Londonderry, Sermon of, viii, 7, 13, 22, 23, 25, 30, 31, 163n, 186, 256.

Bermudas, the, 184.

Beveridge, William, bishop of St. Asaph, 18.

Bibles distributed, 32n, 58, 103, 144, 144n, 219.

Bishop, Edward, 59, 59n.

Bishops, of Anglican church, list of those discussed, 255, 256, 257.

Blackstone, Sir William, 8, 113n.

Bland, A. E., 25n, 258.

Blockgrove, Mr., a slave owner, 126.

Bloom, Mr. and Mrs., slave owners, 126, 138n.

Bloomer, Joshua, missionary to Jamaica, 182.

Board of Trade, 89, 103n, 109, 110.

Bodhams, the, (the Rev. and Mrs. Thomas), 7n.

Bolingbroke, Henry Saint-John, Lord, 37, 37n.

Bolton, Herbert E., 108n, 258.

Book of Common Prayer, *see* Prayer Books.

Books and tracts, distribution of, 13, 17, 29, 32n, 54, 58, 61, 219; analysis of books distributed, 144, 144n, 145; to Indians, 62, 63, 63n, 68, 103, 104, 104n; to Negroes, 126, 128, 131n, 139, 141, 142, 143, 144, 154, 155, 164, 165, 183.

Bone, Mr., a slave owner, 137n.

Bondet, Daniel, missionary to New Rochelle, 136, 136n.

Boston, Massachusetts, one Anglican church in 1701, 32n; Shipley's opposition to closing the port of, 40; "Father of American clergy" in, 108n; Court of Admiralty in, 147n.

Bostwick, Gideon, missionary to Nobletown, 183.

Boum, Boarn, a slave owner, 126.

Bratt, Barnet, a citizen of Albany, 134.

Brant, Joseph, an Indian leader, 50, 94, 94n.

Brant, Molly, 103n.

Bray Associates, viii, 45n, 87, 150, 150n, 151.

Seabury, Jr., 174; Thomas B. Chandler, 169; John Beasley, 175, 176; Joseph Ottolenghe (in Georgia), 20n. *see also* Schoolteachers.
——accused of keeping tavern, 164n; catechist refused, 176, 184; certification of, 73n, 154n, 160n; charges against, 136, 137, 139; Committee for, 55n; difficulty of securing, 165; diligence of, 145; illness of, 146, 146n, 162; in Philadelphia, 20n; opposition to work of, 132, 133, 133n, 134, 135, *See also* Masters; ordained catechist requested, 139; qualifications of, 141, 142, 142n; requested from S. P. G., 139, 141, 142, 164, 184; requested for New York City, 141, 142, 184; salary of (in New York City), 128n, 129, 136, 140, 142, 146n, 152, (in New York colony), 154, 158n, 159, 166, 168n, 175, 176, (in South Carolina), 32n; wife helps in work, 139n.
Catterall, Helen Tunnicliff, 122n, 138n, 155n, 157n, 158n, 170n, 258.
Challoner, bishop, 6n.
Chaplain in ordinary, *see* John Waugh, Thomas Hayley.
Chamberlayne, John, secretary of S. P. G., 31n, 52n, 53n, 130, 196.
Chancellor of Sarum, *see* Henry Stebbing.
Chandler, Edward, bishop of Coventry and Lichfield, 29n, 256.
Chandler, F. B., 164n, 258.
Chandler, Samuel, 28.
Chandler, Thomas Bradbury, catechist at North Castle and Bedford, New York, 169.
Channing, Edward, 125n, 258.
Characteristics,
——of Indians, aloofness of, 187; barbarity of, 24, 26, 33, 34, 40, 41, 42n, 56, 61n, 67, 102, 102n, 116, 218, 224; drunkenness among, 23, 52, 54, 55, 56, 61, 66, 68, 68n, 70, 76, 80, 81, 85; friendly interest of, 16, 16n, 41n, 42n, 58, 59, 60, 62, 63, 64, 67, 71, 72, 73, 73n, 74, 75, 78, 79, 80, 84, 85, 102, 102n, 103, 107n, 108, 111n, 112n, 117n; lewdness and swearing of, 70n; mental

abilities of, 16, 16n, 41, 41n, 42n, 66, 74, 80, 85, 116, 218; nomadic hunters, 65, 76, 96, 98, 107, 113, 119, 218, 224, 243; Secker's estimate of, 218; violence of, 56, 61, 61n, 218;
——of Negroes, adaptive qualities, 5, 7, 85, 119, 146; friendly response of, 136, 139, 156, 165, 171, 175, 176, 177, 178, 179; intelligence of, 5, 20, 45n, 47, 149, 159, 160, 161, 162, 164, 166, 169, 174, 175, 177, 179, 203, 220, 221; uncivilized, 20, 20n, 34, 46, 217, 219; violence of, 5, 35, 131, 132, 133, 136;
——of white colonists; accomplishments of, 35, 42, 43, 44; moral improvement of, 15, 31, 220, 221; religious laxity of, 16, 29n, 39n, 80, 145, 216, 221, 228, 230, 231, 239, 240, 241, 245; uncultivated minds of, 31, 162.
Chapels, 32n, 33; established for Indians, 31, 33, 58, 60, 61, 63, 84, 85, 103, 107. *see also* Churches.
Charity schools, 254; Lady Mico, 161n; Moor Indian, 94; *see also* Schools, Sir William Johnson, Eleazar Wheelock.
Charles II, 125n.
Charleston, South Carolina, 144n.
Charlton, Richard, missionary to New Windsor, and Staten Island, New York, and New York Negro mission, 73, 143, 144, 145, 146, 146n, 147, 161, 162, 163, 164, 165, 182, 183.
Chatham, William Pitt, earl of, 37, 40, *see also* William Pitt.
Checkley, John, missionary to New England, 38n.
Chester, bishops of, *see* William Cleaver, Sir William Dawes, Beilby Porteus.
Chew, Joseph, friend of Sir William Johnson, 101n.
Chichester, bishop of, *see* Francis Hare.
Chickasaw Indians, 39n.
Christ Church, in Philadelphia, 155n.
Christian religion, 131, 133, 136, 142, 154.
Churches, established, 31, 32, 32n, 33, 76, 84, 104, 104n, 105, 105n, 106n, 219. *see also* Chapels.

Farnam, Henry Walcott, 135n, 259.

Fauconnier, Mr., a slave owner, 126.

Five Nations, (Cayugas, Mohawks, Oneidas, Onondagas, Senecas) 52, 54, 57n, 61. *see also* Iroquois Indians.

Flatbush, New Jersey, 61.

Fleetwood, William, bishop of St. Asaph, viii, 11n, 19, 19n, 20, 20n, 21, 21n, 22, 25, 45n, 165, 186, 255; sermon of, 195-212; works of, 19n.

Flick, Alexander C., editor, 263.

Fordham manor, 135n.

Fort Frontenac, (Codroghque) Canada, 80n.

Fort Hunter, New York, 64n, 73, 74, 74n, 75n, 82, 84, 103, 105, 107, 108n, 110.

Fort Johnson, 104.

Fort, King's, 69n.

Fort, Queen's, 64n, 65n, 66n, 67n, 68n.

Fort Stanwix, 101, 101n, 111; treaty of, 100.

Fort, Upper, 83.

Franccan, Andr:, a slave owner, 137n.

France, 136n; colonial participation in war with (1689-1815), 49.

Franciscans, 6. *see also* Roman Catholics.

Franklin, Benjamin, 40, 43n, 45n, 189.

Franklin, William, lieut. gov. of New Jersey, 101n, 115n.

Free thinkers, 240, 241. *see also* Deism, Philosophical deism.

Free Negroes, 5, 131, 137n, 170.

French, translations, 144; dangers of Indian alliance with, 15, 23, 38, 39n, 61, 102n; Indians as allies of, 52, 56, 61n, 65, 77, 102n; ministers, 136n; success of Roman Catholic work, 38, 52, 58, 59, 61, 61n, 67, 78, 102n, 110, 112n; school, 147.

French and Indian war, 82, 93, 102, 172, 193. *see also* Seven Years war.

French Revolution, 8n, 189.

Frink, Samuel, missionary in Georgia, 39n.

Frontenac, Fort (Codroghque) 80n.

Fugitive Slave law, 170.

G

Gage, Gen. Thomas, 100n.

Georgia, catechist to Negroes in, 20n; just treatment of Indians in, 27; missionary to, 39n.

Germain, George Sackville, Lord, 112n.

Gibson, Edmund, bishop of London, 125, 136n, 144n, 147n, 155n, 259.

Gifts, for Indians, 63n, 65, 67, 67n, 69, 70; to church in Albany, 176, 177; to S. P G., 14, 19, 21, 169, 187, 228, 230, 231, 248. *see also* Sir William Johnson.

Gilbert, Sir Humphrey, 25.

Gillies, the Rev. John, 145n, 259.

Gillingham, Richard, 51n.

Glaves, Mr., a slave owner, 137n.

Gloucester, bishops of, *see* Martin Benson, James Johnson, Samuel Halifax, William Warburton, Joseph Wilcocks.

Gloucester, duke of, 19n.

Goodwin, Mary F., 5n, 259.

Gordon, Patrick, missionary to Jamaica, New York, 172.

Governor of New York, 134, 136, *see* Robert Hunter, Lord Bellomont, Lord Cornbury, William Tryon.

Governoua, Mr., a slave owner, 137n.

Great Barrington, New York, 183.

Great Britain, 186; poor white education in, 5, 162; judiciary in, 170; S. P. G. in, 8. *see also* England, London, British empire, British government, British civilization.

Greaton, James, missionary to Huntington, New York, 179, 180.

Green, John, Bishop of Lincoln, 30n, 39n, 256.

Green, Thomas, Lord bishop of Ely, 26, 26n, 256.

Greene, Evarts B., 89n, 122n, 259.

Guinea, 141.

Gulliver's Travels, 50.

H

Hailey, William Malcolm Hailey, Lord, 85n, 259.

205, 207-9, 217, 224; importation of, 138, 141, 146, 170n; Indians as, 16n, 56, 71, 137, 141, 156, 160; instruction of, *see* Instruction; insurrection of, *see* Insurrection; judicial decisions regarding, 151n, 158n, 170, 185, 187; legislative enactments on, 170n, 185; marriage of, *see* Marriage; masters of, *see* Masters; owned by S. P. G. missionaries, 154, 155, 156, 157, 158, 166, 167n; numbers of in colonies, 5, 46n, 122, 137, 138; relations with freedmen, 137; restrictions on, 170; runaway, 170, 170n; separation of children from parents, 170n; skills acquired, 171n; white fathers of, 170n; *see also* NEGROES, Slaveholder, Slavery, Slave Trade.

Slave trade, 30, 34, 39, 121, 122n, 187; capture of Negroes for, 20, 39; Christian teaching as deterrent to, 205, 246; effect on Indians of, 119; evils of, 246, 247; justification of, 35, 36, 36n; legality of, 39, 123; numbers coming from Liverpool, 122n; opposition to, 20, 37, 38, 39, 40, 193; participation by Africans in, 217, 247; profits from, 122n, 187. *See also* NEGROES, Slaveholder, Slaves, Slavery, Emancipation.

Smallpox, 23, 102, 147, 162.

Smith, Joseph, a slave owner, 126.

Smith, William, missionary to Pennsylvania and provost of Philadelphia college, 93, 93n, 98, 99, 99n, 113, 263.

S. P. C. K., viii, 36n, 121, 226; creation of, 11, 87; in expansion of world culture, 4. *see also* Bray Associates, Thomas Bray.

S. P. G., accumulated experience of, 121, 124, 185; as an ameliorative agent, 4, 8, 18, 20, 190; as an organized effort, 227; baptisms by, *see* Baptisms; Books distributed by, *see* Books; catechists for, *see* Catechists; chapels founded by, *see* Chapels; churches founded by, *see* Churches; colleges founded by, *see* King's college; libraries provided by, *see* Libraries; missionaries sent, *see* Mis-

sionaries; part in creation of American Episcopal church, 185, 186; position during American Revolution, *see* American Revolution; position on slavery, *see* Emancipation, Slaveholder, Slavery, Slave trade; publications regarding, 254; sermons for, *see* Sermons; schools of, *see* Schools; schoolmasters furnished by, *see* Schoolmasters; work for Christianization and Education, *see* Instruction; work with Indians, *see* INDIANS; work with Negroes, *see* NEGROES; work with white colonists, *see* White colonists, Masters of slaves;

—financial affairs of, 99, 111, 124, 184, 186, 202, 203; appeals for support of, 6, 6n, 29n, 35, 46, 210, 226, 227, 230-233; contributions to Bray Associates school from, 152; contributions to S. P. G. by Sir William Johnson, 103, 104, 104n, 105, 105n, 106, 106n, 107, 107n; gifts to, 14, 19, 21, 169, 187, 228, 230, 231, 248; income of, 3, 18, 219, 227, 231; salaries of catechists, *see* Catechists; salaries of missionaries, *see* Missionaries; state subsidies discontinued, 4; support furnished by, 31, 32, 32n, 33, 226, 240; treasurer of, 129;

—organization of, Charter, 240, 254; function of executive secretary, viii; list of executive secretaries, 31n; records of, vii, viii, 6n; trustees of, viii, 170;

—program of, viii, 5, 6, 13, 22, 28, 31, 32n, 33, 47, 48, 187, 188, 215, 216, 221-5, 233, 238, 239; conservatism of, 170; middle of the road policy, 170; religious survey made for, 169; success of, 29, 31, 32, 32n, 33, 45, 187, 217, 219; support of humanitarian ideal, *see* Humanitarianism;

—rivalry for religious domination of colonies: with Dissenters, *see* Dissenters; with Dutch, 53, 54, 59, 65, 68; with French, 23, 38, 39n, 61, 67, 77, 78, 80, 110, 112n; with Spanish, 33, 58, 67, 69, 77, 80, 82; with Roman Catholics, 6, 17, 23, 58, 69, 87, 216,

Tomline, Sir George Pretyman, bishop of Lincoln, 42n, 257.

Tories, 19, 174, 181, 181n, 183, 184. *see also* American Revolution, Loyalists, Missionaries.

Towns, in New York colony, *see* Albany, Arlington, Barn Island, Bedford, Brookhaven, L. I., Canajoharie, Cambden, Crab Meadow, Dynderoogby, East Chester, Hempstead, Huntington, L. I., Jamaica, L. I., Johnstown, Langsingburg, Lower Castle, Mohawk Castle, Neufchatel, Newburgh, New Rochelle, New Windsor, Niagara, North Castle, Onondaga, Oneidatown, Oyster Bay, Philipsburg, Poughkeepsie, Rye, St. Choack, Salem, Saratoga, Schenectady, South Side, Shaftesbury, Southampton, Staten Island, Stillwater, Suffolk, Upper Castle, West Chester, White Creek.

Townsend, Epenetus, missionary to Salem, 183.

Tracts, distributed by S. P. G., 29, 104n, 130n, 145, 152; issued by S. P. G., 144n. *see also* Books, Bibles, Prayer Books.

Trade, American, 15, 25; as source of support for S. P. G., 6, 17, 24, 25, 26, 29n, 190, 232; conflicting interests of, 8; depends on virtues taught by religion, 24, 26, 27; fur trade, 55; importance of colonial, 24, 26, 29n, 35, 49, 188, 232; profits from, 8, 25, 26, 27, 29n; religion and, 8, 27, 205, 206, 221; should be the means of spreading religion, 24. *see also* British Empire, Colonies, Slave trade, Wealth.

Trader, British, 31, 49, 55, 64; Dutch, 65, 68, 68n; responsibility for promoting religion, 27; undesirable influence of, 16, 16n, 55, 64; with missionary, 8, 18.

Trade and Plantations, Lords of, 52, 52n, 53.

Translations, for Indians, 26, 54, 58, 59, 61, 62, 62n, 64, 66, 67, 67n, 69, 74, 75, 144.

Trappes-Lomax, Michael Roger, 264.

Trelawney, Sir Jonathan, bishop of Winchester, 228n.

Trevet, Capt., a slave owner, 126.

Trevor, Richard, bishop of St. David's, 39n, 257.

Trimnell, Charles, bishop of Norwich, 18, 19, 29n, 257.

Trinity church, New York City, 71n, 78, 78n, 84, 84n, 97, 125, 125n, 139, 139n, 141, 142n, 144, 151n, 152, 153, 189.

Tryon, William, governor of New York, 117, 117n, 177n.

Tuscarora Indians, 77. *see also*, Six Nations.

U.

Unitarians, comparison of techniques with, 6, 6n. *see also* Dissenters.

United States, 162, 170; Indian policy of, 5. *see also* Episcopal church, American Revolution.

Upper Castle, New York (Canajoharie), 80, 80n, 84, 85, 90n.

Upper Fort, New York, 83.

Urquhart, William, missionary to Jamaica, New York, 56, 56n, 172.

Usher, John, missionary to Bristol, New England, 21n.

Utrecht, peace of, attacked by Fleetwood, 19.

V.

Vandam, Mr., a slave owner, 126.

Vanderhill, Mr., a slave owner, 138n.

Vandressen, Peter, minister of a Dutch congregation in Albany, 135n.

Van'est, Gerrit, citizen of Albany, 135.

Vanghorn, Abrah^m, a slave owner, 137n.

Vanhorn, Cornet, a slave owner, 138n.

Vanhorn, Gerr^d, a slave owner, 137n.

Van Mildest, William, Bishop Llandaff, 257.

van Rensselaer, Killian, 134, 135, 135n.

van Vosse, Mrs., a slave owner, 126.

Vesey, William, commissary of New York and rector of Trinity church, New York City, 31, 71n, 72, 73n, 78,